Aging in the Social Environment

Anissa T. Rogers

Joy Swanson Ernst

Oxford University Press is a department of the University of Oxford.
It furthers the University's objective of excellence in research, scholarship,
and education by publishing worldwide. Oxford is a registered trade mark
of Oxford University Press in the UK and in certain other countries.

Published in the United States of America by Oxford University Press
198 Madison Avenue, New York, NY 10016, United States of America.

© 2024 by Oxford University Press

For titles covered by Section 112 of the US Higher Education Opportunity
Act, please visit www.oup.com/us/he for the latest information about
pricing and alternate formats.

All rights reserved. No part of this publication may be reproduced,
stored in a retrieval system, or transmitted, in any form or by any means,
without the prior permission in writing of Oxford University Press,
or as expressly permitted by law, by license or under terms agreed with
the appropriate reprographics rights organization. Inquiries concerning
reproduction outside the scope of the above should be sent to the Rights
Department, Oxford University Press, at the address above.

You must not circulate this work in any other form
and you must impose this same condition on any acquirer

Library of Congress Cataloging-in-Publication Data
Names: Rogers, Anissa T., author. | Ernst, Joy Swanson, author.
Title: Aging in the social environment / Anissa T. Rogers, Joy Swanson
  Ernst.
Description: First Edition. | New York : Oxford University Press, [2023] |
  Includes bibliographical references and index.
Identifiers: LCCN 2022044914 | ISBN 9780197585092 (paperback) | ISBN
  9780197585115 (ebook) | ISBN 9780197585108 (adobe pdf)
Subjects: LCSH: Older people—Social aspects. | Aging. | Older
  people—Social conditions. | Older people—Care.
Classification: LCC HQ1061 .R5434 2023 | DDC 305.26—dc23/eng/20221003
LC record available at https://lccn.loc.gov/2022044914

Printed by Integrated Books International, United States of America

CONTENTS

Purpose of the Book ix
Acknowledgments xiii
About the Authors xv
To Be of Use is Ageless xvii

Chapter 1
GERONTOLOGY: THE STUDY OF AGING 1
What Is Gerontology? 2
   Population Aging 2
   Consequences of Population Aging 3
Careers in Gerontology 4
Common Theories of Aging 5
   Biopsychosocial Theories 5
   Additional Perspectives on Aging 5
What Is Ageism? 7
Types of Ageism 8
   Middle-Ageism 8
   Neuroageism 8
   Benevolent Ageism 8
   Individual and Institutional Ageism 9
How Culture Influences the Perception of Aging 10
   Media and Literature 10
   Interplay of Complex Factors 11
Consequences of Ageism 12
   Effect on Physical and Mental Health 12
   Effect on Healthcare 12
   Othering 13
   Microaggressions 13
   Effect on Social Policy 14
A More Positive View of Aging 15
   Successful Aging 15
   Optimal Aging 15
   Avoiding Ageist Language 16
Chapter Review 16
Review Questions 18

Chapter 2
BIOLOGY OF AGING 19
Defining Age 20
   Subjective Age 21
   Intersectional Factors That Affect Aging 21
Age and Human Development 22
Cross-Cultural Perspectives on Biological Aging 22
Theories of Biological Aging 23
   Genetic (Programmed) Theory 23
   Wear-and-Tear and Mitochondrial Theories 25
Age-Related Changes by Body System 25
   Skin and Hair 25
   Senses: Hearing and Vision 26
   Musculoskeletal System 27
   Immune System 28
   Endocrine System 28
   Central Nervous System: The Brain 30
      Dementia 30
      Treatment for Dementia 31
Promoting Health and Longevity 33
   Health Disparities and Older Adults 33
   Promoting Health and Well-Being 35
      Nutrition 35
      Physical Activity 36
      Behavioral and Environmental Accommodations 36
Chapter Review 36
Review Questions 38

Chapter 3
PSYCHOLOGY OF AGING 39
Theories of Psychological Age 40
   Erikson's Psychosocial Stages of Development 40
   Peck's Theory of Ego Integrity 42
   Intersectional and Cultural Factors 42

Intersection of Age and Gender 43
  Intersections of Other Characteristics 43
Personality and Emotion 44
  Personality and Aging 44
  Emotion and Aging 45
Learning 46
  Cognitive Plasticity 46
  Preserving Healthy Brain Function 46
  Overcoming Barriers to Learning 46
Mental Health 48
  Depression 48
  Anxiety 49
  Substance Use Disorders 49
  Suicide 50
  Screening and Diagnosis 50
  Treatment 50
    Cognitive Behavioral Therapy 51
    Narrative and Reminiscence Therapies 52
    Medications 52
Resiliency, Creativity, Productivity, and Wisdom 52
  Resiliency 53
  Creativity 53
  Productivity 53
  Wisdom 54
Spirituality 54
Chapter Review 55
Review Questions 57

Chapter 4
SOCIOLOGY OF AGING 58
Social Theories of Aging 59
  Disengagement Theory 59
  Activity Theory 60
  Continuity Theory 61
  Life-Course Model of Social Functioning 61
  Social Convoy Model 61
Social Connectedness 62
  Physical and Mental Health Benefits 63
  Social Connectedness across Cultures 63
Social Connection via Friendships 64
  Evolving Social Networks 64
  Benefits of Friendship 64
  Friendships among LGBT Older Adults 65
  Female Versus Male Friend Groups 65
  Intergenerational Friendships 66
Social Connection via Sexuality and Intimacy 67
  Beliefs about Sexuality in Older Adults 67
  Decreased Sexual Activity 68
  Differences Between Population Groups 68
  Risk of Sexually Transmitted Disease 69
  Influence of Technology 69
Chapter Review 70
Review Questions 71

Chapter 5
DEATH AND END-OF-LIFE ISSUES 72
What Is Death? 73
  Defining Physical Death 73
  Physical Process of Dying 74
  Perceptions of Death 75
End-of-Life Rights and Choices 75
  Right to Die 76
  Death with Dignity Legislation 76
  Hospice Care 77
  Disparities at End of Life 78
Preparing for End of Life 78
Experiencing Grief and Loss 78
  Types of Grief 80
  Theories and Models of Grief 81
    Kübler-Ross Theory 81
    Other Models of Grief 82
  Awareness of Death 83
Memorializing and Taking Care of the Dead 83
  Disposition of Bodies 83
    Green Burials 84
    Organ, Tissue, and Body Donation 85
  Memorialization after Death 85
  Impact of COVID-19 Pandemic on Funeral Practices 86
Chapter Review 88
Review Questions 89

Chapter 6
FAMILY AND CAREGIVING 90

Defining Family 91
Theories of Family and Aging 93
   Family Development Theory 93
   Theory of Intergenerational Solidarity and Conflict 93
   Theory of Intergenerational Ambivalence 93
Familial Roles and Relationships 94
   Marriage and Long-Term Partnerships 94
   Defining a Good Marriage 94
   Divorce 96
   Parents and Adult Children 96
      Adult Children with Challenges 97
      Effects of Increased Longevity 98
   Sibling Relationships 98
   Blended Families 98
      Negotiation of Boundary Ambiguity 99
      Intergenerational Resource Exchange 99
      Filial Norms and Expectations 100
   Multigenerational Families and Households 100
      Demographics 100
      Benefits and Drawbacks of Multigenerational Living 100
   Grandparents and Grandchildren 101
      Role of Grandparents 102
      Caring for Grandchildren 102
   Companion Animals 103
Caring for Older Adults 104
   Adults with Dementia 104
   Informal Care 104
      Rewards and Challenges 105
      Support for Caregivers 106
   Formal Care 106
   Impact on Caregivers 107
   Person- and Family-Centered Care 108
Elder Abuse 108
   Factors That Contribute to Elder Abuse 109
      Caregiving Situations 109
      Intergenerational Ambivalence 110
      Families with a History of Violence 110
   Prevention and Intervention Strategies 111
Chapter Review 112
Review Questions 113

Chapter 7
WORK AND RETIREMENT 114

Work and Older Adults 115
   The Nature of Work 116
   US Labor Trends 116
   Generational Perspective 117
   Ageism in the Workplace 118
      Intergenerational Work Teams 118
      Abolishing Mandatory Retirement 118
      Antidiscrimination Laws 119
   Caregiving and Work 119
Retirement 120
   Sense of Purpose and Longevity 120
   Effects of Retirement 120
   Phases of Retirement 121
Financial Support in Retirement 121
Volunteerism and Community Involvement 123
Lifelong Learning 124
Chapter Review 126
Review Questions 127

Chapter 8
LIVING ARRANGEMENTS 128

Housing and Care Options for Older Adults 129
   Types of Residential Facilities and Communities 131
   Older Adults with Special Needs 131
Aging in Place 132
   The Importance of Place 132
   Research on Aging in Place 133
   Changing Needs over Time 133
Theories and Approaches to Place and Aging 134
   Environmental Gerontology 134
   Geographical Gerontology 135
Older Adults in Urban and Rural Environments 136
The Importance of Neighborhoods 137

Gentrification 138
  Urban Neighborhoods: Challenges, Resources, and Resilience 139
    Detroit 140
    Minneapolis 140
Housing Options for Older Adults 141
  Historical Background 141
  The Housing Continuum 141
  Innovative Solutions 142
    Age-Friendly Communities 142
    Villages 142
    LGBT 65+ Housing Initiatives 142
    Home Sharing 143
    Communal Living 143
    Intergenerational Programming and Communities 143
  Housing for Low-Income Older Adults 144
  Continuing Care Retirement Communities 144
  Assisted Living Facilities 145
  Supportive Housing 145
  Nursing Homes 145
  COVID-19 and Long-Term Care Facilities 146
Living Arrangements of Vulnerable Populations 147
  Older Adults in Prison 147
  Older Victims of Domestic Abuse 147
  Older Adults without Housing 148
Chapter Review 149
Review Questions 149

Chapter 9
COMMUNITY RESOURCES AND CONNECTEDNESS 151
The Importance of Connection 152
  Defining Community 152
  Community Resources 153
  Self-Determination and Social Usefulness 153
  Social Connection and Social Isolation 154
Religious and Spiritual Communities 155
  Spiritual Practices 156
  Benefits of Religious and Spiritual Involvement 157

Recreation and Community Involvement 157
  Sports and Fitness 158
  Travel 159
  The Arts 159
  Volunteer Work 161
  Socializing in Third Places 161
Healthcare Services 161
  Access to Healthcare 162
  Primary Care 163
  Geriatricians 164
  Age-Friendly Healthcare 165
  Treatment Programs 165
Social Services for Older Adults and Their Families 165
  Prevention Services 166
  Adult Day Care 167
  In-Home Personal Care 167
  Protective Services 167
  Support Services 167
  Resource Brokerage and Linkage 168
Chapter Review 169
Review Questions 170

Chapter 10
MEDIA AND TECHNOLOGY 171
Media and Older Adults 172
  News Media 172
  Educational and Entertainment Media 173
  Ageism in the Media 174
  Social Media 174
Technology Use by Older Adults 174
  Access to Technology 175
  Combating Stereotypes 176
  Technology Use for Lifelong Learning 176
  Technology Use for Social Connection and Entertainment 176
  Technology Use to Improve Health 177
  Digital Literacy 178
  Online Safety 178
Technology and End of Life 179
Chapter Review 180
Review Questions 181

Chapter 11
GLOBAL TRENDS IN AGING 182
Global Aging 183
   United Nations Initiatives Related to Aging 183
   Population Aging 184
   Living Arrangements 185
   Life Expectancy and Health 185
   Work and Retirement 186
   Ageism Worldwide 187
Culture and Aging 187
   Cross-National Comparisons 187
   Cross-Cultural Comparisons 188
   Cultural Influences on Aging 188
Aging in the United States in Global Context 189
   US Life Expectancy 189
   Foreign-Born Population 190
Immigration, Migration, and Aging 191
   Who Migrates and Why? 191
   Older Adults in Home Countries 192
   Older Immigrants in Destination Countries 193
      Early versus Late-Life Immigration 194
      Older Refugees Fleeing War and Terror 195
      Legal Status and Threat of Deportation 195
Aging and Climate Change 195
   Climate Change and Migration 195
   Health Impacts of Climate Change 196
   Climate Change and Natural Disasters 196
Chapter Review 198
Review Questions 199

Chapter 12
LEGAL, POLICY, AND ECONOMIC ISSUES THAT AFFECT OLDER US ADULTS 201
Social Policies and Legislation 202
   Social Policy and Aging Policy 202
   History of US Aging Policies 202
   Social Security 203
      Beneficiaries 204
      Retirement Age 204
      Sustainability 205
   Medicare 205
   Medicaid 206
   Affordable Care Act 207
   Older Americans Act 207
   Long-Term Care Services and Supports 209
      Cost of Long-Term Care 209
      Quality of Long-Term Care 210
   Elder Justice Act 210
   Americans with Disabilities Act 211
   Assistance for Low-Income Older Adults 212
Poverty, Inequality, and Cumulative Disadvantage 213
   Poverty Measurement 213
   Who Is Poor? 214
      Variance between Population Groups 214
      Cumulative Advantage/Disadvantage 215
Political Participation and Advocacy 215
   Voting Patterns of Older Adults 215
   Intersection of Politics and Policy 216
   Advocacy Organizations 217
      AARP 217
      Gray Panthers 217
      Leadership Council of Aging Organizations 218
      Other Organizations 218
Chapter Review 219
Review Questions 220

Glossary 221
References 229
Index 265

PURPOSE OF THE BOOK

By 2050, the number of adults aged 60 and over will double. More than ever, students in the helping professions must develop the knowledge, skills, and values needed to work with older adults. The goal of this book is to change the perspective on aging and the aging process while offering broad, introductory level knowledge on gerontology. It examines aging from a holistic, intersectional, strengths-based, life-span perspective to integrate aging into the human development process. The authors aim to challenge stereotypes about aging and help readers understand aging as an integral part of the human experience, rather than a separate process that "others" older adults.

In a changing and aging world, challenges of aging intersect with other challenges such as economic inequality, instability caused by climate change, global patterns of migration, political polarization, and, recently, the pandemic, which highlighted that social isolation is a detrimental and growing concern. Despite growing understanding and awareness of its impact, ageism remains a force in a youth-oriented world. This book examines the aging process from micro, mezzo, and macro lenses. The micro lens looks at individual processes of aging such as biological, emotional, spiritual, and psychological factors along with topics such as health, resilience, sexuality, and creativity as we age. The mezzo lens looks at processes beyond the individual including work, roles, family, caregiving, living arrangements, religious involvement, and healthcare. The macro lens looks at factors such as culture, media, laws, policies, language, and stereotypes about aging.

ORGANIZATION OF THE BOOK

To explore aging-related concepts on the micro, mezzo, and macro levels, the book offers chapters that focus on specific psychosocial and other issues to help readers understand these issues in more depth. Chapters move from individual, micro-level considerations of aging to more macro concepts.

Chapter 1

"Gerontology: The Study of Aging" sets the stage to familiarize readers with the field of aging, why it is important, age-related career options, and common theories used in the study of aging. Chapter 1 also explores ageism and its effects, which provides a foundation for examining ageism in subsequent chapters.

Chapter 2

"Biology of Aging" explores concepts related to the physical aging process from a life-long continuum of human development. Here, different aspects of physical aging are defined and theories about why we age are discussed. This chapter also explores how the aging process affects the body and how well-being can be maximized as we age.

Chapter 3
"Psychology of Aging" discusses theories that explain psychological aspects of aging along with how constructs such as emotion, cognition, and personality continue to develop over time and how aging process and our psychological characteristics interact with one another to shape how we age and adapt to aging. Mental health as well as constructs such as resiliency, creativity, and wisdom are explored in this chapter.

Chapter 4
"Sociology of Aging" explores theories used to describe socialization in older age along with concepts related to social connectedness in later life. This chapter also explores dynamics surrounding friendships and sexuality as we grow older.

Chapter 5
"Death and End-of-Life Issues" takes a deeper look at the physical process of death. It also explores supports, services, and considerations people may need when dying. Theories and types of grief are discussed.

Chapter 6
"Family and Caregiving" discusses the changing nature of family and the theories used to explain the role of family as we age. Family roles and relationships are explored, along with different types of caregiving. Elder abuse and interventions are also discussed.

Chapter 7
"Work and Retirement" describes the nature of work and the workplace as we age. Retirement and financial supports are explored as are work alternatives such as volunteerism and lifelong learning.

Chapter 8
"Living Arrangements" explores housing and care options and innovations for older adults. Theories that explain the role of environment in living arrangements are discussed along with geographical and environmental considerations in living arrangements.

Chapter 9
"Community Resources and Connectedness" focuses on concepts and theories related to community, social connection, and social isolation. Religious and spiritual life is explored along with recreational and other opportunities that can keep people connected as they age. The continuum of social services for older adults is described.

Chapter 10
"Media and Technology" explores the role of media and technology, how we interact with media and technology, and how ageism in the media can affect us in older

adulthood. Media literacy and the ways in which media and technology can be used to help or harm us in older adulthood are discussed.

Chapter 11
"Global Trends in Aging" looks at how the aging population globally affects health, work, retirement, living arrangements, and other psychosocial and economic for older adults. Immigration, climate change, and other issues are discussed.

Chapter 12
"Legal, Policy, and Economic Issues That Affect Older US Adults" covers landmark legislation and social policy that affect older adults. Poverty and its effects on older adults are explored, along with political participation and advocacy for supports that improve life in older adulthood.

ACKNOWLEDGMENTS

We would like to thank the editorial staff at Oxford University Press for their support and guidance throughout the creation of this book. We owe our gratitude to the reviewers who offered their feedback to improve on versions of the book, including Marla Berg-Weger, Laurie Blackman, Willa Casstevens, Shaheen Chowdary, Jamie-Lee Conner, Dana Donohue, Charles Emlet, Karen Fazio, Susan Glassburn, Robert Hesslink Jr., Daniel Kaplan, Patricia Kolb, Daniel Liechty, Gina Maguire, Nicole Major, Dixie McDowell, Victor Molinari, Kyle O'Brien, Benjamin Shamburger, Joyce Weil, Christopher Wellin, and Karen Zellman.

We also thank our colleagues and families for their support throughout the writing and editing process. Joy thanks her mother Anne Swanson for her example of positive aging and her husband Dan Ernst for his encouragement.

ABOUT THE AUTHORS

Anissa T. Rogers, PhD, MA, MSW, LCSW, is Professor at California State University, San Bernardino's School of Social Work. She received her PhD, MSW, and Gerontology Certificate at the University of Utah; MA in Counseling Psychology at Ball State University; and BA in Psychology at the University of Utah. She has held faculty positions in social work at Plymouth State University, University of Portland, and CSUSB.

Joy Swanson Ernst, PhD, MSW is Associate Professor at the Wayne State University School of Social Work. She received PhD at the University of Maryland-Baltimore; MSW at Rutgers School of Social Work; and BA in History at the University of Chicago. She has held faculty positions in social work at Hood College and Wayne State University.

TO BE OF USE IS AGELESS

When we're young so many of us are not yet aware of the connective tissue that links us to our ancestors and elders. We don't see that we come from somewhere and that the elders are of us and we of them. Youth allows us to see ourselves as lone entities too often and independent, like an individual satellite or an island onto our own.

In a contemporary society, many times youth has a way of living in a bubble of indestructibility and a sense of life going on forever. Yet if there is wisdom from gathered years it may be arriving to an awareness that we are all finite. We come closer to feeling and knowing our lives will end. Being in the present with the awareness of the thread that connects us can give us a true appreciation for the preciousness of the gift that is our unique life.

Why don't we value life as it grows toward advancing years? Lives that gain perspective and insight with a multitude of experiences. Lives with knowledge and wisdom.

Stereotyping older adults has permeated our culture for far too long and it is one of the "isms" we have yet to put to rest. "Little old lady" and "weak old man" as tropes of ageism still prevail, unfortunately.

We seem to steal the essence of vitality from older adults when they are forced into retirement (with random target dates) and to leave jobs they are perfectly capable of doing.

Making assumptions about what someone can or cannot do because of their age instead of assessing the capabilities of each individual and not the stereotype. And yes, when there is a slowing down, what about transitioning to other kinds of purposeful work or activism of some form? We have been a throwaway society and label elders useless to the detriment of not just them, but to ourselves. Losing such wisdom that we as a society could gain instead.

Every one of us will pass through the gate of years and find ourselves many ages later and wonder how we got here. How did this happen? It's as if we were asleep all the time of our young lives and suddenly we wonder, am I still of use? Will I still be acknowledged and respected for wisdom gleaned from experience and respected for my abilities? Will I be able to pass on valuable insights to the next generations? Do I have or can I cultivate purpose still? With any luck, we'll get there. To an older, hopefully wiser place, dodging the trappings of humanity and ageism. Do I want to make use of this body no matter what my age? I was born, I got here, so how will I use myself? Age is a number. A number is a label. How does anyone of us want to spend our time, our life? We have a choice, and no one can label that away from us.

—Marsha Breuer, used with the permission of the author

CHAPTER 1

Gerontology: The Study of Aging

Chapter Outline
What Is Gerontology?
    Population Aging
        Consequences of Population Aging
Careers in Gerontology
Common Theories of Aging
    Biopsychosocial Theories
    Additional Perspectives on Aging
What Is Ageism?
Types of Ageism
    Middle-Ageism
    Neuroageism
    Benevolent Ageism
    Individual and Institutional Ageism
How Culture Influences the Perception of Aging
    Media and Literature
    Interplay of Complex Factors
Consequences of Ageism
    Effect on Physical and Mental Health
    Effect on Healthcare
    Othering
    Microaggressions
    Effect on Social Policy
A More Positive View of Aging
    Successful Aging
    Optimal Aging
    Avoiding Ageist Language

Learning Objectives
- Define *gerontology* and explain its importance as a professional field.
- Describe the multidisciplinary nature of gerontology and provide examples of careers in the field.
- Summarize common theories of aging.
- Define *ageism*.
- Distinguish various types of ageism.
- Explain how culture influences perception of the aging process and views on older adults.
- Describe the consequences of ageism at the individual, institutional, and societal levels.
- Describe alternative ways to view aging in a positive light.

Is there a way to view the aging process in a more positive and individualized light than is typically embodied in Western culture? Can individual and cultural perspectives on aging be changed? How do we get to a place where the aging process is viewed as a part of the life span with its own strengths and challenges? These are some of the questions we will introduce in this chapter and explore throughout this book.

WHAT IS GERONTOLOGY?

At its most basic, **gerontology** is the study of aging and older adults. More specifically, it examines all aspects of midlife and later-life development, including the biological, psychological, social, and spiritual facets of growing older. Gerontology is also concerned with the legal, societal, economic, political, and other processes that often occur in response to older populations (Academy for Gerontology in Higher Education, 2019). Gerontology, as a field, also tends to employ its own specialized research methods and processes that attend to unique considerations of conducting research with and for older adults. This includes, for example, how to operationalize gerontological concepts, employ techniques to reach and sample older populations to avoid sampling and other bias and increase generalizability, and choose research designs that are sensitive to characteristics of the populations being targeted, such as when sampling those with physical or cognitive disabilities or those in the older end of the age continuum. As such, gerontology situates aging within the larger social context and considers how older individuals and their environment interact with one another, but it also considers unique aspects of older adult populations along with the heterogeneity of those populations.

Sometimes people confuse gerontology with geriatrics. Gerontology is a multidisciplinary field concerned with physical, mental, and social aspects of aging. **Geriatrics** is a medical specialty focused on providing care for older adults. While it is important to understand how these two fields differ, their common thread is that both aim to better understand the aging process to help older individuals achieve optimal health and quality of life.

Population Aging

Gerontology becomes increasingly important as the world's population ages. With fertility rates declining and life expectancy rates rising, the percentage of people entering

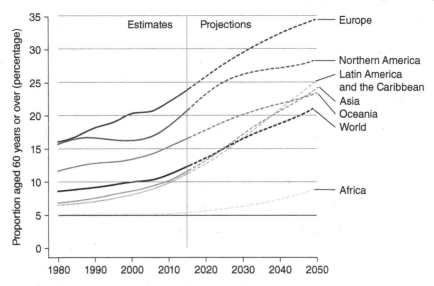

Figure 1.1 Population aging across the globe, 1980–2050
Source: United Nations, Department of Economic and Social Affairs, Population Division (2017). World Population Ageing 2017 Highlights (ST/ESA/SER.A/397).

late life is growing dramatically (United Nations, 2017). This proportional increase of older adults (generally, people aged 60+) compared to younger adults and children is known as **population aging**. It is most prominent in Europe and North America; however, aging populations are increasing in most areas of the globe, including Asia, Africa, Latin America, and the Caribbean (United Nations, 2017; Figure 1.1).

Population aging is occurring at a rapid pace. The number of people aged 60+ worldwide more than doubled between 1980 and 2017, from 382 million to 962 million (Figure 1.2). Further, the population of those 80+ is projected to increase more than threefold, from 137 million to 425 million. Older adults are expected to outnumber 10- to 14-year-olds by 2030 (1.41 billion vs. 1.35 billion, respectively) and adolescents and young adults by 2050 (2.1 billion vs. 2.0 billion). In the United States in 2015, there were 47.8 million people aged 65+ (United States Census Bureau, 2017). Population growth projections estimate that this figure will increase to 98.2 million by 2060 and include 19.7 million people 85 or older.

Consequences of Population Aging

As we will discuss in later chapters, population aging has both negative and positive consequences. For example, there will likely be fewer younger people in the workforce and more retired people, creating labor shortages and fewer contributions to the Social Security system. Demand on the healthcare system will increase and leave fewer caregivers for older adults (Yenilmez, 2015). However, population aging also presents opportunities such as business expansion and adaptation to cater to older consumers; innovative and sustainable housing models for individual and community living; and recrafted roles that allow older adults to engage in various areas of society, including

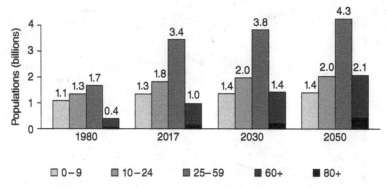

Figure 1.2 Global population aging by broad age group, 1980–2050
Source: United Nations, Department of Economic and Social Affairs, Population Division (2017). World Population Ageing 2017 Highlights (ST/ESA/SER.A/397).

caregiving, volunteering, continued or new employment, and community leadership. These reimagined roles not only benefit us as we age, but they can also address some of the challenges to labor, social, and economic systems that population aging brings (Arensberg, 2018; Gonzales, Matz-Costa, & Morrow-Howell, 2015).

Gerontologists—those who study or work in gerontology—address these issues for both individuals who are aging and their larger social, economic, and physical environments. Gerontologists are also at the forefront of creating and capitalizing on opportunities that arise from population aging.

CAREERS IN GERONTOLOGY

Gerontology is a multidisciplinary field that includes such areas as law, nursing, biology, medicine, economics, sociology, psychology, social work, and political science. This wide scope provides many varied opportunities. Gerontologists establish careers in education, lobbying, architecture, elder law, case management, financial planning, healthcare policy, physical and speech therapy, and assisted living or other housing administration. In fact, gerontology has been a burgeoning field for quite some time, as a result of population aging. More colleges and universities have added gerontology courses and programs over the past few decades, and gerontology certificates and credentials are being increasingly recognized by state licensure boards and employers, who recognize the value of specialized knowledge and skills in later life development. Box 1.1 lists examples of careers in gerontology.

All gerontologists, regardless of their specific job, work to better understand not only the biopsychosocial processes associated with age and aging but also the ways larger societal, political, and economic realms interface with and affect our experiences of age and aging and how older individuals shape these realms. In other words, they strive to understand how we age and how society's reaction to aging and older adults impacts this experience. They also focus on the unique issues of aging, including those related to housing, employment, financial security, physical and mental healthcare, ageism, social isolation, and intergenerational relationships. In so doing, they work to improve services, influence policy, and improve older adults' overall well-being.

BOX 1.1 Examples of Careers in Gerontology

Micro Settings

- Case Manager
- Financial Planner
- Licensed Counselor
- Occupational Therapist
- Physical Therapist
- Research Scientist
- Retirement Planner
- Therapist

Mezzo Settings

- Educator (professor in university-level gerontology program)
- Facility Director (e.g., assisted living, long-term care, memory care, senior center)
- Grief/Loss Group Facilitator
- Health Educator
- Health Promotion Coordinator or Director
- Hospice/Palliative Care Program Director

Macro Settings

- City/County Planner
- Director, Lifelong Learning
- Government Official (department of aging)
- Grant Writer
- Hospice/Palliative Care Policy Planner
- Legislator (city, county, state, federal)
- Medicare/Social Security Program Administrator
- Researcher
- Social Policy Planner

COMMON THEORIES OF AGING

Given the interdisciplinary nature of gerontology, there are myriad ways to examine growing older. In this section, we will focus on theories that are biopsychosocial in nature. These concepts—which can be grouped in terms of biological, psychological, and social lenses—give us a frame of reference to better understand the aging process. We will also discuss perspectives that explore how we define aging and make meaning of it, how we subjectively view and experience it as individuals, and how larger society and formal organizations classify, describe, and treat older adults. These theories will be applied throughout the book as we explore various issues related to aging. Table 1.1 summarizes common theories and perspectives on aging.

Biopsychosocial Theories

As we will see, many biological theories focus on why and how we age. They explore the physical causes of aging, from changes at genetic and cellular levels to the environment's harmful effects on the body. Thus, biological approaches tend to view aging as a process of decline.

Psychological theories aim to explain age in terms of life-span development, emotional and cognitive changes that occur as we age, the role of personality, and how characteristics such as resiliency, creativity, and spirituality may affect aging. Sociological theories aim to explain roles, relationships, and interactions with the social environment. All these theories help us to better understand how aging affects not only the individual but society as a whole.

Additional Perspectives on Aging

Along with theories that help us explain the biopsychosocial processes associated with aging, additional frameworks concentrate on how age and aging affects and is affected

Table 1.1 Common Theories and Perspectives on Aging

Theory/Perspective	Description
Biological theories	Explore the physical causes of aging, from changes at genetic and cellular levels to the environment's harmful effects on the body.
Psychological theories	Explain age and aging in terms of life-span development, emotional and cognitive changes that occur as we age, the role of personality in how we experience aging, and how characteristics such as resiliency, creativity, and spirituality may affect age and aging.
Sociological theories	Explain roles, relationships, and how age interacts with the social environment.
Queer theory	Examines and critiques how we normalize ways of knowing and privilege certain views and behaviors over others, including assumptions we make about age and older adults.
Feminist theory	Explores the experiences of older adults, particularly women and other marginalized groups from an intersectional lens. These theories also explore how culture, history, gender roles, preconceived notions of aging, and the accumulation of past experiences disadvantage and oppress older adults.
Intersectional lenses	Examine how multiple identities and characteristics shape and influence the way we view ourselves and how other view us throughout the life span.
Strengths-based lenses	Emphasize the strengths that come with age, such as resilience and coping skills and focus on the many opportunities that aging brings.
Human development lenses	View aging not as a separate stage of life but as a continuing, adaptive part of life-span development; getting older is a typical part of human development and growth that begins at conception and continues until death.

by other facets in our social environment. Many of these lenses attempt to deconstruct traditional, simplistic, and often discriminatory views of growing older and to reconstruct a richer, more complex, and inclusive discourse.

Queer theory and similar perspectives examine and critique how we normalize ways of knowing and privilege certain views and behaviors over others (Sullivan, 2003). It often is used to consider issues surrounding gender and sexuality, but it is also useful in exploring assumptions we make about age and older adults. For example, this perspective disrupts normalized and stereotyped expectations of what age is and should be and turns a critical eye to assumptions of heteronormativity and able-bodiedness, which often cast older adults in a negative and derogatory light (Sandberg & Marshall, 2017). A queer lens also critiques what it means to "age successfully" instead of to "age typically" or individually.

Feminist theories consider the experiences of older adults, particularly women and other marginalized groups. They also explore how culture, history, gender roles, preconceived notions of aging, and the accumulation of past experiences disadvantage and oppress older adults. Similarly, intersectional lenses examine how multiple identities and characteristics shape and influence the way we view ourselves as we age, as well as how society views and interacts with older adults (Crenshaw, 1989). For example, this approach emphasizes factors such as race, class, ability, appearance, gender identification, and sexual orientation; the ways they intersect with one another and age to affect one's well-being in later life; and how they contribute to inequality throughout the life span (Calasanti & King, 2015).

A common view of age and growing older in many cultures and societies is deficit-based. The focus is on the seemingly negative and stereotypical aspects of aging, many of which relate to bodily decline, change in appearance, and loss of independence.

Strengths-based lenses counter this position by emphasizing the strengths that come with age, such as resilience and coping skills. As such, it focuses on the many opportunities an "aging society" brings. Older adults have much to contribute to society, including their own legacy and their contributions to the health and robustness of their families, communities, and future generations.

A human development lens views aging not as a separate stage of life but as a continuing part of life-span development. In this approach, getting older is a typical part of human development and growth that begins at conception and continues until death. From this point of view, the aging process is adaptive; it is a consequence of previous life experiences and interaction with our environment. The physical, emotional, cognitive, and other changes that occur over the life span are cumulative, and older age is simply a continuation of our development. While we might expect some of these changes, they are by no means guaranteed or look the same from person to person—individuals age in very different ways and experience unique advantages and disadvantages throughout their lives. By viewing growing older in this way, we can move away from the stereotyping that often occurs when we think about older adults (Hanson et al., 2016).

WHAT IS AGEISM?

In many cultures, youth is revered and aging is stigmatized as a state of decline. Older adults are often viewed and treated as a homogeneous group of frail, cranky, and useless people who put a strain on social, health, and other systems. As a result, this population can be vulnerable to biased thoughts and behaviors (Bussolo, Koettl, & Sinnott, 2015; Sadana et al., 2013; World Health Organization, 2015).

The systematic prejudicing, discriminating, and stereotyping of individuals based on age is known as **ageism,** a term first coined by the psychiatrist Robert Butler in 1969 (World Health Organization, 2019). It is a complex phenomenon that is manifested in many ways on micro and macro levels and is expressed cognitively, behaviorally, and emotionally (Iversen, Larsen, & Solem, 2009). It can involve both negative and positive attitudes and behaviors: the former can range from avoiding contact with older adults to discriminatory practices and policies while the latter can include infantilizing older adults by calling them sweet or cute. These attitudes and behaviors are discussed in more detail later in the chapter.

Any age group can experience ageism but none do so more than older adults—particularly women, those who are poor (often older women and people of color), and those with dementia (Rippon et al., 2014). Ageism, and its resulting discrimination, is a deep-rooted problem, particularly in the United States. Indeed, research suggests that it is more pervasive than other "isms," such as racism, sizeism, sexism, and classism, because it is the only one that is universal (Ayalon, 2013). That is, anyone who lives into older age will experience it to a certain degree, depending on his or her environment and circumstances. Ageism also tends to be normalized in our everyday lives, so it is less visible than other types and lacks a specific language for discussing it or its effects (Gullette, 2017). Thus, it is an important concept to understand and apply in gerontology and provides another lens to view age and aging.

To complicate matters, ageism often intersects with other isms, particularly racism, classism, and sexism but also queermisia and transmisia (i.e., homophobia and transphobia). Individuals may face discrimination based on two intersecting characteristics, known as **double jeopardy**, or on three or more, which is **triple jeopardy**. Those who experience racism and sexism typically do so over a lifetime, potentially leading to accumulated damage. Ageism, however, usually is not experienced until later in life and therefore may exacerbate other forms of discrimination and oppression.

We will examine various aspects of ageism throughout this book, such as how it often plays out in different realms (e.g., healthcare and the workplace) and how it is often intersectional in nature.

TYPES OF AGEISM

The study of ageism and its effects is relatively new. As scholars have examined this phenomenon, they have identified different types to better articulate various attitudes and behaviors that can be considered ageist but differ in subtle ways and can have different consequences. The forms discussed here are by no means exhaustive, but they offer different perspectives on how ageism can present and play out in everyday life.

Middle-Ageism

Many people report that ageism begins around middle age, which is when they notice appearance changes such as gray hair, wrinkles, and weight gain (Azoulay et al., 2018). As in all stages in life, women find themselves under more scrutiny for their appearance than men do during this time. Aging can be a status symbol for men, with gray hair and wrinkles being considered distinguished (Calasanti, 2005). But these views are changing in various sectors of society. Middle-aged men used to be thought of as being in their prime; however, they are now deemed obsolete as early as their twenties (Gullette, 2017).

This **middle-ageism** can be seen in the technology industry, where these men are facing unprecedented discrimination for being too old to work in such a rapidly changing field. The rise of entrepreneurs such as Mark Zuckerberg and Bill Gates in their twenties has led to a perception that only young people are effective or successful. Zuckerberg has famously said that "young people are just smarter" (Azoulay et al., 2018).

Neuroageism

This term refers to ageism associated with neurodegenerative diseases that often occur in older age but are not caused by aging. Dementias, Alzheimer's disease, Parkinson's disease, memory problems, and other disorders become linked to aging, and those who suffer from them are stereotyped, dehumanized, and dismissed because they are unable to function "normally" (Gullette, 2017). By associating such conditions with "normal" aging, **neuroageism** only serves to perpetuate the fear of aging and entrench stereotypical beliefs about the aging process and decline.

Benevolent Ageism

Benevolent ageism, sometimes referred to as positive ageism, is based on stereotypes that depict older people as sweet and cute but incompetent (Chonody, 2016; North & Fiske, 2013). While these descriptions seem positive and endearing, they are actually paternalistic and infantilizing, maintain harmful stereotypes and behaviors toward older adults, and "other" them. This type contrasts with **hostile ageism** (or negative ageism), which label all older people as slow, weak, rude, and stubborn.

Individual and Institutional Ageism

Many of the examples previously discussed can be categorized as individual or institutional ageism. Thinking about ageism in terms of these two categories can be helpful, as they point to different ways of addressing it.

Individual ageism refers to our internalized beliefs about age that often lead to discriminatory behaviors between individuals (Kotter-Gruhn & Hess, 2012). Examples include the derogatory language individuals use to describe older adults or hurtful jokes people tell about them. Often, these internalized attitudes are shaped by larger ageist cultural beliefs. Individual ageism can be more overt than institutional ageism because such comments, jokes, and other behaviors are often common and acceptable.

Institutional ageism involves ageist beliefs and behaviors that are embedded in our media, organizations, and larger cultural arenas (Lloyd-Sherlock et al., 2016). Ageism becomes a part of macro-level organizational culture and norms, social policies, and other institutional functions and processes, perpetuating discrimination against older people. Institutional ageism is often more covert than the individual type; because it is part of larger culture, policy, and norms, it is frequently more difficult to detect and address. Examples include discriminatory hiring practices based on age; healthcare policies and practices that systematically discriminate against older people; and pervasive derogatory and demeaning images and portrayals (and the general absence) of older people in media.

Figure 1.3 Ageism in the media
Source: Image Courtesy of The Advertising Archives

> **CASE 1.1**
>
> ### Ageism in Action
>
> Julie is in her junior year at a large university where she majors in psychology. She's in a seminar class with other students who are placed in internships at various sites. Another student is talking about his experiences at a senior center, where he's placed. As the student talks about his day interacting with some of the participants who come for an art class, he refers to them as "cute" and "sweet" and mentions that he makes sure to talk really loudly around them because "old" people can't hear. He then talks about how cute it was that two of the participants were flirting with one another. He went on to describe the participants as "stubborn" because they didn't want to follow his suggestions on how to approach the class.
>
> What types of ageism do you think are at play in this student's comments about the older adults he works with at the senior center? If you were Julie, how could you approach this situation to address the ageism reflected in her classmate's comments?

HOW CULTURE INFLUENCES THE PERCEPTION OF AGING

Views on age and aging are embedded in all cultures, and cultural influences play a big role in shaping our values, attitudes, and social norms on most aspects of life. Generally, ideas on older age are negative and stereotypical in many cultures, which can lead to ageism.

Pervasive cultural beliefs influence our perception of what aging means and how we age. In many societies, particularly in the United States, health is equated with goodness and morality, and people tend to believe they control their own fate. Thus, aging and ill health often are viewed as the consequences of personal failings: physical and cognitive decline is the individual's fault (Calasanti, 2005). These views also exemplify ageism's intersection with ableism. For example, habits like smoking, leading a sedentary lifestyle, and eating poorly may be blamed for not only disease but also the aging process itself. While unhealthy choices can and do contribute somewhat to illness and accelerated aging, many additional and complex factors that are outside of our control influence how we age and experience health and illness. The belief that we control our own fate allows younger people (and some older people) to deny the inevitability of growing older, especially if they feel they have a healthy lifestyle. If aging and illness are perceived to be within our control, judging older people as lazy or undisciplined becomes easier. This view can lead to justifications for ageist or discriminatory behaviors toward older adults, such as withholding healthcare or lifesaving treatments.

Ageism can be found in all aspects of culture, including art, music, language, media, and literature. Let's first consider language. While the term "old" or sayings like "an old hand" or "an old master" can be associated with wisdom, maturity, and experience, much of the terminology used to describe older age tends to be associated with negative and harmful stereotypes. These words include "ancient," "geezer," and "old hag."

Media and Literature

Media also shape our views of age and aging. Many movies, advertisements, and television shows underrepresent older adults, depict them in negative or infantilizing ways, or exaggerate negative labels. Most media in the United States focus on youth, beauty, and sex and do not depict older adults as sexual, capable, intelligent, or valuable. Similarly, literature—particularly children's—often perpetuates negative stereotypes associated with older age (Smith, 2016). Thus, it is not surprising that ageist attitudes often develop at very young ages. Children are exposed to ageism through peers and family members as well as books, movies, and other media, which influence their views about aging and older adults (Hollis-Sawyer & Cuevas, 2013). Developing ageist beliefs while young also shapes self-perceptions and can lead to internalized ageism, meaning that we may hold such ideas about ourselves as we age (Kotter-Grühn & Hess, 2012). Recently, some media and literature have attempted to depict older age in more nuanced ways, and some have grappled with the issue of ageism. However, these efforts fall short of integrating later life into the mainstream.

Interplay of Complex Factors

A commonly held belief is that some cultures, like some Asian and Latinx societies, revere their elders more so than those in the Western world. However, this viewpoint is too simplistic. In reality, beliefs and perceptions of age and aging are complex and ever-changing and vary a great deal depending on the particular culture's political, geographical, and socioeconomical context (see Box 1.2). Research suggests that these factors, along with complex geopolitical and other processes, may be more important to societal views of aging than once thought. Yet even with this variability within and between cultures, research points to cross-cultural commonalities in attitudes about age and aging, including the belief that it brings wisdom as well as decline in physical and cognitive abilities. Factors such as higher educational attainment, stronger emphasis on individuality, less adherence to progressive values, and a lower percentage of

Figure 1.4 Ageism in advertising
Source: Image Courtesy of The Advertising Archives

> **BOX 1.2 Global Ageism**
>
> Ageism exists in every culture. Because of the growing older population, ageism is becoming increasingly more visible. In a study exploring ageism in 28 European countries (Bratt et al., 2018), perceived ageism by younger and older adults showed some interesting results:
>
> - In 14 of 28 countries (Romania, Hungary, Slovenia, Estonia, Sweden, Switzerland, Norway, Denmark, Ireland, Belgium, Finland, France, Portugal, United Kingdom), perceived ageism was highest among younger adults and decreased with increasing age.
> - In the remaining countries, perceived ageism was high for both younger and older adults.
> - The countries studies are marked by egalitarian, modern cultures, where ageism of older adults is deemed unacceptable, so it is more covert.
> - Studies of countries that are more traditional and collectivist, such as Latin American or African countries, may demonstrate different patterns of ageism toward different age groups.
> - Ageism in modern societies may be more prevalent than in traditional societies because of increased separation of age groups, who have fewer opportunities to interact in daily life.
> - Growing political and economic power of older adults in some societies could mean increased ageism toward younger adults.

older adults in a particular culture are associated with more positive attitudes (Löckenhoff et al., 2009; North & Fiske, 2015).

CONSEQUENCES OF AGEISM

Ageism and the discrimination that often follows can have wide-reaching, negative consequences for those who experience it.

Effect on Physical and Mental Health

On an individual level, targets may suffer from low self-esteem, low self-efficacy, decreased productivity, cardiovascular problems, social withdrawal, and other physical and mental health problems (Levy, Ashman, & Dror, 2000; Lou et al., 2012). A lifetime of persistent exposure to ageist attitudes can also lead to internalized ageism as we grow older and can cause self-hatred, social disengagement or withdrawal, and feelings of worthlessness or being a burden (Rivera & Paredez, 2014). Nelson (2005) speculated that this entrenched cultural ageism is a prejudice against our feared future selves, which may explain why people, no matter their age, hold ageist attitudes—we are all fearful of aging and cannot view ourselves as old.

Effect on Healthcare

Ageist attitudes are prevalent in macro settings, such as institutions. The healthcare arena, where older adults often are at their most vulnerable, provides a good example (World Health Organization, 2015). Despite the need and efforts to improve interest in and preparation of the geriatric physical and mental healthcare workforce, there is a growing shortage of geriatricians and other relevant professionals (Golden, Silverman, & Issenberg, 2015).

Ageism also contributes to some healthcare professionals' belief that older adults do not deserve life-saving measures and should be subject to rationed care, especially if it is expensive. Healthcare professionals are trained to "cure" patients; therefore, they may be reluctant to invest time and resources in older individuals who may suffer from difficult-to-manage chronic diseases at higher rates than younger adults and who may not be as likely to recover (Taylor, 2012). Such attitudes have even fueled debates about whether people should simply forego healthcare after a certain age.

These viewpoints disproportionately affect women because they tend to live longer than men (Gullette, 2004, 2017). Studies also have found gender differences in older adults' access to care and treatment. For example, practitioners often view older women's symptoms as psychosomatic, and older women are less likely than older men to receive kidney transplants and diagnosis and treatment for cardiovascular disease (Chrisler, Barney, & Palatino, 2016; Correa-de-Araujo, 2004).

The effect of ageism on healthcare also includes the idea that illness, disability, and depression are "normal" processes of aging; thus, older adults tend to be referred for mental health and other care less frequently than younger people. Similarly, healthcare professionals may not expect older adults to have substance use issues or be sexually active, so attention or referral to substance abuse treatment or sexually transmitted infections may be lacking (McHugh & Interligi, 2015). Older adults' preferred treatment or end-of-life wishes may be ignored or people could be coerced into making unwanted decisions. This is particularly true for those from minoritized groups (Schwenk, 2016). Ageism also contributes to the pharmaceutical push of drugs and other products that target physical, cognitive, and sexual symptoms of aging. Of course, younger people are targeted as well, but treatments for illnesses and "anti-aging" aesthetics are a billion-dollar industry (Fassa, 2019; Gullette, 2017). These stereotypes become self-fulfilling prophesies for many older adults. They may believe they are not capable of following through with dietary or physical changes, improving mental or physical health symptoms, or making their own decisions on healthcare and other issues (Rivera & Paredez, 2014).

Othering
Older adults tend to be thought of and treated as a homogenous group, which can lead to "othering." Othering is defined as viewing or treating a person or group of people as intrinsically different from oneself. The needs, capabilities, characteristics, and issues of older adults are considered to be the same for all and different from those of younger people. Othering older adults perpetuates harmful stereotypes and can lead to decreased interactions between younger and older people. The lack of interactions further reinforces these views and increases the sense of isolation that older adults may feel.

Microaggressions
Another consequence of ageism is feeling traumatized or stripped of one's identity. **Microaggressions**—subtle, indirect, or unintentional actions or incidents directed toward marginalized people (Sue, 2010)—are commonly aimed at older adults and can create insidious, consistent stress. Examples include the following:

- avoiding eye contact with older adults;
- looking at them with a reductive gaze;
- expecting them to move or get out of the way in public;
- excluding them from conversations, such as speaking to their adult children instead of to them;

- infantilizing them (i.e., treating them like children);
- using patronizing language or elderspeak (addressing older adults in a slow, high-pitched voice, as if speaking to a child); and
- making hurtful jokes about age and being older (these are ubiquitous in the media and in commercially produced birthday cards).

These behaviors are often viewed as normal, acceptable, insignificant, or harmless, which can make them more difficult to address (Gullette, 2017).

Effect on Social Policy
With regard to social and other policies, ageism influences whether and how a society should support people as they age. It shapes how we perceive and conceptualize problems, formulate solutions to aging-related issues, and provide services and programs for older citizens (Bussolo, Koettl, & Sinnott, 2015; Sadana et al., 2013; World Health Organization, 2015). Indeed, ageism and discrimination are major barriers to developing and maintaining successful policies. For example, population aging is often viewed negatively; older people are blamed for economic and other problems because they are seen as a drain on resources that take away support from younger people. Older adults can be viewed as burdensome to society; thus, an aging population is viewed negatively in societies with entrenched ageist attitudes. This outlook is reflected in recent debates over Social Security (discussed more later in the book). Although the benefit is known to keep many older adults out of poverty, many legislators and policymakers want to make it more restrictive and chip away at the support it provides.

Rhetoric based in ageist attitudes, such as that older adults are greedy, lazy, dead weight, and stealing resources from our children, often drive policy changes and threaten support for many older adults (Coombs & Dollery, 2004). Similarly, even with laws against age discrimination in the workplace, employers and staff often see older people as ineffective workers who only take jobs away from younger people; as a result, companies may fire older, more expensive workers in favor of cheaper, younger ones (Gullette, 2017).

Figure 1.5 Microaggressions
Source: lemonadeserenade/Shutterstock

A MORE POSITIVE VIEW OF AGING

Numerous efforts have been made to depict growing older in an affirmative manner. A new paradigm of aging and later-life development can be imagined, one that helps to break down stereotypes and reframe later life as a more fulfilling part of the life span.

Successful Aging

The successful aging movement, which was introduced by Rowe and Kahn in the late 1980s, is an example. **Successful aging** consists of three components (Rowe & Kahn, 1997):

- A low probability of disease and disease-related disability
- High cognitive and physical functional capacity
- Active engagement with life

While the concept of successful aging holds promise with regard to describing the unique ways that people age without focusing on decline and disability, it has its critics. Many gerontologists and scholars argue that successful aging may promote another form of ageism by stigmatizing those who do not "age well," particularly minoritized groups who have faced a lifetime of discrimination and barriers to healthcare and other resources that help support healthy aging. In other words, intersectional characteristics greatly impact whether one ages successfully. Many physical declines associated with older age are unpredictable and linked to environmental factors, health disparities throughout the life span, and socioeconomic status. Further, some argue that successful aging does not consider subjective components of aging and that it is a biased, exclusive, and privileged Westernized concept (Martinson & Berridge, 2015). Other scholars wonder if there is room for positive aging that is not "successful" (Gullette, 2017).

A response to these criticisms is to view older age through the aforementioned human development lens; that is, as a typical part of life-span development. Later life development, like other stages, is characterized by some common milestones and experiences. For example, we all expect to find gray hair and wrinkles as we age. However, these commonalities are probably outnumbered by the differences, particularly when we consider that people accumulate a lifetime of unique experiences that affect how later life development unfolds. They have been exposed to different physical environments, experienced different socioeconomic circumstances, had access to different resources, and experienced different levels of privilege and oppression, all of which influence how we age physically, emotionally, cognitively, and spiritually. Because we have unique experiences throughout our lives, we can expect our movement into later life to be unique as well (Bussolo, Koettl, & Sinnott, 2015; Sadana et al., 2013; World Health Organization, 2015).

Optimal Aging

In response to criticisms of successful aging, other terms have emerged to better describe and capture the wide range of what could be considered desirable outcomes in individuals' unique aging processes. "Optimal aging" is one term that has been used to encapsulate the diversity in how people might view their own aging as "successful" or what it means to age well. **Optimal aging** is defined as the capacity to function across many domains (physical, functional, cognitive, emotional, social, and spiritual) to one's satisfaction and in spite of one's medical conditions (Baltes, 1987, 1997).

Figure 1.6 Optimal aging
Source: Rawpixel/Shutterstock

As the definition implies, the heart of optimal aging goes beyond focusing solely on longevity and excellent health and avoiding decline, disability, and illness, which becomes increasingly difficult to do the longer we live. Rather, optimal aging focuses on ways people can optimize their functioning in different areas. It emphasizes the ways people adapt and adjust to changing bodies, health, and circumstances and how people are able to compensate, when needed, to maximize functioning and life satisfaction. Thus, optimal aging does not imply an absence of illness, disease, or disability. Instead, optimal aging highlights the ways people may see problems that often come with usual aging as opportunities for growth and the development of new skills and capabilities (Baltes, 1987, 1997; Wahl & Oswald, 2016).

Avoiding Ageist Language

Given the individual variation in later life development, we can strive for a different paradigm on our lives as we age. Gullette (2017) suggests that an alternative use of language is one way to achieve this shift. We can pay attention not only to ageist language but also change our everyday vernacular regarding development. Gullette (2017) suggests using terms such as "aging into middle years," "aging into old age," "aging past youth," "aging through the life course," and "aging beyond midlife" to help normalize our aging and developmental process, view aging as unifying, and recognize that aging really begins at conception. Life-span development, from birth to death, can also be viewed in terms of progress narratives instead of a process of decline.

CHAPTER REVIEW

What Is Gerontology?
- Gerontology is the study of age, aging, and all aspects of mid- and later life development, including biological, psychological, social, and spiritual facets of growing

older. It is also concerned with the legal, societal, economic, political, and other processes that interface with age and the aging process and that often occur in response to an older population.
- Population aging is increasing globally and has many ramifications for societies. As the population ages, gerontologists work to improve all aspects of life for older adults and their communities.

Careers in Gerontology
- Gerontology is a multidisciplinary field that strives to understand how we age and how to improve our quality of life and well-being as we do so.
- Gerontologists work in many professions, including law, nursing, biology, medicine, economics, sociology, psychology, social work, and political science.

Common Theories of Aging
- Many theories of aging are biopsychosocial. Biological theories explore the causes of aging, from changes that occur on genetic and cellular levels to the ways our environment harms our bodies. Psychological theories help to explain age and aging in terms of life-span development, emotional and cognitive changes, the role of personality, and other factors (e.g., resiliency, creativity, and spirituality). Sociological theories help to explain roles, relationships, and how age and the aging process interact with the social environment.
- Queer, feminist, intersectional, strengths-based, and human development lenses attempt to deconstruct traditional, simplistic, and often discriminatory views of age and growing older. They strive to reconstruct a more complex and inclusive discourse on the process.

What Is Ageism?
- Ageism is the systematic prejudicing, discriminating, and stereotyping of individuals based on age.
- Ageism and its resulting discrimination is a deep-rooted and pervasive problem, particularly in the United States.
- Ageism is the one "ism" that is universal; that is, anyone who lives into older age will experience it to a certain degree, depending on his or her environment and circumstances.
- Ageism often intersects with racism, classism, and sexism, as well as queermisia and transmisia.

Types of Ageism
- Scholars studying ageism have developed specific categories of ageism. These include middle-ageism, neuroageism, benevolent ageism, individual ageism, and institutional ageism.

How Culture Influences the Perception of Aging
- Our cultural context shapes our attitudes, beliefs, and social norms about growing older and the roles we play in society as we age.
- Many cultures view aging in a negative light; this perception is reflected in all aspects of culture, including the terminology used to describe older people and representations of them in literature and media.

Consequences of Ageism
- Ageism can have many consequences, including negative effects on physical and mental health, internalized ageism, and low self-esteem.

- Ageism often results in discrimination in the workplace, across all types of organizations, and in society at large.

A More Positive View of Aging
- Changing society's view of aging and older people involves considering the process as a normal part of the life span, one in which individuals bring their own unique and rich experiences to growing older.

REVIEW QUESTIONS
1. What areas might you see as future opportunities for gerontologists?
2. Discuss strengths and limitations to the common theories used to view aging.
3. Compare and contrast the different types of ageism discussed in this chapter. What might they all have in common?
4. What suggestions could you make to change societal views on aging?

KEY TERMS

gerontology
geriatrics
population aging
gerontologists
queer theory
feminist theory
ageism
double jeopardy
triple jeopardy
microaggressions

middle-ageism
neuroageism
benevolent ageism
hostile ageism
individual ageism
institutional ageism
elderspeak
successful aging
optimal aging

CHAPTER 2

Biology of Aging

Chapter Outline
Defining Age
    Subjective Age
    Intersectional Factors That Affect Aging
Age and Human Development
Cross-Cultural Perspectives on Biological Aging
Theories of Biological Aging
    Genetic (Programmed) Theory
    Wear-and-Tear and Mitochondrial Theories
Age-Related Changes by Body System
    Skin and Hair
    Senses: Hearing and Vision
    Musculoskeletal System
    Immune System
    Endocrine System
    Central Nervous System: The Brain
        Dementia
        Treatment for Dementia
Promoting Health and Longevity
    Health Disparities and Older Adults
    Promoting Health and Well-Being
        Nutrition
        Physical Activity
        Behavioral and Environmental Accommodations

Learning Objectives
After completing this chapter, you will be able to:
- Define physical age and differentiate between chronological age, functional age, and subjective age.
- Describe the relationship between physical age and human development.
- Explain how culture influences the perception of aging.
- Describe common theories of biological aging.
- Provide examples of how aging affects various body systems.
- Describe measures that can promote healthy aging and longevity.

How do our bodies grow, develop, change, and age across our life span, and what factors affect these processes? Gerontologists explore these and many other questions with regard to the biology of aging. Often, physical human development is classified into specific categories such as childhood, adolescence, young adulthood, middle adulthood, and old age. In reality, we all grow, develop, and age in a continuous fashion. Age, as a category or discrete number, is less meaningful but is used to mark various developmental changes.

Still, age as a number tends to be significant in many societies and cultures, and it is important to understand how it is applied and how it can affect us personally, socially, politically, and economically. For example, our age often shapes our self-perceptions, how others perceive us, the roles we assume, and to which benefits and programs we are entitled. As discussed in Chapter 1, older adults may face age discrimination in the workplace and in social and other realms. Thus, understanding how a person's age affects their physical, emotional, and social well-being is important. It is also important to understand how and why our bodies change as we age and how health and well-being can be promoted throughout the life span.

DEFINING AGE
There are two primary ways to define physical age. **Chronological age** refers to the number of years we have been alive (Han et al., 2018). Often, older age is further categorized into young-old (65–74), middle-old (75–84), and old-old (85+) (Zizza, Ellison, & Wernette, 2009). Chronological age is the way most of us define our age. However, many gerontologists posit that chronological age by itself is an incomplete determination of age because it doesn't account for all the factors that influence our functional age.

Functional age refers to our age in relation to our overall health status. Functional age is influenced by many factors, including genetics, presence or absence of disease or chronic illness, and other external forces such as our environment and lifestyle choices, such as diet and nutrition and activity level. Functional age is also influenced by a person's exposure to substances, environmental toxins, and stress (Han et al., 2018; Soriano-Tárraga et al., 2017).

Subjective Age

Subjective age refers to how we perceive and experience ourselves as younger or older than our chronological age. Subjective age is highly individualistic; it varies a great deal from person to person, regardless of chronological or even functional age. Further, subjective age is an important predictor of our health outcomes in later life. Specifically, people who feel subjectively younger than their chronological age compared to those who feel subjectively older tend to have better health outcomes in later life (Kwak et al., 2018).

Research suggests that as we age many of us subjectively feel younger than our chronological age, unless we are struggling with disabling diseases or disabilities, which can cause us to feel older. This is particularly true for people in later life (Rubin & Bernsten, 2006; Shinan-Altman & Werner, 2019). Feeling younger than our chronological age is known as **subjective age bias** (Barak, 2009).

Chronological, functional, and subjective age are interrelated. Our chronological age predicts risks for various diseases and illness as well as physical changes we all will experience to one degree or another. However, many internal and external factors influence our functional and subjective age. Further, our subjective age influences our functional age and vice versa.

Intersectional Factors That Affect Aging

Intersections of age, race, class, and sexual and gender identification influence our functional and subjective age. In addition, our interactions with our environment affect how we age physically and how we perceive our aging bodies. Intersectional and socioeconomic factors influence the availability of resources that can help us feel younger (e.g., gyms, healthcare, cosmetic surgery, healthful foods and environments), how we view our aging bodies (e.g., aging may be seen as more "distinguished" among heterosexual men and more anxiety-provoking for gay men), and how we feel about aging bodies and youthful appearances. For example, in general, white men and women in the United States may be less accepting of aging bodies and more concerned about youthful appearance than people from other groups. Thus, intersectional factors can serve to both privilege and oppress groups of people in later life and result in ageism and discrimination as well as positively or negatively influence subjective aging (Calasanti & King, 2015).

Figure 2.1 Intersectional factors affect aging
Source: Blue Planet Studio/Shutterstock

Socially constructed concepts about aging, which are influenced by intersectional identities, can affect how we age physically. Over the life course, people can internalize negative stereotypes about aging that are reflected in their culture, which can make any physical declines experienced with age more severe. One study found that individuals who held positive beliefs about aging lived 7.6 years longer than those who held negative beliefs. Belief systems can affect aspects of physical aging that include memory, balance, and medication usage (Armstrong, 2020; Levy et al., 2002).

AGE AND HUMAN DEVELOPMENT

Sometimes it can be helpful to use physical age to mark various developmental milestones and anticipate the development of certain physical skills, capabilities, and risk factors for physical issues. However, on an individual level, our bodies grow, develop, and age at different rates, often within wide age ranges. For example, universally, children may be expected to walk somewhere between nine and 12 months, but factors such as culture, nutrition, environment, and physical development all play a role in the development of this skill (Adolph, Karaski, & Tamis-LeMonda, 2009). Children in parts of Africa and India may begin walking earlier in life because their caregivers commonly massage and stretch children's limbs while bathing and prop them in sitting positions, actions that stimulate children's motor skills (Hopkins & Westra, 1988). Similarly, while we all expect to develop gray hair later in life, some people develop gray hair earlier than expected, such as at age 30, while others see their first gray hairs in their 50s. Factors such as smoking, thyroid disorders, and genetic syndromes may contribute to early graying (Zayed et al., 2013). From this standpoint, it is helpful to think of age and human development as a continual process from birth to death that is affected by a wide range of biological, environmental, and other factors.

CROSS-CULTURAL PERSPECTIVES ON BIOLOGICAL AGING

Cross-cultural explorations of biological aging can help us understand how cultural influences and the geographical and socioeconomic environment affect the perception of aging. Like many aspects of human development, internalized cultural values influence our experience of older age. For example, while the onset and symptoms of menopause may be similar across women from different countries and cultures, how women experience these changes often differs. In Western cultures that place a high value on

Figure 2.2 Universalities and individualism in human development
Source: mapodile/iStock

youth, menopause may be viewed as a loss of youthfulness and sexual attractiveness. In Asian countries such as China, menopause may be viewed as "rebirth," a time when energy can be invested in activities other than childcare. Beliefs about menopause, in turn, can affect the way physical changes are experienced (Namazi, Sadeghi, & Moghadam, 2019). Similarly, culture can influence the way we view aging in general. For example, a study on Norwegian older adults found that people tended to respond to physical changes of aging with acceptance. Sense of self was not tied to physical appearance or abilities for people in this study, and growing older was considered a privilege (Kalfoss, 2017).

In studies on memory and cognition, older North American adults tend to demonstrate the **positivity effect** (Carstensen & Mikels, 2005), or a preference toward positive stimuli, such as a stronger memory for faces with happy and pleasant expressions versus faces with angry or neutral expressions. The positivity effect is thought to be dominant in North American culture because of the emphasis on autonomy and independence. However, the positivity is not as prevalent among older individuals in China, perhaps because of the cultural emphasis on interdependence, where negative and positive social cues may be equally important in social situations (Fung, 2013).

THEORIES OF BIOLOGICAL AGING

Senescence can be defined as the process of growing old. It is a result of changes in biological functioning of our bodies over time (Bansal & Tissenbaum, 2015). Our bodies age continuously throughout the life span. In later life these cumulative changes in our immune, cognitive, metabolic, and other functions cause the decline we associate with later age, eventually resulting in death. Often, these changes also bring illnesses associated with later age such as cancer, heart disease, and Alzheimer's disease (Bansal & Tissenbaum, 2015). However, it is important to note that these are not "diseases of old age," as many people assume. Rather, with time, our risk of developing disease increases.

Biological theories of aging attempt to explain the complex biological and genetic processes that contribute to aging, as well as longevity. For decades, scientists have been exploring how biological processes contribute to aging, and currently there are more than 300 theories of biological aging (American Federation for Aging Research, 2019). Many theories have begun to coalesce, offering a more focused perspective on how biology contributes to our aging. Specifically, research suggests that the aging process is due to our biological imperfectness, leading to accumulated damage (Gladyshev, 2014). The most common theories of aging are the genetic (programmed) theory, the wear-and-tear theory, and the mitochondrial theory.

Genetic (Programmed) Theory

Most scientists agree that the aging process is rooted in our cells. Changes, mutations, and impairments in DNA are associated with the physical decline associated with aging and are implicated in disorders that cause premature aging. When DNA replicates, mistakes can occur, changing the DNA sequencing and causing permanent errors. Once a cell's DNA is severely damaged the cell dies or stops replicating, leading to tissue atrophy and dysfunction and the release of inflammatory substances (Field et al., 2018).

Other processes leading to improper protein function, mitochondrial dysfunction, and decline of red blood cell production are also implicated in the aging process (Ben-Zvi, Miller, & Morimoto, 2009; Ross et al., 2014).

Research also suggests that the aging process is influenced by changes in DNA and in **telomeres**, which are nucleotide sequences that "cap" the ends of chromosomes, preventing them from deteriorating or fusing with other chromosomes. Telomeres control how quickly our cells age and die. Researchers have found that higher chronological age is associated with shorter telomeres, and that individuals with short telomeres tend to be at risk for disease (Field et al., 2018). Further, research suggests that a healthy diet and lifestyle can help lengthen telomeres, which can contribute to longer life (Balan, Decottignies, & Deldicque, 2018).

DNA methylation is another process that plays a role in biological aging. DNA methylation is a mechanism used by cells to control gene expression. When a methyl group (molecule consisting of one carbon and three hydrogen atoms) is added to DNA, the function and expression of genes is modified. DNA methylation is vital to cellular processes, including gene suppression, chromosome stability, and embryonic development. Abnormal DNA methylation is associated with various metabolic, autoimmune, and neurologic diseases (Dor & Cedar, 2018; Lou, Hajkova, & Ecker, 2018). Research suggests that DNA methylation can accurately predict functional age.

Programmed aging theory, based on DNA changes, posits that genetically programmed changes occur in cells as the body ages. So many developmental processes are genetically programmed that it makes sense that the aging process would also be programmed. From this perspective, old age and death are caused through an evolutionary process that limits the life span (Goldsmith, 2016a, 2016b). This theory suggests that the aging process is controlled by a master "clock" that determines how and when we age (Mitteldorf, 2016).

The genetic theory incorporates an assumption that the function of the endocrine and immune systems is programmed to decline over time. The endocrine system controls the body's hormonal functions. The immune system recognizes and fights off foreign antigens. Over time, these systems become less effective, which can contribute to the

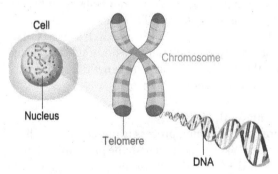

Figure 2.3 DNA and telomeres play a role in aging
Source: Fancy Tapis/Shutterstock

development of conditions such as arthritis, osteoporosis, and cardiovascular disease (Kochman, 2015; Prinzinger, 2005).

The programmed theory of aging has been criticized for its limitations. Researchers point out that if genetics fully explained aging, we would be able to identify the genes responsible for the aging process. Thus, we would have the capability to "turn off" these genes and halt or reverse the aging process. To date, scientists have not been successful in identifying "aging genes." However, some researchers have been able to extend the life span through manipulation of various biological processes, offering evidence that programming may play a role in aging (Kowald & Kirkwood, 2016; Mitteldorf, 2016). Still, a great deal of evidence supports the genetic theory, and it may be that there is an evolutionary advantage to the aging process, such as providing a check on population (Mitteldorf, 2016).

Wear-and-Tear and Mitochondrial Theories

The wear-and-tear theory holds that living takes its toll on the body and that components of cells and tissues simply wear out over time. According to this theory, the cumulative effect of internal and external stresses (such as poor diet, environmental toxins, etc.) is an accelerated rate of cell death.

Mitochondria are called the "powerhouses" of the cell. They are structures within cells that take in nutrients and create energy. The mitochondrial theory of aging holds that aging is caused by free radicals (unstable atoms) that cause damage to cells and their mitochondria, resulting in reduced energy production.

AGE-RELATED CHANGES BY BODY SYSTEM

We experience many physical changes as we age. In this section, we'll discuss common changes that occur within specific body systems.

Skin and Hair

Our skin continually goes through changes throughout the life span. As with other aspects of aging, the extent of these changes is influenced by genetics, molecular and cellular processes, and exposure to the environment. Age-related skin changes involve more than appearance. While many people are familiar with skin changes such as wrinkles and the appearance of dark spots on the skin (solar lentigines), physiological changes can result in a reduced ability for the skin to act as a barrier (Farage et al., 2009). As we age, we lose collagen and elastin fibers, which reduces the skin's strength and results in sagging skin that accompanies aging. Moreover, vascular atrophy can leave people more susceptible to issues like dermatitis, skin tears, and pressure ulcers (Patel & Yosipovitch, 2010).

As we age, our hair also undergoes changes. Continuous structural changes to hair follicles begin at birth and continue throughout the life span. The most commonly recognized age-related changes are graying hair and androgenetic alopecia, which causes male pattern baldness and hair loss in women (Mirmirani, 2015). Hair loss in men is driven by intersectional factors, including age, race, genetics, and hormones. White men with a family history of baldness are most likely to experience male pattern baldness, which can begin as early as the teen years and is at least partly associated with a

Figure 2.4 Aging-related physical changes
Source: FG Trade/iStock

decrease of androgenic hormones. Senescent alopecia (hair thinning with age, usually after age 50) occurs when the hair follicle decreases in size. Further, factors such as smoking and exposure to ultraviolet light, heat from blow dryers and curling irons, and chemicals from hair products and coloring can weaken the hair follicles (Lu et al., 2009; Su & Chen, 2007). As we age, our hair becomes less resilient and is more susceptible to damage.

Graying hair also occurs as we age. Hair color is determined by melanin, which has dark and light pigments, and is formed before we're born. These dark and light pigments blend together in different ways to make our unique hair color. Each hair follicle has a melanin "clock" that is regulated by genes and other factors, and over time, the production of melanin that goes into the hair follicles is slowed and eventually stopped. This exhaustion of melanin happens at a different rate for each hair follicle. For some people this process happens rapidly, while for others it happens over decades. In general, the chance of gray hair coming in increases 10–20 percent every decade after age 30 (Library of Congress, 2017).

Besides being determined by genes, the timing of gray hair appearance is also affected by other factors including the intersection of race and certain physical illnesses. For example, those who smoke, are obese, experience depression, or have autoimmune disorders or iron deficiencies are more likely to gray prematurely than those who do not have these characteristics (Thompson et al., 2019; Shin et al., 2015). Among Asian people, heart disease is associated with premature gray hair, while among white people, premature gray hair is associated with irritable bowel syndrome (Thompson et al., 2019).

Senses: Hearing and Vision

Presbycusis is the medical term for age-related hearing loss. This problem is common but varies a great deal from individual to individual. Like all other physical functions, hearing loss as we age depends on many factors including genetics, aging of the cochlea (the spiral cavity in the inner ear), medical conditions like cardiovascular disease that can limit blood supply to the ear, and environmental exposure to noise

(Yamasoba et al., 2013). Aging-related hearing loss and impairment is associated with issues such as depression, isolation, communication problems, poor quality of life, and increased risk of dementia and mortality (Bowen et al., 2019; Fischer, Weber, & Riechelmann, 2016). Thus, scheduling regular hearing screenings and using preventive measures like wearing ear protection in noisy workplaces or at concerts, for example, is important throughout the life span to mitigate hearing loss in later life.

Vision changes can occur at any point in the life span. Many changes in vision are highly individualistic and are also determined by genetics, environment, and other intersectional factors. Prespbyopia, or the blurring of near vision, is a common development in mid-life, which can worsen with time (Hickenbotham et al., 2012). Cataracts, caused by clouding of the lens in the eye, are commonly associated with age as is macular degeneration, which causes damage to the retina and can cause blindness. Glaucoma, a group of eye conditions that damage the optic nerve, is associated with abnormally high pressure in the eye and is one of the leading causes of blindness in people aged 60+. While these conditions are associated with the aging process, many of them can be prevented or mitigated through regular screenings, good nutrition, and wearing sunglasses. However, intersectional factors such as race, gender, and income can affect people's habits and access to healthcare, which can ultimately affect hearing, vision, and overall health as they age (Desmettre, 2018).

Musculoskeletal System

In general, our muscle mass peaks in early adulthood, after which it begins to decline slowly throughout the life span. Loss of muscle mass and strength is known as sarcopenia. Muscle mass is associated with strength and musculoskeletal function, such as gait speed (the time it takes to walk a specified distance), bone strength, and grip strength. Indeed, our hand grip is a strong predictor of mortality, independent of the presence of disease or other life-shortening factors (American Society for Nutrition, 2019; Cruz-Jentoft et al., 2010; Rantanen et al., 2003).

Figure 2.5 Cataracts are a common age-related eye issue
Source: SERGEI PRIMAKOV/Shutterstock

Further, we tend to lose bone mass as we age, putting us at increased risk for osteoporosis. Osteoporosis is a disease characterized by decreased bone density. Bones become brittle and more fragile, increasing the risk for fractures, a particular concern for postmenopausal women. Approximately one in three women and one in five men aged 50+ will experience fractures caused by osteoporosis (International Osteoporosis Foundation, 2017). Declines in bone density and muscle mass increase the risk for falling, which can result in injury, fractures, disability, and even death (Ungar et al., 2013).

Cartilage also undergoes a variety of structural and mechanical changes as we age. Generally, it becomes softer and erodes, and fluid around the joints decreases, making joints rigid and fragile, sometimes resulting in osteoarthritis. However, not everyone experiences pain or other problems associated with cartilage changes (Fang et al., 2018). Changes in our joints, muscles, and bones all affect our gait speed, which tends to slow as we age, and is a strong predictor of our well-being as we age (Studenski et al., 2011).

Genetics, along with lifestyle factors such as diet, exercise, and substance use, are associated with the extent of muscle and bone loss one may experience with age. For example, studies indicate that men typically have greater grip strength than women, but both see declines in grip strength over time. Further, men and women of all ages in India and Mexico tend to have lower grip strength than men and women from other countries. This difference is likely due to a combination of genetics and access to nutrition across the life span (World Health Organization, 2015).

Throughout the life span, biological factors interact with lifestyle and environmental factors to determine how muscles and bones may change. For instance, consuming a healthful diet, incorporating strength and weight bearing exercises, engaging in core strengthening activities, decreasing alcohol use, improving the quality of sleep, and managing chronic disease can mitigate loss of muscle and bone loss and even improve functioning (American Society for Nutrition, 2019; International Osteoporosis Foundation, 2017). Further, environmental interventions such as improving lighting, securing rugs, using assistive devices, and clearing obstacles around the home can prevent falls and other injuries (Novelli, 2012; Shaw & Claydon, 2014).

Immune System
With age, immune function declines, reducing the body's ability to fight infection. This overall decline is known as immunosenescence, which can compromise the body's ability to effectively respond to other factors such as stress and vaccinations (Lang et al., 2012). This process also can lead to increased inflammation in the body, causing other illnesses and issues such as frailty and atherosclerosis, the build-up of fatty deposits on the lining of the arteries (Aspinall & Lang, 2018).

Endocrine System
The endocrine system is made up of a group of organs and glands that regulate and control body functions by producing and releasing hormones. In general, endocrine function declines with age because hormone receptors become less receptive. However,

levels of hormones themselves may decrease, increase, or remain the same. For example, melatonin, estrogen (in women), testosterone (in men), and growth hormone decrease with age. Cortisol, insulin, and thyroid hormones tend to remain the same or only slightly decrease with age, while hormones such as norepinephrine, epinephrine, and luteinizing hormones typically increase with age (van Den Beld et al., 2018).

A decline in endocrine function can cause various issues including an increase in fat mass and a decline in bone and muscle mass, especially when coupled with issues like illness, inflammation, and malnutrition (van Den Beld et al., 2018). In biological women, a decrease in estrogen and progesterone hormones made by the ovaries leads to **menopause**, or the cessation of the menstrual cycle (confirmed when 12 consecutive periods are missed, with no other apparent causes). Menopause typically occurs between ages 45 and 55, with an average age of 51, but it can happen earlier.

Perimenopause refers to the time frame when the body makes the transition to menopause, with menstruation becoming more irregular. The onset and length of perimenopause varies a great deal, with a typical age range between 35 and 55. Perimenopause can be marked by symptoms such as hot flashes, night sweats, irregular periods, and sleep disturbances. The type of symptoms and the extent to which they are experienced varies a great deal (Ciano et al., 2017; Takahashi & Johnson, 2015).

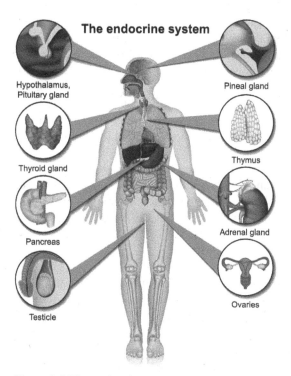

Figure 2.6 The endocrine system
Source: MedicalStocks/Alamy Stock Vector

Hormone replacement therapy (HRT) involves the use of synthetic hormones (mainly estrogen and progesterone) to help reduce the symptoms of perimenopause. HRT carries risks, which vary depending on the timing of the therapy and each woman's genetics, lifestyle, and health status. Synthetic hormone replacement therapy can increase the risk of stroke, breast cancer, blood clots, and heart attack, for example (Manson et al., 2013).

Andropause is the term used to describe a gradual decline in the production of androgenic hormones, especially testosterone, in older males. Testosterone levels generally decrease by about 1 percent per year after age 30, though this percentage varies from individual to individual (Travison et al., 2007). Besides age, levels of testosterone are affected by factors such as stress, obesity, illness, and medication (Bhasin et al., 2010). Lower testosterone levels can lead to decreased sexual satisfaction and a reduction in general well-being (Singh, 2013). Around the mid-30s, many men may begin to notice issues like weight gain and erectile dysfunction, which may be at least partially caused by decreased testosterone. Low testosterone levels can also contribute to other problems such as diabetes, chronic illness, and osteopenia (bone loss), and other chronic illness such as arthritis (Castelló-Porcar & Martínez-Jabaloyas, 2016; Singh, 2013).

Central Nervous System: The Brain
How the brain and cognitive functions change with age vary a great deal from person to person and are affected by many factors, including genetics, nutrition, education, medication, lifestyle, and the environment. Two types of intelligence are affected by aging, but in different ways. **Fluid intelligence** is the ability to think speedily and reason flexibly to solve problems. **Crystallized intelligence** is the accumulated knowledge, skills, and experiences gained over time (Cattell, 1967). Research indicates that a steady decline of **fluid intelligence** tends to occur between the ages of 20 to 80. Conversely, **crystallized intelligence** tends to improve until about age 60 and stabilize until around age 80 (Salthouse, 2010; Simpson-Kent et al., 2020).

As we age, we may experience some decreases in memory, the ability to divide attention among tasks, and speed of information processing. However, other cognitive functions such as vocabulary, comprehension, concentration, and memory for personal and historical facts and procedural tasks (such as driving a car or doing math) tend to improve or at least remain stable over time (Murman, 2015).

Dementia
As we age, our risk of developing dementia increases, though dementia can develop earlier in the life span. **Dementia** is an umbrella term for a set of diseases or conditions caused by changes in the brain that affect cognitive skills such as memory, speech, problem solving, and performing everyday activities. Dementia also can affect emotions, behavior, and relationships (Alzheimer's Association, 2019).

Dementia, like so many issues associated with age, is affected by intersectional factors such as race, gender, ethnicity, environment, and economic status. For example, dementia is more likely to develop in individuals with high incomes, because they tend to live longer than those with low incomes.

There are many types of dementia; some of the more common types are described in Table 2.1.

Treatment for Dementia

While dementia tends to be a progressive disease with no cure, there are various, evidence-based interventions that can help with symptoms. For example, some

Table 2.1 Common Types of Dementia

Type	Description	Symptoms
Alzheimer's disease	The most common type of dementia, making up approximately 60–80 percent of dementia cases. While Alzheimer's disease is not a normal part of the aging process, risk for developing it increases with age. However, Alzheimer's disease can occur at younger ages, which is known as early-onset Alzheimer's disease.	Caused by tangles and plaques in the brain, symptoms of Alzheimer's disease generally progress and worsen with time. Early in the disease process, memory loss and other symptoms may be mild, while later on, memory loss becomes severe and people may not be able to speak, walk, swallow, or respond to their environment, for example.
Creutzfeldt-Jakob disease	A rare but fast developing dementia caused when prion proteins, found throughout the body, begin taking abnormal shape in the brain.	Symptoms of Creutzfeldt-Jakob disease include depression; agitation; confusion; disorientation; issues with memory, planning, and judgment; involuntary movements; and vision problems.
Huntington's disease dementia	A genetic condition that causes dementia through a premature breakdown of the brain's nerve cells, which typically begins in childhood, adolescence, or in mid-life (around the 30s or 40s).	Symptoms of Hunting disease dementia include impaired movement, impulse control problems, trouble speaking clearly, and difficulty focusing and learning new tasks.
Lewy body dementia	The third most common type of dementia caused by protein deposits in nerve cells, similar to Alzheimer's and Parkinson's diseases.	Lewy body dementia is marked by changes in thinking and reasoning, gait imbalances, visual hallucinations, delusions, sleep disturbances, and memory loss.
Mixed dementia	Dementia in which abnormalities of two or more dementias occur simultaneously. The most common form of mixed dementia is Alzheimer's disease and vascular dementia.	Various symptoms may occur, depending on the progression of disease.
Parkinson disease dementia	Dementia that often develops with advanced Parkinson's disease.	Symptoms include irritability, depression, vision problems, sleep disturbances, delusions, and problems with memory and judgment.
Vascular dementia	The second most common type of dementia caused by a lack of blood flow to the brain. A lack of oxygen to the brain can occur with stroke or atherosclerotic disease, for example, and can occur suddenly or gradually.	Symptoms of vascular dementia depend on the cause and location of the damage and can include confusion, disorientation, trouble completing tasks, problems with concentration, and balance and walking problems.

Source: Alzheimer's Association (2019a).

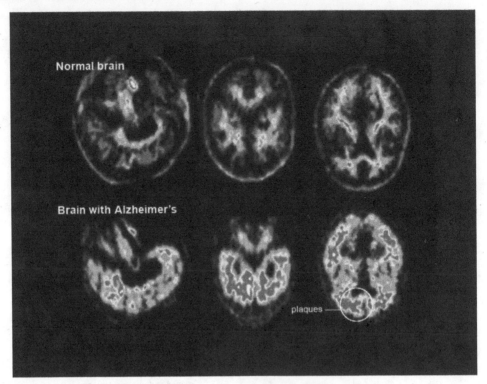

Figure 2.7 Scans of brains with and without signs of Alzheimer's disease
Source: Science History Images/Alamy Stock Vector

medications can help slow the progression of cognitive dysfunction. Various therapies such as cognitive stimulation therapy, validation therapy, and reminiscence therapy often are used with people who have mild to moderate dementia. The goal of these interventions is to stimulate memory, senses, and thinking; validate emotions and experiences; and reduce depression, anxiety, agitation, and restlessness. Other modalities like massage and aromatherapy can be used to stimulate senses and create soothing, comforting environments and physical sensations that can help reduce agitation and other discomfort that often arises with dementia. One such approach is the Snoezelen room, a multisensory space that incorporates various stimulating features such as light, water, color, music, and textures to help facilitate relaxation and communication between people with dementia and their caregivers (Banerjee & Ford, 2018; Dementia Services Information and Development Centre, 2014). Further, in recent decades, dementia care has become increasingly person-centered, meaning care is tailored to the abilities, interests, personality, and cultural and experiential backgrounds of those with dementia. Person-centered care has been shown to be effective in preventing and managing various behavioral and psychological symptoms of dementia in a way that maintains dignity and respect for those receiving dementia care (Alzheimer's Society, 2021).

Figure 2.8 A Snoezelen room
Source: Ciell/Wikimedia Commons/CC BY-SA 2.5

PROMOTING HEALTH AND LONGEVITY

Can aging be slowed or even reversed? Research exploring biological bases for cellular-level, programmed aging has led to efforts to figure out how to "turn off" or reverse these processes and extend the life span. Scientists have been somewhat successful in manipulating the genes and environment of various organisms in a lab setting to extend life. Measures such as dietary restriction, gene alteration, and cellular programming have been shown to add years to the lives of these organisms, but they have not increased their health status. Organisms that have been manipulated by life-extending processes may live longer, but they are not benefitting from better health or less frailty (Bansal & Tissenbaum, 2015; Metaxakis & Partridge, 2013). If these same life extending procedures were applied to humans, it could be that while the life span is increased, we may end up with unsustainable healthcare costs and decreased quality of life for longer periods of time (Bansal & Tissenbaum, 2015). Studies that have examined the current state of increased longevity and its effects on health and well-being have discovered that indeed, people are not necessarily enjoying good health with extended life (Alecxih et al., 2010; Terraneo, 2015).

Health Disparities and Older Adults

As previously noted, individual differences in genetics, lifestyles, intersectional characteristics, and socioeconomic and geographical environments contribute to the speed and nature of age-related changes. For example, people of color often face a lifetime of

CASE 2.1

Daniel's Move

Daniel is 81 years old, lives alone, and has been having issues remembering things like paying his bills and preparing meals. Daniel's adult son, who lives in the same city, has noticed these issues along with other problems like Daniel not taking his medication or taking care of himself or his home. Daniel's son also has noticed that Daniel has lost weight and seems unsteady. When he visited a neurologist, Daniel was diagnosed with moderate dementia, and he and his son decided it would be best for Daniel to move into a care living facility for safety and health reasons. Daniel's son found a facility that practices person-directed care. Upon admission, Daniel received an individualized care plan that addressed Daniel's likes, dislikes, and preferences around areas such as activities, socializing, personal care, sleep patterns, meal preparation and timing, and environmental factors such as temperature, lighting, and noise level that might help Daniel feel more comfortable and mitigate possible cognitive and behavior symptoms associated with dementia. Further, Daniel received a care plan to address his physical health including mobility, pain management, and other disease issues. After several months at this facility, Daniel's son noticed that his father had gained weight, seemed more physically healthy, was socializing and talking more than he had been while at home, and was engaging in some of his old hobbies. Daniel's son also noticed that Daniel's memory had improved a little and the progression of dementia symptoms seemed to have slowed. Daniel noticed that he felt better physically and emotionally. While Daniel admitted he would rather be living in his own home, he appreciated having regular help with his physical and other needs, felt less lonely and enjoyed making new friends and connections, and noticed a sense of relief from his son, who did not seem to be worrying as much about Daniel's well-being.

What are some of the differences in environment between Daniel's home and this care facility that you think contribute to Daniel's overall health and well-being? As an administrator in a person-centered care facility, what factors would you attend to and what services might you offer to provide individualized care and to better support the residents with dementia?

---

compounding barriers and inequities in access to healthcare that contribute to poor health. People who smoke or live in areas with unhealthy air quality are exposed to toxins that affect their health and may accelerate the aging process. Exposure over time to environmental factors such as violence, poverty, discrimination, or forced migration can lead to stress and other physical responses that can cause chronic illness and rapid aging. Intersectional factors like age, race, socioeconomic status, and gender and sexual identity affect not only physical health, but the type and quality of health and other care to which people have access (Calasanti & Giles, 2020).

Falls, pain, diabetes, sensory problems, and diseases such as obstructive pulmonary disease are more likely to develop among people in poorer countries. In these regions, poorer living conditions, lack of adequate nutrition, lack of access to healthcare and other resources, and higher exposure to air and noise pollution contribute to health challenges (World Health Organization, 2015). In the United States, indigenous and immigrant populations continue to have the poorest health outcomes across the life span than other population segments, due to inequities in income, education, health care access, and other intersectional factors (American Society on Aging, 2020).

Access to hearing and vision screening, along with other preventive care, may help to prevent health problems or catch them early enough for effective treatment. However, issues such as disparities in care (especially for people of color), lack of access to care, and cost-prohibitive measures such as hearing aids, cochlear implants, cataract surgery, and technology and devices used to help aid mobility can be out of reach for many older adults, even if they have health insurance. For example, research indicates that Hispanic older adults are less likely to use assistive devices because of cost and lack of awareness of the types of devices and how to use them (Orellano-Colón et al., 2016).

Promoting Health and Well-Being

Health promotion involves a process of empowering people to gain control over and improve their health utilizing a range of social, educational, and environmental interventions (The World Health Organization, 2015). The World Health Organization (2015) proposed recommendations to increase health and well-being as we age. These recommendations include:

- Recognize the diversity and heterogeneity of experiences of older adults;
- Address health disparities;
- Reduce ageist attitudes and stereotypes;
- Empower people in their abilities to face challenges and problem-solve;
- Adapt environments to make them more age-friendly;
- Approach health as comprehensive and holistic; and
- Provide care that is person-centered and enables choice.

Researchers and gerontologists are also interested in the role of behavior, technology, and environmental adaptation that may prevent or mitigate the course of disease and other problems that often arise with age. For example, while much more research needs to be conducted, studies examining the role of nutrition and physical activity in healthy aging are promising.

Nutrition

Good nutrition is important to maintain healthy bone, muscle, neurological, and other biological systems. While our caloric needs decrease with age, our need for most nutrients does not. Malnutrition in older adults is often misdiagnosed or underdiagnosed; thus, opportunities to improve nutrition are missed (World Health Organization, 2015).

Age-related physical changes may compromise diet, appetite, digestion, nutrient absorption, and ability to access and consume a variety of nutritious foods. Some common issues that interfere with good nutrition include:

- Dental problems can make chewing difficult.
- A diminished sense of taste and smell can result in decreased appetite.
- Inflammation or other illnesses can make eating and digestion uncomfortable or painful.
- Limited mobility can make shopping for food and preparing food difficult.
- Food insecurity or lack of access to healthy foods can lead to nutrient deficiencies.

Physical Activity

Physical activity is also important in maintaining health into older age. Engaging in physical activity across the life span is not only beneficial for physical and cognitive functioning and supporting healthy biological processes, but it also has been shown to increase longevity (Arem et al., 2015). For instance, engaging in physical activity throughout the life span and into older age is associated with increased muscle tone, bone mass, cognitive functioning, and decreased risk of chronic illness and disease like stroke, diabetes, and heart disease. Engaging in physical activity is also associated with better social and mental health outcomes, such as increased community engagement, maintenance of friendship networks, and resilience against mental health problems like anxiety and depression (Lachman et al., 2018).

Behavioral and Environmental Accommodations

Accommodations in behavior and the environment can help to improve well-being for older adults with various health issues. For example, training people with macular degeneration to utilize their remaining vision helps to improve mobility and decrease anxiety about falling. For individuals with hearing loss, decreasing background noise, using assistive hearing devices, and looking directly at people during conversations can aid hearing and help to decrease feelings of social isolation (Centers for Disease Control and Prevention, 2018b; Riddering, 2008).

Conducting home assessments for lighting, walkways, and stairways can identify risks for falling and improve visibility and mobility in the home. Preventive measures such as installing nonskid backing to rugs and bathmats, installing railings on stairways, using contrasting colors on washcloths or electrical strips to identify thresholds on tubs or floors, and using shower chairs or tub-transfers can greatly reduce the risk of falls and increase mobility and visibility. Further, technology in the home can be used to monitor activity and collect data to predict risk of falls, which can then be used to modify behavior and the living environment to mediate that risk (Oregon Center for Aging and Technology, 2019). Many of these preventive measures can also be used in public environments such as stores, offices, and shopping centers.

CHAPTER REVIEW

Defining Age
- Chronological age is based on calendar age. Older chronological age is sometimes categorized into young-old (65–74), middle-old (75–84), and old-old (85+) groups.
- Functional age refers to what our age seems to be physically, and it is influenced by factors such as genetics, presence or absence of disease, and environmental and lifestyle factors.
- Subjective age is how a person perceives their age; it can be younger or older than chronological age and is influenced by the presence or absence of diseases and/or disabilities. Subjective age is highly individualistic and an important predictor of health outcomes in later life. Feeling younger than our chronological age is known as subjective age bias.
- Chronological, functional, and subjective age are interrelated. Intersections of age, race, class, and sexual and gender identification also influence functional and subjective age.

Age and Human Development
- Human developmental stages are often categorized as childhood, adolescence, young adulthood, middle adulthood, and old age. In reality, we age in a continuous fashion and age as a number or category is less meaningful.
- The aging process tends to be individualistic and depends on the cultural and socioeconomic context in which we live.

Cross-Cultural Perspectives on Biological Aging
- Cultural influences and the geographical and socioeconomic environment affect the perception of aging.

Theories of Biological Aging
- Changes, mutations, and impairments in DNA are associated with the physical decline associated with aging and are implicated in disorders that cause premature aging.
- The aging process is influenced by changes in DNA and in telomeres, nucleotide sequences that "cap" chromosomes and prevent the end from deteriorating or fusing with other chromosomes. Higher chronological age is associated with shorter telomeres. Individuals with short telomeres tend to be at risk for disease.
- DNA methylation is another process associated with biological aging. Abnormal DNA methylation is associated with various metabolic, autoimmune, and neurologic diseases.
- Programmed aging theory, based on DNA changes, posits that genetically programmed changes occur in cells as the body ages.
- The wear-and-tear and mitochondrial theories are other common theories of aging.

Age-Related Changes by Body System
- Age-related changes to skin include the appearance of dark spots, reduced skin strength that results in wrinkles and sagging, and thinning skin, which reduces the skin's ability to act as a barrier. Hair undergoes structural changes that can result in baldness, graying, thinning, and weakening of the follicles.
- Age-related changes in hearing and vision are common. Hearing or vision loss or impairment are highly individualistic and are influenced by genetics, the environment, and intersectional factors.
- Muscle mass, which is associated with strengths and musculoskeletal function, declines slowly throughout the life span. We also tend to lose bone mass as we age, increasing the risk for fractures. Immune and endocrine system functioning also tends to decline with age, compromising our ability to fight infection and produce hormones.
- Aging may lead to a steady decline in fluid intelligence, the ability to think speedily and reason flexibly to solve problems. Aging may also lead to an increase in crystallized intelligence, accumulated knowledge, skills, and experiences. Other cognitive skills such as vocabulary, comprehension, concentration, and memory for personal and historical facts and procedural tasks tend to improve or at least remain stable over time.
- As we age, the risk of developing various types of dementias increases.

Promoting Health and Longevity
- Physical aspects of aging can be slowed or made less problematic through changing certain health behaviors and environmental contexts. These measures include providing access to resources that help older adults improve health and navigate their environments in safe ways that reduce the risk of injury.

REVIEW QUESTIONS
1. What are different ways that we define older age and what are some of the strengths and limitations to these definitions?
2. Compare and contrast the main theories that explain why we age.
3. Discuss how culture influences our experiences with the aging process.
4. Describe ways that health promotion can be utilized to increase well-being as we age.

KEY TERMS

chronological age
functional age
subjective age
subjective age bias
positivity effect
senescence
telomeres

menopause
perimenopause
andropause
fluid intelligence
crystallized intelligence
dementia

CHAPTER 3

Psychology of Aging

Chapter Outline
Theories of Psychological Age
    Erikson's Psychosocial Stages of Development
    Peck's Theory of Ego Integrity
    Intersectional and Cultural Factors
    Intersection of Age and Gender
    Intersections of Other Characteristics
Personality and Emotion
    Personality and Aging
    Emotion and Aging
Learning
    Cognitive Plasticity
    Preserving Healthy Brain Function
    Overcoming Barriers to Learning
Mental Health
    Depression
    Anxiety
    Substance Use Disorders
    Suicide
    Screening and Diagnosis
    Treatment
        Cognitive Behavioral Therapy
        Narrative and Reminiscence Therapies
        Medications
Resiliency, Creativity, Productivity, and Wisdom
    Resiliency
    Creativity
    Productivity
    Wisdom
Spirituality

Learning Objectives

After completing this chapter, you will be able to:

- Describe well-known theories of psychological age and provide examples of cultural and intersectional factors that affect psychological aspects of aging.
- Explain how personality and emotion develop and evolve as we age.
- Explain how cognitive plasticity benefits older adults, and list activities and strategies that enhance cognitive function and learning in this population.
- Describe issues related to mental health and the aging process.
- Explain how resiliency, creativity, productivity, and wisdom affect and are affected by the aging process.
- Describe how spirituality can influence and play a role in later life.

Like other aspects of aging, psychological aspects of the aging process are complex. It is inaccurate to assume that aging inevitably includes declines in memory, learning, creativity, and productivity. It is also inaccurate to assume that aging automatically results in negative changes in personality and mental health. Many individual, social, cultural, economic, historical, environmental, and other factors influence how we respond psychologically to the aging process. In this chapter, we will examine some of the more prominent psychological concepts as they pertain to the aging process: cognition, emotion, learning, mental health, and resilience. When considering psychological aspects of later life, there are a few ways to approach the subject. One deals with psychological changes as we age, and the other focuses on how we adapt and change throughout the life span. These approaches to understanding the psychological aspects of aging are interrelated, and both will be explored.

THEORIES OF PSYCHOLOGICAL AGE

Most theories of psychological age attempt to explain the aging process in terms of mental, emotional, and motivational processes and how our personality may develop over time. Psychological theories help in understanding the changes that occur as we age through the life span and how we cope with the changes that we might experience. There are myriad ways to conceptualize psychological aging; in this chapter we will discuss a few well-known theories.

In the twentieth century, many theorists viewed older age as a time of decline (Baltes, 1987). Some of the more common life-span theorists that focused on psychological aspects of development include Sigmund Freud and Jean Piaget, whose stage theories highlighted the importance of personality and cognitive development in infancy, childhood, and adolescence. Erik Erikson was one of the first theorists to articulate processes of psychosocial development past adolescence into later life.

Erikson's Psychosocial Stages of Development

Introduced in the 1950s, Erikson's theory consists of eight sequential stages that consist of unique developmental tasks to be mastered (Table 3.1). The way in which an individual approaches the tasks in each stage provides the foundation for their development and

Table 3.1 Erikson's Psychosocial Stages

Stage	Age	Tasks
1: Trust vs. Mistrust	Birth to 18 months	Infants and children learn they can get needs such as love, food, and shelter met through their caregivers. If needs aren't met, mistrust develops.
2: Autonomy vs. Shame and Doubt	18 months to 3 years	Children learn how to do things and accomplish tasks independently, giving them a sense of self-confidence. If children aren't encouraged to or are punished for doing things independently, self-doubt can develop.
3: Initiative vs. Guilt	3 to 6 years	Children are active in their environments, taking initiative to learn and explore and, consequently, developing interests and goal-directed behavior. Children who are discouraged to engage in this behavior can lack confidence and initiative to shape their lives.
4: Industry vs. Inferiority	6 to 12 years	Children seek to be productive and successful through playing, learning, and mastering tasks, which leads to industriousness. Children who experience repeated failures may develop feelings of inferiority.
5: Identity vs. Identity Confusion	Adolescence (12 to 18 years)	Adolescents explore who they are and their sense of identity, trying out roles and integrating these into their sense of self. Adolescents who don't get to explore roles or who have difficulty integrating roles into their identities may experience confusion about who they are.
6: Intimacy vs. Isolation	Young Adulthood (18 to 40 years)	Young adults explore intimacy and closeness in their relationships, learning to sacrifice and compromise with others. Young adults who are unable to establish intimacy with others are at risk for isolation as they become adults.
7: Generativity vs. Stagnation	Adulthood (40 to 65 years)	Adults invest in work, family, community, and future generations and are concerned with the well-being of others. Adults who cannot do this may struggle to look past themselves and become self-absorbed and stagnated, unable to be productive for the sake of others.
8: Integrity vs. Despair	Older Age (65 to death)	Older adults reflect on their lives and take inventory of their successes. People who feel satisfied with their lives develop a sense of well-being and peace, while those who don't may feel despair and regret lost opportunities.

Source: Adapted from Erikson, 1950.

how they proceed to the next stage. The tasks in each stage consist of opposing psychological constructs, so that one can successfully or unsuccessfully complete tasks before moving on to the next stage (Erikson, 1950).

Erikson's stages 6 through 8 consider tasks to be mastered in emerging adulthood through later life to ensure optimal well-being. Erikson's wife, Joan Erikson, added a ninth stage of development for continued aging that incorporates aspects from all the previous stages of development challenges (Orenstein & Lewis, 2020).

According to Erikson, mastering tasks successfully in earlier stages of development is important for tackling tasks successfully later in life. Likewise, struggling with tasks earlier in life complicates later development. An individual can overcome these complications to successfully complete tasks but might need help to overcome past difficulties to improve well-being later in life. For instance, if in stage 5 a person struggles to develop a strong identity, they may struggle with tasks in later stages and be more likely to experience isolation, stagnation, and despair. Conversely, developing a strong identity helps to provide tools and skills that promote the formation of strong, healthy relationships, generativity in one's career and personal life, and ultimately, integrity.

While the sequence of development is universal and fixed, resolving developmental issues can be a fluid, lifelong process, and issues from previous stages can resurface later, triggered by life events. Individuals progress through these developmental stages regardless of whether or not issues have been resolved, and upon advancing to later stages must often reintegrate tasks from previous stages (Orenstein & Lewis, 2020).

Erikson's theory has been criticized for being too limited and not taking into consideration intersectional, socioeconomic, or cultural factors and their influence on development. Further, Erikson's theory, along with many of the established stage theories and similar gerontological theories, are criticized for treating older adults as if they are a homogenous group with similar developmental trajectories. Individual development is complex and unique and cannot be reduced to a set of proscriptive tasks. Consequently, Erikson's theory may lack relevance for certain populations.

Peck's Theory of Ego Integrity
Another theory that explores psychological, emotional, and social aspects of older age is Robert Peck's theory of ego integrity (Peck, 1955, 1968). This theory describes how we attain ego integrity and well-being as we age through tackling three distinct tasks:

- *Ego differentiation versus work and role preoccupation*: Self-worth is measured through family, friendships, and community investment rather than career successes and physical abilities. Older adults must negotiate changing roles that occur when children leave the home, one retires, or one develops new friendships or interests, for example.
- *Body transcendence versus body preoccupation*: Older adults compensate physical limitations and body changes that can occur with age with cognitive, social, and emotional skills and growth.
- *Ego transcendence versus ego preoccupation*: Older adults focus on securing the future for younger generations and making life more meaningful and gratifying for others rather than being preoccupied with death and one's own legacy.

The work of these tasks, and ultimately attaining ego integrity, requires older adults to move beyond work and individual identities to reflect on life and spirituality from a more holistic perspective (Berk, 2011).

Intersectional and Cultural Factors
As with Erikson's theory, Peck's theory is criticized for not taking into consideration some of the intersectional and cultural factors that influence development. For instance, life-span development entails a series and accumulation of transitional changes rather than discrete ones. That is, we do not necessarily wake up one morning and notice we have entered into a new stage. Also, age is not the only variable that causes change. Instead, many aspects of our lives contribute to change, and we are more apt to notice gradual shifts that slowly raise our awareness to how we are changing, which may or may not be directly related to age.

Further, intersectional factors contribute to age-related psychological changes and states that are shaped over time and in individual, unique ways. For example, facing a lifetime of discrimination, oppression, and other marginalizing experiences can influence development and how one approaches tasks and ego transcendence. Thus, many gerontologists suggest that we enlarge our view of psychological aging (as well as other aspects of aging) to include queer, feminist, and race gerontological perspectives. Intersectional dynamics and their influence on psychosocial development can be more thoroughly considered by recognizing how factors such as race, gender, culture, history, socioeconomic status, and the sociopolitical context influence psychological development throughout the life span.

Intersection of Age and Gender

Feminist gerontology tends to focus not only on how the intersection of age and gender affect psychological development over time, but it also considers the power dynamics of factors such as race, ethnicity, ability, sexual orientation, and socioeconomic status influence, as all these factors play a role in our psychological state at any point in the life span (Hooyman et al., 2002).

Feminist theory and feminist gerontology highlight the double standards of growing older that place female-identified people at a disadvantage over male-identified people and that can affect people psychologically. Many feminist scholars argue that older people are treated as a homogenous group, when in reality, a great deal of variability in characteristics, experiences, and other factors define individuals in older age, just as they do across the life span. Moreover, people of different genders place different psychological meanings on age and the aging process, and different societal expectations placed on people because of gender identification as they age affect psychological and emotional well-being differently (Lazar, 2017). For example, men, women, transgender, and gender-fluid individuals experience different standards related to their aging bodies and appearances; aging typically adds to the male-identified person's social capital and detracts from that of female-identified people.

This effect on social capital and the worth society places on people because of their gender and age can have a strong influence on how one adapts to aging psychologically (Settersten & Hagestad, 2015). These gendered expectations have even more serious ramifications for older adults whose gender identification falls outside of the strict male-female binary imposed by society. For example, many transgender older adults, if they transitioned early in life, have faced lifelong discrimination in housing, employment, healthcare, and other sectors. This discrimination often continues into later life and can create problems as people retire and experience changing healthcare, personal care, and housing needs. This discrimination and the barriers and hardships it creates can have consequences for the psychological well-being of transgender older adults, particularly related to issues that include anxiety, depression, loneliness, and suicidal ideation (SAGE, 2020).

Intersections of Other Characteristics

Intersections of other characteristics beyond gender, such as race, ethnicity, ability, weight, socioeconomic status, and sexual orientation add even further complexities to how people adapt psychologically to the aging process. Like gender, these intersectional characteristics are often a source of inequality for individuals over the course of the life span, the effects of which accumulate with age. For instance, race and socioeconomic status are associated with varying experiences related to discrimination; cultural, social, and economic capital; and access to resources and opportunities such as housing, employment, and healthcare. These experiences accumulate throughout

Figure 3.1 Intersections of age, gender, and other characteristics influence our experiences
Source: Igor Alecsander/iStock

the life span, affecting one's experiences and psychological well-being in later life as well as the psychological and other outcomes of aging and life in later years (DiPrete & Eirich, 2006).

Another approach to understanding psychological (and other) aspects of aging is queer theory generally and queer gerontology specifically. These lenses allow us to examine how socially constructed parameters on what "normal" aging is affects how we perceive ourselves and how others view us as we age, as well as the consequences associated with deviating from or challenging that norm. **Queer gerontology** is a specific approach to understanding older adulthood that assists in the examination of heterosexist and other dominant norms that define what it means to be older (Hughes, 2006). It shines a critical light on the ways in which various "isms" such as heterosexism, ableism, sexism, sizeism, and racism affect individuals as they age, particularly if their identities are at odds with the dominant norms. Embedded in white, male, young, heterosexual norms are powerful political, economic, and other forces that can influence how one experiences aging in various realms such as housing, employment, retirement, relationships, healthcare, and social roles. These experiences, in turn, can have psychological consequences such as loneliness, anxiety, and depression that can lead to issues with well-being and even higher mortality rates for those who do not adhere to dominant norms of aging (Heaphy, 2007).

PERSONALITY AND EMOTION

As with other aspects of aging, many stereotypes persist about personality, emotional state, and aging. In this section we'll examine those stereotypes and discuss how reality often differs.

Personality and Aging

Western culture is replete with negative stereotypes about older adults, as a group, as becoming cranky, stubborn, and unable to adapt, among other negative traits, as age increases. However, how (and whether) our personality traits change and are expressed over the life span is more complicated than these stereotypes would suggest.

Research over the past several decades has suggested that personality traits, in general, remain somewhat stable over the life span. If one is conscientious, extroverted, easygoing, and has a positive outlook when younger, then one will tend to have the same disposition when older (Edmonds et al., 2013; Friedman, Kern, & Reynolds, 2010). In particular, personality traits of conscientiousness and stability of mood were found to be stable across eight decades by one study (Harris et al., 2016). Other research indicates that while personality characteristics tend to remain stable over the life span, circumstances such as declining health, restricted access to resources, and stress-inducing experiences that affect one's lifestyle and ability to interact with the social and physical environment can affect personality traits and how they are expressed. Similarly, one's personality traits also influence how one adapts to changing circumstances (Mueller, Wagner, & Gerstorf, 2017). For instance, if one has approached life with a generally positive outlook over the years, one will likely respond with the same outlook when facing physical or other problems that will inevitably occur with time. However, even a person with an unwavering positive outlook can have this positivity challenged if a string of negative circumstances overwhelms one's resources or ability to cope.

Other research indicates that perhaps our universal personality traits are activated and expressed at different times throughout the life span. Specifically, some traits are more useful than others at different developmental stages with regard to ensuring that our needs are met. For example, cross-cultural observations indicate that while overall, personality traits tend to remain stable regardless of context, certain characteristics tend to be more prominent at certain ages. Those younger than 30 years of age tend to display more extroversion and adventurousness than those 30+, while older individuals tend to display characteristics of trust, self-control, and dutifulness more often than younger individuals. It may be that extroversion is more useful when we are younger and are seeking jobs or partners, for example, and dutifulness is more important when we are fulfilling our familial or community commitments (Noftle & Fleeson, 2010).

Emotion and Aging
With regard to the study of emotion and age, one of the most frequently examined concepts is the positivity effect (discussed briefly in Chapter 2). Recall that the positivity effect refers to the notion that as we age, we are more likely to remember and have a preference for positive information than negative information and shift away from a negativity bias that is more prevalent in younger years (Carstensen & DeLiema, 2018). Thus, older adults are more likely than younger adults to report feeling positive (Gurera & Isaacowitz, 2019). One reason for the positivity effect may be socioemotional selectivity theory. This theory that suggests that our perceptions of how much time we have remaining in life influence how we view our goals and what types of experiences we seek out. Specifically, if we view our time as short, then we are more motivated to choose positive experiences instead of novel, potentially negative experiences that may advance more long-term goals but delay positive experiences (Carstensen, Isaacowitz, & Charles, 1999). With regard to emotional development as we age, there may be a paradox; while we see some general physical

declines as we age, emotion and emotional experiences are likely more complex and not necessarily apt to follow the same trajectory of decline (Mather, 2012).

LEARNING

Some aspects of cognition and aging as they relate to the brain were discussed in Chapter 2. Here we will explore cognition as it relates to learning.

As discussed earlier, cognitive functioning tends to be relatively stable as we age, though variability exists due to a range of factors. For instance, **neurodiversity** is the range of differences in individual brain function regarded as normal variations within the population. Other factors contributing to variability in brain function include an individual's access (or lack of access) to healthcare and nutritious food. Conditions such as dementia and cognitive deficits resulting from a stroke also contribute to variability in brain function in older adults.

Multiple factors influence cognitive functioning throughout the life span, such as medications, physical activity, mental health, illness and disease, diet and nutrition, and lifelong sleep habits and patterns (Hayes et al., 2015; Scullin & Bliwise, 2015; Vandewoude et al., 2016). Research also indicates that exposure to prolonged stress, such as stress that results from long-term experiences with trauma and/or discrimination, can have adverse effects on cognition as we age. Specifically, prolonged stress can interfere with our ability to process information or retain memories (Marshall et al., 2015).

Cognitive Plasticity

Cognitive plasticity, or the brain's ability to change and adapt physically and functionally throughout the life span, benefits us as we age. This ability is also helpful for individuals who experience a health or other problem that affects cognitive functioning (Bherer, 2015). While researchers once believed that brain activity slowed with age, neuroimaging has shown that older adults tend to use both sides of the brain for completing tasks and decision-making, while younger people tend to use only one side. Thus, older adults may make more efficient and adaptive use of their brains and be less prone to errors in their thinking than younger individuals (Phillips, 2011).

Preserving Healthy Brain Function

Remaining engaged in learning, working, socializing, hobbies, and other cognitive activities throughout the life span helps keep the brain healthy and cognition functioning well. The "use it or lose it" adage applies to cognition; the more we use our cognitive abilities for learning, remembering, and problem solving, the more likely we are to keep our cognitive functions strong. This is why engaging in activities such as puzzles, memory games, and narrative storytelling can keep our brains sharp as well as assist those with dementia cope better with symptoms.

Overcoming Barriers to Learning

Some cognitive issues can be mitigated through environmental or other adjustments. For example, if hearing or eyesight problems create barriers to learning, changes in lighting or sound or the use of assistive devices can help a great deal. Learning and memory can be enhanced when new content is connected to past experiences (Gawlowska et al., 2017).

Figure 3.2 Engaging in activity is one way to maintain brain health
Source: Fat Camera/iStock

Further, adjustments in the approach to learning can improve cognitive function. The **theory of selective optimization with compensation** posits that employing the strategies of selecting fewer but important goals, pursuing goals in optimized ways, and applying compensatory means to overcome barriers can assist in learning and other cognitive functions for those who face limitations (Baltes & Baltes, 1990). For example, someone who can no longer drive might compensate by finding alternative transportation options or a person who is experiencing mobility problems may compensate by using assistive devices or getting help with certain activities.

CASE 3.1

Joel's Accident

Joel is a 67-year-old man who broke his neck in a work-related accident. He went through months of rehabilitation and had to retire, sell his home, and move into an assisted living facility. While he was not paralyzed by the injury, Joel had to relearn to walk and do other activities. For about two years, Joel felt anxious and depressed, mostly due to the losses he experienced because of the accident, especially the loss of his social network at work and his hobby of photography. Initially, when Joel moved into his new assisted living apartment, he refused to go to physical therapy, engage with other residents, or use his computer or other equipment for photography. After therapy with a mental health counselor, Joel found ways to compensate for problems caused by his injury. For example, he started using an electric wheelchair, purchased photography equipment that he could manipulate with limited use of his hands, and found alternative transportation to visit family. He also used social media and other platforms to engage with his friends from work and share his photography.

If you were working with Joel in a health or mental health capacity, what other ways might you think of that would allow Joel to compensate for his limited mobility issues that would allow him to reengage in social and other activities? How do you think this compensation might help his physical and mental health?

Figure 3.3 Compensation can help people with quality of life
Source: adriaticfoto/Shutterstock

MENTAL HEALTH

In the United States, about 14 percent of people aged 50 and older struggle with mental health issues, including substance use disorders. This is lower than the rate for younger adults (22.2 percent for age 26 to 49 and 25.8 percent for age 18 to 25) (National Institute of Mental Health, 2019). Given that life expectancy is increasing, adults experiencing mental health problems will live with these struggles for longer periods. Further, older adults often experience complex, chronic, and comorbid physical and mental illness (Renn, Arean, & Unutzer, 2020). While evidence does not suggest that mental illness has increased among older cohorts, a growing older population means more people with mental health issues, which could strain healthcare and mental health systems (Center for Behavioral Health Statistics and Quality, 2017). In the following sections, we will discuss a few of the more common mental health problems experienced by older adults. Box 3.1 at the end of this section offers a global look at mental health and aging.

Depression

Many people erroneously associate older age with depression. It is often assumed that aging brings with it mental, physical, social, and economic decline, so depression is inevitable. Certainly, various issues such as illness, disability, isolation (especially the isolation that occurred with the COVID-19 pandemic), and the persistent discrimination that BIPOC and other people face sometimes bring insurmountable challenges. However, as we have discussed, not everyone responds to these issues in the same way, like developing depression, and we often do not discuss the resiliency that many people demonstrate in the face of adversity.

As with rates of mental illness in general, rates of depression among older adults are actually somewhat lower than rates among younger adults. For adults aged 50+ in the United States, approximately 4.8 percent had a major depressive episode in the past year and 9.8 percent had a minor depressive episode. This percentage has not changed substantially over the decades (Center for Behavioral Health Statistics and Quality, 2017). However, depression among older cohorts may present differently than among younger cohorts, so there is the possibility that depression among older adults is under-assessed and reported. For example, older individuals with depression may not display as much sadness as younger individuals. Instead, older individuals may present with more apathy, reduced interest in normal activities, and physical symptoms such as fatigue and pain, which may be viewed as a normal part of the aging process by both older individuals and healthcare professionals (Whiteford et al., 2013). This may make it more likely that older adults experiencing symptoms of depression will visit their primary care physicians complaining of physical or other symptoms. Further, physicians lacking training in aging-specific issues may be more likely to overlook these symptoms as part of a mental health problem.

Anxiety

Anxiety issues are common among individuals of any age. For older adults, anxiety disorders are estimated to affect approximately 1.2 percent to 15 percent of those living independently and 3.2 percent to 20 percent of those living in residential settings (Creighton, Davison, & Kissane, 2016). The most prevalent anxiety disorders among older individuals include agoraphobia, specific phobias, panic disorder, social anxiety disorder, and generalized anxiety disorder (Canuto et al., 2018).

Like people of all ages, symptoms of anxiety disorders can be mild or severe and can be extremely debilitating. Research suggests that anxiety disorders may be linked to an increased risk of developing cognitive issues and disorders like dementia as well as an increased risk for mortality. Like other mental health issues, a lifetime of dealing with trauma, poverty, violence, discrimination, health disparities, and other issues can increase the risk of people developing anxiety-related symptoms later in life (Miloyan, Byrne, & Pachana, 2015; Ostir & Goodwin, 2006; Petkus et al., 2016).

Substance Use Disorders

Substance use disorders among older adults are increasingly common and must be understood from the viewpoint of how individual, environmental, and cohort factors affect the development of such disorders. For example, those in the baby boom generation (those born between 1946 and 1964) came of age in the 1960s and 1970s when attitudes about substance use were changing, and it was more common for people to use psychoactive drugs for various reasons. Consequently, those in the baby boom cohort have higher rates of substance use disorders than older cohorts that came before them. Further, as we age, environmental and social stressors can make us more susceptible to developing substance use disorders, and physical and metabolic age-related changes can lower our tolerance for substances and make us more vulnerable to overdose (Blow & Barry, 2012). Further, as with other mental illnesses, substance use disorder is often overlooked and underdiagnosed among older adults (Le Roux et al., 2016).

While the use of any illegal substance is a growing problem among older adults, the misuse and abuse of alcohol and prescription drugs is more prevalent. Alcohol is the most used drug among people aged 65, with approximately 65 percent of those in this age group reporting high-risk drinking (defined as exceeding daily guidelines). A large percentage (80 percent+) of older adults use at least one prescription medication, increasing the risk that prescription and nonprescription medications and dietary supplements will be mixed, causing dangerous drug interactions (National Institute on

Drug Abuse, 2020). The rate of cannabis use among older adults is increasing, possibly due to its legalization across the United States. Cannabis use increased by 250 percent among those aged 65+ in the past decade, which could lead to increasing problematic use of the drug (Han et al., 2017).

Suicide
In the United States, rates of suicide for people, regardless of age, have been increasing over the past few decades. According to the Centers for Disease Control and prevention (2018), the United States has seen over a 30 percent increase in suicide rates over the past 20 years. Those aged 45 to 64 have the highest rates of suicide (20.2 per 100,000), followed by those aged 85+ (19.1 per 100,000). The suicide rate for all people aged 65+ is 17.4 per 100,000, making the rates for older adults higher than the average for all age groups in the United States (14.8 per 100,000) (Drapeau & McIntosh, 2018).

Among those aged 65+, men and women attempt suicide at about the same rate (45 vs. 43 per 100,000). However, men (approximately half) in this same age range are much more likely to complete suicide than women (approximately 1 in 7) because they tend to use more lethal means (Choi et al., 2017). With regard to race, the highest rates of suicide occur among older American Indian/Alaskan Native men followed by Caucasian males, which is over four times the national rate (World Health Organization, 2018).

Screening and Diagnosis
Thorough assessments can help differentiate between mental and physical health problems and the comorbidity of the two. Certain physical illnesses can cause symptoms similar to a mental health issue. In other cases, a mental health issue could be a harbinger to a physical problem, such as dementia (Weintraub & Mamikonyan, 2019; Wise et al., 2019). Attention to how physical and mental illnesses may be related is an especially important part of care for older adults.

Many tools exist to help screen for a wide variety of physical and mental health problems and to more accurately diagnose illness. For example, the geriatric depression scale (GDS) (Yesavage et al., 1983) comes in both long (30 questions) and short (15 questions) forms and has been used extensively with older adults in different settings such as acute and long-term care. The GDS can be used with older adults who are ill or who have mild to moderate cognitive impairment. The Mini-Mental State Exam (MMSE) is a common tool to assess cognitive functioning and impairment. The MMSE is a short, easy-to-administer questionnaire that measures a person's comprehension, short-term memory, orientation to place and time, and ability to solve problems. The MMSE alone is not used to diagnose dementia, but it is a helpful tool that physicians, mental health professionals, family members, and others can use to determine if problems in cognitive functioning are present. Often, the MMSE is used to determine if someone may need further testing for potential problems (Dementia Care Central, 2020).

Treatment
Over the past few decades, a great deal of progress has been made in understanding mental illnesses and developing effective treatments. Treating mental health problems in older adults must take into consideration historical, generational, individual,

physical, psychosocial, and other factors. For instance, among many families and cultures and across generations, mental health issues come with stigma that can be a barrier for seeking treatment. Many older adults view mental health issues as private matters to be handled within the family, not by outside professionals. Additionally, comorbid physical issues, along with the use of various medications, can make treatments for some issues complex and difficult (Conner et al., 2010). Nonetheless, many effective psychotherapeutic and psychopharmacologic treatments are available for older adults dealing with mental health issues. Common psychotherapeutic approaches such as psychodynamic, cognitive behavioral, and interpersonal therapies are also effective in treating mental health problems, as are techniques using meditation and mindfulness (Mitchell & Pachana, 2020).

Cognitive Behavioral Therapy

Cognitive behavioral therapy (CBT) is particularly effective in treating issues like anxiety, depression, and sleep disorders among older adults. CBT also is useful for older adults who are experiencing mental health issues alongside physical health issues. For example, it is not uncommon for people with chronic obstructive pulmonary disease (COPD) to experience symptoms of anxiety and depression. CBT can be effective in helping people manage negative emotions and make positive changes in behavior and thoughts related to COPD, which in turn can help ease the symptoms of COPD (Zhang, Yin et al., 2020).

Healthcare providers may confuse symptoms of physical illnesses with those of substance use disorders. Further, substance use disorders can put older adults at risk for physical health problems such diabetes, high blood pressure, and congestive heart failure. Interventions such as CBT, group treatment, individual and family counseling, psychotropic medications, and case management, as well as addressing loneliness and isolation and creating linkages with medical and other support services, can all be helpful in treating substance use disorders among older adults (National Institute on Drug Abuse, 2020).

Figure 3.4 Therapy can be a useful tool to improve mental health
Source: No System Images/iStock

Narrative and Reminiscence Therapies

Psychotherapeutic approaches often used with older adults, including those with dementia, include narrative and reminiscence therapies. **Narrative therapy** supports older adults in recounting dominant life stories that are important to their identities and the problems with which they have struggled. The goal of narrative approaches is to help people reconstruct meanings to promote problem-solving and a positive self-identity (Biassoni, Cassina, & Balzarotti, 2019). **Reminiscence therapy** (also called life review therapy) helps older adults reflect on and review their lives with the goal of taking stock, addressing unresolved issues, and highlighting past events and accomplishments (Rubin, Parrish, & Miyawaki, 2019). For individuals with dementia, this type of therapy may involve using sensory experiences to help them remember events, people, and places from their past.

Medications

Psychotropic medications may be effective in the treatment of various mental illnesses, but because of metabolic and other physical characteristics of older adults, medications must be chosen and used with caution. Particular areas of concern are how the drugs are metabolized, determining effective doses, and possible drug interactions. For example, some evidence suggests that symptoms of certain mental illnesses are exhibited differently in older adults versus younger individuals, so careful assessment of symptoms and accurate diagnosis are important to ensure that appropriate medications are prescribed.

RESILIENCY, CREATIVITY, PRODUCTIVITY, AND WISDOM

A person's adaptability, resiliency, creativity, and productivity are highly individualistic and influenced by intrinsic and extrinsic intersectional characteristics and by experiences over the life course. Some people bring adaptability and resiliency into their later years, allowing them to live happy, well-adjusted lives well into old age. For others, the aging process can bring challenges that are impossible to overcome, regardless of their ability to cope and adapt. Some people find their creativity and productivity increased

---

BOX 3.1 Global Perspectives on Psychological Aging

- Globally, more than 20 percent of older adults have a diagnosed mental or neurological disorder. These disorders account for nearly 7 percent of disabilities among this population.
- Mental health issues are underrecognized and underreported among older adults and medical and mental health professionals who provide care for this population. Regardless of nationality or ethnicity, stigma associated with mental illness plays a role in under-utilization of treatment.
- Older adults in many countries around the world have faced (sometimes over the course of their lifetimes) problems and events such as war, crime, poverty, violence, genocide, migration, oppression, discrimination, political upheaval, natural disasters, effects of climate change, and a lack of resources such as food, housing, and healthcare. All of these factors put older adults at risk for developing mental health problems.

Source: World Health Organization, 2017b.

with age, while others experience the opposite. Learned coping skills, access to resources and support systems, and cumulative lifetime experiences, affect how we age as much as our personality, physical and socioemotional characteristics, and genetics.

Resiliency

The **crossover effect** exemplifies how intersectional factors can influence our life trajectories with regard to resiliency. Research has demonstrated that throughout the life span, Black people have higher mortality rates than whites, until about the age of 75–80, when a crossover effect occurs and the mortality rates for Blacks become lower than that of whites. Higher mortality rates for Blacks throughout much of the life span can be linked to a variety of factors including disparities in housing, employment, healthcare, and other resources as well as experiences with overt and covert racism and oppression. Researchers theorize that if one can survive a lifetime of disparities and oppression that typically shorten the life span, then selective survival mechanisms or resiliency come into play and that person likely will live a long life (Roth et al., 2016).

Another way intersectional resiliency into older age is demonstrated is through double and triple jeopardy (discussed in Chapter 1). While these concepts are often used to refer to health disparities, they can also be used to describe any adverse outcome for people with intersectional identities. For example, many older women have experienced a lifetime of lower wages and other discrimination because of their gender, and they face additional discrimination because of their age. And older, Black, transgender women have likely faced a lifetime of discrimination because of race, and gender and will experience further discrimination based on age. People who identify as gay, lesbian, bisexual, queer, or pansexual also face issues as they age that add to those related to their sexual identities (Feagin, 1991). Resiliency is often cultivated as people experience different life circumstances, which can be an asset with advancing age.

Creativity

Related to resiliency, creativity can be considered as our ability to be flexible, to innovate, and to be adaptable in our thinking. Some research suggests that this type of thinking tends to decline before early adulthood (Kim, 2011). However, much of this research focuses mostly on memory, executive function, and cognitive control, which may not be fully reflective of creativity. Further, other research has not validated these findings (Li et al., 2015; Lu et al., 2010). Some evidence suggests that innovative and divergent thinking (the ability to generate creative ideas by exploring many possible solutions) remain intact as we age (Palmiero, 2015). Creative thinking is also linked to learning. Thus, new learning can enhance creative thinking. History is replete with creative thinkers who achieved remarkable success later in life. Notable examples include fashion designer Vera Wang, who launched her business at age 40 and recently celebrated the 30th anniversary of her brand. Other examples are the artists Salvador Dali and Pablo Picasso, who produced paintings right up until the time of their deaths (Dali at age 84 and Picasso at age 91).

Productivity

Many people believe that productivity declines with age. In the United States and other capitalist societies, productivity is often equated with the ability to produce economically (Landers & Kapadia, 2017). This lens invalidates the plethora of ways people are productive. Many older adults who are retired or employed part time remain productive in activities such as caregiving, volunteering, providing informal help to family or friends, and producing artistic and other creative works (Carr, Fried, & Rowe, 2015). Productivity in older age is important, and it is an aspect of aging that can be encouraged and supported. Productivity typically results in increased physical, cognitive, and social engagement. In addition, research suggests that productivity is associated with positive health outcomes, including reduced risk of disease and mortality, delayed decline in physical functioning, and improved self-rated health (Lee & Jean Yeung, 2019).

Wisdom
Wisdom, as a concept, is complex and multifaceted. While it is difficult to define, many theories have attempted to better understand wisdom, where it comes from, and how it is exhibited. These theories suggest that wisdom is often expressed in several key ways, including emotional stability, prosocial attitudes and behaviors, reflection and self-understanding, value relativism and tolerance, social decision-making and pragmatic knowledge of life, and acknowledgment of and dealing effectively with uncertainty (Meeks & Jeste, 2009). Research suggests that the development of wisdom is associated with age. Specifically, people who are older have had more time to gain experiences that can lead to wisdom (Li & Durgin, 2017), particularly with regard to increased empathy, altruism, emotional stability, and social reasoning (Oxman, 2018). Wisdom can not only be personally helpful, leading to better physical and mental health, but it also likely serves an evolutionary role benefitting humans overall as older adults' wisdom contributes to the health and well-being of younger people (Jeste & Lee, 2019).

SPIRITUALITY

Religion and spiritual practices are discussed in Chapter 9, but here, we will take a look at how spirituality can affect aging and what role it might play in later life. While spirituality can be an important part of one's life regardless of age, research has explored how spirituality may support the aging process and influence quality of life in later years.

Spirituality, as a concept, is multidimensional and deeply personal. It is often shaped and influenced by a person's life experiences and belief system and reflects a person's understanding of life and the meaning ascribed to it. Spirituality also is often associated with trust in a transcendent source such as nature or a higher power. Research on spirituality in later life suggests that spirituality helps to support mental health and quality of life. Spirituality can help people find meaning in their lives and experiences as they age, including experiences with change, loss, and grief caused by death, declines in health, or the loss of roles, for example. Spirituality can also improve quality of life by promoting resiliency, creating positive social exchanges and social networks, and shaping and supporting a positive outlook on the aging process and what it means to be older (Chen et al., 2017; Cohen, Thomas, & Williamson, 2018).

Spirituality continually evolves over time as it is influenced by new experiences and circumstances. Age-related and culture-specific experiences can serve to challenge and transform spirituality in ways that prompt individuals to grapple with and reconsider existential questions as well as to reconsider what it means to engage meaningfully in life and with others. Spirituality in later life can help increase coherence between our perceptions and interpretations of life and the approaches we bring to living (Janhsen et al., 2021).

Figure 3.5 Spirituality can help improve quality of life in later years
Source: AscentXmedia/iStock

CHAPTER REVIEW

Theories of Psychological Age
- Psychological theories of aging attempt to explain the mental, emotional, and motivational processes associated with aging and how personality may develop over time. Psychological theories of the aging process help us to both understand the changes that occur with aging through the life span as well as how we cope with the changes that we might experience with age.
- Erik Erikson was one of the first theorists to theorize about aging past adolescence into later life. Erikson's theory of psychosocial development consists of eight sequential stages that consist of unique developmental tasks to be mastered. How one approaches the tasks in each stage influences and provides the foundation for one's development and the way in which one proceeds into the next stage. The tasks in each stage consist of opposing psychological constructs, so that one can successfully or unsuccessfully complete tasks before moving on to the next stage.
- Robert Peck's theory of ego integrity describes how people attain ego integrity and well-being as they age through tackling three distinct tasks. These tasks include ego differentiation versus work and role preoccupation, body transcendence versus body preoccupation, and ego transcendence versus ego preoccupation.
- Intersectional factors also contribute to age-related psychological changes and states that are shaped over time and in individual, unique ways. Because of this, we must view psychological aging (as well as other aspects of aging) from queer, feminist, and critical race and gerontological lenses.

Personality and Emotion
- Ageist stereotypes suggest that as we age, we become cranky, stubborn, and unable to adapt, among other negative traits. However, research suggests that the relationship between personality traits and age is complex.
- Research over the past several decades suggests that it is likely that personality traits, in general, remain somewhat stable over the life span and that circumstances such as declining health, restricted access to resources, and stress-inducing experiences that

affect one's lifestyle and ability to interact with the social and physical environment can affect personality traits and how they are expressed. Further, it is likely that universal personality traits are activated and expressed at different times throughout the life span.
- As we age we may be subject to the positivity effect, or the tendency to remember and have a preference for positive information instead of negative information and shift away from a negativity bias that is more prevalent in younger years. This is related to the socioemotional selectivity theory, which suggests that our perceptions of how much time we have remaining in life influence how we view our goals and what types of experiences we seek out.

Learning
- Cognitive plasticity, or the brain's ability to change and adapt physically and functionally throughout the life span, tends to benefit people as they age and can help if people experience a health or other problem at some point in our lives that affects cognitive functioning.
- Many factors can influence cognitive functioning throughout the life span and as we age such as medications, physical activity, mental health, illness and disease, diet and nutrition, and lifelong sleep habits and patterns. Further, exposure to prolonged stress, such as stress that results from lifelong experiences with discrimination, can have adverse effects on cognition throughout the aging process.
- The theory of selective optimization with compensation posits that employing the three strategies of 1) selecting fewer but important goals; 2) pursuing the goals in optimized ways; and 3) applying compensatory means to overcome barriers can assist in learning and other cognitive functions when we face limitations.

Mental Health
- Rates of depression among older adults are somewhat lower than that in younger adults. Older adults with depression may not display as much sadness as younger individuals but instead display more apathy, reduced interest in normal activities, and physical symptoms such as fatigue and pain.
- Anxiety disorders are common among older adults, with the most prevalent being agoraphobia, specific phobias, and panic disorder.
- Substance use disorders are increasingly common among older adults and are influenced by individual, environmental, and cohort factors.
- The suicide rate for all people aged 65+ is 17.4 per 100,000, making the rates for older adults higher than the average for all age groups in the United States (14.8 per 100,000) (Drapeau & McIntosh, 2018).
- Suicide rates for people of all ages are increasing. Among those aged 65+, the highest rates of suicide occur among older American Indian/Alaskan Native men followed by Caucasian males, which is over four times the national rate.
- Effective psychotherapeutic and psychopharmacologic treatments are available for older adults with mental health issues, some of which are especially effective with older adults. These include narrative and life review approaches that utilize a person's life experiences in the treatment process. Complex biological and physical issues must be considered when using psychotropic medications in treatment of mental illness among older adults.

Resiliency, Creativity, Productivity, and Wisdom
- As we age, adaptability, resiliency, creativity, and even productivity are highly individualistic and influenced by intersectional characteristics and experiences over the life course.
- The crossover effect, which refers to Blacks having higher mortality rates than whites until about the age of 75–80, when they then have lower mortality rates than whites, is an example of resiliency among older Black people.
- Older people who have survived double and triple jeopardy (the phenomenon of several intersectional characteristics contributing to discrimination and oppression) exemplify another form of resiliency in older age.
- Our ability to be flexible, innovate, and adaptable in our thinking is one way to think about creativity. Research suggests that we don't necessarily lose our creative abilities as we age.
- Many older adults often engage in productive activities such as caregiving, volunteering, part time or contract work, providing informal help to family or friends, and other forms of social engagement, which is associated with positive health outcomes.
- Wisdom tends to come with age, when people can use their experiences to develop more empathy, altruism, emotional stability, and social reasoning.

Spirituality
- Spirituality is multidimensional and influenced by a person's life experiences and belief system. It often reflects a person's understanding of life and the meaning ascribed to it.
- Spirituality is associated with good mental health and quality of life in later years.
- Spirituality can help people make sense of their experiences as they age, including those that cause change, grief, or loss. Spirituality can also help people build resiliency, become more socially connected, and reevaluate their sense of self as they age.

REVIEW QUESTIONS
1. What are some of the strengths and limitations to the theories discussed in this chapter as they apply to later adulthood?
2. Describe characteristics of personality, emotion, and learning in later life.
3. Describe some mental health issues for older adults and treatment options and considerations.
4. How can resiliency, creativity, productivity, and wisdom be used in working with older adults to improve quality of life?
5. Articulate how spirituality can be beneficial to people in later life.

KEY TERMS
feminist gerontology
queer gerontology
neurodiversity
cognitive plasticity
theory of selective optimization with compensation
narrative therapy
reminiscence therapy
crossover effect

CHAPTER 4

Sociology of Aging

Chapter Outline
Social Theories of Aging
    Disengagement Theory
    Activity Theory
    Continuity Theory
    Life-Course Model of Social Functioning
    Social Convoy Model
Social Connectedness
    Physical and Mental Health Benefits
    Social Connectedness Across Cultures
Social Connection via Friendships
    Evolving Social Networks
    Benefits of Friendship
    Friendships Among LGBT Older Adults
    Female Versus Male Friend Groups
    Intergenerational Friendships
Social Connection via Sexuality and Intimacy
    Beliefs About Sexuality in Older Adults
    Decreased Sexual Activity
    Differences Between Population Groups
    Risk of Sexually Transmitted Disease
    Influence of Technology

Learning Objectives
After completing this chapter, you will be able to:
- Describe five social theories of aging.
- Explain the importance of social connectedness and relationships in older age.
- Describe the benefits of friendships for older adults and list some of the issues that influence the ability to form and maintain friendships in later life.
- Explain how ageist beliefs promote false perceptions about sexuality in older adults and how these beliefs can contribute to negative health outcomes.

The sociology of aging is concerned with how our social life changes as we age, including how friendships, intimate relationships, social networks, and other types of connection evolve and change. The sociological perspective seeks to understand how a person's social life affects well-being during the aging process. Social connectedness affects all aspects of life, including physical and mental well-being. How we establish and maintain relationships with others forms the foundation of all cultures, values, and belief systems. Further, social interaction and engagement are at the core of how we form beliefs about ourselves and others, including beliefs about what it means to age well. In this chapter, we will explore social theories of aging based on the personal social dynamics of later life. We'll also examine various aspects of social connectedness in older age.

SOCIAL THEORIES OF AGING
Several theories and models are commonly used to explain social aspects of older age. The theories and models discussed in this section were created to help explain how our social lives are affected by aging and the social environment, and how the interplay of these factors affects an individual's well-being.

Disengagement Theory
One of the first theories to describe social aspects of the aging process was **disengagement theory** (Cumming & Henry, 1961), which posits that we naturally remove (disengage) ourselves from certain social roles, such as professional and familial roles, as we age. According to this theory, older adults have an increased inclination to seek solitude and engage in reflection and contemplation by reducing time spent on social activities and roles. Disengaging from these roles is seen as beneficial for society because by disengaging, older adults open up roles for younger individuals, such as employment opportunities. Disengagement is also seen as beneficial to older individuals because they have more time to create a peaceful inner world that will be comforting at the end of life. This theory holds that if a large amount of time is spent in social interactions, older adults could become distracted from the real work of growing older, which entails introspection.

Disengagement theory has long been criticized by gerontologists as being too simplistic to explain the social needs, roles, and behaviors of people as they age, particularly people with varying cultural backgrounds and experiences. This theory is also criticized for promoting stereotypical and ageist beliefs about the social roles and interactions of older adults. For instance, a belief that older employees are being selfish by not retiring at a certain age to make room for younger adults in the workplace is seen as an ageist view. Similarly, disengagement theory may promote ageist stereotypes of older adults needing to "act their age" by not participating in certain social roles as they did when they were younger (Hasworth & Cannon, 2015). Research on the physical and mental health benefits of social engagement in later life undermines the main arguments of disengagement theory. Later in this chapter, we will explore the importance of social connectedness throughout the life span with respect to well-being.

Activity Theory

Activity theory (Havighurst, Neugarten, & Tobin, 1968) suggests that aging adults remain active and engaged in social lives and roles rather than dropping out of life activities. For many older adults, their level of social interest and involvement remains similar to that at earlier stages of life. If disengagement occurs, it is likely due to factors outside the individual's control, such as changes in health, employment, financial status, or because of discrimination or other issues that lead to a shift in social interactions and patterns. Activity theory suggests that it is important to avoid being sedentary and isolated in later life, as an active social life is important to maintain health, self-esteem, and life satisfaction.

Activity theory has been criticized for potentially placing unreasonable pressure or expectations on people to remain socially active as they grow older (which is similar to the critique of successful aging discussed in Chapter 1). Indeed, some argue that disengagement theory was developed in response to the overly optimistic view of activity theory (Hasworth & Cannon, 2015). As with successful aging, those who cannot remain socially active, engaged, or productive in older age may be blamed or stigmatized. Another form of ageism may result by maintaining that older adults who do not maintain previous levels of social engagement (or who do not become socially engaged in later life) are not "aging well." This type of expectation ignores intersectional factors that often create barriers for older adults in becoming or remaining active later in life. For example, successful, active social aging is often equated with performing physical

Figure 4.1 Activity theory: remaining active is important to well-being
Source: filadendron/iStock

activities at a level similar to that of younger adulthood. Not only is that expectation unreasonable for many, but it negates the experiences of older adults who must manage chronic illness or disability (Sandberg & Marshall, 2017). Thus, the definition of successful, active social aging is criticized for being too narrowly defined and culture bound. Like successful aging, activity theory may also downplay subjective factors and alternative cultural and contextual factors that affect social engagement in later life.

Continuity Theory

Continuity theory emphasizes the roles that personality and past behaviors play in our social lives as we age (Atchley, 1989). Specifically, relationships, social roles, and patterns of social behavior and engagement established early in life help to predict what an individual's social life will look like in older age. According to continuity theory, adults tend to maintain patterns of behavior related to social engagement throughout the life span. This continuity is seen as helping people cope with and adjust to the developmental changes experienced through the decades. Continuity theory suggests that as we grow older we reflect on our past activities, learning, and other social engagement tasks. We take this contemplation into our later years, which informs and shapes how we socially engage (or choose not to) later in life.

One criticism of continuity theory is that it does not necessarily explain how major life events, such as a debilitating illness or major life changes, may alter the trajectory of our social development later in life, both positively and negatively. However, the theory does suggest that older adults have the capacity to adjust to such events in ways that will not radically change their social development.

Life-Course Model of Social Functioning

The **life-course model of social functioning** is similar to continuity theory in that it acknowledges the importance of prior experiences and how they shape social functioning in later adulthood. These experiences may be personal events or more macro events that cohorts or broader society might experience at any one time. Both theories regard social, cultural, political, and historical contexts as important across the life span, as well as experiences with discrimination, oppression, and privilege that are intertwined with intersectional identities. For example, lesbian, gay, or bisexual people who grew up in the 1940s or 1950s experience their larger social contexts across the life span much differently than those born decades later. When other identities (e.g., socioeconomic status, race, ability, weight, gender) are considered along with sexual identity over different time periods, we encounter vastly different social experiences. Contextual and other experiences we have early in life influence our experiences later in life, including the way we engage and interact in our social lives (Hasworth & Cannon, 2015).

Social Convoy Model

The **social convoy model** (Antonucci, 2001), like the socioemotional selectivity theory (Carstensen, Isaacowitz, & Charles, 1999) discussed in Chapter 2, helps to explain changes in social needs and relationships as people age. This model posits that individuals are embedded in social networks (convoys) throughout the life span. These networks provide the reciprocity (give and take) of needed social support. In this model, three circles represent the various levels of closeness of other people to an individual.

Figure 4.2 Social convoy model
Source: monkeybusinessimages/Shutterstock

The inner circle consists of those who are closest and provide the most social support, such as partners, parents, and children. The second (middle) circle consists of people such as close friends, uncles and aunts, and cousins. The last (outer) circle consists of people who provide more limited social support such as neighbors, coworkers, and members of recreational social groups or religious congregations. According to the model, as we age, the outer circles begin to decline, as do the number of convoys. Thus, we are left with convoys that are closest to us, such as children, partners, siblings, and close friends. Relationships with people such as coworkers and more distant friendships begin to fall away as we shift roles and activities, as when we retire or stop participating in certain social groups.

Both socioemotional selectivity theory and the social convoy model posit that adults refine their social networks throughout the life span to achieve emotional goals that change over time. Both theories suggest that social networks decrease with age but that connections with close social networks remain stable and even increase. However, the social convoy model suggests that social network changes are due to changes in social roles, such as the changes related to retirement. The socioemotional selectivity theory suggests that changes in social networks are more deliberately chosen by individuals as they age due to shifts in priorities that determine which relationships are most important when there is a sense of limited time left in life.

SOCIAL CONNECTEDNESS

The extent to which we are socially connected and engaged throughout the life span is dependent on many factors. Continuity theory and the life-course model highlight some of the ways in which intersectional, cultural, social, political, and historical factors throughout a person's life can affect how they engage with others and larger society in later years. Other chapters discuss social connectedness as it relates to the family, partnerships, and caregiving (Chapter 6), the workplace and retirement (Chapter 7), and the community (Chapter 9). Here, we will explore social connectedness in later life through friendships and various forms of intimacy.

Physical and Mental Health Benefits

Social connectedness is one of the most basic of human needs and is critical to mental and physical well-being. When needs for love, belonging, inclusion, and acceptance are not met through social interactions and relationships, we are at risk for experiencing isolation and loneliness that contribute to higher rates of illness and mortality (Maslow et al., 1970). Social connectedness protects against physical and mental illness and disease, improves self-esteem, sense of fulfillment and purpose, and bolsters physical functioning (Al-Kandari & Crews, 2014; Wakefield et al., 2020). Conversely, poor physical and mental health often contribute to increased isolation, loneliness, and disconnection (Ambrey, Bosman, & Ballard, 2017). Consequently, social connectedness is even more important as individuals age and experience changing bodies, social roles, and other developmental and social shifts. Strong social lives can bring great fulfillment in later years and contribute to mental and physical health.

Given how important social connection is for well-being, it is important to realize that in the United States, more than 30 percent of people aged 45+ report feeling lonely, and 25 percent of those aged 65+ are considered socially isolated. Factors such as disability (including hearing loss), living alone, chronic physical and mental illness, poverty, lack of access to resources, and social network loss through death, divorce, relocation, and estrangement, can place people at risk for social isolation (National Academies of Sciences Engineering and Medicine, 2020). Consequently, gerontologists and other helping professionals and policymakers focus on ways to increase formal and informal social supports and resources that can increase overall well-being.

Social Connectedness across Cultures

Cross-cultural studies (Ajrouch et al., 2017; Antonucci, Lansford, Schaberg et al., 2001; Fiori, Antonucci, & Akiyama, 2008) of older adults in the United States, Mexico, Lebanon, France, Germany, and Japan used the convoy model to examine older adults' friendships from the inner circle (very close relationships), the middle circle (not very close, but still important), and the outer circle (important, but less close). These studies found some universal patterns in friendships, as well as cultural differences. The studies all underscore the fact that social networks do not necessarily shrink later in life and that culture plays an important role in shaping individual and societal expectations about social engagement in later years:

- In all countries studied, declining fertility rates, changing economic landscapes, and other variables make it increasingly difficult to keep family units intact as a means of social and practical support.
- Universal social network patterns emerged for older adults in all countries studied, but cultural differences meant that some patterns were more prominent in certain areas. For example, a close, family-focused pattern was common in Japan, where people had few close relationships outside of marriage, while in the United States, patterns emerged of extensive, diverse, and close friendships outside of marriage and the primary family unit.
- In the United States, large social networks maintained earlier in life tended to shrink as people age. Conversely, in other countries such as Mexico, Japan, and

Lebanon, smaller social networks maintained earlier in life tended to expand with age. Older adults in Germany and France who were widowed or ill had the smallest social networks of all the countries studied.
- Many older adults from various countries reported poor mental health and a lack of emotional support associated with familial social networks that were perceived as negative, while older adults in Japan reported no such association between a lack of familial support and poor mental health.

SOCIAL CONNECTION VIA FRIENDSHIPS

Friendships are important at all life stages and we can gain new friendships at any time, whereas it is more likely to gain new family members earlier in life through birth and marriage (Blieszner, Ogletree, & Adams, 2019). In this section, we will explore the nature and importance of friendship as one form of social network in older adulthood.

Evolving Social Networks

Research and personal experience show that the specific nature of social engagement and connectedness tends to evolve and change over the course of the life span depending on intersectional characteristics, life circumstances, living arrangements, and other variables. For example, chronic illness or retirement may make it difficult or less desirable to maintain former social networks, including friendships. Further, while the social convoy model suggests that core social networks (e.g., spouses) tend to be more important than non-core networks (Lee & Szinovacz, 2016), dissolution of the core network through divorce, death, relocation, or other factors may necessitate seeking more support from friends. Some research indicates that support from friend groups may be even more desirable than support from core networks because we can choose our friends (Sias & Bartoo, 2007). If a relationship with a friend becomes more negative than positive, we can choose to distance ourselves or even sever ties with that person.

Benefits of Friendship

The benefits of friendships, at any stage in life, are numerous. In fact, friendship is often referred to as the "social glue" that promotes cohesion and social inclusion (Pahl, 2000). Friend networks may buffer negative relationships with close network members such as spouses and children. Friend networks can help increase self-esteem through cultivating a sense of competence, accomplishment, and well-being (Adams & Blieszner, 1995). Further, friends tend to mitigate the effects of stress and provide resources that help us respond to problematic situations (Walen & Lachman 2000). As with social connectedness in general, close friendships provide benefits through reciprocity in satisfying social needs; mutual emotional and instrumental support and caregiving; increased cognitive, physical, and mental health; and companionship and people with whom we can share interests and activities (de Vries, 2018; ten Bruggencate, Luijkx, & Sturm, 2018). The positive effects of friendship networks hold true for older adults, regardless of demographics and other characteristics.

Friendships among LGBT Older Adults

The roles that friends play and the importance of those roles may differ between different groups of older adults, depending on their backgrounds, experiences, and unique circumstances (Nguyen et al., 2016). For instance, LGBT older adults benefit from strong social networks; in general, strong social networks are associated with better physical and mental health and less disability (Fredriksen-Goldsen et al., 2013). For many, friends become their core social network and are often important sources of social support. In some cases, LGBT older adults have become estranged from biological family members or do not have children. This group may be more motivated than heterosexual older adults to maintain friendships with ex-partners to maintain ties with social networks outside of the core network (Eeden-Moorefield et al., 2011; Fredriksen-Goldsen, Kim et al., 2013).

In some studies, transgender older adults have been found to have larger, more diverse friendship networks than nontransgender older adults. This may be because many transgender older adults have sexual identities that vary across the continuum, so opportunities to develop friendships in diverse communities may be more plentiful. Further, transgender older adults are more likely to have children and more likely to be living with someone than nontransgender older adults (Erosheva et al., 2016). However, other studies have found that transgender older adults are more socially isolated than their nontransgender counterparts (Fredriksen-Goldsen et al., 2011; Witten, 2003).

Female Versus Male Friend Groups

Women tend to have larger, more diverse friendship networks than men (McLaughlin et al., 2010) for many reasons. Women tend to outlive men, so for heterosexual women, friends become a part of the core network after spouses have died or the number of eligible male partners has dwindled. Also, some heterosexual women may prefer or need the social support of friends over spouses or male partners, such as when a male partner is too ill to provide support or does not share the same interests. Older women are more likely than older men to state that they have a best friend. Women's ability to develop close friendships and weather difficult friendships may also contribute to the importance, maintenance, and longevity of friendships in later life (Antonucci, Lansford, & Akiyama, 2001). Further, friendship networks in which women can confide appear to protect against mental health issues such as depression (Antonucci, Lansford, & Akiyama, 2001).

Often, married men rely on the friendship networks of their female partners and find fewer opportunities to develop close friendship ties. This may, at least in part, be related to gender roles in which men are not encouraged to cultivate intimate friendships, particularly male friendships, also known as **homosociality** (Lee & Szinovacz, 2016). Research suggests that men, in many cultural contexts, are discouraged from displaying physical affection (e.g., hugging) toward their male friends or from verbally expressing their love or appreciation for male friends. It may be more difficult for men to form and maintain close, socially supportive same-sex friendships on which they can rely into older age (Anderson & Fidler, 2018).

Men often participate less frequently in formal social groups and activities than women (Nurmi et al., 2018), so this likely limits opportunities for men to make friends. Thus, many men may miss out on the protective elements that close, intimate friendships

Figure 4.3 Friend groups provide important connection in later life
Source: kali9/iStock

can provide, which may contribute to the shorter life spans of men compared to women. However, shifts in social roles, such as when men become grandfathers, can provide ways in which men (and women) find new ways to engage in intimate social networks (Mann, Tarrant, & Leeson, 2016).

Intergenerational Friendships

Intergenerational friendships can provide benefits for all ages, including helping to reduce ageism (for both younger and older adults). Indeed, the benefits of intergenerational friendships include all the benefits of friendship in general plus additional benefits that same-age friendships cannot offer. Unique benefits include offering inspiration and different perspectives on life, providing role models or mentors and a sense of

---

CASE 4.1

Happy Hour

Mark is 74 years old and lives alone in a small town. He recently retired from his teaching job at a local university, which is where he did most of his socializing and networking with friends and colleagues. During his 20 years of teaching, Mark developed several close friendships with other male instructors and administrators at the university. On a regular basis, while Mark was still teaching, he and his friends would meet for happy hours at local bars and restaurants. After Mark retired, he and his friends kept their regular happy hour meetings. This allowed Mark to maintain his social connections and get updates about what was happening at the university. These meetings also allowed Mark's friends to get updates on Mark's life and to help him with things like house maintenance and other issues with which he might need support. For example, Mark needed to undergo a medical procedure and asked one of his friends to drive him to and from the appointment. His friends also checked up on him after the procedure.

What do you see as some of the advantages to Mark's regular happy hours with his male friends? In what ways could you, as a health or mental health professional, encourage more social interaction and networking among older men?

Figure 4.4 Intergenerational friendships are important at every stage of life
Source: Fly View Productions/iStock

being valued, offering opportunities to keep up with trends, and a greater appreciation for different experiences (Levy & Thayer, 2019). Intergenerational interaction has the added benefit of reducing stereotypical thinking about age, as getting to know people on a deeper level helps to challenge assumptions, simplistic thinking, and preconceived notions about groups of people (Leedahl et al., 2020).

SOCIAL CONNECTION VIA SEXUALITY AND INTIMACY

Intimacy is a sense of closeness with another person. While we typically think of intimacy as having a sexual component, there are at least four types of intimacy: physical, intellectual, emotional, and spiritual. This means that sexuality is only one aspect of connecting with another person.

According to the World Health Organization, sexuality and intimacy is multifaceted, and encompasses "sex, gender identities and roles, sexual orientation, eroticism, pleasure, intimacy and reproduction. Sexuality is experienced and expressed in thoughts, fantasies, desires, beliefs, attitudes, values, behaviors, practices, roles and relationships. While sexuality can include all of these dimensions, not all of them are always experienced or expressed" (World Health Organization, 2006, p. 5). This definition can include emotional, behavioral, cognitive, and physical aspects of sexuality and intimacy.

Beliefs about Sexuality in Older Adults

Ageist notions of sexuality and intimacy in later life include the belief older adults have no interest in or need for sexual activity or intimacy. Reproductive purposes aside, and regardless of age, older adults still value intimacy, regardless of the form it may take. Different forms of intimacy fulfill needs related to safety, security, attachment, belonging, and closeness (DeWitte & Mayer, 2018; Kolodziejczak et al., 2019). Further, healthy physical and emotional sexual intimacy contributes to overall well-being (Fileborn et al., 2017; Verschuren et al., 2010).

Much of the research conducted on sexuality and intimacy in later life focuses on a narrow range of activities such as sexual intercourse, employs limited definitions of sexuality, and utilizes standards of sexuality that are often used to study younger populations.

These representations of sexuality are often used to define successful aging, so that aging well or successfully means that one remains sexually active in these narrowly defined ways well into older adulthood (Kolodziejczak et al., 2019). The concept of successful aging tends to encompass a notion of narrowly defined **heteronormative sexuality** (i.e., a worldview that promotes heterosexuality as the normal or preferred sexual identity or orientation) and **heterohappiness**. From a queer theory perspective, Marshall (2018) discusses heterohappiness as a way that popular culture cultivates an image of aging and sexuality (as well as other aspects of aging) in a rigid, heterosexual (and often white) way. In this view, older adults are able, active, healthy, attractive, and sexually active. However, defining sexuality in these terms and couching it in successful aging does not capture the rich and varied intimate needs, complexities, and realities of older adults (or any adult for that matter).

Decreased Sexual Activity

Research does indicate that older adults report less engagement in sexual activity (such as intercourse) than younger adults, and many older adults report less sexual desire as they age (Kolodziejczak et al., 2019). Many and varied psychological, cognitive, biological, and relational reasons contribute to older adults' decreased sexual desire and their less frequent engagement in sex; some are part of "normal" aging and some are not. Many of these reasons can apply to younger people as well. For example, pain and/or chronic illness that leads to cardiovascular or metabolic conditions can make sexual activity difficult or uncomfortable, as can functional disabilities or limitations, vaginal dryness stemming from menopause, or erectile dysfunction caused by health or psychological issues. Certain medications and medical treatments, such as chemotherapy, can create physical limitations to sexual intercourse (Allen & Desille, 2017; Merghati-Khoei et al., 2016). Further, stress, depression, body image issues, and relational conflict can contribute to a decrease in sexual desire.

Many causes of decreased sexual desire and activity in later life can be mitigated. For instance, medication can help with erectile dysfunction, lubricants can help with vaginal dryness, and therapy can help with relational and mental health issues (Cherpak & dos Santos, 2016; National Institute on Aging, 2021). Further, many people find that exploring other forms of intimacy that do not entail intercourse, such as kissing, caressing, masturbation, body contact, and other displays of affection, are just as fulfilling and satisfying. Given some of the factors that can cause problems with sexuality later in life, it is not surprising that research indicates that good health and an emotionally close relationship with a partner are associated with an active sex life in later years (Traeen et al., 2018).

Differences Between Population Groups

Studies suggest that older men, regardless of sexual orientation, report more frequent sexual activity and sexual thoughts than older lesbian, bisexual, and heterosexual women. Some of the differences in sexual activity between men and women can be explained by older men (particularly heterosexual men) having access to partners more often than women (Kolodziejczak et al., 2019; Lee et al., 2016). However, even older women who have female partners report less sexual activity and thoughts than older men (Sandberg, 2013). Many women, regardless of sexual identity, turn to other women in later in life for a range of physical, emotional, and other intimacy needs (Diamond, 2016; Ghisyawan, 2016).

Nonintercourse activities have been found to be prevalent for both older men and older women (Kolodziejczak et al., 2019). For example, research indicates that both older men and older women benefit from and place importance on emotional intimacy, particularly in advanced age (Fileborn et al., 2017; Sandberg, 2013).

While many ageist assumptions about older adults and sexuality exist, particularly for older women, many older adults feel that the quality of their sexuality improves with age, their definition of sexuality expands (e.g., to include more than just intercourse), and that many worries related to sexuality decrease with age (e.g., issues related to pregnancy and body image) (Fileborn et al., 2015; Taylor et al., 2016).

Risk of Sexually Transmitted Disease

Though many worries related to intimacy and sexual activity decrease with age, the risk of contracting sexually transmitted infections (STI) does not. Indeed, STIs have increased dramatically among older adults in the past decade, particularly among those who are divorced or widowed (Smith et al., 2020). A report by the Centers for Disease Control and Prevention (2020b) indicates that cases of chlamydia, gonorrhea, and syphilis have increased significantly in recent years. For example, between 2008 and 2017, rates of STIs increased by 275 percent in Montana and 240 percent in Wyoming. STIs create health problems in and of themselves and can also increase the risk of other health problems such as cancer and heart disease. An increase in common STIs among older adults also brings with it risk for increased rates of HIV infection.

The reasons for this increase in STIs among older adults include that older adults tend not to use condoms because pregnancy is no longer an issue and also because older adults tend to underestimate their risk for infection (Centers for Disease Control and Prevention, 2020b). Research indicates that many healthcare practitioners do not perceive older adults as being sexually active, so topics surrounding sexuality and STIs are often not discussed with older patients (Schaller, Traeen, & Kvalem, 2020).

Influence of Technology

Technological advances have helped older adults increase intimacy and social connection (see Chapter 10 for further discussion on media and technology). Older adults

Figure 4.5 Sexuality and intimacy continues into older age
Source: Davids'Adventures/Shutterstock

seeking companions or sexual or marriage partners may rely on social media, dating sites for older adults, and video conferencing applications to meet and form relationships with others. Older adults (particularly those who live in rural areas) have increasingly been turning to dating and other sites to find potential companions and partners (Smith & Duggan, 2013; Wion & Loeb, 2015).

Older adults also participate in online social groups based on shared interests such as hiking, travel, gardening, gaming, and grief support. Online meeting platforms and video conferencing apps became a very important means of connection for people, including older adults, who had become isolated or widowed due to the COVID-19 pandemic. This technology not only has helped connect people, but it has been a helpful tool in combating isolation and loneliness. Technology can also offer additional resources and support to older adults in areas of sexuality that can help increase their intimate and partner satisfaction (Fileborn et al., 2015).

CHAPTER REVIEW

Social Theories of Aging
- Social theories of aging help explain social aspects of older age and how people's social lives are affected by age and the social environment, which in turn affect well-being.
- Disengagement theory, a foundational social theory of age, posits that we naturally remove, or disengage, ourselves from certain social roles, such as professional and familial roles, as we age.
- Activity theory, another foundational theory of social age, suggests that we remain active or engaged in our social lives and roles as we age. Our level of social interest and involvement remains similar to that at earlier stages of life, and if we disengage, it is likely because of factors outside our control, such as changing health, economics, discrimination, or other issues that cause us to shift our social interactions and patterns.
- Continuity theory suggests that relationships, social roles, and patterns of social behavior and engagement established early in life help to predict what our social lives in older age will look like. We tend to maintain patterns of behavior related to social engagement throughout the life span, which also help us cope and adjust to the developmental changes we experience through the decades.
- A life-course model of social functionality acknowledges the importance of prior experiences and how they shape our functioning in later years. This model acknowledges that social, cultural, political, and historical contexts are important across the life span as well as experiences with discrimination, oppression, and privilege that are intertwined with intersectional identities.
- The social convoy model of social age posits that we have social networks, or convoys, in which we are embedded throughout our lives and that provide the reciprocity, or give and take, of needed social support.

Social Connectedness
- Social connectedness is an important human need and is critical to our mental and physical well-being. Without social connectedness, we are at risk for loneliness, isolation, and higher rates of illness and mortality.

- Factors including disability, living alone, chronic physical and mental illness, poverty and lack of access to resources, and social network loss through death, divorce, relocation, and estrangement all can place people at risk for social isolation.

Social Connection via Friendships
- Friend networks in older adulthood are important and serve many purposes including buffering negative family relationships; increasing self-esteem; mitigating the effects of stressful situations; providing mutual emotional and instrumental support and caregiving; increasing cognitive, physical, and mental health; and providing companionship and shared interests and activities.
- Women, who on average outlive men, tend to have larger, more diverse friendship networks than men. Men also often are discouraged from cultivating intimate friendships with other men, known as homosociality.
- Intergenerational friendships can provide benefits for all ages, including reducing ageism (for both younger and older adults), offering inspiration and different perspectives on life, providing role models or mentors and a sense of being valued, and offering opportunities to keep up on trends and a greater appreciation for different experiences.

Social Connection via Sexuality and Intimacy
- Ageist assumptions about older adulthood often include that older adults have no desire for and are not engaged in sexual or intimate activities. Further, much of the research on sexuality in older age is modeled on rigid, stereotypical, and heteronormative standards sexuality of younger adults.
- Many older adults report less desire for sex and that they have less sex than in their younger years. However, many older adults report that the quality of their sexual and intimate lives is better than in younger years.
- The risk of STIs among older adults has increased dramatically in recent years, partly because older adults underestimate their risk for contracting STIs and because they tend not to use condoms or other protective measures.
- Technology has helped many older adults build and maintain social and sexual relationships, which has increased many older adults' sense of connection.

REVIEW QUESTIONS
1. Compare and contrast different theories of social aging. What are some of the pros and cons to each? How do you view your own aging from these theories?
2. Discuss ways that culture might affect friendship and social connectedness.
3. Explore factors that might affect sexual intimacy and connection (e.g., physical, social, cultural).

KEY TERMS

disengagement theory
activity theory
continuity theory
life-course model of social functioning

social convoy model
homosociality
heteronormative
heterohappiness

CHAPTER 5

Death and End-of-Life Issues

Chapter Outline
What Is Death?
   Defining Physical Death
   Physical Process of Dying
   Perceptions of Death
End-of-Life Rights and Choices
   Right to Die
   Death with Dignity Legislation
   Hospice Care
   Disparities at End of Life
Preparing for End of Life
Experiencing Grief and Loss
   Types of Grief
   Theories and Models of Grief
      Kübler-Ross Theory
      Other Models of Grief
   Awareness of Death
Memorializing and Taking Care of the Dead
   Disposition of Bodies
      Green Burials
      Organ, Tissue, and Body Donation
   Memorialization After Death
   Impact of COVID-19 Pandemic on Funeral Practices

Learning Objectives

After completing this chapter, you will be able to:
- Define death and describe the process of physical death.
- Describe hospice care and explain options for death with dignity for terminally ill individuals and the legal issues involved.
- List and describe the legal documents used to state end-of-life and after-death wishes.
- Name and explain the types of grief and well-known theories of grief.
- Describe how bodies of the deceased may be handled and ways that family and friends memorialize loved ones after death.

Loss, grief, and death are all part of being human. How we experience age-related changes, loss, grief, and the inevitability of our own death is highly individual. In this chapter, we'll explore the issues surrounding death and dying as an important part of the human experience.

WHAT IS DEATH?

The question "What is death?" is complicated. It can be asked in a philosophical sense, such as, "What does it mean to die?" Answers to this question rely in large part on factors such as a person's religious and spiritual beliefs, cultural background, personal experiences, and other factors related to their upbringing and environment. Or it can be asked in a literal sense, such as, "What needs to happen to be declared dead?" In short, death is the permanent cessation of all the vital functions of the body. We will all die eventually, and while there are many causes of death, our bodies undergo relatively the same processes and changes as we die.

Defining Physical Death

The definition of death, or what we consider physical death and how to declare someone physically dead, has changed over the centuries, even up to recent years. Further, the definition of death has been influenced by factors such as technology, social practices, and cultural values, which in turn affect aspects of death such as grieving, medical interventions, organ donation, and other ethical and legal issues associated with the end of life (Sarbey, 2016).

Not long ago, death was declared using medical standards such as fixed pupils and the absence of a pulse or breath (doctors would hold a mirror under the nose to look for condensation). These signs of death were part of the cultural definition of death, and physicians' practices to declare death mirrored those cultural perceptions. As technology developed, cultural conceptions and medical standards related to death began to diverge. For example, those undergoing heart or lung transplants would not show signs of heartbeats or respiration (respectively) but would most likely be very much alive. Similarly, those on artificial life support systems would still be alive while not showing some of the standard signs of life (Sarbey, 2016).

Due to advances in medicine and technology, a group at the Harvard Medical School developed criteria for brain death in the 1960s, which described an irreversible coma or total unresponsiveness and cessation of breathing, reflexes, and heartbeat. However, this definition of death could not scientifically or logically explain physical death. Complicating matters were cases of people being kept alive for decades through artificial means; definitions of death were played out in courts as family members fought over whether their loved ones were dead and whether they should be kept on life support and in permanent vegetative states. Two of the most famous cases that helped to shape contemporary definitions of death were Karen Ann Quinlan and Terri Schiavo. Karen lapsed into a coma in 1975 and remained alive for 10 years through artificial means. Her adoptive parents fought in court to have Karen removed from life support, but the courts intervened. Later, the case of Terri Schiavo, who remained in a coma from 1990 to 2005, resulted in a court battle between her husband and parents around Terri's right to die (Kennedy, 1976; Sarbey, 2016; Weijer, 2005). These cases also helped to shape and propel the "right to die" movement, discussed later in this chapter.

More recently, the standard for physical death has become more precise, leading to a uniform definition of total brain death. Death, according to this definition, includes the criteria of irreversible cessation of circulatory and respiratory functions as well as the entire brain, including the brain stem. This definition also states that total brain death may not be necessary but is sufficient to declare death (Sarbey, 2016).

Physical Process of Dying

What happens to our bodies when we die? The physical process of dying depends on factors such as medications, disease process, and the use of life-sustaining measures, for example. Further, the process of death can occur in a matter of hours or take weeks. While the dying process varies from person to person, it is typical to observe common physical signs that death is imminent (Lamers, 2017):

- Physical changes such as weight loss, skin tone changes, a drop in body temperature and blood pressure, and a decrease in activity such as moving, speaking, eating, and drinking;
- Breathing changes, such as periods of slowed or stopped breathing alternating with rapid breathing (known as Cheyne-Stokes breathing). Noisy breathing and frequent coughing often occur as fluids accumulate in the throat; the gurgling sound may be referred to as the "death rattle."
- Cognitive changes such as alternating periods of unconsciousness and alertness as well as experiences of delusions, illusions, and hallucinations. Toward the end of life, many people will lapse into a coma. Despite states of unconsciousness, it should be assumed that the person can hear as the sense of hearing is typically the last of the senses to decline.

After death, our bodies, as complex ecosystems, undergo a series of biological changes. Once the heart stops beating, cells are deprived of oxygen and chemical reactions cause toxic byproducts to accumulate inside cells. Upon death, decomposition occurs. Tissues and cells are "self-digested" via a process known as **autolysis** in which enzymes break down cells and cellular components. Fluids begin to settle in the body, aided by gravity, which changes the color of the skin. Body temperature cools and protein filaments become locked in place, causing rigor mortis. With the immune system shut down, the microbiome in the intestines begins to digest tissue (Martinez et al., 2019).

Perceptions of Death

Many years ago, family members and loved ones would die at home, and those left behind had to deal with it directly by being present during death and handling the body of the deceased. Death was viewed as a natural part of living (Aries, 1981). More recent medical and technological advances have resulted in the ability to prolong life, and there has been a shift in the way most people view death. Medicine seemed to promise an escape from death, or at least the ability to live longer and postpone the inevitable. Dying and death for the most part moved from the home to hospitals and long-term care facilities, and bodies are often whisked away shortly after death. In most cases, loved ones rarely have the opportunity to be with the body until a viewing in a funeral home, and sometimes, not at all (Cassel, 1997).

Our language reflects a societal discomfort with death, as words such as "passed away" or even flippant terms such as "kicked the bucket" are used instead of simply saying that a person has died. While fear and discomfort around death are still common, hospice and increasing end-of-life options have contributed to an increased ability among some people to accept death as a natural part of life.

END-OF-LIFE RIGHTS AND CHOICES

Over the past several decades, widely publicized court cases, along with advances in medical technology, have focused more attention on end-of-life rights and choices. Before we discuss important issues, events, and legislation, we need to understand some basic terminology related to end of life:

- **Active euthanasia**: causing death by active means, such as administering or injecting a lethal dose of a drug.
- **Passive euthanasia**: causing death by withdrawing or withholding life-prolonging medical treatment such as a ventilator or feeding tube.
- **Medical aid in dying** (also called physician aid in dying): a physician or other medical professional provides a mentally competent, terminally ill patient (upon the patient's request) a prescription for a lethal dose of medication, which the patient intends to take to end their life.
- **Assisted suicide** (also called assisted death or assisted dying): a person, usually a physician, takes some type of action (such as providing drugs) to help a patient end their life. In recent years, supporters of right-to-die choices have omitted the word "suicide" from end-of-life discussions because it may misrepresent the intentions and philosophy of end-of-life choices (Starks, Dudzinski, & White, 2013). The term may still be used by various legislative bodies and medical organizations.
- **Voluntary stopping of eating and drinking (VSED)** is the conscious act of intentionally ceasing eating and drinking, with the goal of ending one's life.

Right to Die

In 1980 the Hemlock Society was founded, which focused on the right to die or death with dignity, the idea that a terminally ill individual has the right to choose to end their life. In 2003, The Hemlock Society split into two organizations, the Final Exit Network (https://finalexitnetwork.org), which focuses on death with dignity education, and Compassion and Choices (https://compassionandchoices.org), which focuses on legislative change. Hemlock Society founder Derek Humphry wrote the book *The Final Exit* in 1991, which discusses assisted and other methods of suicide and was very controversial at the time of its publication.

Another prominent proponent of assisted suicide was Dr. Jack Kevorkian, a physician who assisted in the deaths of 130 terminally ill people between 1990 and 1998. In 1999, Dr. Kevorkian was sentenced to prison for 25 years but was released in 2007 upon an agreement to never assist in another death (Biography, 2019).

Right to die movements generated by organizations such as the Hemlock Society and people like Dr. Kevorkian and Derek Humphry ignited debate about end-of-life choices and gave voice to arguments in favor of rights for terminally ill people to gain control of end-of-life decisions, including ending their own lives. These arguments are based in the premise that advances in technology can result in prolonging life to the point that terminally ill people experience needless pain and suffering. In many ways, consistent with queer theory, these movements challenged our thinking on what a "normal" death is, who is in charge of overseeing the death process, and how we ought to experience it.

Death with Dignity Legislation

End-of-life movements have led to the passage of legislation supporting rights for terminally ill people to die and renewed emphasis on end-of-life options. For example, ten US jurisdictions have statutes allowing physician aid in dying, with

Figure 5.1 Derek Humphry (*left*) and Jack Kevorkian (*right*)
Sources: Derek Humphry/Wikimedia Commons/CC BY-SA 3.0 and Dfree/Shutterstock

Oregon being the first in the United States to pass Death with Dignity legislation in 1997, which allows qualified terminally ill adults to voluntarily request and receive prescription medication to hasten their deaths. In addition to Oregon, the other nine states that have statutes in place to safeguard the practice are California, Colorado, the District of Columbia, Hawaii, Maine, New Jersey, New Mexico, Vermont, and Washington. While some sites list Montana as an additional state that allows physician aid in dying, it does not have a statute in place. Rather, the Supreme Court ruled that nothing in state law prohibits physicians from honoring the wishes of terminally ill, mentally competent patients by prescribing medication to hasten death. Other countries such as Belgium, Canada, Colombia, Luxembourg, Switzerland, and The Netherlands also have legalized assisted death practices (Dignitas, 2019).

Hospice Care
Further, in the 1960s, Cicely Saunders introduced the concept of hospice care to the United States and opened the first hospice in the United Kingdom. **Hospice** is care provided to terminally ill people, who, in a doctor's opinion, have fewer than six months to live. Hospice care focuses on comfort for the patient and quality of life for the patient, family, and caregivers. This approach to end-of-life care may take place in the home or in a facility such as a hospital, assisted living residence, or specialized hospice center (National Hospice and Palliative Care Organization, 2019). Hospice includes holistic care from an interdisciplinary team of physicians, nurses, social workers, volunteers, and spiritual advisors who focus on medical, physical, emotional, and spiritual needs and support of the dying person without utilizing disease-focused treatments or interventions such as chemotherapy.

Hospice care incorporates **palliative care**, which is medical care that aims to provide relief from pain and other symptoms of serious illness. For patients not under hospice care, palliative care may be provided along with curative treatments. In a hospice setting, palliative care is the primary type of care for the terminally ill. The goal is to keep the patient as comfortable as possible.

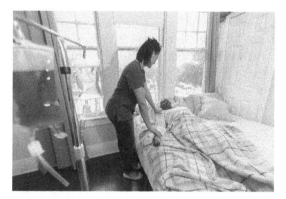

Figure 5.2 Hospice care
Source: SDI Productions/iStock

Disparities at End of Life

It is important to note that, as with healthcare disparities throughout the life span, people of color are likely to experience disparities at the end of life. For example, in the United States, Black patients are more likely than white patients to die in a hospital, and Blacks are less likely than whites to be informed of end-of-life choices or to engage in end-of-life planning. Research suggests that these patterns are driven by factors such as cost and inequitable access to alternative services, a lifetime of discrimination in healthcare settings, mistrust of healthcare professionals, and cultural and religious beliefs and traditions that influence end-of-life practices (Orlovic, Smith, & Mossialos, 2019).

PREPARING FOR END OF LIFE

Increasingly, people are making end-of-life choices earlier in life, so that they have more control over what happens to them in various medical situations. Most people are familiar with **do not resuscitate (DNR) forms**, also called allow natural death (AND) forms, which direct medical personnel to forgo resuscitative measures in cases of cardiopulmonary arrest. These orders can be used in or out of the hospital.

More frequently, people are utilizing more comprehensive tools to make end-of-life choices that may be necessary in a variety of medical situations. **Physician orders for life-sustaining treatment (POLST) forms**, also called medical orders for life-sustaining treatment (MOLST), are used to indicate wishes regarding specific treatments commonly used during medical emergencies. These instructions remain with the person and can be accessed by physicians regardless of where the person may be during a medical event. Typically, DNR and POLST forms are used by seriously ill individuals, but many people who are not experiencing serious illness keep them on file with their physicians.

Advance directives are legal documents used to communicate a person's wishes about medical treatment when they cannot communicate on their own. The two main types of advance directives are a living will and a durable power of attorney for healthcare. Many healthcare providers suggest that their patients, regardless of health status, have advance directives on file. A **living will** is a document that states wishes for medical care when a person is in a terminal condition or persistent vegetative state and is unable to communicate decisions. A **durable power of attorney for healthcare** is used to appoint a representative (surrogate or proxy) who will make healthcare decisions for a person who is temporarily or permanently unable to communicate or make these decisions on their own (Compassion and Choices, 2019).

EXPERIENCING GRIEF AND LOSS

Bereavement is the period of grief and mourning following the death of a beloved person or pet. How long this period lasts depends on factors such as how close you were to the individual who died, if the death was anticipated or unexpected, and other factors. **Grief** is the personal response to loss. It is often experienced as a

CASE 5.1

Joyce's Diagnosis

Joyce is 60 years old and recently has been diagnosed with a terminal illness. While Joyce is maintaining her regular activities without too much pain or discomfort, she knows that as the disease progresses, she will likely experience debilitating pain and eventually will need help with daily care. Joyce has talked with her medical team about hospice care, but she also wants to learn more about physician aid in dying should her quality of life deteriorate significantly, especially if pain becomes unmanageable. Joyce wants to spend as much time as possible with family and friends, but she also does not want to suffer or have her life prolonged through artificial means. Joyce wants to maintain control over her healthcare decisions as the disease progresses.

If you were Joyce's family member or a member of her medical team, what conversations do you think would be important to have with Joyce right now? How could you best support Joyce as she makes decisions about her care and end-of-life choices?

---

strong, sometimes overwhelming, emotional response to a real or perceived loss (Mayo Clinic, 2020). **Mourning** describes the ways in which grief is outwardly expressed, which are influenced by cultural, religious, ethnic, and other intersectional factors. Grief can be expressed quietly and privately or it can be expressed through elaborate public rituals or symbols such as wearing black or lowering a flag to half-staff.

There are other types of loss that occur in life in addition to losing a loved one. Common losses include the loss of jobs, health, abilities, supports, possessions, independence, relationships, friendships, and various roles. These can leave people with feelings of grief similar to those that occur after a death. The models discussed in this chapter can help us make sense of the grief process, regardless of the cause.

Figure 5.3 Grief is a unique experience
Source: Rawpixel.com/Shutterstock

Types of Grief

People react differently to loss, depending on intersectional factors such as personality, coping skills, personal resources, life experiences, and cultural backgrounds. Grief may be experienced as a physical, mental, or emotional reaction, often a combination of all three. With regard to loss through death, research suggests that additional factors like social and gender roles, perceived relationship with the deceased, values and beliefs, mode of death, and number of losses can affect the way a person experiences or expresses grief. These intersectional characteristics can influence the outcomes of the grief process and the ways in which people adjust to loss or death (Milic et al., 2017).

Grief is part of living, and typically people move through the experience of grief in ways that allow them to carry on their usual relationships and functioning at some point. This is often referred to as **uncomplicated grief** or uncomplicated bereavement. That doesn't mean the pain of loss doesn't resurface or that people don't struggle with the loss at various times, such as at the anniversary of a loss. Uncomplicated grief acknowledges the vast array of cognitive, emotional, and behavioral responses to loss; these are all considered "normal" or not out of the ordinary. Typically, people work through loss and grief in their own time, in their own way, and often with the help of informal or formal support networks such as partners, friends, or a therapist. Often what is helpful to people in the grief process is reassurance that the range of emotions one might feel is okay, as the intensity of emotions and reactions to loss can be scary and overwhelming at times.

The outcomes of uncomplicated grief can be contrasted with those of **complicated grief**, now also known as prolonged grief (or prolonged grief disorder), which refers to grief or bereavement that can be problematic for people and require additional support or intervention. Sometimes people have difficulties coping with loss or experience prolonged periods of distress that create adjustment problems long after a loss occurs, to the point where they experience long-term disruptions in their relationships or daily functioning. Complicated or prolonged grief may be associated with symptoms like a sense of disbelief or anger related to the loss; recurring, unrelenting painful emotions; or intrusive thoughts of or preoccupation with the loss years after it occurs (Aoyama et al., 2018; Howarth, 2011). Complicated or prolonged grief tends to be associated with certain factors as well as unusual or problematic circumstances associated with loss that can be challenging for people, making the grief process more difficult. For example, previous loss, the death of a child, lack of social support, high-profile losses (like those covered in the media), and loss accompanied by multiple stressors (like loss of family members and pets in a fire that also destroys the home and belongings and creates a financial hardship) can put people at risk for complicated or prolonged grief (Aoyama et al., 2018; Lobb et al., 2010). As another example, many people who experienced the death of a loved one during the COVID-19 pandemic that began in the United States in 2020 found they were unable to be with loved ones as they were dying or allowed to hold or attend memorial services because of the ban on social gatherings and the need for social distancing. These types of conditions can bring risk of complicated or prolonged grief.

Another issue that can complicate grief is when people are denied the opportunity to grieve. **Disenfranchised grief** (Doka, 2002) refers to situations when people's reactions to loss are unacknowledged by others around them or by larger society. Every culture holds its own traditions and rules that guide which losses can be grieved, who can grieve them, and in what ways they can be grieved. Socially sanctioned losses are allowed be grieved, and only those losses that are grieved in socially sanctioned ways will receive acknowledgment and support, both informally and formally through support networks and laws and policies. Disenfranchised grief occurs when people experience losses or grieve in ways that are not socially acceptable. For example, in the United States, it is generally agreed that family members (that is, those with biological or marital ties) have a right to grieve the deaths of other family members. Family members get time off work, social support, and financial benefits when they experience a loss of a family member. However, a loss of a relationship that is not socially sanctioned or legally recognized may not be acknowledged or supported. For example, this may occur among partners who choose not to marry; are lesbian, gay, bisexual, or transgender; or who are estranged or divorced. People may lose pets, pregnancies, close friends, coworkers, foster children, children of significant others, or even possessions such as a home. Losses like these may get little to no acknowledgment, financial benefits, time off work to attend the funeral or make necessary arrangements, or control over decision-making processes about the deceased after the loss.

Grief can also be disenfranchised when losses occur under socially unacceptable circumstances like death that results from suicide, violence, or self-neglect. For example, the death of a partner from a drug overdose may be seen differently than if the partner dies from an illness. Or, in the case of gun violence, the deaths of the perpetrator and the victim will be viewed and treated differently, having ramifications for surviving family and friends. Further, grieving and bereavement are socially sanctioned. Cultures define parameters for grief such as how long grief should last, in what ways it should be demonstrated, and how it should be acknowledged by others. If we deviate from those parameters, we may be diagnosed with a mental illness or lose social support.

Theories and Models of Grief

Over the years, many theories and models have been developed that attempt to explain our experience with death, loss, and grief. One of the first and most recognized (and often most misapplied) theories is Elisabeth Kübler-Ross's theory of death and dying (1969).

Kübler-Ross Theory

Elisabeth Kübler-Ross (1926–2004) was a Swiss American psychiatrist who conducted hundreds of extensive interviews with dying patients. Through listening to patients expressing their feelings, thoughts, and experiences related to the dying process, she noticed that many people's reactions to dying followed a predictable pattern. Kübler-Ross used these interviews to develop her five stages of grief model (Kübler-Ross, 1971):

- *Stage 1: Denial*, usually occurs when a person first learns of imminent death. The person may be in shock or deny that a diagnosis is correct.
- *Stage 2: Anger*, involves experiencing intense feelings of anger or hostility. A person may lash out at others or a higher power, and question why he or she deserves to die.

- *Stage 3: Bargaining*, involves attempts to bargain with a doctor or a higher power to restore health.
- *Stage 4: Depression*, occurs when the person may begin to turn inward and grieve losses.
- *Stage 5: Acceptance*, occurs when the person achieves a sense of peace and may begin to resolve unfinished business and bring closure to their lives.

After publication of her original research, Kübler-Ross later adapted her view to note that the stages do not reflect a sequential, linear process. People may experience the stages in no particular order. Some may skip stages or move back and forth between stages. Others may get stuck in a stage or experience two stages simultaneously.

Kübler-Ross's model has been widely used to not only describe the dying person's experience but to describe other experiences of grief and loss. The model can be helpful in understanding that there is huge variation in how people react to loss. However, the model has been criticized for being too simplistic and prescriptive. The model also may not address cultural, spiritual, or other intersectional diversity that people may bring to the dying process. Thus, the model may not capture the unique, complex, and nuanced experiences that often come with grief and loss.

Other Models of Grief

Since the development of the Kübler-Ross model, many other models have emerged to expand on our thinking about the grief and loss process:

- *Continuing bonds model*: Grief is viewed as a process in which we create lasting attachments to whatever it is we have lost. We create things like symbols or memories or we use objects to connect us to our loss and we develop a new, different relationship with the lost person, pet, object, or opportunity we have lost (Klass, Silverman, & Nickman, 1996).
- *Dual-process of coping model*: Grief is viewed as a process of dealing with two types of stressors: those related to the loss and those related to restoration. People oscillate between coping with these stressors as they learn to adapt with the loss. They oscillate between being preoccupied with grief and reengaging with a transformed world (Stroebe & Schut, 2010).
- *Tasks of mourning model*: Working through grief involves dealing with four tasks of mourning: accepting the reality of the loss, processing the pain of the loss, adjusting to an environment without whatever it is we have lost, and emotionally relocating and memorializing whatever it is we have lost (Worden, 2009).
- *Adaptive grieving model*: Grief is viewed as highly individualistic and complex, and its expression is dependent on personality, culture, and other intersectional variables. Grieving reflects an individual's use of cognitive, behavioral, and affective strategies to adapt to loss. Adaptive grief follows one of three patterns: intuitive grieving, marked by a heightened experience and expression of emotion, including a desire to talk about the loss; instrumental grief, marked by a cognitive approach to grief and a need to control emotion and focus on tasks and problem solving; and blended grief, marked by a combination of affective and cognitive strategies to cope with loss (i.e., utilization of both intuitive and instrumental grieving) (Martin & Doka, 2000).

Awareness of Death

While not a theory that explains the grieving process, a more recent theory examines how we. cope with the awareness of our own deaths using concepts from Freud's psychodynamic theory. Terror management theory (Greenberg, Solomon, & Pyszczynski, 1997) suggests that because we have the capacity for self-awareness and can reflect on the past and future, we know that we will die. This death awareness can cause paralyzing fear and anxiety, so we must utilize defense mechanisms to manage these emotions and keep death thoughts at bay.

There are two main defenses people use to do this. One is the **proximal defense**, or a mechanism people use to suppress death thoughts and deny personal vulnerability. Examples of proximal defenses include exercising more, eating a healthy diet, or stopping smoking. These behaviors may offer a sense of control over health, decreasing feelings of vulnerability and anxiety over a premature death. The second is the **distal defense**, which is used after people have successfully suppressed death thoughts. This defense comes through building a worldview, or system of beliefs and practices, that gives meaning to life and death, thereby reducing anxiety about death. For example, we may believe we are contributing something meaningful to the world through our work or actions, building a legacy that will be remembered by the generations after us, or ending up in a better place after death because of our good deeds. According to terror management theory, without these defenses to reduce anxiety about death and dying, terror would paralyze us and we would not be able to function in our daily lives.

MEMORIALIZING AND TAKING CARE OF THE DEAD

The ways in which we handle bodies and memorialize people after death vary a great deal, depending on intersectional factors like culture, tradition, access to resources and technology, religious and spiritual beliefs, environmental constraints and considerations, and individual and familial preferences and circumstances. With advances s in technology, knowledge, and resources as well as changing views on death, more options than ever exist for memorializing loved ones and handling their bodies after death.

Disposition of Bodies

There are myriad ways of handling a body after death, including burial, cremation, and body donation, among others. Burial of a body used to be the preferred method of body disposition in the United States and Canada as well as other parts of the world. Increasingly, however, cremation has grown in popularity and has recently become the preferred method of choice in both countries. For example, in 2004, 31 percent of people were cremated in the United States and 52 percent in Canada. By 2020, that percentage increase to 55 percent and 73 percent respectively. As of 2020, Nevada (79.8 percent), Washington (78.0 percent), and Oregon (77.6 percent) had the highest rates of cremation in the United States, while Kentucky (33.4 percent), Alabama (31.4 percent), and Mississippi (26.0 percent) had the lowest rates (Cremation Association of North America, 2020).

Part of the reason for the increase in cremation rates has to do with economics. Cremation is less expensive than burial. In 2020, the median cost of a funeral (with viewing, transportation, burial, etc.) was $7,360. The average cost of a direct cremation (without a viewing and casket) was $1,100 (World Population Review, 2020). Of course, either method can be far less or more expensive, depending on the options that are chosen for each. Another reason for the increasing popularity of cremation includes the freedom and flexibility it allows for loved ones. For example, ashes from cremation can be easily transported and divided up among loved ones, who may want to keep or scatter them in different locations. Further, the immediacy of a burial is removed with cremation, which means that loved ones can be afforded more time to plan memorial services or gatherings. With advances in technology, more options for ashes exist besides saving, burying, or scattering them in meaningful locations. Depending on one's financial resources, ashes can be transported into space, turned into diamonds, made into art or decorative pieces, or placed in a biodegradable urn that is buried as used as a nutrient for growing trees or plants (National Cremation, 2020).

Environmental concerns are yet another reason for cremation's rise in popularity. Embalming fluid used in many burials contains toxic chemicals such as formaldehyde, ethanol, and methanol, which end up in the soil and water supply. Land scarcity and the unsustainable use of materials for caskets, like metals, plastics, and hardwoods, not only take a toll on natural resources because of demand but take a long time to decompose (National Cremation, 2020). Cremation also has its environmental challenges, however. It requires the burning of fossil fuels, and mercury can be emitted into the atmosphere through the burning of dental amalgam fillings. New biocremation methods and technologies have been developed to address these concerns, such as using water, heat, pressure, and potassium hydroxide (lye) to reduce the body to ash (Cremation Institute, 2020).

Green Burials

Along with more environmentally friendly cremation practices has come similar practices for burials. Green burials, as they are commonly referred to, seek to reduce the environmental impact of burial practices. The goals of green burials are

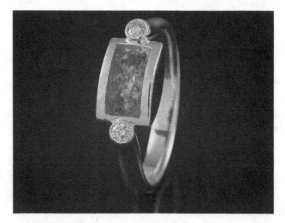

Figure 5.4 Ashes encased in a ring
Source: posteriori/iStock

to conserve natural resources, reduce carbon emissions and damage through the use of toxic chemicals, and protect funeral workers' health. This can be accomplished through the use of nontoxic and biodegradable materials in urns, caskets, shrouds, and the embalming process, for example, instead of more commonly used materials like plastic, metal, exotic wood, and formaldehyde (Green Burial Council, 2020).

Other green burial practices now exist that help reduce the footprint of burials on the environment. For example, conservation cemeteries are areas of land where vaults, headstones, pesticides, embalming chemicals, lawns and mowing, and other nonsustainable burial practices are prohibited. These areas are considered conservation areas and are left in their pristine state. Area maps and markers are used to identify the location of loved ones. Hybrid cemeteries are conventional cemeteries that allow bodies to be buried without vaults (Green Burial Council, 2020). In addition, people can choose to have their bodies placed in biodegradable pods that nourish trees or turned into compost that can be spread to provide nutrients to the soil.

Organ, Tissue, and Body Donation

Still other options for body disposition include organ, tissue, and whole-body donation for a variety of purposes. For example, some people choose to donate part or all of their bodies for transplants or medical or research use, or bodies can be donated to outdoor "farms" where scientists conduct forensic research on body decomposition under different natural circumstances to aid in solving murders. People can become organ and tissue donors by completing an application online or by mail, through an app, or at the local motor vehicle department. Each state has its own registry that is uploaded into a national database. Typically, organ and tissue donation occur after death, but some organs and tissues can be donated while a person is alive, such as kidneys, lungs, skin, bone, and blood (Health Resources and Services Administration, 2021).

Bodies also can be donated for plastination, a process through which water and fat in the body is replaced with plastic so that the body is preserved for various uses. One use is to display bodies in various poses for the Body Worlds exhibit that has traveled the world. Still other people have chosen cryonics, allowing their bodies to be frozen with the hopes that science will one day be able to revive and restore them to their original selves.

Memorialization after Death

There are many ways to memorialize loved ones. In the United States, funerals tend to be the most common way to honor loved ones, typically with a viewing of the body or in the presence of cremated ashes, a service at a funeral home or church, and the burial or scattering of ashes. However, many other mourning and memorializing traditions exist based on diverse ethnic, spiritual, and religious beliefs and practices (see Box 5.1 for examples). In addition, in the past few decades, many more unique ways to memorialize the dead have become popular.

Figure 5.5 Body plastination
Source: Photo Inspiration/Shutterstock

In lieu of the traditional memorial service, some people have opted to hold more personal, intimate gatherings or do things that are more meaningful for those who want to honor the person who has died. These include activities like holding parties that celebrate the life of the loved one; creating photo displays or quilts of the loved one; creating memorial trees with notes to the loved one; collecting memorial stones with notes of condolence written on them; making memorial jewelry; creating online memorial social media sites; holding movie or dinner nights with family and friends to honor the loved one; planting trees or giving to charities in the name of the loved one; keeping altars in the home to honor the loved one; and getting tattoos with the image or a memory of the love one. "Fun funerals" are increasingly popular, where people engage in fun activities during the viewing, burial, or scattering of ashes like signing or painting the coffin or engaging in sports, swimming, or barbequing instead of a formal, sit-down service.

Recently, funeral homes have been offering unique options in lieu of the typical funeral service. For example, families can choose to have their loved one embalmed and posed in scenes that reflect the loved one's favorite activity. A body might be dressed in the person's favorite outfit and staged on a chair with a controller and a TV, surrounded by chips and drinks. Or a person might be posed in a scene reflecting the loved one's favorite sport. These scenes can be surprisingly lifelike and provide an alternative to the usual viewing of a body in a casket.

Impact of COVID-19 Pandemic on Funeral Practices

Funeral homes also have been offering drive through services, where one can view the body from the car or a walk-up window. This mode of viewing the body can be useful for people with limited mobility or who do not want to participate in a religious ceremony associated with the funeral, for example. Drive through services also became useful during the COVID-19 pandemic, when social distancing became necessary and people couldn't attend services but still wanted to see the body before burial or cremation. With continual shifts in our perspectives on death, the ways we choose to memorialize and handle our dead will continue to change.

BOX 5.1 Cultural and Religious Traditions at Death

- In eastern Indonesia, bodies of the dead are laid out in special rooms in the family home, where they are symbolically fed and cared for and considered part of the family's life. Funerals are lavish and tend to involve whole villages and last for weeks (Topsfield & Rosa, 2020).
- People from different areas in the Philippines have different ways of handling their dead. In the northwest area, the Benguet blindfold their dead and sit them next to the main entrance of the house. The Caviteño near Manila bury their dead in hollowed-out tree trunks. Those in the north bury the dead under the kitchen (Nobel, 2013).
- Buddhists in Mongolia and Tibet perform sky burials in which bodies are returned to the earth by separating the body into smaller pieces and laying them on mountain tops to expose them to vultures, animals, and natural elements (Humphrey, 1999).
- The Balinese hold lavish funeral processions where bodies are cremated to release the soul to inhabit a new body (Meadows, 2020).
- In the Jewish tradition, cremation, embalming, and viewing the body typically are not allowed. From death until burial, which takes place as quickly as possible, guards watch over the body and study Jewish texts in memory of the person. The body is bathed in warm water to purify it; women may wash men and women, but men may only wash men. The body is then wrapped in a shroud, or white garment, and placed in a wood casket to return to the earth in its most natural state. After the burial, it is customary for the family to sit Shiva (to mourn) for seven days, though some have shortened this time and sit Shiva for one to three days (Klug, 2020).
- Old Irish wake and funeral customs consist of women washing, preparing, and laying the body out in a room of a house. Candles are lit and clay pipes are placed in the room, where men take a puff. Clocks are stopped at the time of death and mirrors are turned around or covered. The body is not left alone until after burial, and crying cannot begin until after the body is prepared so it does not attract evil spirits that could take the soul of the deceased. The lead keener, the person who wails or sings in grief for a deceased person, also recites poetry. Wakes last two or three nights and include a celebration with food, tobacco, and liquor. Laughter, singing, crying, and sharing of stories are common.

Figure 5.6 Shiva call candle
Source: Bryan Firestone/Shutterstock

CHAPTER REVIEW

What Is Death?
- The definition of physical death has changed over the centuries and is influenced by factors such as technology, social practices, and cultural values, which in turn affect aspects of death such as grieving, medical interventions, organ donation, and other ethical and legal issues associated with the end of life.
- The legal cases of Quinlan and Schiavo from the mid-1970s to early 2000s have helped reshape how we define death and think about end-of-life issues and spurred the birth of right-to-die movements.
- The standard for physical death recently has become more precise, leading to a uniform definition of total brain death and includes the criteria of irreversible cessation of circulatory and respiratory functions as well as the entire brain, including the brain stem. This definition also states that total brain death may not be necessary but is sufficient to declare death.
- The physical process of dying depends on factors such as medications, disease process, and the use of life-sustaining measures, for example. While the dying process varies from person to person, it is typical to observe common physical signs that death is imminent.

End-of-Life Rights and Choices
- Over the past several decades, the United States and other countries have seen the proliferation of end-of-life organizations, movements, and legislation including the Hemlock Society, Compassion and Choices, the Final Exit Network, Death with Dignity, and others that provide support and choice at the end of life including the legalization of physician aid in dying.
- Hospice care can be provided to terminally ill people who are determined to have fewer than six months to live. Hospice care incorporates palliative care, which is medical care that aims to provide relief from pain and other symptoms of serious illness. The goal of hospice and palliative care is to keep the patient as comfortable as possible.

Preparing for End of Life
- Various legal documents allow individuals to specify their wishes regarding medical treatment at end of life. The two main forms of an advance directive are the living will and durable power of attorney for healthcare.

Experiencing Grief and Loss
- Grief is the personal response to loss, mourning refers to how grief is expressed, and bereavement refers to the timeframe in which grief and mourning happen.
- Uncomplicated grief refers to grief that has been processed to the point that allows people to carry on their usual relationships and functioning at some point. Complicated grief refers to grief or bereavement that can be problematic for people to the point they may need additional support or intervention. Disenfranchised grief refers to situations when people's reactions to loss are unacknowledged by others around them or by larger society.
- Several models exist that help to explain the grief process including Kübler-Ross's stage model; the continuing bonds model; the dual-process of coping model; the tasks of mourning model; and the adaptive grieving model.

- Terror management theory helps explain how people cope with the awareness of death using Freud's concepts of defense mechanisms.

Memorializing and Taking Care of the Dead
- Myriad ways of memorializing and handling bodies after death exist including burial, cremation, fun funerals, and organ and body donation, among others. Factors such as culture, tradition, access to resources and technology, religious and spiritual beliefs, environmental constraints and considerations, and individual and familial preferences and circumstances all affect how we handle and honor the dead.

REVIEW QUESTIONS
1. Describe the process of physical death.
2. Discuss end-of-life options for terminally ill people.
3. Compare and contrast theories of grief. How can they be helpful in working with people who are grieving?
4. Discuss ways bodies can be handled after death. How have these changed over time?

KEY TERMS

autolysis	living will
active euthanasia	durable power of attorney for healthcare
passive euthanasia	bereavement
medical aid in dying	grief
assisted suicide	mourning
hospice	uncomplicated grief
palliative care	complicated grief
do not resuscitate (DNR) form	disenfranchised grief
physician orders for life-sustaining treatment (POLST) form	proximal defense
	distal defense
advance directive	

CHAPTER 6

Family and Caregiving

Chapter Outline
Defining Family
Theories of Family and Aging
    Family Development Theory
    Theory of Intergenerational Solidarity and Conflict
    Theory of Intergenerational Ambivalence
Familial Roles and Relationships
    Marriage and Long-Term Partnerships
    Defining a Good Marriage
    Divorce
    Parents and Adult Children
        Adult Children with Challenges
        Effects of Increased Longevity
    Sibling Relationships
    Blended Families
        Negotiation of Boundary Ambiguity
        Intergenerational Resource Exchange
        Filial Norms and Expectations
    Multigenerational Families and Households
        Demographics
        Benefits and Drawbacks of Multigenerational Living
    Grandparents and Grandchildren
        Role of Grandparents
        Caring for Grandchildren
    Companion Animals
Caring for Older Adults
    Adults with Dementia
    Informal Care
        Rewards and Challenges
        Support for Caregivers
    Formal Care
    Impact on Caregivers
    Person- and Family-Centered Care

Elder Abuse
    Factors That Contribute to Elder Abuse
        Caregiving Situations
        Intergenerational Ambivalence
    Families with a History of Violence
    Prevention and Intervention Strategies

Learning Objectives

After completing this chapter, you will be able to:
- Define family and describe the changing nature of the family structure.
- Summarize theories used to describe the role of family as people age.
- Describe familial roles and relationships within various family systems.
- Differentiate between informal and formal care and describe some of the challenges associated with each type of caregiving for older adults.
- Define elder abuse and list several prevention and intervention strategies.

The roles that older adults play in their families are as many and varied as older people themselves. Awareness of the variety and complexity of family relationships and the types of support that people may need as they age helps us approach each older adult as a unique individual. Awareness of the types of caregiving that older persons give and receive over the life course and the associated challenges aids our efforts to create programs and policies that will improve quality of life.

DEFINING FAMILY

During the twentieth century, family studies focused on the traditional nuclear family (married heterosexual parents with a male breadwinner and female caregiver) (Ganong & Coleman, 2018). By century's end, however, this arrangement had declined while rates of divorce and single parenthood had risen (Figure 6.1). Increased longevity has also affected family structure, as more families now contain multiple generations for longer periods. For example, children born in 2000 are more likely than people born earlier to have living grandparents when they are 30 (Bengtson, 2001).

These and other changes meant that a more holistic and inclusive definition of family—one that considers the different types of family ties, the quality of these relationships, and the roles within them—was needed. From this perspective, a **family** is a collection of relationships determined by "biology, adoption, marriage, and ... social designation and existing even in the absence of contact of affective involvement, and, in some cases, even after the death of certain members" (Blieszner & Voorpostel, 2016, p. 328).

Families and family relationships grow and change throughout the life course. They not only influence early development but also significantly influence how people experience older age (Stowe & Cooney, 2014). These connections make life meaningful,

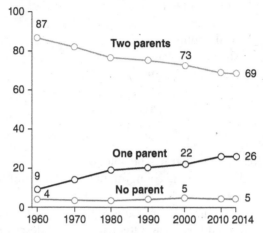

Figure 6.1 Decline in two-parent households, 1960–2014
Source: Parenting in America. "The Two-Parent Household in Decline, 1960-2014." Pew Research Center, Washington, DC (December 14, 2015) https://www.pewresearch.org/social-trends/2015/12/17/parenting-in-america/st_2015-12-17_parenting-12/

give it purpose, and provide many benefits (Thomas, Liu, & Umberson, 2017). The ways people rely on and are nourished and sustained by **kinship** ties depend on location (both geographic and social), economic realities, life history, social identity, and expectations shaped by cultural norms, family tradition, and shared narratives. **Fictive kin** is a term used to describe consensual family-type relationships, not bases on blood ties or marriage, that are mutually beneficial to family members (Nelson, 2014).

Two major components of family relationships are support and **caregiving**, which we will discuss throughout this chapter. Older adults fulfill important roles here: they may provide financial or emotional support and assume caregiving duties for their

CASE 6.1

Long-Distance Relationships

At age 89, Anne lives independently in her single-family home. She walks with a cane, and drives during daylight to church, exercise class, and the grocery store. She receives some informal help with occasional household chores (changing lightbulbs and moving furniture) and transportation after dark from friends and neighbors. Her two daughters and daughter-in-law, who live in other states, visit her periodically, take her out for meals and shopping, and help with household chores.

Anne also travels to their homes; she can navigate the airport with mobility assistance. She needs and appreciates the care and companionship provided by her family members, but she does not need regular caregiving and values her independence.

What should this woman and her children do to plan for her future care needs, and what impact does the distance between them have?

spouses, adult children, grandchildren, or other family members. Many, though, require this same help as they age. Their need for family grows because other social connections diminish (through death, distance, or estrangement) and formal resources may be prohibitively expensive, fail to meet the need or desire to remain as independent as possible, or simply not exist (National Academies of Sciences Engineering and Medicine, 2016). Family ties—however defined—will therefore become increasingly important in the support and well-being of people as they age (Bengtson, 2001).

While family members can protect and support older adults, they can also be a source of stress (Gullette, 2017). The need for care can overwhelm even the strongest families and have a significant impact on members' physical, mental, and economic well-being. In the worst cases, family members abuse, neglect, or exploit older adults. These issues have become more apparent as the population of older adults grows.

THEORIES OF FAMILY AND AGING

Theories of family and aging help in thinking about family processes and roles. They provide a cognitive map that allows us to see people in the context of their lives.

Family Development Theory

Family development theory, which arises out of life-span and life-course theories, "focuses on transitions into and out of family roles across the family life cycle," as well as the timing of and challenges associated with these changes within and across generations (Blieszner & Voorpostel, 2016, p. 329). This theory also examines the transmission of parenting styles across generations, the enduring effects of a stressful family environment during childhood, and opportunities and constraints imposed by both personal and structural factors that can influence well-being in older age (Blieszner & Voorpostel, 2016).

Theory of Intergenerational Solidarity and Conflict

The theoretical framework of **intergenerational solidarity and conflict** provides insight into positive and negative dimensions of family relationships, such as opportunities and barriers for family interaction and integration and isolation. This model has six conceptual dimensions:

- affection and closeness
- type and frequency of contact
- agreement in opinion and values
- giving and receiving support across generations
- expectations regarding obligations and family norms
- geographic proximity, which provides opportunity for cross generational interaction (Bengtson, 2001).

Thus, it looks at the different and often complex dimensions of relationships within and across generations and has practical applications in examining relationships such as those between grandparents and grandchildren (Blieszner & Voorpostel, 2016).

Theory of Intergenerational Ambivalence

The theory of **intergenerational ambivalence** was developed in recognition of the space between solidarity and conflict. Family relationships, particularly those between older parents and their adult children, are often characterized by mixed or contradictory feelings. This framework is helpful when considering changing family roles connected to family development over the life span, especially those regarding support and caregiving obligations (Blieszner & Voorpostel, 2016).

FAMILIAL ROLES AND RELATIONSHIPS

Across generations, family networks are characterized by their diversity and complexity, and the ongoing patterns of these relationships shape the experience of growing older (Bengtson, 2001). Family systems are defined by marriage and other partnerships, divorce and the ending of adult relationships, the formation of stepfamilies, single parenthood, and the associated living arrangements. Decisions that people make in their youth and middle age determine who is available to care for and support them in their later years. Single or divorced older adults without children do not have built-in family to depend on for care in later years. LGBT older adults may not have children to help with informal care.

Marriage and Long-Term Partnerships

Marriage and other long-term partnerships have a major impact on people's quality of life. These relationships define an individual's life context, affect their well-being throughout adulthood, and become more important with advancing age (Thomas, Liu, & Umberson, 2017). The aging of the US population, along with the demographic changes in family, means that more and more adults will enter the later part of their lives with romantic histories that may be complicated by transitions in and out of marriage or other forms of partnership.

The reasons for and roles within marriage have varied over time by social class, race, ethnicity, and culture, and the expectations with which older adults entered marriage have shifted due to increased diversity of the population and changing norms. Many of today's older adults were influenced by religious teachings and social norms that reserved sexual activity and procreation for marriage, although attitudes toward premarital sex became more favorable from the early 1970s forward (Harding & Jencks, 2003). Marriage had economic benefits for women who were not socialized to enter high-paying careers.

Although the gap has narrowed, since the mid-twentieth century fewer African American women than white women have married, largely due to structural reasons (e.g., higher rates of unemployment and incarceration) that limited the availability of Black men. These lower rates of marriage have had consequences for the well-being of middle-aged and older African American women who will retire with significantly less accumulated wealth (Addo & Lichter, 2013).

Many non-Western cultures prize collective (family and community) over individual well-being; in some cases, marriages are arranged to form an alliance that benefits both families (see e.g., Al-Krenawi & Jackson, 2014). The roles that men and women occupied within their marriage may range from traditional expectations (e.g., husband as breadwinner) to a more egalitarian sharing of earning money, raising children, and maintaining the home.

Defining a Good Marriage

Research on what constitutes a "good" marriage focuses on traditional marriages between a man and a woman; there is less research on other forms of partnership. In one study (Kaslow & Robison, 1996), heterosexual couples married between 25 and 46 years identified the following traits as essential to a long-term, satisfying marriage: belief that marriage is a partnership, love, sense of responsibility toward each other, enjoyment of their shared lives, religious beliefs about the sanctity of marriage, closeness from shared experiences over the life course, appreciation of closeness and comfort, and continuing sexual attraction.

More recently, a study based on nationally representative data found that the older married couples and those in cohabiting relationships (a much smaller group) reported similar relationship qualities. Positive qualities included measures of happiness, emotional satisfaction, physical pleasure in relationship, ability to be open about worries, and satisfaction with time spent together. Negative qualities included measures capturing the extent to which partners criticize and make demands on each other (Brown & Kawamura, 2010).

Happy marriages are associated with better mental health, in part because marriage makes economic, social, and health-promoting resources available to people over the life course and takes on more importance as people age (Thomas, Liu, & Umberson, 2017). A study based on a nationally representative sample from the National Social Life Health and Aging Project reveals that those in high-quality marriages had fewer depressive symptoms than those in all other categories (widowed, never married, divorced/separated, and low-quality marriages). However, perceived family support, family strain, and friend strain were all significantly associated with depressive symptoms (Stokes & Moorman, 2018). Perceived family support outside marriage was associated with fewer depressive symptoms only for the never married, highlighting that the role of other family members takes on added significance for older adults if they are widowed, divorced, or never married. Figure 6.2 illustrates marital history of adults aged 60 and older.

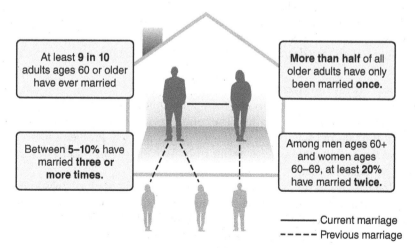

Figure 6.2 The marital history of older adults (ages 60+)
Source: US Census Bureau, 2016 American Community Survey, 1-year estimates

Divorce

For a variety of reasons, marriages often end in divorce. The increase in divorce over the past 50 years has had a profound influence on family structure, composition, and history; the consequences play out over the life course and affect quality of life and well-being for people as they age (van der Pas, van Tilburg, & Silverstein, 2013). Divorce and other relationship changes over the life course influence life outcomes; they may also lead to changes in household composition, confusion about relationships and family boundaries, and the introduction of stepparents and step siblings (Ganong & Coleman, 2018). Divorce and separation are disruptive but viewing them from a **strengths perspective**—which highlights people's "capabilities, assets, and positive attributes rather than problems and pathologies" (Langer, 2004, p. 614)—demonstrates that many people develop new relationships that are more fulfilling and nurturing than their previous ones.

Today's older adults were young at a time when divorce was less common and expectations about family roles were more narrowly defined. The overall divorce rate has decreased since 2000, in part because younger adults have delayed getting married. The rate of divorce doubled for adults aged 50 and older between 1990 and 2010, with the greatest number of divorces occurring for those between the ages of 50 and 64. Those who divorce are more likely to have less income, be less educated, to be nonwhite, and to have more than one previous marriage (Brown & Lin, 2012). The divorce rate for those over 50 has remained relatively steady since 2008 (Stepler, 2015).

Divorce can have both advantages and disadvantages. Longer life expectancy and greater acceptance of divorce can mean that people are less likely to remain in unfulfilling or abusive relationships and that their life satisfaction will increase postdivorce (Bourassa, 2015). Greater labor force participation by women means they are less likely to remain in an unsatisfactory relationship for economic reasons. The disadvantages are increased family conflict, divided family loyalties, and the need to draw upon adult children for support (including caregiving).

Divorce among middle aged adult children may affect their older parents. They might have fewer resources to devote to caring for their parents while tending to other needs. Grandparents may lose access to their grandchildren depending on custody disputes or relocation; conversely, they may need to assume a greater role in raising their grandchildren than they desire, as discussed later in this chapter.

Parents and Adult Children

Relationships between older adults and their adult children arise from the shared experiences of living and growing together. The connection, shaped by the past relationship, can be affectionate and supportive or stressful and conflicted. Problems between older adults and their adult children may result from how their family addressed problems and challenges in the past.

While many think that younger family members draw upon the wisdom of their elders and the different generations respect and mutually support each other, the reality of most families is much more complicated and may differ by cultural expectations. As needs arise, family members must work out how to support, relate to, and help each other. The theory of intergenerational ambivalence helps explain relationships between older adults and their adult children in terms of support and caregiving (Lowenstein, 2010):

older parents report better quality relationships with their children than their children report with them (Birditt et al., 2015). Understanding a "quality relationship" includes considering the connection's importance and its positive and negative features.

The **intergenerational stake hypothesis** states that parents of adult children are more emotionally invested in and report higher quality ties with their adult children than with their parents, even though this may vary with different children (Birditt et al., 2015). Older adults' dependency on their adult children often increases as people age. This switch in roles can be challenging for many adult children as they determine the best way to help their parents maintain independence while also providing care and support (discussed in more detail in the section "Caring for Older Adults").

Notable shifts in relationships between parents and their adult children have occurred as larger social and economic forces affect the timing of marriage, formation of families, the number of children in families, and increased longevity. For example, the number of boomerang children—adults who return to their family home because of financial pressures such as housing costs, student loan debt, and lack of well-paying jobs—has increased over the past 20 years. The number of adult children who have never left home is even higher. These adult children and their older parents must develop new ways of interacting to live together (Fry, 2017).

Adult Children with Challenges

Adult children with mental health challenges or substance use disorders may be conflicted about their relationships with their parents, especially if they depend on them for shelter and financial and emotional support. This dependency may also be a source of abuse (discussed further in the section "Elder Abuse"). On the other hand, parents may regret the situation that has led to their child's struggles yet welcome the opportunity to provide care and support. Research about **support exchanges** suggests that, while the parents worry about their children, they do not necessarily view helping them as negative. These children often remain close by or even share a residence with their older parents. One study found that "aging parents were more likely to receive emotional support and advice, and no less likely to receive practical help from children with problems than children without problems" (Huo et al., 2017, p. 456).

Figure 6.3 Father and son
Source: kupicoo/iStock

Effects of Increased Longevity
Increased longevity has led to a newly observed "wrinkle" in the demographics of aging: families may include parents over 80 years old, with children who are also older adults. Researchers at the University of Massachusetts-Boston have conducted a study of very old parents and their children who are at least 65 years old. While these relationships can be rewarding, they also are a cause for concern for the "old" child's well-being because both parent and child may have unmet health needs (Burger, 2018).

Adult children may die before their older parents. The death of an adult child can represent a loss of social support and companionship, caregiving, or access to grandchildren. Little research on how to help older adults understand and respond to the death of an adult child exists. The loss is painful and compounded by other losses that tend to occur in the latter part of life, including the deaths of spouses and friends and age-related bodily changes (Walter & McCoyd, 2015).

Sibling Relationships

We pay less attention to sibling connections in later life than to relationships between older parents and their children. Greif and Woolley (2016) have found that sibling relationships in adulthood are characterized by a combination of "affection, ambivalence, and ambiguity" (p. 5) and that "these often-gray relationships have many ambivalent and ambiguous aspects during families' life spans" (p. 73). Sibling relationships vary by gender, birth order, number of siblings, age range, presence of step and half-siblings, context, culture, and time. Life events, such as the death of a sibling or parent, may bring survivors closer together. The need to provide care to aging parents often requires estranged siblings to communicate with one another, while their parents' deaths may remove a reason for siblings to remain connected (Greif & Woolley, 2016).

Family ties often continue to keep people bound in some way as they age. Even in middle age and later adulthood, memories of childhood experiences may affect how people relate to their siblings. Some parents, unintentionally or not, may have favored one child over another or feel that one needs protection from the other. Sibling rivalry may continue into adulthood. Parents may interfere in the siblings' relationships (Greif & Woolley, 2016).

Moving away from the perspective of the traditional nuclear family, siblings may also include half-siblings (siblings who share one biological parent) and stepsiblings (a relationship formed when a parent remarries or starts a household with a partner who has children from previous relationships). Questions related to families and caregiving, such as who bears responsibility for the care of different family members (e.g., aging parents, family members with disabilities, and dependent children), cannot be answered without considering the sweeping changes to family composition and relationships that have occurred since the mid-twentieth century.

Blended Families

The complex romantic histories of many older adults mean that it is now common for couples to separate or divorce, for children to grow up experiencing these breakups, and for adults to form new families. People may decide to have children without a partner, such as through adoption, egg or sperm donors, or surrogacy. In fact, nontraditional families are now more common than those with a traditional nuclear family structure and are widely accepted even if deficit-based comparisons to nuclear families persist among family researchers (Ganong & Coleman, 2018).

A **stepfamily**, also called **blended family**, is one of these so-called nontraditional types. The definition of the term has evolved over time to describe a family in which "at least one of them has a child (or children) from a previous relationship" (Ganong & Coleman, 2018, p. 8). When divorce was less common, most of these families were formed when a widowed parent remarried and the new partner assumed parental duties. Today, blended families are those where one or both parents, who may be in a same sex or heterosexual relationship, have children from a previous relationship and may have children together as well (Mayntz, 2019).

Challenges within stepfamilies include ambiguous role definitions and divided loyalties. The responsibilities of stepparents may require negotiation over time (Ganong & Coleman, 2018). Consider the difference in roles between being a stepfather to a bereaved child (e.g., he's the "new" father) and being one to a child whose father remains involved. Think also about how the connections between stepfamily members change over time and what sense of obligation these family members feel toward each other. Understanding these relationships requires factoring in "relationship duration, gender, repartnership status, emotional closeness, and health of parents," among other things (van der Pas, van Tilburg, & Silverstein, 2013, p. 1068).

Older adults with stepfamilies often count these relatives as part of their support networks. Three common themes lend understanding to what happens in stepfamilies during the latter part of life, particularly as they determine expectations and responsibilities for care and support (van der Pas et al., 2013). These themes are negotiation of boundary ambiguity, intergenerational resource exchange, and filial norms and expectations.

Negotiation of Boundary Ambiguity
Negotiation of boundary ambiguity refers to how people clarify uncertainties of role expectations (van der Pas et al., 2013). Adult children must determine how to relate to their parents' new partners and vice versa. Consider a divorced father who remarries at age 60, when his children are adults. The way in which his wife and children develop and maintain a relationship (and whether she has children and her relationship to them) will influence the type of caregiving support the stepchildren give her if she outlives their father. Determining these responsibilities will depend upon how the children and their stepmother can discuss feelings associated with what might be difficult or distressing memories of their parent's divorce. Competing demands from the children's mother may also limit their availability to their stepmother.

Intergenerational Resource Exchange
Intergenerational resource exchange focuses on how family members exchange resources such as time, money, and emotional support and nurturance over time (van der Pas et al., 2013). Conflict between generations may be more pronounced and strained in stepfamilies because they are often formed after members have lived through difficult circumstances such as discord and separation. These circumstances can create a legacy that affects the resources available to the older adult. A stepparent with a long and close relationship with a stepchild likely has more "capital" to draw on than one who has a more distant or difficult relationship.

Filial Norms and Expectations

The third theme, **filial norms and expectations**, refers to expectations of culture and society in terms of families' responsibilities toward their members (van der Pas et al., 2013). The roles and norms within families, including expectations for providing care and companionship, depend on how family members define boundaries. Today, tolerance toward diverse family forms means that boundaries are less defined by traditional nuclear family roles. Instead, the needs and preferences of family members determine boundaries, which depend on the duration of relationships and whether stepparents have a history of living with their stepchildren (Suanet, van der Pas, & van Tilburg, 2013).

Multigenerational Families and Households

Relationships across multiple generations are important due to increased longevity and because families have fewer children in each generation. People now have more living "vertical" kin; that is, there are more three-, four-, and even five-generation families (Seltzer, 2019). Longer, healthier lives mean that grandparents and even great-grandparents are participating in a range of family activities, including providing childcare and support to younger generations.

Demographics

The number of Americans in multigenerational living rose from 12 percent in 1970 to 20 percent in 2016. The Great Recession of 2007–2009 sparked an increase that has slowed but not diminished. One in five Americans now lives in a multigenerational household, where two or more adult generations or grandparents and grandchildren under 25 years of age live together (Cohn & Passel, 2018). The increase in shared households stems from a more diverse US population, with multigenerational families being a tradition of some ethnic and cultural groups. Higher costs of housing and need for caregiving also contribute to this increase.

Benefits and Drawbacks of Multigenerational Living

Even if they do not share a household, members of multigenerational families have relationships that are diverse in structure and function; these structures can enhance and, in some cases, replace the functions of the traditional nuclear family. Therefore,

Figure 6.4 A multigenerational family
Source: monkeybusinessimages/Shutterstock

different generations may be available for help and support (Seltzer, 2019). These family members are an important part of a support network, especially during a family crisis such as illness.

However, as with stepfamilies, these arrangements may lead to unstable family ties. As a result, the availability of family members, such as grandparents or adult children, to provide care may be limited. Weak and unstable family ties are compounded by the scarcity of economic resources available to support families of all types (Seltzer, 2019).

While there are challenges, benefits of household sharing for all family members include help with child and elder care, lower expenses, and stronger intergenerational family ties (Cohn & Passel, 2018). For people 70 and over, sharing a household with younger generations may have economic advantages and reduce social isolation. A lens of diversity helps us appreciate the ways that intergenerational family members support each other and the impact of that support. For example, a study of older Chinese immigrants who joined their adult children and their families in the United States found that those with greater family support and less family conflict were less depressed. These results suggest that acculturation (e.g., learning English) was less important to these older immigrants than strong and supportive family ties (Sun et al., 2018).

Multigenerational living also requires negotiating boundaries and setting household rules around sharing finances and managing expectations around time spent together and apart, such as meals. Families that live in smaller homes may especially have difficulty with expectations about privacy and even determining a schedule for the bathroom.

Families with the means to create separate living quarters for their older family members allow the different generations to maintain independence and privacy while still being near enough to regularly share meals and assist each other. Developers have created homes that are specifically designed for multigenerational living, which often include separate living quarters with small kitchens to be used by older family members (Snelling, 2016).

Grandparents and Grandchildren

Grandparents' influence on their grandchildren's lives and what it means to be a grandparent partly depend on the age cohort of the grandparent, cultural expectations, and economic and social realities.

CASE 6.2

Multigenerational Living

The situation of Amy, a Philadelphia pastor who lives with her husband, two school-age children, and mother-in-law Judy in their five-bedroom home, illustrates the benefits of multigenerational households. Judy cooks one night a week, watches the children after school and on occasional evenings so Amy and her husband can have a date night, and offers advice and support. The children know their grandmother, and she has support, companionship, and built-in family caregiving for when she may need it (Lawrence, 2012).

What are some of the possible drawbacks of this arrangement?

Role of Grandparents

Most grandparents experience joy and happiness in their role, and grandparents of the twenty-first century are involved with their grandchildren in many ways. An AARP (2018) survey of 2,654 adults aged 38 through 85+ revealed that most grandparents are a source of financial and social support and play the traditional role of providing wisdom and guidance to their grandchildren. Most of the sample were also accepting of their diverse grandchildren; those in multiracial families want to have good relationships with their grandchildren's parents and other grandparents. In addition, they want their grandchildren to know about their shared cultural heritage (David & Nelson-Kakulla, 2019). Most of the older adults surveyed said that their relationships with their grandchildren were beneficial for their social, mental, and physical well-being (David & Nelson-Kakulla, 2019).

The survey also underscores the challenges grandparents face. Distance and busy schedules create barriers to seeing grandchildren, with 30 percent of the respondents saying that they do not have enough time with their grandchildren. The COVID-19 pandemic was difficult for grandparents separated from their grandchildren. However, communication with technology, such as texting and video chat, helps strengthen and maintain connections.

Family configurations may create other challenges. Children born outside of marriage and whose custodial parents, usually their mothers, have different partners over the course of their lives may not be well-connected to their grandparents. This may represent a loss of potential support for both parties.

Caring for Grandchildren

The AARP survey revealed that 1 in 10 grandparents lives with their grandchildren and that 5 percent serve as the primary caregiver (David & Nelson-Kakulla, 2019). Assuming this role is part of **kinship care**, in which relatives and family friends raise children when the parents are unavailable or unable to care for them. Approximately 2.7 million children, or one in eleven, are being raised by individuals, mostly grandparents, other than their parents. One in five African American children will spend a portion of their childhood in kinship care (Annie E. Casey Foundation, 2012).

Figure 6.5 A child with her grandparents
Source: Dean Mitchell/iStock

Grandparents may assume the caregiver role because of parental drug addiction, mental illness, teenage pregnancy, incarceration or when Child Protective Services has removed a child from their parents due to abuse or neglect. Although living with grandparents can increase children's well-being by providing a stable, permanent home, it can also result in financial, health, and social stress for grandparents who assume the caregiving role. Some grandparents may have difficulty adjusting to the role or dealing with special needs children.

The stage of life for both the grandparent and the grandchild influences how the former incorporates the role of primary caregiver into his or her life (Conway, Jones, & Speakes-Lewis, 2011). Younger grandparents who are still in the workforce may be parenting their own children or caring for aging parents while simultaneously having to think about their grandchildren's education and childcare. Older grandparents must adjust their retirement plans. One common concern about the ability of grandparents to take on this role concerns the relationship between the stress caused by caregiving and the age of the grandparent relative to the grandchildren.

Ageism can create assumptions that younger grandparents are better caregivers than older grandparents. Yet a study of African American grandmothers found that the older grandmothers experienced less emotional and caregiving strain than the younger ones, though the level of the children's behavioral problems increased the strain of caregiving for all grandparents. This study suggested that grandmothers in later phases of the life cycle are more likely to be oriented to maintaining close relationships, which are important to both their interpersonal and cognitive well-being. Thus, they may be more likely to employ emotional regulation that enables them to preserve rather than strain relationships (Conway et al., 2011).

For the past 30 years, a growing area of attention and concern within the child welfare and aging fields is the needs of grandparents who serve as their grandchildren's primary caregivers. Recognition of the need for specialized help has resulted in special programs that raise awareness of the public benefits available, such as assistance with income support, food, medical care, housing, and childcare (Annie E. Casey Foundation, 2012).

Kinship navigator programs have been developed to assist grandparent and other kin caregivers involved in the formal child welfare system in accessing these services and supports (Pandey et al., 2019). One study showed that a program using **peer navigators** (experienced grandparent caregivers trained to support others) plus interdisciplinary teams of professionals to assist with complex issues were effective in increasing family protective factors, including family functioning, social support, concrete support, knowledge of child development and parenting, and better nurturance and attachment (Pandey et al., 2019).

Companion Animals

Pets, or companion animals, are another important type of family support for many older adults. Over 57 percent of households own a pet, and 38.4 percent have dogs. The vast majority (>80 percent) of pet owners consider their pets as family (American Veterinary Medical Association, 2018). Animal companionship can improve quality of life in community-dwelling older adults and for those who live in assisted living via interventions such as visits from specially trained dogs (Hughes et al., 2020). Dog ownership increases physical activity and helps reduce social isolation, which improves psychological health (Ikeuchi et al., 2021).

There can be drawbacks to pet ownership. Some people may have unhealthy relationships with their pets that permit them to avoid needed human interaction. In rarer instances, people may engage in animal hoarding, which creates unhealthy living conditions and may present a danger to the community (Fine, 2019). When older pet owners need caregiving, their caregivers need to provide for the care of the pet. The pet may provide motivation for the care recipient to get or stay well; on the other hand, concern about the pet may cause the older adult to avoid needed hospitalization or other care (Bibbo, 2019).

CARING FOR OLDER ADULTS

Most of the care provided to older adults is **informal care** by family members, including spouses (who may have their own challenges related to health, cognition, or mobility), adult children, grandchildren, other relatives, and friends. **Formal care** is provided full or part time in the older adult's home by paid care providers such as home health aides, in adult day centers, or in long-term care facilities such as assisted-living residences and nursing homes.

Caregiving includes assistance with **activities of daily living (ADL)**, such as getting in and out of bed, using the toilet, dressing, grooming, and eating. Caregiving also includes assistance with **instrumental activities of daily living**, which are activities needed to live independently in the community, such as shopping, cooking, and paying bills. The increased longevity of older adults means that more people fall into the category of "oldest old," which is the population that will most likely need help due to physical health, limited mobility, and cognitive impairment.

Reasons for care include deterioration due to long-term health problems such as congestive heart failure or diabetes, or the aftereffects of a stroke or a fall that results in a broken hip. People with lifelong cognitive or developmental disabilities are also living longer and need care as they age (Kirkendall, Waldrop, & Moone, 2012). Finally, many family members provide care at the very end of life. Each caregiving experience is unique and shaped by the past relationships and present realities of both the people giving and receiving care. Organizations such as those listed in Table 6.1 offer advocacy, information, referral, and support for caregivers.

Adults with Dementia

The population of people with Alzheimer's disease—a type of dementia that robs individuals of their short-term memory and impairs their abilities to perform activities of daily living—was 5.8 million in 2019 and is expected to increase to 14 million in 2050. The onset of Alzheimer's requires families to plan for how to care for a person who will at some point be unable to care for themselves (Alzheimer's Association, 2019). Currently, 16 million people provide unpaid care to those with this disease and other dementias.

Informal Care

The responsibility for paying for and providing care to older adults most often falls to their spouses, adult children, or other relatives. Family caregivers in the United States provide long-term services and support to at least 17.7 million individuals, and the economic value of their unpaid care was estimated to be $470 billion in 2013 (Reinhard et al., 2015).

Table 6.1 Resources Related to Caring for Older Adults

Organization	Website	Description
Alzheimer's Association	https://www.alz.org/	Information on disease process, caregiving, and long-term care planning for individuals with Alzheimer's disease
Caring Across Generations	https://caringacross.org/	Advocacy and education to raise awareness of the need for better support and policy on caregiving issues
National Center on Elder Abuse	https://ncea.acl.gov/	Information on research, practice, policy, and education and training with respect to elder abuse
National Institute of Aging Caregiver Resources	https://www.nia.nih.gov/health/caregiving	Articles and tips on long-term care, long-distance caregiving, advanced care planning, and Alzheimer's disease
Next Avenue	https://www.nextavenue.org/channel/caregiving/	Articles and advice on caregiving including policy
The Conversation Project	https://theconversationproject.org/	Guidance to families in making decisions about caregiving

People become informal caregivers for many reasons. Spouses provide care out of love, attachment, and a profound sense of obligation connected to their vows of "for better or for worse" and "in sickness and in health." Adult children and other family members may also have a sense of duty, or they have promised to never put their loved one in a nursing home. They also want their loved ones to be happy and comfortable in familiar surroundings and may question whether paid caregivers can provide quality, personalized care.

Rewards and Challenges

Unlike professionals, many caregivers have little preparation for their role. When the need for regular caregiving arises, challenges occur. Much caregiving involves assistance with shopping, meal preparation, and household tasks, in addition to providing companionship. Caregiving also makes unexpected physical, intellectual, and emotional demands. When adult children assume caregiving roles, they take on tasks of a very intimate nature (e.g., bathing, assisting with toileting, grooming, and dressing) with parents who must relinquish control, modesty, and dignity. Caregiving requires a role reversal: the child assumes responsibilities for the well-being and health of the parent (O'Donnell, 2016). Long-distance caregivers, or those who live more than an hour away from the older person, often must arrange in-home and respite care, help with finances, and address emergencies (National Institute on Aging, n.d.).

Research shows that for most family caregivers, the rewards of caregiving outweigh the stress it causes (Stepler, 2015). The circumstances and expectations of caregiving are "extremely variable" (National Academies of Science, Engineering, and Medicine, 2016, p. 4); they are shaped by society, culture, tradition, education, socioeconomic status, access to healthcare, employment history, and necessity.

Many older adults and their families fail to make adequate caregiving plans and are thus unprepared for its challenges. A survey of 1,004 adults revealed that many Americans face both lifestyle and financial demands due to caring for an elderly relative or friend (Northwestern Mutual Life Insurance Company, 2018). Caregivers make tradeoffs that include sacrificing time with their partners, children, and other family members. Many do not plan for the costs that they will incur from providing caregiving and for their own care in the future. Human services professionals who work with older adults and their families must often help them have difficult conversations about expectations, wishes, and boundaries.

Support for Caregivers

The need to support informal caregivers is often overlooked or minimized (National Academies of Sciences Engineering and Medicine, 2016). Many caregivers have their own challenges and concerns. Caregiving is often difficult and lonely work. The burden falls disproportionately on women, with adult daughters providing two-thirds of the care. They are more likely than other family members to leave their careers to care for their aging parents, and the lost earnings make their own retirement less secure (Feinberg, 2014b).

A subpopulation of caregivers—again, primarily women—do double- and triple-duty; that is, they work in long-term care as nurses or nursing assistants and have children and/or older adult family members who require care. A study of these caregivers found that spousal support influences how they can cope with their multiple caregiving duties (DePasquale et al., 2018).

Family caregivers often must assist with more advanced medical care. An AARP study revealed that the role has dramatically expanded "to include performing complex medical/nursing tasks of the kind once provided only in hospitals" (Reinhard, Levine, & Samis, 2012, p 1). Many of those surveyed reported that they received little support from healthcare professionals in managing medications (including those intravenously administered) and performing complex wound care.

Formal Care

Some older adults do not have family members or friends who can provide care, or they have conditions that make formal care the only realistic option. People can receive formal care in their homes part or full time; this care is provided by visiting nurses, other healthcare professionals such as occupational therapists, and home health aides. Some older adults live with relatives but attend adult day centers, which provide activities, meals, and medication monitoring and other nursing care and allow primary caregivers to work at paid jobs or to take a break. Some adults move to assisted living facilities (discussed in Chapter 8), where they can receive some formal care (e.g., assistance with ADL, meals, and transportation). The most "formal" of formal care is a nursing home that provides around the clock assistance.

Whatever the type, formal care is expensive (Table 6.2). The government programs that assist with paying for in-home and nursing home care have different restrictions such as income tests and many families do not qualify. The United States lags behind other developed nations in covering the cost of long-term care. Washington State is one of the first states to provide a state-funded long-term care insurance program (Bunis, 2019). The Family and Medical Leave Act (FMLA) provides 12 weeks of unpaid leave to employees of government agencies and those in eligible corporations (those with 50 or more employees). However, many cannot afford to lose income. New York City provides city employees six weeks of fully paid leave only for the birth or adoption of a child, not for taking care of sick family members (O'Donnell, 2016).

Table 6.2 Estimated US Monthly Costs for Long-Term Care, 2021

Type of Care	Cost: National Median
Home Health Aide (40 hours)	$4,680
Home Health Aide (168 hours – 24/7)	$19,656
Adult Day Care	$1,690
Assisted Living	$4,500
Nursing Home – Semiprivate Room	$7,800
Nursing Home – Private Room	$8,910

Source: Genworth., 2021.

An additional concern regarding formal care is that the number of potential home care workers is small relative to those who will need care. Much of the formal care labor force is comprised of younger workers and immigrants, and many American communities do not have enough people available to take on caregiving jobs, which are low-paying, difficult, and often isolating (Poo, 2015; Spetz et al., 2019; Stein, 2019).

LGBT people may face discrimination by formal caregivers and may delay or avoid formal care due to their fear of judgment or abuse. In describing future long-term care needs, LGBT adults aged 55 and older described their desire to find LGBT-inclusive residential care. Their fears of dependence, dementia, mistreatment, and social isolation were compounded by their fear of having to conceal their identities in order to receive care (Putney et al., 2018).

Impact on Caregivers

Many researchers have studied the difficulties of caring for persons with dementia, with other serious medical challenges, or at the end of life. Research now includes the development and evaluation of interventions designed to improve care by training and supporting caregivers (see, e.g., Griffin, et al., 2015). Boltz (2015) describes a family-centered, function-focused care intervention that provides training and support for family caregivers of persons with dementia who are hospitalized to promote recovery of abilities to perform activities of daily living and walking abilities after discharge from the hospital. Another example is the memory support program for families dealing with a recent diagnosis of dementia that offers education, behavioral management, future planning, linkages to resources, and caregiver support. It pays attention to the need to build trust with African American older adults who have experienced systemic racism in the healthcare system (Clark et al., 2018).

Two related concepts capture the impact of caregiving: caregiver burden and caregiver stress (Hoffmann & Mitchell, 1998; Llanque et al., 2016). **Caregiver burden** is defined as the intolerable strain produced by caregiving; family researchers and gerontologists have been exploring this phenomenon since the 1960s (Hoffmann & Mitchell, 1998). **Caregiver stress** is defined as "the unequal exchange of assistance among people who stand in close relationship to one another, which results in emotional and physical stress on the caregiver" (Llanque et al 2016).

Whether caregiving is a burden relates to the nature of the situation and the availability of resources rather than the recipient's condition. Lack of support affects well-being, as does the caregiver's perception of how the caregiving influences his or her emotional well-being, ability to socialize with friends and participate in other activities, and relationships with other family members. Two caregivers who are dealing with similar situations, such as a father with Alzheimer's disease, have different experiences of caregiving and experience burden differently; for example, research shows that adult daughters who are caregivers for their older parents often experience more stress than adult sons (Hoffman & Mitchell, 1998). Care recipients may fear being a burden, which may lead them to ignore or minimize their needs, even as their abilities to perform household chores or easily move around diminish.

Studies of **dyads** (pairs) of older adults and their caregivers illuminate the impact of caregiver burden. One study of almost 200 dyads found that caregivers' reports of feeling burdened by their obligations and the care recipients' concerns about being a burden independently predicted unmet needs for care. These results suggest that "older adults who are transitioning to needing help ... would benefit from explicit discussions with family regarding concerns about being a burden. Open discussions with caregivers, who may also have concerns about their own abilities to provide adequate help, may help families navigate complex decisions about obtaining needed supports. Ideally, such care recipient–caregiver discussions about help needed should be routinely incorporated into healthcare provider visits" (Nieuwenhuis, Beach, & Schulz, 2018, p. 1).

The quality of care that an older adult receives at the end of life may depend on the nature of the relationships they have with their caregivers over the life course. A study of mothers in hospice care and the adult daughters caring for them explored areas of agreement and disagreement between how each described the relationship and the caregiving experience. While most pairs reported close friendships that were characterized by compassionate care and the idea that they were cherishing their limited time together, a small percentage reported that very strained and difficult relationships over the life course affected the quality of care (Solomon, Hansen, & Baggs, 2018).

Person- and Family-Centered Care

Caregiving should involve the caregivers' and families' wishes. The concept of **person- and family-centered care (PFCC)** is an "orientation to the delivery of healthcare and supportive services that considers an older adult's needs, goals, preferences, cultural traditions, family situation and values" when making decisions about care (Feinberg, 2014a, p. 97). It keeps older adults and their families in the center of care and helps ensure that services are delivered from the recipient's perspective. It also considers needs beyond medical and physical health concerns by considering, for example, individual preferences regarding food, daily routines, and activities (Feinberg, 2014a). The principles of PFCC are not always easy to carry out in practice, particularly in providing care for older adults with dementia. Assessments that assist older adults and their families in finding optimal caregiving strategies that fit the realities of their lives are helpful (Molony et al., 2018).

ELDER ABUSE

In some cases, the burden of caregiving results in mistreatment. **Elder abuse** affects an estimated 1 in 10 older adults (Acierno et al., 2010). The growing population of older adults means that this number will increase dramatically (Pillemer et al., 2016). Understanding the circumstances that may lead to elder abuse—as well as concern about the availability of caregivers and their abilities—helps us think about how to promote well-being in all older adults. This section expands on information presented earlier in the chapter to address the complicated issue of elder abuse.

No single accepted definition of elder abuse exists. The World Health Organization (WHO) defines it as "a single, or repeated act, or lack of appropriate action, occurring within any relationship where there is an expectation of trust, which causes harm or distress to an older person" (World Health Organization, 2017a, para. 1). The concept of "trust relationship" focuses on expectations and norms around obligations, respect, and affections due to marriage or filial or family ties. It can extend to formal relationships with paid caregivers, attorneys, financial planners, and other professionals (Bonnie & Wallace, 2003). **Polyvictimization** (being subjected to more than one type of abuse or neglect) is also common (Ramsey-Klawsnik & Miller, 2017). Self-neglect is not included in all definitions of elder abuse; however, it is a serious problem that may be rooted in complex family dynamics and traumatic life-course events. Table 6.3 defines forms of elder abuse.

Elder abuse also includes criminal acts such as serious violence, fraud, medical neglect, and even murder, which are appropriately addressed by the criminal justice system. However, far more common are situations where "family members can neglect their partners' or parents' needs, belittle or exclude them socially, threaten institutionalization, or demand money" (Gullette, 2017, p. 22). These actions are not criminalized, but they all can be considered abusive. Elder abuse has many short- and long-term consequences, including poor emotional and physical health (Acierno et al., 2017), nursing home placement, and death.

Factors That Contribute to Elder Abuse

The **ecological model** focuses on interacting individual, family, community, and societal factors that affect human behavior. This model is useful in understanding how older adults may be vulnerable to abuse and what factors contribute to it (Bonnie & Wallace, 2003; Schiamberg & Gans, 2000). Table 6.4 lists risk factors at different ecological levels, highlighting the situations that are conducive to elder abuse (Johannesen & LoGiudice, 2013; Pillemer et al., 2016).

Caregiving Situations

Some caregiving situations can put older adults at higher risk of abuse, particularly if the caregiver also has health problems or a complicated past relationship with the

Table 6.3 Types of Elder Abuse

Type of Abuse	Definition
Physical	Intentional use of physical force that results in illness, injury, pain, or functional impairment
Emotional	Infliction of mental pain, anguish, or distress
Sexual	Nonconsensual sexual contact of any kind
Financial	Misappropriation of money or property
Neglect	Failure to provide food, shelter, protection, or necessary healthcare
Self-Neglect	Failure to perform self-care tasks to a degree that endangers own health or safety

Source: National Center on Elder Abuse, n.d.

Table 6.4 Risk Factors for Elder Abuse

Ecological Level	Risk Factors
Individual victim	Cognitive impairment Functional impairment Poor physical or mental health Behavioral problems Prior trauma or interpersonal violence Absence of a protective spouse
Perpetrator	Caregiver burden/stress Poor mental health Substance misuse
Older adult victim/perpetrator relationship	Older adult dependency upon perpetrator for daily care Perpetrator dependency upon older adult for economic resources
Family system	Family disharmony Conflicted relationships
Home environment	Victim-perpetrator shared living arrangement Low household income
Social environment	Low social support Social isolation

recipient (Twomey, 2018). Advocates have warned against focusing solely on caregiver stress as a cause of elder abuse because it does not adequately account for abuser characteristics, such as mental illness or substance use (Brandl & Raymond, 2012). One group that is particularly vulnerable is older persons with dementia, particularly those who display aggressive behavior or who are difficult to manage. A study of 129 family caregivers for older persons with dementia found that over two-thirds had engaged in psychological abuse and one-fifth in physical abuse. Almost one-third had neglected the older person (Wiglesworth et al., 2010). Similar studies have revealed high levels of abuse resulting from caregiver stress; one study had caregivers keep online diaries that revealed they were most abusive when their care recipients displayed aggressive behaviors (Pickering, Yefimova, & Maxwell, 2018).

Intergenerational Ambivalence

The previously discussed theory of intergenerational ambivalence fits with many of the situations involving elder abuse. Smith (2015) studied low-income older women (some recruited from community services and some from elder abuse services) who live with their self-described "difficult" adult children, many of whom were sons who were unemployed and had problems with mental illness and substance abuse. This study revealed themes of boundary violations, mothers' feelings of shame and blame for their children's behavior, and difficulty in making the adult child leave.

Families with a History of Violence

The diversity and complexity of intergenerational families is more intricate in families in which violence exists (Band-Winterstein, 2015). Some older adults have families with a history of domestic and family violence; the older adult may have been the victim and/or the perpetrator. Some older women were physically abused by their husbands throughout their marriages but remained in the relationships for a variety of economic and social reasons, including a desire to keep the family together and a lack of resources. Their children may have witnessed the violence or were themselves victims of abuse by one or both parents. Many older women did not have ready access to community resources such as domestic violence shelters when they were younger; even today, programs that serve victims of domestic violence are not always responsive to older people's needs (Crockett, Brandl, & Dabby, 2015).

A qualitative study of older women and their abusive adult children provides insight into how long-term patterns of abuse in families create situations of elder abuse (Band-Winterstein, 2015). Both the older women and their children felt that they were victims of the circumstances that had led to the elder abuse. In some cases, the latter used their childhood experiences of abuse to explain their behavior. The study's author concluded that "from the point of view of all the participants, victimhood was found to be a central motif, which characterized the formation of reciprocal relationships in these families. By placing themselves in the victim role, the adult children created a retrospective narrative accounting for their lack of interest or abusive behavior toward their parents. The victim role was a relief for the adult children, as it released them from the obligation of caring and the normative expectation to be sensitive to their parents' needs" (p. 130).

Prevention and Intervention Strategies
Professionals, advocates, researchers, and policymakers in the elder abuse field have taken many steps to inform the public about the issue, including ways to prevent it. Prevention strategies include addressing ageism, using background checks and abuse registries to prevent those with a history of abuse from being hired as paid caregivers, encouraging older adults to make their caregiving wishes known with advanced care planning, and raising public awareness (National Center on Elder Abuse, 2019).

The Supports and Tools for Elder Abuse Prevention (STEAP) Initiative provides resources for individuals and communities to learn the signs of elder abuse, prevent social isolation, and serve as "friendly visitors" to isolated older adults (USC Center on Elder Mistreatment, 2017). The WHO and the International Network for the Prevention of Elder Abuse launched World Elder Abuse Awareness Day in 2006; today, many communities around the world observe it with public events and social media campaigns.

Programs funded by the Older Americans Act (discussed in more detail in Chapter 9), provide preventive services to those aged 60+ through state, county, and regional offices for the aging. These systems use educational programs, caregiver support groups, and public service announcements to address spouse and partner abuse in cases where the victim is not functionally disabled or cognitively impaired and where the abuse has not escalated to the level of a crime (Ernst & Brownell, 2013). Other programs train professionals (e.g., healthcare practitioners, social workers, and members of the clergy) and community members (e.g., employees of senior centers and financial institutions) to recognize signs of potential abuse (Gironda et al., 2010).

In most states, professionals are legally mandated to report suspected elder mistreatment to Adult Protective Services (APS), which serves older adults and adults with disabilities who are at risk of being abused. While APS responds to and investigates all reports, including those of self-neglect, there is great variation among states in terms of eligibility criteria, definitions of elder abuse used, and relationships with other service providers, including the criminal justice system (Bobitt et al., 2018).

APS uses a service philosophy that upholds client **self-determination**, the right of people to make decisions on their own behalf, whenever possible. Some older adults who are mistreated by relatives do not want them arrested or held responsible because they depend on them for care. As mentioned earlier, not all programs serving victims of crime, domestic abuse, or family violence are equipped to work well with older victims. However, some communities have developed programs targeted to older victims, such as ones providing legal assistance and social services (Rizzo, Burnes, & Chalfy, 2015).

Multidisciplinary teams containing professionals and agencies with various areas of expertise have also been created to address elder abuse. These innovations and developments in legal, medical, and social service settings aim to improve responses to elder abuse so that the older adults' many needs can be met. Such teams vary in their purpose, format, and professional "home," but they all share the goal of improving services across many systems (Pillemer et al., 2016).

CHAPTER REVIEW

Defining Family
- The quality of family relationships significantly influences how people experience older age.
- A holistic and inclusive definition of family is necessary to account for different types of family relationships.
- Increased longevity means that family relationships are more likely to extend over many generations.

Theories of Family and Aging
- Theories to understand families and age include family development theory, intergenerational solidarity and conflict, and intergenerational ambivalence.

Familial Roles and Relationships
- Family networks are characterized by both their diversity and their complexity across generations.
- Many older adults have histories that may be complicated by transitions in and out of marriage and other forms of partnership.
- Relationships with adult children can be a source of support or stress, depending on the nature of the past relationship.
- Relationships with siblings may be a source of support and/or stress as people age.
- Stepfamilies are now more common than traditional nuclear families, which in some cases has led to confusion and ambiguity as people determine expectations about relationships as they age.
- The number of multigenerational households has increased due to greater population diversity, higher cost of housing, and the need for caregiving of both younger and older household members.
- Many grandparents are primary caregivers to their grandchildren. While this arrangement keeps families together, it can cause caregiver strain depending on the grandparent's age and economic and social realities.

Caring for Older Adults
- Most of the care that older adults receive is informal. The availability of family members and the nature of family relationships determine who can provide care and support. Women assume most informal care responsibilities.

- Formal care is provided by a variety of healthcare professionals and agencies in the older adult's home, in adult day centers, and in assisted living centers and nursing homes.
- Unmet needs for caregiving are a major challenge to older adults, families, and society.

Elder Abuse
- Elder abuse includes actions that harm or distress older persons and that occur in relationships of trust. Types of elder abuse include physical abuse, sexual abuse, emotional abuse, neglect, financial abuse, and self-neglect.
- Risk factors for elder abuse include both individual characteristics of the older person and the abuser, as well as characteristics of their relationship and living situation.
- Strategies to prevent elder abuse include educating the public and having professionals involved with older adults.
- Interventions addressing elder abuse include Adult Protective Services, services for victims of domestic violence, and other community-based services for older adults. Multidisciplinary teams of professionals can address the complex nature of many elder abuse situations.

REVIEW QUESTIONS
1. How do theories related to family processes and roles contribute to your understanding of parent-child and sibling relationships in later life?
2. What are some ways to create supportive relationships between grandparents and grandchildren?
3. How would you advise someone who needs to assume an informal caregiving role for their 90-year-old mother who can no longer live alone independently?
4. What factors are associated with elder abuse and neglect? How does your awareness of these factors inform the advice you would give the same caregiver?

KEY TERMS

family
kinship
fictive kin
caregiving
family development theory
intergenerational solidarity and conflict
intergenerational ambivalence
strengths perspective
intergenerational stake hypothesis
support exchanges
stepfamily
blended family
negotiation of boundary ambiguity
intergenerational resources exchange
filial norms and expectations
kinship care
peer navigator
informal care
formal care
activities of daily living
instrumental activities of daily living
caregiver burden
caregiver stress
dyads
person- and family-centered care
elder abuse
polyvictimization
ecological model
self-determination

CHAPTER 7

Work and Retirement

Chapter Outline
Work and Older Adults
    The Nature of Work
    US Labor Trends
    Generational Perspective
    Ageism in the Workplace
        Intergenerational Work Teams
        Abolishing Mandatory Retirement
        Antidiscrimination Laws
    Caregiving and Work
Retirement
    Sense of Purpose and Longevity
    Effects of Retirement
    Phases of Retirement
Financial Support in Retirement
Volunteerism and Community Involvement
Lifelong Learning

Learning Objectives

After completing this chapter, you will be able to:
- Describe the nature of work for older adults and the challenges they face in the workplace.
- Explain the effects and phases of retirement.
- Describe the components of financial support for retired adults and the financial challenges that many retirees face.
- Provide examples of volunteerism and community involvement by older adults and explain the benefits of this type of activity in later life.
- List some options for lifelong learning and barriers older adults face in pursuing learning opportunities.

In the United States, what we do for a living is often inextricably linked to our identity. Work is important for financial support, but perceived productivity is often viewed as a reflection of an individual's merit, status, character, responsibility, and independence. Work can also be a way to develop skills, gain social recognition, and engage with and contribute to our communities (Gheaus & Herzog, 2016). Given that many people spend so much of their time working, it makes sense that we want our work to be meaningful and satisfying. Being unable to work or unable to be productive in general not only affects a person's financial stability, but also their self-perception and sense of value to society. In this chapter we will explore work and other activities in later years, including retirement, volunteerism, continued learning, and other avenues of productivity, in light of how these activities affect health, well-being, and quality of life as we age.

WORK AND OLDER ADULTS

As discussed in Chapter 1, the global population is aging rapidly, which has an effect on careers, roles in the workplace, and workforce trends. People aged 65+ represent the fastest growing segment of US labor force participation, with the percentage aged 65+ in the workforce steadily increasing over the past several decades. From 1970 to 2000, those aged 55+ were the smallest segment of the labor force. In the 1990s, the number of older workers began to steadily increase while the number of younger workers began to decrease. By 2003, those in older age groups no longer had the smallest representation (Toossi & Torpey, 2017), and by 2019, approximately 20 percent (10.5 million people) of those aged 65+ were employed at least part time. So in 2019, almost 7 percent of the workforce consisted of older adults, compared to only 3 percent in 2000 (Pew Research Center, 2019c).

From 2014 to 2024, the growth rate of those aged 75+ in the workforce is estimated to be approximately 86 percent compared to 5 percent growth for the labor force as a whole. Part of this growth has been fueled by the baby boomer generation, whose numbers used to exceed those in other generations, so it will decrease with subsequent generations (Toossi & Torpey, 2017).

The Nature of Work

The nature of work has a long history in terms of how its meaning and purpose have evolved over time. That discussion is beyond the scope of this chapter. However, work, employment, and career development also mean different things to different people depending on intersectional factors such as age, race, gender, and socioeconomic status. For example, when agriculture was the main form of work for many people, men and women of all ages participated because this was necessary for their survival.

In the mid-ninteenth century, the concept of men being the family providers emerged and many women (primarily white women), depending on socioeconomic status, took on domestic and household tasks instead of working outside the home. This shift may have occurred in part because of the establishment of labor laws that attempted to protect workers, particularly women and children, from the harsh and dangerous conditions in factories.

In the 1970s, views on gender roles were changing. Increased technology and changing economics also played a role in more women (again, mainly white women) participating in the workforce (Hannan & Kranzberg, 2017).

Until recently, many people tended to stay in the same job or industry. It is much more common now for people to change jobs frequently, to pursue varied career paths, or even to not pursue a career (Lyons, Schweitzer, & Ng, 2015). This is because many employers no longer provide any kind of long-term employment security, people are more concerned about work-life balance, and many are responsible for their own professional development. These issues, along with socioeconomic, technological, and other factors, continue to change the labor force (Gallup, 2021).

US Labor Trends

In the United States, workers aged 55+ tend to be concentrated in management, sales, service, production, and construction sectors. Further, individuals aged 55+ are the group that makes up the largest percentage (approximately 25 percent) of self-employed workers. Self-employment, has become an increasingly popular choice for older adults. After retiring or being laid off from a full-time job, many older adults find opportunities to engage in entrepreneurship and build new businesses that they did not have the time or financial means to do earlier in life. Still others engage in **encore careers**, or careers that are developed in the pursuit of new, meaningful work in later life (Freedman, 2007).

For many reasons, often financial, retirement is not an option for some older people, nor is it necessarily desirable. Increasingly, people are redefining work, productivity, and what human development means in later years. Approximately 27 percent of those aged 55+ work part time, compared to 18 percent of workers in younger age groups. Common part-time positions for older workers include jobs in retail stores, hospitals, offices, restaurants, food concessions, libraries, theaters, and in product promotion (AARP, 2021).

Part-time work can be a good alternative for those who want or need to supplement their income or who want to stay involved in the workforce as a way to remain physically, mentally, and socially active. However, part-time employment usually does not offer health insurance or other benefits, so for older adults who need more financial support or benefits, a part-time job may not be sufficient. Still, many older adults take

Figure 7.1 Bridge jobs provide useful and meaningful work for some older adults
Source: LightField Studios/Shutterstock

CASE 7.1

Claudia's Encore Career

Claudia had a 25-year career as an executive in a large corporation. She enjoyed the challenges of the work, but she was growing tired of the long hours at the office, which made it difficult for her to pursue other interests, including travel. When Claudia was younger, she had wanted to explore a career in non-profit work, but she chose the corporate world for various reasons. When Claudia decided to retire from her corporate job, she found a full-time position in a nonprofit organization that allows her to travel as part of the job and to utilize her talents in program development. This organization also will offer opportunities for Claudia to transition to part-time work if and when she decides she wants to reduce her hours but remain working.

What advantages does this new job offer Claudia over full retirement? What employment-related patterns does this career shift reflect given the discussion on work in later life?

---

a **bridge job** (paid work that spans the time between full-time employment and retirement); some people in bridge jobs are also collecting Social Security or pension benefits from a former employer.

Generational Perspective

Older workers' views on and experiences with work will depend on their generation, combined with intersectional factors. For example, a Black woman who graduated from high school and began working a minimum wage job in the 1970s likely faced racism, sexism, pay disparities, and a lack of benefits and job opportunities. This woman will have very different options for retirement and financial and other types of supports in later life than a white man in the same situation. While racism and sexism would still be factors for those who entered the workforce in the 2000s, differences in the workforce, labor and employment policy, and economic and sociopolitical landscape, among other factors, would affect the financial situation of these people in later life.

Ageism in the Workplace

Ageism in the workplace, particularly bias against older workers, is a persistent and harmful problem that affects all industries and labor sectors. Research suggests that outdated, negative attitudes about older workers are pervasive, as is the discrimination that often results from negative stereotypes about older adults. Employers as well as younger coworkers often think that older workers are less healthy, educated, skillful, and productive than younger workers (World Health Organization, 2021).

In reality, older workers often bring skill, knowledge, experience, connections, consistency, and a strong work ethic to their jobs; they also tend to stay in positions longer and take fewer days off than younger workers. Many older workers pick up new skills easily, bring a diverse perspective to multigenerational teams, play a critical role in training other employees, and attract new business and customers with their experience, knowledge, and personalized attention, among other benefits (Columbia Public Health, 2021). It is important to note that age does not predict ability in the workplace, nor can age predict one's interests or level of performance. Factors such as cognitive and physical abilities, which affect a person's ability to perform particular jobs, are highly individualistic and are influenced by a variety of factors such as genetics, health and fitness status, and other characteristics (Lipnic, 2018).

Age discrimination becomes even more of a problem when intersectional factors are taken into consideration. The diversity of older workers has continued to increase over the decades. For example, the racial diversity of older workers has increased over time, with Latinx, Asian, and Black workers making the most gains. Thus, older workers of color often face double discrimination based on age and race, and older women of color often face the triple threat of age, race, and gender discrimination (Lipnic, 2018).

Ageism is costly for workers, their families, employers, and the economy as a whole. Discriminatory practices based on age can be expensive for companies that continually need to recruit and train employees, and they affect the financial stability of workers and their families, who may need to rely on other sources of income or public aid to support themselves (Gurchiek, 2018).

Intergenerational Work Teams

Research suggests that exposing workers, particularly younger workers, to older workers helps to reduce ageist stereotypes. This also holds true to help dispel ageist stereotypes about younger workers. For example, work completed by intergenerational teams allows workers to experience and benefit from the diversity and range of skills, knowledge, and competence of the entire group.

Abolishing Mandatory Retirement

Since age is not a reliable predictor of an individual's skills and abilities, abolishing mandatory retirement ages is another way to combat ageism in the workplace. However, many countries, including those with large percentages of older workers, still have mandatory retirement ages for many government and business segments. Research suggests that mandatory retirement ages do not increase job opportunities for younger workers, which is the main reason they were implemented. (In some industries, they were implemented for safety reasons). Instead, these mandates tend to reduce older workers' ability to remain financially stable and contribute to the economy and the vitality of organizations (Work Health Organization, 2021).

Antidiscrimination Laws
Antidiscrimination laws can also combat ageism in the workplace. Over the years, many countries have enacted laws that prohibit age discrimination in the workplace, but the enforcement of these laws varies widely. Further, even when such laws are in place, ageism in the workplace can be difficult to prove, and many countries such as China, India, and Nigeria still do not protect workers from age discrimination based on age. Table 7.1 lists examples of countries with laws in place to protect older workers.

Caregiving and Work
With the aging of the population, caregiving for a spouse or relative can be a barrier to employment and postemployment activities for older adults. Women are still primarily responsible for caregiving, both for young children and older parents, so many women who provide care have to pass up promotions, take leaves of absence, leave the workforce, or cut back on work hours, which affects their overall income, long-term earnings, and investment in Social Security and retirement programs (National Alliance for Caregiving, 2020).

Intersectional factors such as gender, race, and socioeconomic status can further complicate a person's ability to work while acting as a caregiver by adding issues that include discrimination and lack of resources or support (Feinberg et al., 2011).

Women, members of minority groups, and people from other vulnerable groups can be particularly susceptible to economic downturns and other situations that can cause problems for those in the workforce. For example, in 2020 when the COVID-19

Table 7.1 Examples of Antidiscrimination Laws to Combat Workplace Ageism

Country	Law
Australia	The Age Discrimination Act 2004 (ADA) prohibits discrimination in employment on the basis of age and covers workers of all ages. It also protects citizens from ageist behavior in other areas such as education, housing, and securing services.
European Union	The EU framework for equal treatment in employment and occupation enacted in 2000 bans discrimination on the basis of age in employment.
Japan	The Older Persons' Employment Stabilization Law of 1971 obligates companies to ensure employment until the age of 65.
Peru	Article 2.2 in the Peruvian Constitution prohibits age discrimination in the workplace.
Philippines	The Anti-Age Discrimination in Employment Act of 2016 protects the employment of people based on skills, abilities, knowledge and qualifications rather than age; prohibits arbitrary age limitations in employment; and promotes the rights of workers of all ages to be treated fairly in areas such as benefits, compensation, and opportunities.
Russia	Russia's Labour Code prohibits age discrimination in employment.
Tanzania	The Employment and Labour Relations Act of 2006 promotes equality and prohibits discrimination at the workplace based on a variety of characteristics, including age.
United States	The federal Age Discrimination in Employment Act (ADEA) of 1967 prohibits age discrimination in the workplace and promotes the employment of older workers.

Adapted from: Age Discrimination Info, 2018; Australian Human Rights Commission, 2020; Europa-Kommissionen, 2021; Lipnic, 2018; Sakuraba, 2008.

pandemic caused much of the US business sector to close, along with schools and adult and child daycare centers, women, those from low-income groups, and people of color were disproportionately affected. Mothers and caregivers were at risk of losing their jobs or work hours once daycare facilities, schools, and other support resources closed because they had to give priority to their caregiving responsibilities.

RETIREMENT

While the concept of retirement has been around for centuries, it is not a universal concept and its meaning is affected by culture. For example, a study by Sone (2008) to examine why people in Okinawa, Japan live, on average, seven years longer than people in other parts of the world found that not only do their health and social behaviors differ from those of many other people, but the idea of retirement, as we think of it in Western culture, does not exist.

Sense of Purpose and Longevity

The researchers in the Sone study wondered if people who had *ikigai*, translated as purpose in life, would live longer than those who do not. After examining various health, stress, disease, and other behaviors and characteristics of 43,000 people, the researchers found that those who had a sense of purpose were more likely to have a partner and to be educated, employed, and to outlive those who did not. An important takeaway from this study is that while many people plan for and dream of a retirement, in which they spend time traveling or pursuing other hobbies or interests, what actually increases longevity and health is a sense of purpose. While enjoying our time is important, focusing only on recreational activities in retirement does not seem to be the key to a long life. Rather, engaging in activities that connect us to others, provide structure to our days, keep our minds active and challenged, and help us feel a part of something bigger than ourselves helps us live longer (Pasricha, 2016).

Effects of Retirement

People experience various effects of retirement depending on the circumstances, timing, and other factors in their lives. For example, while many people equate early retirement with choice and financial stability, sometimes early retirement is prompted by corporate downsizing, job instability, lack of support and resources, or a lack of job satisfaction, among other factors. Illness, caregiving obligations, and other personal or family circumstances may also prompt early retirement. Even if planned, early retirement can have detrimental effects on health, finances, self-efficacy, social status, and other individual, familial, and social factors (Topa, Depolo, & Alcover, 2018).

Mandatory retirement still exists in many government and business sectors, which may be perpetuating outdated ideas and stereotypes about older workers. For example, firefighters, airline pilots, law enforcement officers, and air traffic controllers all have mandatory retirement ages between 55 and 60 years old. Even in sectors where antidiscriminatory laws apply, older workers can be pushed into retirement (Gokhale, 2004).

Many studies have examined the effects of retirement on characteristics such as physical and mental health, financial stability, and social connectedness, among others. These effects can be difficult to examine because the experience of retirement, like so many other aspects of aging, is highly variable, individualistic, and inextricably linked to many intersectional and psychosocial characteristics. However, it is not surprising that a great deal of research finds that retirement, in general, often has detrimental effects, with the exception of those who work in physically strenuous jobs (Mazzonna & Peracchi, 2015).

For some people, postponing retirement may have a positive effect on health, mental health, and other areas of life (Bertoni, Brunello, & Mazzarella, 2018; Heller-Sahlgren, 2017). For example, Robinson et al. (2020) found that for their sample of 42 Black men, work positively contributed to their perceptions of themselves as men. Work was not only a financial vehicle for them to support their families but provided a way for them to be physically and socially active and to build self-efficacy and self-esteem. Conversely, a lack of work contributed to depression, low self-esteem, feelings of anger, and even suicidality.

Phases of Retirement

Researchers who study retirement have identified phases or transitions that people tend to make as they plan for retirement and leave the workforce. Atchley and Barusch (2004) describe a model that consists of eight phases: preretirement, honeymoon, immediate retirement routine, rest and relaxation, disenchantment, reorientation, retirement routine, and termination of retirement.

The preretirement phase includes both a remote aspect, when early discussions of retirement happen and a near aspect, when retirement is approaching and a date for leaving the workforce has been set. The honeymoon phase is when people start doing everything they have wanted to do in retirement; this phase is usually temporary. Often the activities involved in the honeymoon phase, such as travel, can be expensive, so not everyone is able to engage in the honeymoon phase. Once the honeymoon phase is over, people tend to settle into a stable, immediate retirement routine.

Many people take some time for rest and relaxation, which often involves a temporary decline in activity, especially if the honeymoon phase was particularly active. As retirement progresses, people generally settle in to a regular routine, but some will become disenchanted with retirement. This can happen due to unexpected events such as the death of a partner, needing to resume caretaking duties, or other events that can disrupt or change a person's original plans. When disruptions occur, people can reorient and either adjust to retirement or terminate retirement by returning to work because of financial concerns, wanting to return to work, or other factors.

FINANCIAL SUPPORT IN RETIREMENT

The concept of government entities or employers providing financial support for people after a certain age or a certain amount of time in service has existed for a long time in various parts of the world. Typically, this financial support has been tied to a person's years of service or employment. A labor market perspective suggests that pensions and other types of retirement support not only provide a financial safety net when participation in the workforce ceases, but that they provide incentives that promote productivity, reward longevity in the workforce, and penalize (in many pension situations) remaining in the workforce too long (Dorsey, Cornwell, & Macpherson, 1998). Table 7.1 lists examples of pension and other retirement plans developed in various eras.

As Table 7.2 indicates, in the United States, pensions, Social Security benefits, and retirement savings plans have been a key financial support for retired workers for a long time. Those workers who are fortunate enough to have reliable employment that pays well and who are able to save, rely on what is known as the "three-legged stool" for their financial support in retirement—savings, pensions, and Social Security income (Cutler, 1996). Further, Social Security and some employer-sponsored programs provide financial support for workers and their family members, at any age, in cases of disability and death. However, these benefits are provided only to employees (or family members in certain cases) who have been participating in the workforce and have paid taxes into the federal Social Security system, among other requirements.

There are groups of people who are not covered by these benefits, such as undocumented immigrants, even when they are participating in the workforce. For others,

Table 7.2 Pension/Retirement Benefits Throughout History

Year and Location	Description
13 BC: Roman Empire	Caesar Augustus, Emperor of the Roman Empire, offered soldiers who had served 20 years a retirement sum 13 times their annual salary.
1592: England	Parliament established a pension for soldiers who had become disabled.
1684: London	A Port Authority official receives the first ever pension.
1776: United States	US Congress created pensions for those serving in the US Army.
1779: United States	Disability pensions were created for US Navy personnel.
1857: New York	Disabled police officers receive pensions.
1875: United States	American Express offers the first private-sector pension plan.
1889: Germany	Chancellor Otto Von Bismark establishes pensions.
1910: Europe	Municipal workers in France, Spain, Sweden, Belgium, Germany, the Netherlands, and the United Kingdom were covered by retirement plans.
1920: United States	The Federal Employees Retirement Act was enacted to provide pensions for all civil service employees aged 70+ after 15 years of service; all mechanics and postal workers age 65+; and all railway clerks aged 62+.
1930: United States	All federal workers, and many state and local government employees, are covered by pension benefits.
1935: United States	The Social Security Act is enacted, signed by President Roosevelt, which created a system of payments for retired workers aged 65+.
1974: United States	The Employee Retirement Income Security Act (ERISA) is enacted. This federal law established standards and protections for voluntary retirement and health plans. These standards included plan information, vesting and benefit accrual, responsibilities for those managing plans, and participant rights.
1983: United States	The Social Security Act is amended, raising the retirement age from 65 to 67 for those born after 1959 and to make payments taxable.
2006: United States	The Pension Protection Act is enacted, which expanded on the protections of ERISA and improved workers' options for retirement funding.
2011: United States	Approximately 51 million workers have 401(k) accounts, which are offered to employees by employers through payroll withholding. Employers often match some or all of employees' contributions, which are taxed after money is withdrawn after retirement.

Sources: American Society of Pension Professionals and Actuaries, 2021; Social Security Administration, n.d.b; US Department of Labor, 2021.

Social Security benefits alone are not sufficient to support them in retirement. Many people, regardless of employment status, are not able to save enough money to completely support themselves in retirement. Millions live in poverty in older age, and many older adults cannot retire because of a lack of financial support. Women, on average, tend to make less than men, even when they have the same qualifications and are doing the same job. Consequently, women, particularly those who live alone or are the primary earner for the family, contribute less to Social Security over time and thus receive a lower Social Security benefit upon retirement (American Academy of Actuaries, 2021).

The majority (51 percent to 75 percent) of unauthorized or undocumented immigrants and workers are estimated to contribute approximately $13 billion per year into Social Security through their taxable income, yet they are not eligible to receive Social Security payments upon retirement or becoming disabled (New American Economy, 2021). (See Chapter 12 for a more detailed discussion on Social Security.)

The age of eligibility for collecting retirement benefits has changed with changing economic, demographic, sociopolitical, and other circumstances. When the Social Security Act was passed in 1935, 65 as a retirement age was in place under the German system of social insurance. However, the European precedent was not the main factor in deciding the US retirement age. Rather, it was determined based on the age used by most US pension systems and by actuarial data that showed that age 65 would allow for a system that would be self-sustaining with only modest levels of payroll taxation (Social Security Administration, 2021). Over the years, the age at which people can collect Social Security and other benefits has been reexamined, especially given increased life expectancy and fluctuations in the numbers of people in each retiring cohort, which affects how the Social Security system can be financially sustained.

VOLUNTEERISM AND COMMUNITY INVOLVEMENT

Volunteering and community involvement are important to many people throughout the life span. However, for many older adults, retirement provides more available time and energy to devote to volunteering and investing in their community. The percentage of US adults aged 65+ who report volunteering has remained steady over the years, with approximately 26 percent to 28 percent reporting that they engage in some form of volunteer activity each year (United Health Foundation, 2020).

Research suggests that engaging in volunteer activities, at least monthly, is associated with improved health and well-being, including improved working memory, improved social and cognitive activity, enhanced quality of life and life satisfaction, increased longevity, and decreased disability (Guiney, Keall, & Machado, 2021; Jiang et al., 2019). Volunteering is also associated with improved mental health outcomes such as reduced symptoms of depression and decreased feelings of loneliness and isolation (Americorps, 2019). Given the many benefits of volunteering and community engagement, it is important to think about ways for older adults to participate in these types of activities, including those in skilled nursing facilities, those with family or work obligations, and those with physical and/or cognitive limitations (Sellon, Chapin, & Leedahl, 2017).

Like volunteerism, community or civic engagement is important throughout the life span, and older adults may be able to devote more time to these activities than they could when they were younger. Engaging in activities such as voting, activism, political

Figure 7.2 Volunteerism and civic engagement are meaningful ways for older adults to remain socially engaged
Source: SolStock/iStock

involvement, maintaining informal and formal connections with community groups, and contributing to various aspects of community through philanthropy, participating in the arts, and contributing to boards and organizations are just a few examples of how civic engagement occurs in all stage of life (Martinson & Minkler, 2006).

Civic engagement and participation are associated with better physical, cognitive, and mental health as well as increased well-being and social connection. They also help build and maintain social capital (Proulx, Curl, & Ermer, 2018; Varma et al., 2016). The level of civic participation tends to vary by generation and educational achievement; younger adults are less likely to be civically engaged than older adults, and those with higher education levels tend to be more civically engaged than those with less education. These differences may be accounted for because many younger adults may not know how to engage with their communities, and those who attend college are more able to engage in organizations and causes that are linked to their campuses. People with higher levels of education tend to form social networks that can help them remain engaged after graduation.

LIFELONG LEARNING

Learning is an important part of adult life, just as when we are younger. It can play an important role in retirement or if we choose to stay employed, keeping our minds active. Research indicates that lifelong learning is important for many facets of well-being. Learning is important for memory, cognitive stimulation, self-confidence, sharpening coping abilities, continuing growth of brain cells, helping us feel in control of our environment, instilling hope, and increasing life satisfaction, among other benefits (Boulton-Lewis, 2010; Nicoll, 2003; Oliver, Tomas, & Montoro-Rodriguez, 2017). Even with age- or disease-related cognitive and processing changes, older adults learn as well as their younger counterparts (Nicoll, 2003).

Adults learn differently than younger people, using past experiences for context and linking new information to prior knowledge. Self-directed learning is a central concept in how adults learn. This means keeping the locus of control with the learner, thereby increasing feelings of competence and life satisfaction with learning (Cercone, 2008).

A number of barriers can impede the pursuit of continued learning:

- Age-related issues such as slowed cognitive processes or other physical barriers may erode people's self-confidence in learning new skills or information.
- Educational programs may be too expensive for some people.
- Language barriers may make learning difficult.
- Mental health issues such as depression or social anxiety may erode people's confidence or motivation to attend classes, workshops, or social functions.
- Technological limitations such as lack of access to a computer or internet or lack of knowledge of how to use technology may pose barriers for those who want to use online educational resources (Laal, 2011).

Lifelong learning can happen in many ways. Older adults can earn a high school equivalency diploma, complete a certificate- or degree-level college or university program, or take noncredit courses or workshops offered by colleges, senior centers, or community centers. They can pursue self-guided learning activities by joining clubs or special-interest groups or learning new skills on their own.

One example of how adult learners can continue their education is a national educational network called the Osher Lifelong Learning Institute (OLLI). OLLI has 124 institutes, housed in universities around the country, that provide educational opportunities such as social events, classes, travel, and cultural enrichment for those aged 50+. OLLI instructors typically are university faculty members or retired educators who offer courses in their field or specialization. While OLLI opportunities are fee-based, many older adults can find learning opportunities that are free or low cost through sources such as in-person and online courses or workshops offered at libraries and senior/community centers.

Figure 7.3 Learning is a lifelong endeavor
Source: monkeybusinessimages/Shutterstock

CHAPTER REVIEW

Work and Older Adults
- People aged 65+ represent the fastest-growing segment of labor force participation in the United States.
- Work, employment, and careers also mean different things to different people depending on intersectional factors such as age, race, gender, generation, and socioeconomic status.
- Older workers' views on and experiences with work and retirement depend on their generation and how intersectional factors affect generational dynamics.
- Caregiving can be a barrier to employment and postemployment activities for older adults.
- In the United States, workers aged 55+ tend to be concentrated in management, sales, service, production, and construction sectors.
- People aged 55+ make up approximately 25 percent of self-employed workers in the United States, more than any other age group.
- About 27 percent of those aged 55+ work part time, compared to 18 percent of workers in younger age groups.
- Ageism in the workplace is a persistent problem that affects all business sectors. In spite of this, older workers often bring skill, knowledge, experience, connections, consistency, and a strong work ethic.
- Research suggests that exposing younger workers to older workers helps to reduce ageist stereotypes.

Retirement
- Research shows that longevity is linked to having a sense of purpose in the later years.
- People can experience various effects of retirement depending on the circumstances and timing and other factors in their lives.
- Atchley's and Barusch's model of retirement consists of the phases of preretirement, honeymoon, immediate retirement routine, rest and relaxation, disenchantment, reorientation, retirement routine, and termination of retirement.

Financial Support in Retirement
- Financial support for retirees has been tied to years of service or employment.
- In the United States, Social Security payments do not provide enough income for some older adults and many live in poverty.

Volunteerism and Community Involvement
- Between 26 percent to 28 percent of those aged 65+ report engaging in some form of volunteer activity.
- Volunteering and civic engagement are associated with improved health and well-being, as well as improved mental health outcomes.

Lifelong Learning
- Lifelong learning is important for many facets of our well-being including memory, cognitive stimulation, self-confidence, sharpening coping abilities, continued growth of brain cells, helping us feel in control of our environment, and increasing life satisfaction.

- Barriers can impede the pursuit of learning in later years. These barriers include cognitive and physical barriers, mental health issues, financial barriers, language barriers, and issues related to access to or use of technology.

REVIEW QUESTIONS
1. Describe various options to full retirement and their socioeconomic benefits.
2. Discuss what ageism in the workplace might look like and some of ageism's consequences on both the older adults who experience it and for the organizations where it occurs.
3. Explore opportunities for volunteerism, civic engagement, and lifelong learning for older adults. How do these opportunities benefit older adults and their communities?

KEY TERMS
encore careers				bridge job

CHAPTER 8

Living Arrangements

Chapter Outline
Housing and Care Options for Older Adults
    Types of Residential Facilities and Communities
    Older Adults with Special Needs
Aging in Place
    The Importance of Place
    Research on Aging in Place
    Changing Needs Over Time
Theories and Approaches to Place and Aging
    Environmental Gerontology
    Geographical Gerontology
Older Adults in Urban and Rural Environments
The Importance of Neighborhoods
    Gentrification
    Urban Neighborhoods: Challenges, Resources, and Resilience
        Detroit
        Minneapolis
Housing Options for Older Adults
    Historical Background
    The Housing Continuum
    Innovative Solutions
        Age-Friendly Communities
        Villages
        LGBT 65+ Housing Initiatives
        Home Sharing
        Communal Living
        Intergenerational Programming and Communities
    Housing for Low-Income Older Adults
    Continuing Care Retirement Communities
    Assisted Living Facilities
    Supportive Housing

Nursing Homes
COVID-19 and Long-Term Care Facilities
Living Arrangements of Vulnerable Populations
Older Adults in Prison
Older Victims of Domestic Abuse
Older Adults Without Housing

Learning Objectives
After completing this chapter, you will be able to:
- Describe some common housing and care options for older adults.
- Define aging in place and describe the types of research that have been conducted about this approach.
- Name and explain theories about the role of environment in aging.
- Compare and contrast the experience of aging in urban and rural areas.
- Describe qualities that make neighborhoods safe, healthy environments for older adults.
- List common housing options for older adults and describe innovative living options that have emerged.
- Describe the challenges associated with living arrangements for older individuals who are incarcerated, homeless, or a victim of domestic abuse.

Place matters for older adults, and where people live influences how they age. Some people live in the same home where they spent many of their adult years, raising a family and building strong connections to a community. Others decide to downsize and move to smaller living quarters or to communities specifically designed for older adults. Still others will relocate at retirement or to be near children and grandchildren. A small percentage of older adults will live out their lives in nursing homes because their care needs become too complex for them to remain at home. In this chapter, we'll examine the various types of living arrangements of older adults in urban, suburban, and rural areas. We'll also discuss how economic and social forces affect the types of living arrangements that are available to them.

HOUSING AND CARE OPTIONS FOR OLDER ADULTS
Needs and preferences for living arrangements change as people age. People may need alter their homes or move because of a reduced ability to perform physical tasks such as climbing stairs or doing lawn care. They might relocate to better meet their needs for companionship and assistance. With creative thinking, we can work toward the ideal of living arrangements that will allow people to live as independently and as safely as possible in a variety of settings where they can remain connected to others in the community.

For reasons ranging from economic to emotional, many people want to stay in the homes where they have lived for years. They want to maintain their routines and how they go about activities such as shopping, cooking, doing paid and volunteer work, socializing, and participating in leisure, community, and religious activities. Some may continue to live in apartments or houses where there is a mismatch between their needs and their environment. People with lower incomes often face more challenges and have fewer choices as they age.

Where people live during their later years reflects their needs, values, life circumstances, and desire to maintain a sense of belonging (Wahl, Iwarsson, & Oswald, 2012). Ideally, people can live as independently and safely as possible, with dignity, and where their self-determination is honored. However, frailty, cognitive impairment, or other health- and aging-related vulnerabilities may make their homes incompatible with their needs. Disparities in income and wealth and whether people own or rent their homes also influence living arrangements and options for people as they age. Many older adults must pay a large percentage of their income toward housing expenses, leaving less for food, healthcare, and other needs (Joint Center for Housing Studies, 2019).

In 2017, the majority of the 50 million adults aged 65 and older lived either alone or with their spouse or partner. The percentage of older adults living alone increases with age. By 2038 the number of people aged 80 and above who live alone is projected to be 10.1 million (Joint Center for Housing Studies, 2019).

People's responsibilities, needs, family relationships, and cultural preferences influence their living arrangements. Although the majority of adults aged 65+ live in small households, the number of multigenerational households has increased (see Chapter 6). Multigenerational living is more common among nonwhite families, including more recent immigrants to the United States (Cohn & Passel, 2018; Joint Center for Housing Studies, 2019). The number of adult children who continue to live with their parents has increased. Some older people provide a home for adult children with disabilities or for grandchildren.

The availability and accessibility of community support and healthcare services affect living arrangements (see Chapter 9), as do laws and policies that address the needs of older adults (see Chapter 12), particularly those related to affordable housing (Stone, 2018).

Figure 8.1 Many older adults live alone
Source: Wavebreakmedia/Shutterstock

Types of Residential Facilities and Communities

About three percent of adults aged 65 and older live in group quarters, which include nursing homes, jails, and prisons. The percentage increases with age, with 10.6 percent of people aged 85 and older living in residential settings known as **long-term care** facilities. Long-term care is the mix of services to meet a person's health or personal care needs. **Nursing homes**, also called skilled nursing facilities, are for those who need both medical and personal care (Roberts et al., 2018). Recent data show that 1.4 million people over the age of 65 live in nursing homes, while another 750,000 live in **assisted living** settings, which provide personal care and other services that assist people with **activities of daily living** (ADLs) (Harris-Kojetin et al., 2019).

ADLs include eating, bathing, dressing, grooming, and using the toilet. **Instrumental activities of daily living** (IADLs) include cooking, cleaning, transportation, laundry, and managing financial affairs. The ability to perform these activities contributes to quality of life and may diminish due to illnesses and/or chronic conditions that limit a person's ability to perform these tasks (Edemekong, et al., 2022).

Independent living communities, also called active adult communities and senior communities, provide a range of housing options that may include apartments, condos, townhomes, or single-family dwellings. Generally, residents can function independently and may have access to common areas such as a gym, pool, clubhouse, or an on-site medical clinic. These communities may also offer services such as organized events and outings and transportation to grocery stores, medical facilities, and local businesses.

The term **continuum of care** describes the range of housing and healthcare and personal care services available as a person's needs change from being able to care for oneself to needing significant help with ADLs. Older adults may become unable to manage everyday activities when a chronic health condition or disability worsens or when a sudden event such as a stroke or fractured hip necessitates ongoing care. This continuum accounts for the needs of older adults ranging from those who are completely independent to those who are dependent (Rowles & Teaster, 2015). Keeping people out of institutions reduces the cost of government-funded programs such Medicare (health insurance for adults aged 65+ and some persons with disabilities) and Medicaid (health insurance for low-income persons). Medicare and Medicaid are discussed in Chapter 12.

Older Adults with Special Needs

Many adults with developmental and other disabilities will outlive their aging parents who are their caregivers, and there is shortage of comprehensive community-based care for them as they age (Koenig, 2015). In the United States, an estimated 31 percent of the 1.5 million people who are homeless are over the age of 50 (Gass, Mahan, & Balfour, 2018). In 2017, 12 percent of the approximately 1.5 million individuals in prison in the US (state and federal prisons) were age 55 or older, with and 2.8 percent over the age of 65 (Bronson & Carson, 2019). Due to sentencing policies of the 1990s that called for longer sentences and life imprisonment for those with three or more felonies in some states, the number of people who will age and die in prison has increased. Others will be released after many years of incarceration with needs for support and resources, including housing.

AGING IN PLACE

Understanding the impact of place in the daily lives of older adults helps determine ways to improve their situation (Cutchin 2018). **Aging in place**, the ability of people to age in their own home and community safely, independently, and comfortably, reflects the values and goals of people and public policy (Harvard Health Publications, 2018). While retirement, the wish to move to a warmer environment or less expensive location, family needs, or health problems prompt some people to move, many people value living where they feel a sense of connection and belonging and a sense of control or agency (Wahl, Iwarsson, & Oswald, 2012). From an intersectional lens, people in marginalized groups will want to remain in communities where they feel safe and can access the support they need. However, economic and social forces can persuade people to relocate. For example, people who identify as LGBT will move to locations purposely established to create a welcoming community (Bitterman, 2020).

As a social policy, aging in place prioritizes public policies that help people stay in their homes and out of institutions (Golant, 2018). However, the power of this concept may complicate older adults' decisions about where they live and whether those places meet their needs. Older adults' choices about whether to age in place may affect their family members and influence the quality of their neighborhoods and communities. Large numbers of older adults who are concentrated in urban neighborhoods with older dwellings may not be able to keep up with maintenance or upgrades, leading to depressed housing values and less tax revenue, and eventually vacant housing if younger buyers are not available when they are ready to sell (Golant, 2018).

The Importance of Place

Rowles (1983), an early researcher on the importance of place to older adults, coined the term "autobiographical insideness" to describe the deep attachment of a group of adults aged 75 and older to the small community in rural Appalachia where they had lived most or all their lives. Rowles contrasted the attachment of these "old old" people with those in a "young old" age group (those aged 65–74) who did not have the same deep connections, highlighting the diversity of attachment to place elaborated in many subsequent studies. Rowles used **ethnography**, an approach to qualitative research that relies on extensive observation, in-depth interviews, and

Figure 8.2 Enjoying time for conversation
Source: kali9/iStock

the collection of documents and other research evidence to develop a deep understanding of a phenomenon.

According to Rowles (1983, 1993), the role of place in aging includes the physical attachment to the place, the social identity connected to the place, and how place is linked to personal history and the passage of time. Familiarity with the physical space—both the home and surrounding neighborhood—leads to automatic behaviors and responses that are important sources of stability and well-being. People acquire and apply certain rules and norms, such as watching television in a favorite chair or regularly interacting with neighbors, such as seeing the same people walking their dogs every morning. As time passes, the places where people live may become more important because they are symbols of identity that give meaning to life and buffer against losses later in life. For example, the rooms where important life celebrations and events occurred and mementos such as photos, collectibles, and memorabilia are important expressions of who people are.

Research on Aging in Place
Research on aging in place has focused upon three areas (Golant, 2018):

- *The meaning of place for older adults.* This encompasses personal preferences and their feelings about their home, their neighborhood, and the available social and support networks.
- *Strategies that people use to remain in their homes.* These include modifying living spaces, having a family member move in to provide care, or making do with a less-than-adequate living situation.
- *Public policies focused on aging in place*—are these policies beneficial and cost effective?

This research draws attention to both the benefits and challenges of aging in place, particularly when people need assistance with their care and support. In the United States, 27 percent of adults aged 60 and older live alone (Ausubel, 2020). Sometimes this is due to death of a spouse or partner, while others have lived alone for most of their adult lives. While many who live alone have supportive social networks, social isolation affects about 24 percent of older adults, who may or may not live alone (National Academies of Sciences Engineering and Medicine, 2020). **Elder orphans**, defined as "aged, community-dwelling individuals who are socially and/or physically isolated, without an available known family member or designated surrogate or caregiver," are a particular concern (Carney et al., 2016, p. 1). How well these elder orphans fare will depend upon their health, cognitive status, and economic and social resources.

Changing Needs over Time
Needs for support, companionship, and assistance change. Major changes in living arrangements can create psychological, emotional, and spiritual challenges. Sometimes, adult children feel they must relocate to the older adult's home or community to provide care, which has implications for their social and long-term financial well-being (Golant, 2018). Particularly as people move into their eighth and ninth decades of life, their changing capabilities alter the way they interact with and survive (or ideally thrive) in

their homes and communities, changing their relationships with familiar spaces and places (Cutchin, 2018).

As they age, people may lose the ability to perform physical tasks related to home or yard maintenance. Homes may develop structural or mechanical problems, and repairs are expensive. Features such as steep stairways and high shelves will no longer match the physical capabilities of the person living there. For example, a home in which the only bathroom is on the second floor may work for a couple in their eighties until the husband's stroke makes climbing the stairs impossible. Installing a first-floor bathroom would make it possible for them to stay in their home, but remodeling might be unaffordable or impractical. Nurses, occupational therapists, and others may undertake a home safety assessment that involves an assessment of the older person with respect to physical health, medication use, cognitive status, and mobility plus an assessment of actual and potential risks in the home, such as loose area rugs and other hazards for tripping (Edelman & Ficorelli, 2012).

Neighborhoods (discussed later in the chapter) also play a role in aging in place. Many want to remain in their communities to stay close to friends, family, and familiar places, even if they need to move to different housing to better meet their needs for transportation, recreation, and amenities that make physical activity, social interaction, cultural engagement, and ongoing education possible (Wiles et al., 2011).

THEORIES AND APPROACHES TO PLACE AND AGING

Theories have evolved that address the relationship between aging adults and their environment.

Environmental Gerontology

Environmental gerontology is concerned with how the physical environment influences the aging process and people's sense of belonging to a place and their **agency**, or the proactive and reactive behaviors used to adjust to their environment (Wahl et al., 2012). **Environmental press** refers to how the constraints of the environment influence the ability to adapt as personal competence changes with age (Lawton & Nahemov, 1973). For example, loss of mobility, such as the ability to maintain a treasured garden, and cognitive decline, manifested for example by repeatedly forgetting to turn off the stove, require changes. People adapt in different ways, such as hiring someone to help with gardening, but changes can result in feelings such as sadness about losing the ability to care for one's yard (Wahl et al., 2012). This theory helps us see that "strategies for reducing environmental press may include adapting one's current residence or relocating to a more supportive environment" (Perry, Andersen, & Kaplan, 2014, p. 76).

Wiseman (Perry et al., 2014; Wiseman, 1980) focused on factors that influenced older people's decisions to move and how larger social forces affect residential options. These factors included tangible resources such as wealth, the cost of living, and the housing market, and intangible resources such as ties to community and the emotional capacity to handle a move. He noted differences between a full-time move outside the community, seasonal moves (when people, sometimes called "snowbirds," go to warmer locations in the winter) and moving to a new location in the same community and pointed out that moves are influenced by both voluntary and involuntary factors. Often, an event such as a fall exposes vulnerabilities and precipitates a move.

> **CASE 8.1**
>
> ### An Involuntary Mover
>
> Marian, who was single for her entire adult life, taught in international schools in Poland, Japan, and England before she ultimately settled in midlife in New York City, where she worked as a reading specialist. Her social life included singing in a choral society and being active in her church, which had a large and active ministry for single adults. In retirement, she spent her summers in a vacation area in upstate New York and enjoyed traveling, especially to Hawaii. As she aged, she also experienced some episodes of major depression and was hospitalized for several weeks when she was 73. At age 81, she fell in her apartment and could not get up. She lay on the floor for two days until a concerned friend, who had not heard from her, stopped in to check on her. This event resulted in her move to an assisted living facility near her sister's home in the Midwest.
>
> What are the benefits and drawbacks for Marian of this major life change?

In Wiseman's terms, an "involuntary mover" is forced to relocate due to changing functional abilities or family needs. "Involuntary stayers" are those who are "unable to relocate despite significant concerns about care and environmental needs related to physical and financial limitations" (Perry et al. 2014, p. 77).

Litwak and Longino (1987) focused on the progression of types of moves that generally occur after retirement. The "amenities move" helps people achieve things that they want in retirement, such as a home near a golf course in a warmer climate. The second and third moves are "necessary adaptations to increased needs and typically involve relocations that bring older adults closer to family or under the care of formal service providers" (Perry et al., 2014, p. 77). This work showed that relocation in later life involved both making adaptations based on changing personal priorities and developing needs.

Geographical Gerontology

The field of **geographical gerontology** draws attention to the impact of "place, space, scale, landscape, and territory" on older adults and the aging process, focusing on where people live and the meanings of those places from dwelling to neighborhood all the way to region of the world (Skinner, Andrews, & Cutchin, 2018, p. 3). It recognizes that the impact of the close physical and social environment that includes both the home and the surrounding territory. In a city, this includes the apartment building, street, or block; in the suburbs, this might include a cul-de-sac, townhouse development, or gated community; in rural areas, home may be on a country road and the nearest neighbors are farther away. Geographical gerontology also considers the impact of migration patterns, climate change, environmental hazards, and public policy on the quality of the immediate environment and the availability of different housing options.

Zoning laws that limit neighborhoods to single-family dwellings provide an example of the impact of public policy on housing options. These laws have impeded development of multifamily housing and the creation of accessory apartments, or auxiliary dwelling units, that allow multiple generations to live near each other while maintaining some boundaries and privacy (Joint Center for Housing Studies, 2019). In 2019, the city of Minneapolis eliminated the single-family zoning law, which allows for a greater variety of homes available across the city (Kahlenberg, 2019). This change is an example of an age-friendly policy that will increase living options in neighborhoods in many cities and suburban areas (Joint Center for Housing Studies, 2019).

OLDER ADULTS IN URBAN AND RURAL ENVIRONMENTS

Living arrangements and options vary by location in urban, suburban, and rural areas, in addition to other intersectional characteristics including race, gender identity, sexual identity, and social class. Over 80 percent of the population of the United States, including those age 65 and older, lives in urban areas. People aged 65 and older comprise 13.8 percent of the urban population and 17.5 percent of the rural population.

The US Census Bureau defines "urbanized areas" as places of 50,000 or more people and "urban clusters" as places where there are at least 2,500 and fewer than 50,000 people (Ratcliffe et al., 2016). The term "urban" refers to small cities, suburban areas, and large cities. "Rural" areas are those not defined as urban, and can range from remote, sparsely populated areas where much land is undeveloped to areas that are close to more densely populated areas (Ratcliffe et al., 2016).

In the United States, many younger people have migrated from rural areas and small towns to more populated areas with better job opportunities. Since 1980, the percentage of older adults living in rural areas has increased (Figure 8.3). The states with the largest percent of rural older populations are Vermont and Maine, where over 60 percent of the population is over the age of 65. Older adults comprise over 50 percent of the rural populations in Arkansas, Mississippi, Montana, South Dakota, and West Virginia (Symens Smith & Trevelyan, 2019).

In rural areas, most older adults live in single-family homes, which may not be optimal for aging in place (Stone, 2018). Older adults in rural communities, who are

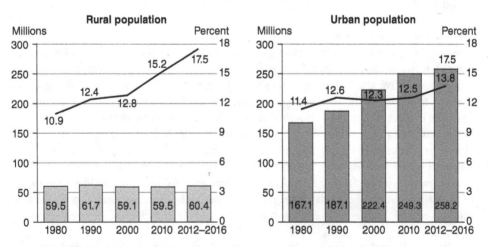

Figure 8.3 Population size and percentage 65 years and over by rural and urban status: 1980 to 2012–2016

Source: US Census Bureau. Taken from US Census Bureau, American Community Survey Reports, ACS-41, "The Older Population in Rural America in the United States: 2012–2016". US Government Printing Office, Washington, DC, 2018.

accustomed to their self-reliance and independence, may find it especially difficult to maintain their homes and to get help they need to stay there. People in rural areas benefit from being part of communities that have relied on the willingness of residents to support each other in times of need (Kaye, 2017).

In rural areas services such as hospitals and healthcare providers are geographically dispersed, and access to services such as supported housing, rehabilitation services, nursing homes, and specialized medical care are more limited than in urban areas. Since 2010, many rural hospitals have closed (Kaufman et al., 2016). Some of these challenges also apply to certain suburban and urban areas.

The isolation of older and vulnerable adults with dementia and their caregivers in rural areas also raises concern. A study of visiting nurses and social workers in rural Ontario, Canada found that they often struggled with how to respond when vulnerable older adults were being mistreated by their caregivers, most often adult children. The mistreatment was often the result of disruptive behaviors created by dementia. The workers struggled when caregivers refused services and situations seemed risky and there were few options that would make the older adult safer (Lindenbach et al., 2019).

THE IMPORTANCE OF NEIGHBORHOODS

People spend more time in their homes and neighborhoods as they age, and the importance of these environments increases. As a place where people live and interrelate, a neighborhood is often described by traits or characteristics rather than by precise geographical boundaries (National Geographic, 2019). Urban neighborhoods may be defined by who lives there (e.g., demographic characteristics such as race, ethnicity, age, and income level of the residents) but also the type and quality of housing and the physical environment. Other important characteristics that affect older people are the sense of whether the neighborhood is a supportive community; the availability of reliable public services such as transportation, sanitation, and police; and the presence of amenities such as shops, libraries, and parks.

People who are no longer working, particularly if they have limited resources, are tied to their immediate neighborhoods in ways that people who work are not. Neighborhoods influence whether living arrangements provide a safe and secure home that allows older adults to live where they can easily access services and supports such as food, healthcare, and socialization (Finlay, Gaugler, & Kane, 2020). Particularly when people experience loss of mobility, such as the ability to drive, the neighborhood takes on even more importance in the daily quality of their lives.

Naturally occurring retirement communities (NORCs) are places from apartment buildings to whole neighborhoods where there is a large proportion of older adults. While NORCs were not originally designed with the needs of older adults in mind, many are conducive to promoting healthy aging due to their political, social, and economic environments, and city governments have encouraged policies and programs to support them (Masotti et al., 2006). NORCs comprised largely of immigrants, ethnic minorities, African American, or LGBT adults can also support culturally specific needs.

When 121 people from two low-income, multicultural neighborhoods in New Zealand were asked to describe what aging in place meant to them, many stated that they were attached to their neighborhoods and that they wished to stay in the same geographic community, even if their current house or apartment became unsuitable (Wiles et al., 2011). Important neighborhood features included the familiarity of shops and health and other services, the knowledge of resources, and the connections with people. Features of neighborhoods associated with healthy aging are walkability, being compact (residences and businesses in proximity), accessibility (public transportation and barrier free sidewalks), plentiful resources, and healthy air (Mather & Scommegna, 2017). Figure 8.4 summarizes these features and their relationship to physical health.

An intersectional lens helps us see urban neighborhoods as places where people in groups that have been sidelined or ostracized have banded together for familiarity, protection, and support. LGBT persons and persons from immigrant groups have also clustered in urban neighborhoods due to needs for support and community. "Gayborhoods" such as Greenwich Village in New York or the Castro in San Francisco grew out of needs for community, protection, and support during the early to mid-twentieth century. Today, shifting social attitudes toward LGBT individuals and economic and social forces have altered the character of some of these neighborhoods and led to the creation of LGBT-affirmative communities in other urban neighborhoods (Bitterman, 2020).

Gentrification

Gentrification changes the character of a neighborhood through the influx of more affluent (and often younger and whiter) residents and the services and amenities that the new residents desire. Gentrification raises cost of living, including rent, so people may need to find less expensive housing in less supportive communities. Gentrification has influenced the well-being of long-time residents of low-income urban

Neighborhood Features	Self-Rated Health	Physical Limitations	Cognitive Function	Heart Disease Risk	Obesity	Physical Activity
Walkable – More intersections sidewalks, and crosswalks; few cul-de-sacs or dead end streets; residents view walking in the neighborhood as pleasant and easy.	▲	▼			▼	
Compact – A diverse mix of residences and businesses (mixed land use) in walkable proximity.		▼		▼		▲
Accessible – Public transportation on the street, and/or barrier-free and well-maintained streets and sidewalks.		▼				▲
Safe – Residents consider their neighborhoods safe.		▼				▲
Plentiful Resources – Public transit on the street; community centers, parks, and libraries; well-maintained public spaces such as sidewalks.			▲			
Healthy Air – Low concentrations of fine particulate matter air pollution that can be inhaled and damage organs, including the brain.			▲			

Figure 8.4 Neighborhood features related to healthy aging in place
Source: Table from Mark Mather and Paola Scommegna, "How Neighborhoods Affect the Health and Well-Being of Older Americans," Today's Research on Aging no. 35 (2017), https://www.prb.org/resources/how-neighborhoods-affect-the-health-and-well-being-of-older-americans/. Used with permission.

neighborhoods who are members of ethnic groups, immigrants, or LGBT individuals. A study that combined data from the National Health and Aging Study and the National Neighborhood Trends Study found that gentrification's impact on the self-rated health and mental health of both economically vulnerable and higher income older residents of gentrifying is negative (Smith, Lehning, & Kim, 2017).

Urban Neighborhoods: Challenges, Resources, and Resilience
In the United States, "a legacy of structural racism, segregation, and economic disinvestment has resulted in older minorities disproportionately inhabiting, and therefore aging, in stressor-laden urban neighborhoods" (Massey 1998, as cited by Fritz, Cutchin, & Cummins, 2018, p. e109). Most larger cities have a range of vibrant neighborhoods that provide amenities such as libraries, restaurants, parks, and social services. However, other urban neighborhoods are characterized by physical decay, high crime, and a limited number of quality formal services. Fewer concerned family members or younger neighbors who are available and suitable to provide informal assistance live near the older adults who remain (Finlay et al., 2020; Portacolone, Perissinotto et al., 2018).

The difficulties of living in changing and high crime neighborhoods illustrate how an emphasis on aging in place can keep people in difficult situations rather than helping them to achieve maximum well-being. Living to be very old in these neighborhoods is different than growing old in a socially cohesive urban neighborhood. Examples of these challenges raise awareness of what social workers, visiting nurses, and other helping professionals may encounter, as illustrated in Box 8.1. However, the strengths and resilience of older adults living in distressed urban neighborhoods are important to keep in mind as well as learning about services provided by neighborhood organizations and informal networks that are committed to remedying neighborhood conditions.

BOX 8.1 Heat Wave

The book *Heat Wave* by sociologist Eric Klinenberg examined the high rates of death among older adults in Chicago during the heat wave of July 1995 and illustrated the impact of social isolation. Klinenberg compared two neighborhoods on the West Side of Chicago and found that the physical and social environment, including what he called the "cultural practices" of the neighborhood, affected whether residents took responsibility for ensuring the well-being of older adults. In many cases, health problems limited their mobility and made it difficult for them to leave their homes to access designated cooling centers or other public places with air conditioning.

The mortality rate in North Lawndale was many times that of the adjacent community of South Lawndale. North Lawndale, characterized by abandoned buildings, little commercial activity, violent crime, degraded infrastructure, low population density, and the dispersion of families that weakened social support systems, made older residents particularly vulnerable. South Lawndale, characterized by busy streets, heavy commercial activity, residential concentration, a relatively low crime rate, and much more public engagement and collective life, appeared to provide benefits for the elderly. Older adults in neighborhoods that were less socially cohesive were more likely to die of heat exhaustion (Klinenberg, 2015).

CASE 8.2

Marie: Challenges and Resilience in a High-Crime Neighborhood

Marie, an African American woman, was vigorous and energetic through her ninth decade, but at 95, she was confined to a wheelchair and to her apartment, having outlived her family and supportive social network. Service providers did not communicate well with each other, and frequently changing home care attendants exploited or ignored her. A report of elder abuse did not result in intervention to protect her from further mistreatment. The neighborhood had evolved from a predominantly African American population to one that was mostly Latino. The people that Marie had felt more comfortable with were now gone. Nurtured by her faith, Marie took initiative to protect herself and was proud of her ability to put herself to bed each night (Portacolone, 2017).

Question: What community-level strategies are needed to enhance well-being for Marie?

Detroit

Qualitative research conducted in Detroit, Michigan, illuminates how older adults can lose trust in the neighborhoods in which they live (Fritz, Cutchin, & Cummins, 2018). Detroit lost population decline over the latter half of the twentieth century and into the twenty-first century. The city became majority African American and experienced a housing crisis, disinvestment, and bankruptcy. Study participants took photos that illustrated their neighborhood-based stressors. Their photos of abandoned and decayed housing, unmaintained lots and alleys, dumping, and stray dogs represented how the neighborhood's physical features were no longer able to provide reliable safety, security, and a pleasant living environment. Changes in property ownership and renters who did not adhere to social norms of caring for property, noise control, and supervision of children added to the loss of trust, as did the unreliable city services (e.g., nonfunctioning streetlights and unresponsive police) (Fritz, Cutchin, & Cummins, 2018).

Minneapolis

Low-income older adults in four different neighborhoods in Minneapolis, Minnesota described ways in which place can both provide support and create challenges (Finlay et al., 2020). Study participants valued security and the ability to feel comfortable in their home surroundings. Depending on conditions inside and outside of their dwellings, some found it difficult to maintain important social connections while simultaneously living in safe surroundings. Physical and safety hazards included mounds of snow on sidewalks outside, heavy traffic, and home conditions that increased risk for falls and exacerbated health problems. Many study participants wanted to remain in their robust multiracial and multigenerational communities, but their housing did not meet their changing needs, they could not afford home repairs, and neighborhood crime levels made them feel less secure. Others who lived in subsidized or transitional housing did not feel at home in places where they were subject to rigid rules about home décor and inspections. Despite challenges, many demonstrated resilience and creativity as they negotiated the challenges created by their neighborhoods and communities (Finlay et al., 2020).

Seeking out and working with the community-based organizations that work to address the needs of even these most vulnerable older adults is vital. Minneapolis, Detroit, and other cities have numerous community-based organizations that provide support and well-resourced communities for older adults.

HOUSING OPTIONS FOR OLDER ADULTS

As helpers and advocates, we need to respect people's right to self-determination when we are asked to assist with people's decisions about where to live. We need to look for opportunities to question our own assumptions of what makes for the "best" living arrangement, challenge the assumptions of others, and develop alternatives that offer solutions to the challenges we have identified.

Historical Background

From colonial times in America through the early twentieth century, families cared for older persons. The only "senior housing" that existed was the almshouse or poorhouse, institutions set up by local governments to care for older adults with no other supports. The almshouses evolved into "old people's homes" and eventually many became nursing homes that provided long-term care (Haber, 2016). Over the past 100 years, living options have expanded due to changing demographic patterns and public and private efforts, including housing designed specifically for older adults.

The Medicare and Medicaid programs begun in 1965 included provisions for federal government funding for long-term care and provided new resources for nursing homes. More recently, Medicaid has provided funds to support community-based care for aging in place (discussed in Chapter 12) (Stone, 2018).

During the 1960s and 1970s, concern about meeting the specialized needs of older adults led to the development of age-segregated housing by both the public and private sectors. These housing options included "over 55" retirement communities and "senior citizen" apartments, mostly in urban areas that offered recreational options and services to meet needs for support and socialization. During this time, for-profit companies and not-for-profit organizations recognized the opportunities in building housing for older adults such as **continuing care retirement communities (CCRCs)** (Stone, 2013). These communities offer a range of housing and care options on the same property, including independent living, assisted living, and skilled nursing care.

As time has passed, public policy has focused on efforts to promote aging in place, as the fastest-growing household type will consist of persons in their eighties (Joint Center for Housing Studies, 2019).

The Housing Continuum

As discussed earlier, people remain in homes for reasons that include personal preference, not having the means to move, or because the type of place they want to live is not available. Those who stay in homes they have owned for many years may have lower housing costs because their mortgages are often paid off. However, a substantial percentage of older adults have difficulty paying for maintenance, taxes, and other expenses on a fixed income. Many who rent or are still making mortgage payments also face significant burdens due to cost of their housing (Joint Center for Housing Studies, 2019). These costs create precarious housing situations for older adults.

Housing cost burdens, in addition to cultural practice and preference, contribute to the large number multigenerational households in the United States, particularly among immigrant families, including mixed-status households that contain both US citizens and undocumented residents. As discussed in Chapter 11, immigration enforcement and anti-immigrant attitudes have increased the possibility of detention and deportation of family members who provide economic support for both their older parents and their children. The social and economic disruption resulting from deportation contributes to housing insecurity (Warren & Kerwin, 2017).

Innovative Solutions
The growing number of very old people who are aging alone without a family network for support, and the availability and affordability of different housing options in both rural and urban areas, are areas of concern that require creative solutions and assistance from both government and the private sector (Stone, 2018). People without a strong support network may need help from paid or formal care. The challenge for older adults living alone is there may be no one to notice when something goes wrong.

Many older adults cannot afford options such as continuing care communities or they are not satisfied with the lifestyle that these options provide. Over the past several decades, older adults and their entrepreneurial and creative allies have devised innovative solutions that meet the needs for autonomy and support for people as they age. Still, a particular challenge is meeting the needs of low-income seniors.

Age-Friendly Communities
The Age-Friendly Community Initiative focuses on ways to improve the social and physical environments of neighborhoods to contribute to health and well-being and allow people to remain in their communities (Greenfield et al., 2015). Over 400 communities in the United States have made commitments to actively work toward becoming "age-friendly" (AARP Livable Communities, 2020).

Villages
"Villages" are consumer-driven membership organizations that rely on both volunteers and paid help to provide a variety of services and activities in cities such as Boston, Denver, and Las Vegas and smaller towns and rural areas across the United States. They are a promising model for helping people age in place, though it is unclear if they can address the extensive health and social service needs of people who are more frail and more isolated. Village members are predominantly white and female (Stone, 2013). Englewood Village in Chicago serves a community that is predominantly African American and where over half of the residents live below the poverty line. It provides one example of how the model has been adapted in different communities (Jaffe, 2017).

LGBT 65+ Housing Initiatives
Awareness of the needs of LGBT persons who are 65+ for housing options and communities that respond to their unique issues has increased over the past several decades. Earlier in life, these individuals often hid their sexual orientation or gender

identity due to fear and stigmatization. Many were victims of harassment and violence. Even though society is more open and accepting, many LGBT persons have experienced renewed discrimination as they look for housing to meet their aging-related needs, and they fear mistreatment in residential settings. Several housing initiatives focused on LGBT 65+ adults have emerged because they lack access to housing options that are affirming and nondiscriminatory and that also meet individual needs for care. Providers of housing initiatives noted the need for safe spaces and opportunities for community engagement and social support and that there is a limited capacity of LGBT-friendly residential settings aimed at 65+ adults (Ranahan, 2017).

Home Sharing

Some persons who wish to continue to live independently take in boarders or participate in home sharing programs that match them with persons who need affordable housing. The experience can be mixed. At worst, some boarders exploit or abuse the older persons with whom they live (Portacolone, 2017); at best, they provide companionship that reduces loneliness and increases well-being and safety. Other benefits include assistance with daily living and valuable intergenerational exchanges. Potential challenges include loss of privacy and control, the older person's discomfort with the boarder's substance abuse or mental health challenges, differing standards of cleanliness, and communication about cultural differences. Arrangements facilitated by third parties such as community-based agencies help with communication around rules and expectations (Martinez et al., 2020).

Communal Living

Other communal living arrangements offer solutions to isolation and the need for acceptance. Woody (2016) describes plans for a friendly and accepting communal living space for "lesbian, gay, bisexual, transgender, queer and same gender-loving (LGBTQ/SGL) older persons" who are in living situations where they do not feel welcome (p. 108). This model, known as Mary's House, will provide single rooms plus shared common areas for 65+ adults who are independent but can benefit from organized wellness activities, transportation, and help in accessing community services.

Intergenerational Programming and Communities

Intergenerational programming that brings residents together with children, youth, and university students through arts activities, tutoring, or service activities is one promising means to reduce social isolation and provide meaningful activities for residents while at the same time promoting understanding and reducing ageism among younger generations (Generations United and Leading Age, 2017). Bridge Meadows in Oregon is an example of an intentionally created intergenerational community that provides housing and support for 65+ adults and families with foster children. The older adults who live in the housing complex agree to mentor or support the children for a set number of hours per month; they also receive help with daily tasks from the children's parents (Beato, 2013). All residents are expected to participate in community activities. Box 8.2 addresses innovative intergenerational living arrangements that focus on nursing homes and assisted living.

BOX 8.2 Innovative Intergenerational Living

In 2012, Gea Sijpkes, director of Humanitas, a home for 160 older adults in Deventer, the Netherlands, allowed Onno Selbach, a university student, to move in. This was a unique response to externally created needs and a vision of better long-term care for older adults. In 2012, the Dutch government restricted eligibility for funding for long-term care to adults over the age of 80 who had an urgent care need, thus reducing the demand for the long-term care homes such as Humanitas. As a result, Humanitas decided to focus on what the residents can do, what they want, and their happiness, as opposed to simply caring for them.

Selbach's only guidelines were that he had to organize one meal per week and spend time with the residents. Sijpkes managed the concerns of family, staff, and board members and eventually expanded the program to six students. The benefits of having young adults among the residents began to emerge. The residents appreciated how their presence made Humanitas a livelier and more joyful place. They enjoyed the companionship of the students. Hearing about their lives (and romances) gave them topics of conversation and helped them reminisce about their younger years. Residents became less preoccupied with matters such as doctors' appointments, medications, and the losses that are part of aging (Arentshorst, Kloet, & Peine, 2019).

Judson Manor, an assisted living center in Cleveland, Ohio, undertook a similar program. Students from the nearby Cleveland Institute of Music live rent free in exchange for providing free concerts for the residents. Many friendships have formed between students and some of the residents, who appreciate their presence (Jansen, 2015).

These programs offer a way to think about how to "open up" segregated, institutionalized settings into places where intergenerational relationships can be formed, grow, and flourish. Programs that bring college students together with older adults can generate ideas for other programs that meet community needs and that encourage a view of aging that focuses on quality of life as much as quality of care.

Housing for Low-Income Older Adults

Rental units financed by the US Department of Housing and Urban Development (HUD) that provide affordable housing for older adults with low incomes are another option in some communities. Some buildings are restricted to residents aged 62 and older, while other publicly funded housing supports people who have aged in place. HUD finances service coordinators who "provide supportive services and wellness programming on a voluntary basis to older adults with various social and health care needs" (Stone, 2018, p. 232).

Continuing Care Retirement Communities

Continuing care retirement communities (CCRCs) provide an option for older adults with financial resources who wish to live in a setting that can provide for them as their needs change as they age. CCRCs, which sometimes have affiliations with religious denominations, offer independent living units such as apartments or cottages, assisted living, and skilled nursing care in one location. Some of these communities also provide units for specialized dementia care. Average entrance fees of $329,000 plus monthly fees of $2,000–$4,000 per month make this option unaffordable for most older adults; however, some CCRC's run on a rental model where rents are between $3,000 and $6,000 per month for independent living units (AARP, 2019). Some CCRC's have been developed to specially meet the needs of the LGBT community; an example is Stonewall Gardens in Palm Springs, California (Gallagher, 2020).

Assisted Living Facilities

People may move to assisted living when they can no longer safely function independently. Assisted living, which is regulated by individual states, provides housing, personal care services, and healthcare to individuals who need help with daily activities but who do not need 24/7 skilled nursing care. Assisted living facilities vary in size, cost, and services offered, which include group meals, assistance with medication management, recreational services, and transportation, among other things. Board and care homes are smaller homes in residential areas that have been adapted for the needs of a small number of residents (e.g., between 2 and 10), while larger facilities can serve a greater number of residents (National Institute on Aging, 2017).

Supportive Housing

Supportive housing, developed in the 1970s, combines the complex housing and services needs of people who are aging with physical, cognitive, and developmental disabilities. It offers an alternative to the residential institutions where many people with disabilities used to age.

Table 8.1 summarizes supportive housing options in terms of type of housing, ownership, the funder, the level of services provided, and who gets paid to provide services. This helps us think about options for those aging with any type of disability, no matter when the onset occurred (Koenig, 2015).

Nursing Homes

Nursing homes provide long-term, formal care for less than 5 percent of aged 65+ adults. While many provide short-term care for rehabilitation, they are home for the majority who live there. Many nursing homes have an institutional rather than a home-like atmosphere. The Federal Nursing Home Reform Act of 1987 set forth minimum standards of care and legal rights for residents. Although the legislation highlighted the importance of person-centered care, it resulted in structured procedures for ensuring patient health and safety rather than prizing choice, dignity, and purposeful daily living (Fagan, 2013). An additional challenge is that the quality of care provided by nursing homes can vary by factors including for-profit or not-profit status, the percentage of residents who receive Medicaid, and the racial and ethnic makeup of the residents.

Table 8.1 Supportive Housing Options Matrix

Housing Type	Housing Ownership	Housing Funder	Service Funder	Service Level	Service Provider
House	Single-family	Individual	Individual	Call-in	Family
Apartment	Condo	Family	Family	Weekly	Roommate
Group Home	Joint ownership	Donors	Donors	Part-time daily	Neighbor
Shared Apartment	Rental	Agency	Agency	Full-time daily	Volunteers
Room	Organization	Bank	State	24 hour daily	Nonprofit
Dormitory	Government	Government	Federal	48 FTE	Government

Source: Koenig, 2015.

Most older adults are reluctant to enter nursing home care due to concerns about loss of autonomy and concern that they will receive poor quality care and are being abandoned by their families.

Advocates to improve nursing home care for older adults have offered innovative solutions to change the culture of care. This **culture change movement** has raised awareness of the highly regimented and misery-inducing atmosphere of some nursing homes, where adherence to schedules is prized, turnover of staff is frequent, and problems such as poor-quality care and even risk for abuse and neglect are not uncommon. The culture change movement shifted the thinking to highlight the "home" rather than the "nursing" aspect of nursing homes (Koren, 2010).

The Pioneer Network and the Green House Model are examples of the culture change movement. The Pioneer Network, established in 1997, focuses on leadership, education, and public policy advocacy to encourage long-term care models that practice flexibility in provision of care and foster self-determination for residents. It advocates change from a medical, institutional model of elder care to one that prizes empowerment and self-determination to make life more humane and meaningful for older adults even when they can no longer live independently (Fagan, 2013). This movement addresses ageism by encouraging meaningful roles for people into their eighth and ninth decades and beyond. The Pioneer Network strives to create nursing homes that treat people as unique individuals, rather than diseases and conditions to be managed (Fagan, 2013).

The Green House Model divides nursing homes into "households" of 8–12 residents (referred to as "elders") and self-managed teams of certified nursing assistants who manage the daily operation of the household. The model fosters dignity and self-determination by prioritizing resident preferences for how they spend their time and allowing for more freedom of movement and choice in, for example, when they wake up, what they eat, and how and when they bathe. Like other models of culture change, the Green House model, requires changes in a nursing home's physical environment, organizational development, and psychosocial practices that can be difficult to sustain without supportive leadership (Fagan, 2013).

While the culture change efforts are laudable, relatively few nursing homes have made the significant changes recommended by this movement, and quality of care across nursing homes remains uneven (Fagan, 2013).

COVID-19 and Long-Term Care Facilities

Residents of long-term care facilities and their families were significantly affected by the COVID-19 pandemic. Although data are not complete, as of spring 2021, about 8 percent of residents of US long-term care facilities had died from the virus. In US nursing homes, nearly 10 percent of residents died because of COVID-19 (COVID Tracking Project, 2021).

Due to concerns about the spread of infection and the disease's disproportionate impact on older adults, congregate care ranging from independent living to skilled nursing care had to employ strict procedures. Family members and other visitors were not allowed to see residents for many months, and efforts to help them maintain contact via telephone or tablets were difficult to implement in many facilities due to lack of access to proper equipment and shortage of staff who could facilitate virtual visits.

Facilities had to develop procedures for isolating residents who were infected. Recreational and therapeutic activities were also curtailed (Centers for Disease Control and Prevention, 2020a).

LIVING ARRANGEMENTS OF VULNERABLE POPULATIONS

Aging often confers new challenges and vulnerabilities on people who are dealing with situations that for some have been lifelong. We need to understand and address the needs of aging prisoners, older victims of domestic violence, and homeless older adults, among others, whose challenges are tied to their living arrangements. The growth of the population of adults over the age of 65, and the increase in the numbers of people who are 85 and older, means that service systems (discussed in Chapter 9) encounter these challenges daily.

Older Adults in Prison

About 180,000 of the incarcerated persons in the United States are age 55 or older. Between 2007 and 2010, the population of prisoners aged 65 and older in the United States grew 94 times faster than the total population of sentenced persons (Human Rights Watch, 2012). As a result, prisons must address age-related healthcare needs, which include Alzheimer's disease and other dementias as well as conditions such as cancer, heart disease, diabetes, and frailty. Many prisons are not equipped to meet needs of older adults who have difficulty with the regimentation and restrictions of prison life and the need for care and protection in a stressful, harsh, and dangerous environment where older persons are often victimized (Maschi, Viola, & Sun, 2012).

People growing older in prison often experience "accelerated aging," and declining health conditions at an earlier age. Caring for older prisoners with extensive medical needs is expensive for state budgets. Compassionate release policies allow people to be discharged into the community before the end of their sentence if they are sick or dying. However, only a fraction of older prisoners benefits from these policies because of the public's reluctance to release people who have committed serious crimes, even if they are so ill their imprisonment no longer serves a purpose of deterrence, retribution, incapacitation, or rehabilitation (Human Rights Watch, 2012). Some nursing homes will not take those who are released, and no family members are available to care for them.

Older Victims of Domestic Abuse

Older victims of domestic abuse at times need to alter their living arrangements, whether on a permanent or temporary basis. Older women may be "invisible" as victims and survivors of intimate partner abuse, and they are not particularly well-served by either the domestic violence or the adult protective services system (Crockett, Brandl, & Dabby, 2015), They may be reluctant to use shelters for abuse victims where they must live with younger women and their children (Beaulaurier, Seff, & Newman, 2008). A movement to develop shelters for victims of elder abuse has gained momentum over the past decade. Shelter programs, while not yet widely available, are often housed within long-term care settings, giving those settings added expertise on elder abuse that can serve all residents. These programs can buy time to address problems and devise safe and sustainable solutions to housing needs (Levin, Reingold, & Solomon, 2020).

Older Adults without Housing

In October 2019, four homeless men were murdered while sleeping on the streets of Chinatown in New York City. One was 83 years old (Sandoval et al., 2019). This gruesome story underscores the persistent problem of homelessness in the United States, its dangers, and the growing number of older adults who are homeless.

The geriatric homeless population (defined as those aged 50 and older) is very diverse. Reasons for homelessness can be a combination of medical, economic, political, and social factors. Some older persons have lifelong persistent mental health, substance abuse, and health issues that have contributed to instability throughout their lives and have "aged into" their homeless status (Harvie & Rumore, 2018). Others are homeless due to unemployment or unavailability of affordable housing. Loss of employment in late middle age can result in loss of medical coverage and even bankruptcy, from which it is difficult to recover (Gass et al., 2018).

Some individuals are homeless for the first time in later life. Those who have lived "on the edge" for much of their lives may be better equipped to cope with homelessness than those for whom a cascading series of events in late life led to their homeless status (Burns & Sussman, 2018). Bruder (2017) describes adults in their 50s and 60s who live in RVs or campers and migrate from one area of the country to another doing seasonal labor such as harvesting crops or working in Amazon warehouses, for low wages and few benefits. Some lost their permanent housing due to foreclosures during the Great Recession in 2008.

Shelters and other transitional housing arrangements often are not suitable for the older persons without housing. Shelters can increase distress and restrict autonomy (Finlay et al., 2020). For example, a shelter that relies on providing employment services/vocational training cannot help a person in their eighth decade who can no longer work. Programs that provide transitional care assume a transition to independence that is not possible for an older person who requires extra services. Assisted living facilities may resist taking formerly homeless individuals with substance abuse or mental health problems (Harvie & Rumore, 2018). Clearly, being unhoused compounds the challenges of the aging process.

Figure 8.5 Older unhoused man sleeping on the street
Source: APIWAN BORRIKONRATCHATA/Shutterstock

CHAPTER REVIEW

Housing and Care Options for Older Adults
- The quality of family relationships significantly influences how people experience older age.

Aging in Place
- Where people live reflects their needs and values and influences their quality of life as they age.
- Aging in place is the ability of people to age in their own home and community safely, independently, and comfortably and reflects both values and goals about where people should live as they age.

Theories and Approaches to Place and Aging
- Theories of environmental and geographical gerontology provide important information about the impact of multiple levels of the environment including home and neighborhood on how people age.

Older Adults in Urban and Rural Environments
- While most older adults live in urban areas, rural areas contain a higher percentage of older adults.
- Residential options and services for older adults are limited in rural areas.

The Importance of Neighborhoods
- Urban neighborhoods that are walkable, accessible, resource-rich, and safe support efforts to age in place while unsafe and resource-poor neighborhoods create obstacles to maintaining independence.

Housing Options for Older Adults
- The range of living options available for older adults depends upon whether they have resources.
- While most older adults live independently in single-family homes or apartments in the community, others reside in congregate housing such as assisted living and nursing homes.

Living Arrangements of Vulnerable Populations
- Older adults who are incarcerated, victims of domestic violence, or unhoused require special consideration from service systems.

REVIEW QUESTIONS
1. What are benefits and drawbacks to aging in place? What are some considerations to consider when an older adult is considering a move?
2. Compare and contrast environmental gerontology and geographical gerontology.
3. Describe features of urban neighborhoods that support aging in place.
4. What are important features of housing for older adults who need assistance and support due to declining health and mobility?

KEY TERMS

- long-term care
- nursing homes
- assisted living
- activities of daily living
- instrumental activities of daily living
- independent living
- continuum of care
- aging in place
- ethnography
- elder orphans
- environmental gerontology
- agency
- environmental press
- geographical gerontology
- naturally occurring retirement communities
- gentrification
- continuing care retirement community
- supportive housing
- culture change movement

CHAPTER 9

Community Resources and Connectedness

Chapter Outline
The Importance of Connection
    Defining Community
    Community Resources
    Self-Determination and Social Usefulness
    Social Connection and Social Isolation
Religious and Spiritual Communities
    Spiritual Practices
    Benefits of Religious and Spiritual Involvement
Recreation and Community Involvement
    Sports and Fitness
    Travel
    The Arts
    Volunteer Work
    Socializing in Third Places
Healthcare Services
    Access to Healthcare
    Primary Care
    Geriatricians
    Age-Friendly Healthcare
    Treatment Programs
Social Services for Older Adults and Their Families
    Prevention Services
    Adult Day Care
    In-Home Personal Care
    Protective Services
    Support Services
    Resource Brokerage and Linkage

Learning Objectives

After completing this chapter, you will be able to:

- Articulate concepts and theories related to community, social connection, and social isolation.
- Describe older adults' participation in religious and spiritual communities.
- Explain how recreational activities and community involvement serve as a source of support and social connection for older adults.
- Define health and describe the continuum of healthcare services available to older adults.
- Describe the continuum of social services for older adults and their families.

Because of the importance of connectedness across the life course, we must recognize the variety of ways in which older adults are connected to their communities. As they age, people draw upon a variety of community resources. They also desire meaningful ways to be socially active and engaged in community activities (Szanton et al., 2016).

This chapter addresses the many ways in which people access support and nurture connections. We'll discuss older adults' participation in religious and spiritual communities and their involvement in recreation and hobbies, from sedentary to active. We'll explore how older adults interact with the healthcare system and the social services and other resources available to older adults and their families. This chapter will also highlight innovative programs and activities that provide support, belonging, and sustenance for the diverse 65+ population.

THE IMPORTANCE OF CONNECTION

The nature and quality of social relationships that older adults establish and maintain as they move through the life course shapes their experience of aging. People need support from their families and communities, and they must be able to develop new connections and sources of support to address issues such as loss and isolation.

Defining Community

A precise definition of **community** is hard to pin down. One definition is "a group of people with diverse characteristics who are linked by social ties, share common perspectives, and engage in joint action in geographical locations or settings" (MacQueen et al., 2001, p. 1929). Throughout life, people belong to multiple communities that are based on geographical location, on social networks of people with shared interests, or a combination of the two (Greenfield et al., 2018). For example, churches and other religious organizations share a physical space (a building or meeting location) but are also comprised of multiple social networks.

Neighborhoods that can provide a sense of community and well-being help people age in place. Urban neighborhoods for healthy aging in place have plentiful resources including public transportation, community centers, parks, libraries, and well-maintained public spaces such as sidewalks (Mather & Scommegna, 2017). These characteristics support people of all ages, but as discussed in Chapter 8, as people reach their seventh, eighth, and ninth decades, their immediate surroundings and the local community take on more importance.

Communities based on shared interests or other common characteristics provide a sense of identity. Throughout the twenty-first century, the importance and influence of virtual communities, such as those established on social media, has increased, and has in some cases replaced face-to-face interactions (Greenfield et al., 2018).

Community gerontology is a framework that aids our understanding of communities as essential **mezzo-level** settings for the diversity of experiences people have as they age (Greenfield et al., 2018). This framework views individuals, families, and small groups (the **micro-level** setting) as embedded in communities that may have lasting impact on health and well-being. Smaller groups also influence quality of communities; for instance, older adults who regularly gather in locations such coffee shops help make a neighborhood more supportive and conducive to well-being. Communities are in turn immersed in **macro-level** social contexts (e.g., government at all levels; regional, national, and global issues; and social forces) that shape resources such as health and social services available at the local level.

Community Resources

Community resources can strengthen connectedness among residents across the life course. Ideally, the resources available for the older members of a community also counteract the powerful forces of ageism and other "isms" that affect older adults. Ageism leads us to think of older people as a homogeneous group with similar—and stereotyped—needs and services. We need to expand our thinking about what people need and value and about what provides social connection for a diverse population of older adults. For example, do older adults need and want intergenerational or age-segregated opportunities? Or both, each at various times?

The principles underlying services and supports for older adults are connected to values (anti-ageism, inclusion, mutual aid, protection for vulnerable citizens, opportunities for growth, freedom to participate or not participate) related to being connected. As we work with older adults, we limit our thinking if we only consider help they may need. Individuals and communities should also consider what people gain from being connected as part of a community.

Self-Determination and Social Usefulness

Self-determination theory addresses the need for relatedness (connection to others), autonomy (the ability to make decisions for oneself), and competence (the feeling that one can accomplish one's goals) while promoting the well-being of others (Gottlieb & Sevigny, 2016). This theory provides a framework for "appreciating why and how older adults internalize socially useful identities and benefit from expression of their social usefulness" (p. 337).

People often gain a sense of vitality and confidence while serving others. The concept of **social usefulness** explains why older adults seek connections, such as volunteer work that promotes the well-being of others. Older adults want to be needed, welcomed, and validated for who they are and the work they do. These connections contribute to the sense that they are leaving a legacy (Gottlieb & Sevigny, 2016).

Social Connection and Social Isolation

Social connections to others strongly influence people's health and longevity. Social isolation, loneliness, and poor social relationships can increase the risk of harmful outcomes including health problems, dementia, depression, and death (Holt-Lunstad, 2017, 2018).

Community identity and resources can contribute to resilience (the ability to deal with the difficulties in life) as people age (Kwong, Du, & Xu, 2015). For example, healthcare providers and staff can potentially identify social isolation and loneliness in healthcare settings (National Academies of Sciences Engineering and Medicine, 2020). While isolation can be debilitating throughout the life course, it is especially dangerous for older adults who do not have the support of family or others. Ideally, community resources can help even the most socially isolated older adults.

The COVID-19 pandemic shed light on the power of informal resources and informal networks to help people in times of need (see Box 9.1). Stay-at-home orders, quarantines, and social distancing physically isolated many people while attempting to protect them from infection. Many, especially those living alone, were separated from activities that made them feel connected, such as attending religious services, going to restaurants and coffee shops, and gathering with friends. In some neighborhoods and communities, the pandemic prompted informal efforts to address the impact of isolation. For example, residents of apartment buildings started checking on one another. Neighbors recognized that their older neighbors were alone and worked to get groceries delivered to those who could not or would not go out.

The most socially isolated older adults face barriers to accessing and using community resources in some communities. The social and physical environments of certain neighborhoods, particularly those in low-income areas, create obstacles. For example, a study of older adults in Richmond, California, found that participants were fearful of leaving their residence due to drug trafficking, violence, or other criminal activity. Unsafe and unsanitary conditions and buildings in disrepair keep visitors and service providers away. These are some of the challenges facing vulnerable older adults (Portacolone, Perissinotto et al., 2018).

Figure 9.1 Socially distanced visit during the pandemic
Source: Piksel/Shutterstock

BOX 9.1   COVID-19 and the Technology Divide

The COVID-19 pandemic highlighted both the need for community and the micro- and macro-level influences on community. Many older people communicated with family, friends, and social groups through online platforms only; virtual participation in communities using video conferencing and social networking accelerated. Technology reduced social isolation and maintained connections. However, some older adults lacked access to technology and internet, or their physical or cognitive conditions (e.g., hearing loss or dementia) precluded their use of technology. The divide between technology "haves" and "have-nots" had serious consequences during the pandemic and continues to affect access to resources and social connections (Graham, 2020). Improving access to technology and the internet can be addressed through macro-level interventions, such a city providing free or low-cost internet access to its citizens, which would in turn strengthen community ties.

RELIGIOUS AND SPIRITUAL COMMUNITIES

Religious and spiritual communities are important resources. **Religion** refers to organized and institutional traditions of faith and worship, while **spirituality**, described as a sense of connection to other beings, the universe, or something sacred or larger than oneself, involves people's search for what holds meaning for them (Peteet, Al Zaben, & Koenig, 2019). **Faith**, a related concept, is strong belief in and relationship with God or a higher power and is often associated with the doctrines, traditions, and values of a specific religion (Victor & Treschuk, 2020).

Religious communities and institutions (churches, synagogues, mosques, and other religious organizations) provide both resources and a sense of connectedness for many older adults and may increase in importance as people age. The Religious Landscape Study of 35,000 adults provides an overview of religious involvement in American life (Pew Research Center, 2015a). In the United States, most adults affiliated with a religion are Christians, with the majority identifying as Evangelical Protestants, Catholics, or mainline Protestants. Adults affiliated with non-Christian religious traditions (Jewish, Muslim, Buddhist, Hindu, and others) are a smaller group (5.9 percent) than those who are unaffiliated with any religious group (22.8 percent). The subset of "religious nones" had grown to 26 percent by 2018 and is projected to continue its increase (Pew Research Center, 2019b).

The religious landscape study found that 48 percent of 65+ adults attend religious services at least once per week (Pew Research Center, 2015a). While Christianity is the most dominant religious tradition in the United States, the diversity of beliefs and religious institutions has increased. Being actively affiliated (attending at least once a month) with a religious group is linked to higher levels of civic engagement (voting in elections and participation in community groups, charity groups, and labor unions) (Pew Research Center, 2019a).

Adults aged 65 and older are more likely than other age groups to attend religious services at least once a week, to participate in other religious activities (prayer and study groups), and to say that religion is very important to them. Table 9.1 compares importance of religion and attendance at religious services and participation in other religious activities by race and ethnicity. The US population has become less religious

Table 9.1 Importance of Religion and Participation in Religious Activities by Race and Ethnicity (Adults 18 and older)

Race/Ethnicity	% who state religion is "very important"	% attending religious services at least once a week	% participating in religious activities
White	49%	34%	22%
Black	75%	47%	39%
Asian	36%	26%	17%
Latino	59%	39%	27%
Mixed/Other	54%	34%	26%

Source: Pew Research Center, 2015a.

over time, and the number of US adults who do not identify with any organized religion is growing. This suggests that religion may take on less importance as currently middle-aged and younger adults grow older. However, patterns of involvement may change as people age (Pew Research Center, 2015a).

Spiritual Practices

Many older adults who do not adhere to a particular religious tradition regularly engage in spiritual practices such as meditation, yoga, or tai chi alone and with the support of community resources such as health clubs, community centers, and informal groups. If current trends continue, the number of people 65+ who identify themselves as not affiliated with a particular religion will continue to grow, and many will still engage in spiritual practices (Pew Research Center, 2015a). What remains to be seen is whether the diminishment of connections to a formal religious community will correspond with increasing social isolation or whether people will find different communities with which to connect.

Figure 9.2 An outdoor yoga class
Source: Fat Camera/iStock

Benefits of Religious and Spiritual Involvement
Religious and spiritual involvement support health and well-being as people move into the later decades of their lives. "More often than not, people experience positive benefits from their faith" (Faigin & Pargament, 2010, p. 165). People use religious resources to promote self-efficacy (belief in one's ability to succeed in a particular situation) and to cope with losses later in life. Actively participating in a religious community is "vital involvement" that promotes social commitment and community engagement and contributes to health in later life (Woźniak, 2015).

Studies of the meaning and impact of religious involvement among various US population groups illustrate how it serves as a community resource for older adults. One study that examined differences among older white, Black, and Asian Christians in the United States conceptualized religious involvement as "spiritual connectedness" provided by membership in a religious community (Lee & Zhang, 2018, p. 323). Spiritual connectedness is a meaningful measure of religiosity for older adults who are no longer able to attend church activities due to functional limitations. This study found that spiritual connectedness reduced the negative effects of functional limitations such as depression on Black Christians but not on white or Asian Christians. When compared with whites, Asians reported more frequent church attendance but lower levels of spiritual connectedness, and higher levels of functional limitations and depression. Within ethnic groups, such as Chinese Americans, migration status also plays a role in the degree of religious involvement, such as church attendance, and the impact of that involvement, which may include help with feelings of displacement from their countries of origin (Lee & Zhang, 2018).

The strong connections between religious involvement and health and psychological well-being result from three factors (Woźniak, 2015):

- *A sense of coherence and predictability* in times of serious illness and crisis. Prayer and other religious rituals give people tools for navigating a crisis.
- *A sense of personal control and empowerment.* Especially for those experiencing loss of functional abilities (e.g., diminished mobility, hearing, and eyesight), the religious community can provide both active support and ways of interpreting their circumstances that help them feel more hopeful when dealing with losses associated with age.
- *A supportive community and forgiveness.* Religious organizations often provide support for members, such as providing meals for bereaved families or outreach to people who are homebound. They help people adopt positive behaviors and provide spiritual support and counseling. Affirmations about forgiveness can help people cope with the negative effects of guilt about fractured relationships, regret about choices made, and resentments that have accumulated over their life course (Woźniak, 2015).

RECREATION AND COMMUNITY INVOLVEMENT
Adults engage in a wide variety of recreational and community activities that foster connectedness, well-being, optimism, and personal growth as they age (Heo et al., 2017). Many people engage in the activities they have enjoyed throughout their lives, such as sports and fitness activities, travel, involvement in the arts, and volunteer work.

In retirement, older adults may explore new interests and activities. Differences in income and available resources, personal preferences, cultural expectations, health status, caregiving responsibilities, and ageism help determine the types of recreational activities that people prefer and to which they have access. Adults aged 65+ participating in recreational activities that some would consider them "too old" to do offers narratives that counter assumptions about age-related decline.

Sports and Fitness
Older adults participate in a range of sports and fitness activities that are beneficial for both social connections and health. Some engage in vigorous pursuits such as surfing, triathlons, body building and mountain climbing. These older adults resist stereotypes and counter the idea of inevitable frailty in later life. There is a risk that these examples further shape stereotypes by setting up expectations that people should be able to do anything they set their mind to, ignoring the realities of aging-related losses in muscle strength and endurance that affect many individuals. In addition, poor health and loss of social networks can interfere with continued athletic participation. Social and financial constraints, as well as the lack of community recreational resources, can also hinder involvement in health-promoting activities.

Participation in activities such as team sports and group exercise increases life satisfaction, optimism, and social integration (Ryu et al. Heo, 2018). For example, numerous retirement communities are built around golf courses. Regular golfing has been shown to lower risk of stroke, heart attacks, and early mortality (American Heart Association, 2020), and golf provides a pleasant experience and sense of community (Stenner, Mosewich, & Buckley, 2020). However, although public golf courses exist, access to golfing is reserved for those with resources to play at mostly private courses and clubs where costs are high.

In many cities and towns, community centers, YMCAs, and senior centers offer a variety of fitness activities based on age group and/or fitness levels. Many gyms and health clubs have members aged 65+, and many parks and recreation departments and community fitness centers make efforts to engage and involve older adults in organized sports and leisure activities. For example, pickleball, which is easily learned and less physically strenuous than tennis, has gained popularity among older adults, and communities have responded by building courts and designing programs (Ryu et al., 2018). Other activities such as yoga, Pilates, and tai chi have also become popular.

Older women may benefit from the sense of accomplishment and the camaraderie offered by participation in team sports such as softball. However, some must overcome constraints such as lack of confidence or caregiving responsibilities to participate. Communities must address structural constraints to participation in team sports that may include a shortage of facilities and resources when teams for older adults "compete" with other age groups in securing places to play (West et al., 2019).

The desire to maintain health and well-being and give back to the community, along with entrepreneurship, can help diverse community members. Peggy Howard Moore, an African American woman, trained as a yoga teacher in her 60s. Moore and her daughter developed a yoga studio in Chicago that intentionally welcomes all members of the community, including those who are 65+ and people of color, and offers free classes to the community (Moore, 2017).

People enjoy a wide variety of activities throughout their lives and into their later years. Other people take up new sporting activities as they make life transitions such as retirement or when they want to feel less isolated. Those who work with older adults must be aware of and address the individual, interpersonal, and structural constraints to participation in activities.

Travel

Many 65+ adults travel on their own and in organized tours. Road Scholar (formerly called Elderhostel) is a nonprofit educational travel organization for 50+ adults that offers trips and educational programs all over the world. These programs are categorized based on ability level, not age. Road Scholar also offers tours aimed at grandparents and grandchildren and offers Caregiver Grants to provide travel experiences as respite for family caregivers (Moses, 2018). "Voluntourists" travel to work on projects such as building homes for low-income individuals through organizations such as Habitat for Humanity or conservation-related activities such as repairing facilities and refurbishing trails in state and national parks (Horngren, 2016).

Some travel independently, while others forge connections and community on a more informal basis. Some people who travel in their recreational vehicles (RVs) do seasonal work in agriculture or campgrounds or work in warehouses during the holidays to supplement their retirement savings (Farrell, 2016). Some are economically dependent upon this way of living. A portion of this group lost jobs and sometimes their homes in their 40s or 50s, and now travel across the country, staying at RV campsites and supporting themselves by doing seasonal labor (Bruder, 2017).

The Arts

Involvement in the music, theater, and other creative and artistic endeavors adds joy and meaning to life and fosters connection. Both receptive (e.g., as an audience member) and participatory engagement in the arts are associated with short- and long-term well-being in that they help people stay engaged in the community and to deal with age-related change and loss (Tymoszuk et al., 2020). Regular attendance at concerts and the theater and frequent visits to museums are associated with long-term well-being, though access to these activities requires personal interest, financial resources, and community availability (Tymoszuk et al., 2020). Active engagement in dance, expressive writing, music, theater, and the visual arts promotes a sense of well-being, contributes to cognitive health, motivates, and provides social support (Noice, Noice, & Kramer, 2014).

Many people actively participate in music programs, theater performances, and the visual arts. Regularly making music, especially playing a musical instrument, may help prevent cognitive decline (Mansens, Deeg, & Comijs, 2018). Some formal programs are intergenerational, and some are established specifically for older people. Both professional and amateur musicians, actors, and artists continue to engage in their lifelong vocations well into their eighth and ninth decades. These programs provide connections in the community, foster well-being, and combat age-based and other stereotypes. Organizations in cities, the suburbs, and small towns sponsor programs; resources of money, time, and talent vary by community. For example, EngAGE provides residents of apartment communities in California, Oregon, and Minnesota with free programming for active participation in theater, visual arts, music performance, and other forms of creative expression. This program benefits a primarily low-income and racially and ethnically diverse group of older adults (average age 77) (EngAGE, 2020).

Music programs such as orchestras or choral groups provide a means for creative expression and build upon community resources. The Young@Heart Chorus in Northampton, Massachusetts for adults aged 70+ began in 1982 in a senior housing project. Now, people from across the community participate. The group performs a wide repertoire of music styles several times per year. Their performances (and a 2008 documentary film) counter ageist stereotypes (Partners for Livable Communities, 2020). Intergenerational community orchestras and choruses offer children, college students, and adults of all ages ways to connect through a shared love of music; however, organizers need to encourage interaction across generations and offer structure that will ensure meaningful participation (Sutherland, 2018).

Many communities have arts programs that encourage older participants to both create and appreciate art. For example, the LGBTQ-friendly Hannan Center in Detroit, Michigan, a city which is 80 percent African American, provides classes in the visual arts and exhibition space for a diverse group of 65+ adults. Art classes and visits to art museums also foster connection and community for individuals living with mild cognitive impairment or dementia and their caregivers (Lamar & Luke, 2016).

Figure 9.3 Many older adults enjoy creative arts such as pottery
Source: BGStock72/Shutterstock

Volunteer Work

Many community-based organizations that provide social, educational, health-related, and recreational services depend on the work of volunteers. Almost one-quarter of those aged 65+ engage in some sort of formal volunteer work (US Bureau of Labor Statistics, 2016). Some older adults have volunteered throughout their lives, while others take up volunteer work as they transition into retirement. People most often volunteer for religious, educational, youth-service, or social and community service organizations (US Bureau of Labor Statistics, 2016). Some formal volunteer opportunities are connected with AmeriCorps Senior, a federal program that includes the Senior Companion program, Foster Grandparents, and RSVP, a network of volunteer programs (Americorps, 2020).

Outcomes of volunteering include higher self-rated health, increased life satisfaction, and reduced depression (Morrow-Howell, 2010), and it may have more positive effects than working or caregiving because it is "socially valued, publicly recognized, and more discretionary than working or caregiving" (p. 465). Volunteering may also be valuable as other social roles are lost, such as when people are widowed. The value of volunteering is connected to the type of work, the number of hours served, and the value of the connections made. Most research on older volunteers does not address dimensions of diversity including race, ethnicity, immigration status, disability, and institutionalization (Serrat et al., 2020). One study of volunteers for a Senior Companion Program highlights both the challenges (transportation, dealing with community emergencies, and family caregiving) and benefits (training, stress relief, and peer support and socialization) for culturally and linguistically diverse older adults (Cao et al., 2021).

Socializing in Third Places

Third places is a term coined by sociologist Ray Oldenburg (Butler & Diaz, 2016). It describes places where people socialize outside of home and work. Third places are locations such as neighborhood restaurants and coffee shops where people congregate and socialize, creating support and connections (Finlay, Gaugler, & Kane, 2020). Some choose these settings rather than age-segregated locations such as senior centers due to perceived ageism, heterosexism, language barriers, marginalization, or discrimination often associated with age-specific locations (Dunkle, 2018; McCarron et al., 2020; Torres & Cao, 2019).

HEALTHCARE SERVICES

Healthcare services are designed to diagnose and treat injury and disease and help people manage chronic conditions. The World Health Organization's (2020) definition of **health** as "a state of complete physical, mental and social well-being and not merely the absence of disease or infirmity" suggests a broad mandate for healthcare services. An even more inclusive definition of health adds the concept of "flourishing" to include purpose and meaning in life to view the concept of health more fully. The Flourishing Measure consists of questions (Table 9.2) in six domains that assess a range of factors that contribute to health (VanderWeele, McNeely, & Koh, 2019).

The diseases and functional impairments that accompany the aging process mean that people need more healthcare resources as they age, and adults 65+ are the largest consumers of healthcare services in the United States due to age-related needs and the

Table 9.2 Flourishing Measure and Questions

Domain	Question/Statement
Happiness	1. Overall, how satisfied are you with life as a whole these days?
	2. In general, how happy or unhappy do you generally feel?
Mental and physical health	3. In general, how would you rate your physical health?
	4. Overall, how would you rate your overall mental health?
Meaning and purpose	5. Overall, to what extent do you feel the things you do in your life are worthwhile?
	6. I understand my purpose in life.
Character	7. I always act to promote good in all circumstances, even in difficult and challenging situations.
	8. I am always able to give up some happiness now for greater happiness later.
Close social relationships	9. I am content with my friendships and relationships.
	10. My relationships are as satisfying as I would want them to be.
Financial stability	11. How often do you worry about meeting normal monthly living expenses?
	12. How often do you worry about safety, food, or housing?

Source: VanderWeele, McNeely, & Koh, 2019.

availability of Medicare (government-funded health insurance; see Chapter 12). Healthcare takes place in doctors' offices and outpatient clinics, hospitals, long-term care facilities, and in the home. The healthcare continuum ranges from preventive services to acute care to rehabilitative services in an **inpatient** setting. Some surgical procedures, diagnostic tests, and rehabilitative services such as physical therapy are provided on an **outpatient** basis. The challenges posed by the COVID-19 pandemic greatly expanded the use of **telemedicine**, which enables remote diagnosis and treatment using electronic communication (Mehrotra et al., 2020).

Many community-based services also promote health, prevent disease, and slow the progression of conditions such as osteoporosis or diabetes. Examples of preventive services are blood pressure checks, health fairs, and exercise and recreational activities. Communities provide emergency medical services (EMS) that respond to immediate health emergencies and address other health-related issues and potentially harmful situations. For example, EMS can make referrals to Adult Protective Services (see Chapter 6) in cases of self-neglect based on observations made in the home related to problems such as expired medications, empty refrigerators, signs of hoarding, or presence of vermin (Rosen et al., 2017).

Access to Healthcare

Access to regular, high-quality healthcare services helps people maintain their independence as they age. While most older adults access healthcare services regularly, internal and external constraints can impede access. Human services professionals' understanding of what health-related community resources exist, how they function and relate to each other, and who is eligible for the resources, helps ensure that people get the care they need.

While Medicare provides adults aged 65 and older with health insurance coverage, intersectional factors such as race, gender, sexual orientation, and immigration status affect whether people have adequate insurance or use healthcare services (Balakrishnan & Jordan, 2019; McCarron et al., 2020). Residents in rural areas may have to travel long distances to get to doctors' offices and hospitals. Overall, when compared to other countries, people in the United States have less access to primary care physicians and greater needs with respect to chronic, preventable health conditions such as hypertension and diabetes (Tikkanen & Abrams, 2020).

The Andersen model of healthcare utilization categorizes the barriers to and incentives for using formal healthcare resources into 1) predisposing characteristics; 2) enabling resources, and 3) need for services (Andersen, 1995). Predisposing characteristics include intersectional factors such as age, gender, education, occupation, and ethnicity in addition to health beliefs and psychological characteristics such as mental dysfunction or cognitive impairment. These characteristics influence how people determine when they should seek healthcare and where they should get it. Factors promoting access to care include personal knowledge, higher income, health insurance, and a regular source of care. Doctors' offices, clinics, and hospitals near the places where people live and work enable access, if people also have access to transportation (Lehning, Kim, & Dunkle, 2013). Under the Andersen framework, people are more likely seek help (meet needs) if their healthcare services address barriers related to predisposing factors such as language, accessibility, and knowledge of patients' culture and life circumstances.

Primary Care

Healthcare for older adults must often address complex care needs of multiple conditions that are exacerbated by factors related to living conditions, family situations, and availability of resources (Aronson, 2019). Ideally, individuals have a primary care physician who knows their medical history and coordinates their care. The **patient-centered medical home** is a model of care that focuses on making sure that people receive necessary care, coordinated by a primary care doctor (American College of Physicians, 2020). This model addresses overall well-being as much as treating specific conditions, and physicians and other staff recognize and address the nonmedical reasons that interfere with medical care. As a result of the Affordable Care Act (see Chapter 12), Medicare funds an annual wellness visit with a primary care provider during which a conversation about health history, health behaviors, and disease prevention can occur (Resnick, 2018).

Many older adults have their most consistent connection to formal community resources through their primary care physician's office. Good models of primary care practice involve home visits and emphasize keeping people in their own homes and avoiding hospitalization. Ideally, these practices can also address social issues, help with transitions to and from the hospital, and manage complex care needs. Practices vary with respect to whether they can provide this help and who (e.g., doctor, nurse practitioner, social worker) provides this help. Attention to these factors can help patients with multiple health problems achieve better outcomes (Donelan et al., 2019). Care coordination can be particularly challenging when the practice deals with a high proportion of patients who are dealing with social problems such as financial challenges, food and housing insecurity, family discord, or violence.

Geriatricians

Geriatricians are primary care doctors who have additional training and specialize in the care of older adults and the diseases and conditions that affect them. They are skilled in communicating with patients and families and working as part of an interdisciplinary team. Geriatricians provide holistic care that incorporates prevention and focuses on quality of life. These doctors practice across multiple settings (office, clinic, hospital, and long-term care) and can focus on difficulties that can arise during transitions in care. Geriatricians understand how normal, age-related physiological changes in organ systems interact with disease processes. They know how to address end-of-life issues through advance care planning and help patients understand the risks and benefits of medical interventions such as feeding tubes and ventilators. They also recognize cognitive decline, including distinguishing different types of dementia, which is critical in helping older adults and their caregivers make suitable plans for care needs (Lester, Dharmarajan, & Weinstein, 2019).

Unfortunately, due to ageism in the medical profession and the fact that geriatricians are among the poorest compensated group of physicians, there are fewer geriatricians today than 20 years ago, even as the number of people who are aged 85+ has increased dramatically (Lester et al., 2019). Most medical schools do not require students to take specialized courses in geriatrics, and some graduate from medical school with as few as twelve teaching sessions on older patients (Aronson, 2019).

A projected 19.6 million Americans aged 85+ will comprise 4.7 percent of the US population in 2060, up from 6.7 million and 2 percent of the population in 2020 (Vespa, Medina, & Armstrong, 2020). The increase in life expectancy, coupled with the US shortage in geriatricians and primary care physicians, has spurred advocates and organizations concerned about the quality of care to encourage older adults to advocate for themselves. Ideally, people are connected to a medical practice or primary care doctor who can recognize and address the nonmedical reasons that interfere with meeting healthcare needs.

Figure 9.4 A geriatrician and older patient
Source: Prostock-Studio/Shutterstock

Table 9.3 The 4Ms of Age-Friendly Care

The "M"	Characteristics of Care
What Matters	Healthcare providers encourage patients to share concerns, goals, wishes, needs, and life experiences.
Medication	Providers regularly review all medications prescribed to watch out for harmful interactions and side effects that may affect cognitive function, mobility, or quality of life.
Mentation	Providers discuss memory and mood to assess cognitive function and address dementia, depression, and other cognitive and mental health issues.
Mobility	Providers address the need for patients to stay active to maintain health and independence and to safely navigate their environment.

Source: John A. Hartford Foundation, 2020.

Age-Friendly Healthcare

By defining the essential elements of **age-friendly healthcare** the Age-Friendly Health Systems initiative gives people tools with which to communicate with their doctors about their needs and wants with respect to their care (John A. Hartford Foundation, 2020). This model (Table 9.3) advocates for healthcare providers who are skilled in listening and responding to the concerns, needs, and life experiences of those under their care, in addition to paying attention to medication, cognitive function, and mobility. Given the intersectional identities that are sometimes hidden from providers, this advice will improve care. For example, the growing group of transgender older adults are at risk that they will see providers who are unable (due to lack of knowledge or experience) or unwilling (due to religious objections) to provide healthcare services that will meet their needs, resulting in harm (Perone, 2020).

Treatment Programs

A number of programs provide treatment or intervention to resolve or ameliorate problem situations such as alcohol or drug addiction or mental health issues. Treatment services include inpatient and outpatient health services and long-term care provided in residential facilities. Older adults may continue to receive services for lifelong mental health challenges or may receive treatment to address problems that arise in association with the aging process.

SOCIAL SERVICES FOR OLDER ADULTS AND THEIR FAMILIES

Social services for older adults address a continuum of needs. The programs and agencies created to help people navigate life as they age are collectively known as the **aging network**, which is "an approach that seeks to balance national standards, a consistent structure, and core services with opportunities for local innovation based on the needs of individual communities" (Yonashiro-Cho, Meyer, & Wilber, 2017, p. 298). The Older Americans Act, first passed in 1965 and last reauthorized in 2020, provides the administrative structure and funding for each state. Through the OAA, each state has an Office on Aging and organizes services and programs for those aged 60+ years through Area Agencies on Aging (Colello & Napili, 2020). Some services are provided via a local department of aging, while others, typically for adults meeting income guidelines, are provided by the local department of social services (Ernst & Smith, 2015).

As described previously with respect to health, the Andersen model highlights predisposing characteristics and enabling factors that explain why people access and use social services, such as elder abuse services or adult day care, and other community-based resources (Barker & Himchak, 2006). Lack of knowledge makes it difficult to access services, and values of independence and self-sufficiency make it hard for some people to accept services. For some older adults, cognitive impairment and/or mental illness may prevent them from realizing that they need help and complicate their ability to access it. Social isolation and lack of a support network can also hinder access to services or result in services that do not help. As with health services, the neighborhood environment and the structure of available services can affect a person's ability to access and accept social services.

Formal community resources strive to enhance well-being and provide support while upholding values of autonomy and self-determination. Older adults must often obtain assistance from family, friends, or paid help to remain in their homes in the community. Unless they lack the cognitive capacity to make decisions with respect to their health and well-being, people are free to reject services that family members and professionals see as needed. Thus, those who provide social services need skills in engagement, assessment, and treatment. They must also have knowledge of resources and be able to engage in multidisciplinary work (Yonashiro-Cho, Meyer, & Wilber, 2017).

Specific services vary by community and may be provided by government agencies or nonprofit or for-profit organizations. The types of services include nutrition, personal care, disease prevention and health promotion, legal services, transportation, family caregiver support, help with enrollment in Medicare benefits, and in-home personal care. Some services are free or low-cost to those meeting income guidelines. Categories of service include prevention services, adult day care, protective services, support services, and resource brokerage and linkage.

Prevention Services

Prevention services are meant to prevent social isolation and health problems that become more common as people age. **Primary prevention** services are aimed at whole populations to prevent the occurrence of health or social effects before they occur. **Secondary prevention** efforts aim to identify health or psychosocial problems at their earliest stages, and **tertiary prevention** programs manage diseases or problems once they have been identified to slow further disease progression or physical or mental decline.

Senior centers, which are one model of community-based services, are often the focal point for the delivery of services funded by the Older Americans Act. They provide services directly and may serve as the gateway to a range of preventive services including exercise and fitness, hearing testing, falls prevention programs, and health promotion events such as diabetes education. Some help with tax preparation and with navigating applications for the Medicare prescription drug benefit. However, due to negative stereotypes about senior centers and lack of interest among adults who are aged 60–75, participation in traditional senior centers has declined, which may affect the availability of these services in the future (Pardasani, 2019).

Subsidized meal programs aim to prevent problems associated with inadequate nutrition. Senior centers and other venues such as adult day care programs provide nutritious meals and opportunities for socialization. The Meals on Wheels program delivers prepared meals to people who are homebound (Siegler et al., 2015).

Adult Day Care

Adult day care services provide organized, tailored care and social engagement and support for people who cannot be left alone during the day. Services vary by location, but adult day care centers generally provide social and health-supporting services, and some provide specialized services for persons with dementia. These centers often provide transportation as well. Adult day services are associated with positive outcomes for people receiving care, including improvement in mental health and social contacts, and their caregivers, including the reduction of caregiver stress (Ellen et al., 2017).

In-Home Personal Care

In-home personal services run the gamut from help with household tasks such as cooking and cleaning to home health services that help people manage chronic conditions, functional disabilities, or cognitive impairment. Community resources that provide these services include independent contractors and for-profit and nonprofit organizations. The cost of services often prevents people from accessing the in-home help that they need, and public funding for in-home services is limited to those with low incomes. Some eligible adults who are assessed as needing nursing home–level care can access Medicaid waivers that reallocate resources originally designated to paying for care in institutional settings to pay for home healthcare (Ernst & Smith, 2015).

Protective Services

Adult Protective Services (APS, discussed in Chapter 6) responds to and investigates allegations of physical and sexual abuse of older and dependent adults, neglect by caregivers, financial exploitation, and self-neglect. Older victims of interpersonal violence can also access services for victims of domestic violence, such as community-based shelters and hotlines. Although in the past some of these services focused on younger and middle-aged women, many have expanded their scope of practice to address the needs of older victims. Services that can provide both legal and psychosocial assistance to community-dwelling older adults who do not meet criteria for APS are also helpful in marshalling support, such as protective orders, for older adults being abused or victimized by members of their family (Burnes, Rizzo, & Courtney, 2014).

Support Services

As described in Chapter 6, caregiving can be difficult and lonely work. The need to support caregivers can be overlooked, and caregivers may have difficulty accessing services. Caregiver support programs, funded partially by the Older Americans Act, exist in many communities.

Respite care provides relief for caregivers from 24/7 demands. Respite can include adult day care and in-home care, as well as overnight stays for care recipients in facilities, which allow the caregiver to take a break or even a short vacation.

Caregiver **support groups** bring caregivers together on a regular basis so they may learn from each other's experiences and benefit from time spent with others in similar circumstances (Family Caregiver Alliance, 2017). The Alzheimer's Association provides support groups for caregivers of persons with dementia. These groups can help caregivers address some of the challenges particular to Alzheimer's disease and other dementias, such as wandering, combative behavior, home safety, and the care recipient's desire to continue driving. They also provide education about disease processes so that caregivers will know what they might expect in the future (Alzheimer's Association, 2020).

Legal and financial counseling can help when those needing care can no longer handle their own legal or financial affairs.

Resource Brokerage and Linkage

Getting information about community resources and accessing services can be challenging due to different eligibility rules, costs, location, and other barriers. Older adults living alone who have few family supports may have difficulty in accessing and coordinating care when they need it. Older adults who live alone with mild cognitive impairment or Alzheimer's disease, may be in precarious situations if they are trying to preserve their independence when at the same time no one is available to help them organize different types of assistance such as home healthcare, transportation, or home maintenance (Portacolone, Rubinstein et al., 2018).

Local departments of social services manage programs that provide financial assistance to eligible low-income citizens, including many who are 65+. These programs include the Supplemental Nutrition Assistance Program (SNAP), the Low Income Home Energy Assistance Program (LIHEAP), which helps with energy costs, and the Temporary Assistance for Needy Families (TANF) program that often supports grandparents caring for grandchildren (Ernst & Smith, 2015).

Many communities offer services, often via their Area Agencies on Aging, which provide information about community services including caregiver support and long-term care. Information and referral can take many forms, including walk-in services, resource fairs, and hotlines.

Through the "No Wrong Door" initiative, people can receive information about supports and services for long-term care provided by Medicaid, the Older Americans Act, and the Department of Veterans Affairs at a variety of access points including hospitals and community-based agencies. This initiative recognizes the difficulty for caregivers and others in navigating access to long-term services and support. The goal is to provide a one-stop system with a single standard process that allows people to tell their story once rather than multiple times with multiple services (Administration for Community Living, 2020).

CASE 9.1

The Benefits of Social Engagement

At age 73, Diana enjoys her life in the suburbs of Washington, DC where she lives in a small house that she bought after divorcing her husband when she was 55. She retired from the faculty of a small college seven years ago. Now, she enjoys daily walks, sewing, reading, and gardening. She plays tennis twice a week and sings in an acapella group. She sees her daughter and two granddaughters regularly and has a large circle of friends. She combines her love of traveling and learning with trips sponsored by educational organizations.

Since her divorce Diana has dated and has had a few longer-term relationships. She is open to more dating, but she is content with being single. The enforced isolation and limits to social activity of the pandemic were difficult, but she made the most of it. She sewed and sold face masks during the pandemic and kept in touch with family and friends via Zoom. While the pandemic put some of her travel plans on hold, she recently completed a hiking and rafting trip in the Grand Canyon.

Pain in Diana's right knee hampered her enjoyment of her last trip. Her doctor has recommended total knee replacement surgery. The doctor predicts a full recovery where she could renew her tennis playing and traveling. Except for having her two children, Diana has never even been hospitalized. She now finds herself worried about who will help her after her stay in the hospital and rehab because she will not be able to drive for up to eight weeks.

How do Diana's activities benefit her? What would you suggest to Diana to make sure she has support after her knee surgery?

CHAPTER REVIEW

The Importance of Connection
- A community is a group of people that share social ties, common characteristics, and perspectives, and that may be linked to a geographic location or setting.
- Communities based in geographic space, such as a neighborhood, take on increasing importance as people age.
- People seek connections based on self-determination and the desire to be socially useful.
- Social connections influence health and longevity, while social isolation increases the risk of harmful outcomes, including barriers to accessing and using community resources.

Religious and Spiritual Communities
- Involvement in religious and spiritual communities often provides resources and connections for people as they age.
- Over time, older adults have demonstrated decreased affiliation and involvement with formal religious communities.
- Connections between religious involvement and health and psychological well-being include a sense of coherence and predictability, reframing of aging-related losses, and material and emotional support in times of loss.

Recreation and Community Involvement
- Adults engage in a wide variety of recreational and community activities that foster connectedness, well-being, optimism, and personal growth as they age.
- Older adults participate in a wide range of group and individual sports and a variety of fitness activities.
- Many older adults travel on their own or as part of organized tours, that are geared toward their interests and needs.
- Involvement in music, theater, creative expression, and dance can add to joy and meaning in life, and many organizations provide programs targeted to older adults or for intergenerational participants.

- Older adults who volunteer contribute to a range of social, educational, health-related, and recreational services in the community.
- Third places are informal spaces for people to gather and socialize and provide safe spaces for diverse community members.

Healthcare Services
- The definition of health encompasses physical, mental, and social well-being and flourishing, or a sense of purpose and meaning in life.
- Access to regular, high-quality healthcare services and a connection to a primary care physician helps people maintain optimal functioning and address age-related health changes.
- Ageism in the medical profession and poor compensation contributes to the shortage of geriatricians, who specialize in the care of older adults and the diseases and conditions that affect them.
- Factors related to individual and community characteristics impede access to high-quality healthcare for some older adults.

Social Services for Older Adults and Their Families
- The aging network addresses a continuum of needs and provides services in the areas of prevention, intervention, protection and support, and resource brokerage and linkage.

REVIEW QUESTIONS
1. What are the major sources of social connection for older adults? What advice would you give to someone who is concerned about maintaining social connections as they grow older?
2. Considering declining involvement in formal religion, what do you see as major sources of spiritual connection and support for older adults in the future?
3. What are some advantages and challenges for older adults in obtaining high-quality primary medical care?
4. Provide examples of primary, secondary, and tertiary prevention services.

KEY TERMS

community
community gerontology
mezzo level
micro level
macro level
self-determination theory
social usefulness
religion
spirituality
faith
third places
health
inpatient
outpatient
telemedicine
patient-centered medical home
geriatrician
age-friendly healthcare
aging network
primary prevention
secondary prevention
tertiary prevention
senior center
adult day care
respite care
support groups

CHAPTER 10

Media and Technology

Chapter Outline

Media and Older Adults
    News Media
    Educational and Entertainment Media
    Ageism in the Media
    Social Media
Technology Use by Older Adults
    Access to Technology
    Combating Stereotypes
    Technology Use for Lifelong Learning
    Technology Use for Social Connection and Entertainment
    Technology Use to Improve Health
    Digital Literacy
    Online Safety
Technology and End of Life

Learning Objectives

After completing this chapter, you will be able to:
- Describe how older adults interact with various types of media and how ageism in the media influences perceptions of older adults.
- Describe how older adults use various forms of technology and explain some of the challenges around access and digital literacy.
- List some ways in which technology can have a positive or negative effect at end of life.

Media and technology play an important role in our lives. Older adults have witnessed the birth and proliferation of technology, including the widespread use of computers, tablets, smartphones, and other devices. They have also witnessed the evolution of media from a limited range of print and broadcast sources to today's vast variety, which includes print and online news sources and social media. Teens and younger adults have grown up using the abundance of technology and media sources. Regardless of a person's age, all users of media and technology are influenced by them, can benefit from them, and can also be harmed by them. In this chapter, we will explore how older adults use media and technology and how they affect well-being in later life.

MEDIA AND OLDER ADULTS

The term **media** refers to means of mass communication, such as radio, television, newspapers, magazines, and online sources such as websites, podcasts, and blogs. All types of media offer the potential to provide information, but they also have the ability to spread misinformation and perpetuate stereotypes.

News Media

Print media such as newspapers and magazines have been a significant mode of obtaining information, education, and entertainment for a long time. Radio news began in 1920, and television news broadcasts began in 1940. Today, due to technology use, news is increasingly being disseminated online. As might be expected, older adults get most of their news from TV and print sources, while younger generations rely primarily on online sources. Still, the majority of all adults, regardless of age, get their news from modalities other than print. Approximately 86 percent of adults get their news online at least sometimes or often, 68 percent via TV, and 50 percent via radio. This compares to 32 percent of adults who get their news in print form (Pew Research Center, 2021).

The source of news matters in shaping personal opinions, and with so many sources of news currently available, there is a real need for people to be able to differentiate legitimate, fact-based sources from those that spread misinformation with the goal of swaying opinions on social and political issues. Increasingly, various news sources present biased arguments, manipulate information, and report inaccurate or false data or facts. Media consumers in younger age groups (18–29) rely more frequently on social media sources, which may or may not be credible. Adults aged 50+ rely more heavily on cable, local, and network TV sources, some of which may present biased coverage.

Research indicates that those who rely primarily on social media for their news tend to be less engaged with the news, less likely to follow news closely, and less likely to be knowledgeable and understand issues deeply than those who get their news from TV, print, radio, or reputable digital news outlet sources. They are also more likely to be exposed to made-up "news" and to believe misinformation and conspiracy theories. While older adults are also susceptible to misinformation from biased sources, research indicates that younger adults may be in more danger of these problems because they likely do not diversify their news sources as much as those in older groups (Pew Charitable Trust, 2020).

Educational and Entertainment Media
Podcasts and blogs are popular with people of all ages, and older adults can find many that are geared toward their interests. People of all ages have access to online content that can be educational, entertaining, and helpful for personal and professional growth. Podcasts and blogs can be a way for older adults to gain information on topics of interest as well as to find support and community. Older adults who want to blog can contribute their knowledge and skills to those who want to follow their writing. One example of a blog specifically targeted to an older adult audience is the AARP *Bulletin* (https://www.aarp.org/bulletin/), which focuses on current events from a national and state perspective.

For older adults who want to learn more about health-related topics, many sites exist that provide reliable, accurate, and research-based information that cater to older populations and health-related concerns. Examples include:

- NIH Medline Plus, Older Adult Health: https://medlineplus.gov/olderadulthealth.html
- Health in Aging Foundation: https://www.healthinaging.org/health-aging-foundation
- Very Well Health: https://www.verywellhealth.com/healthy-aging-4014711

Figure 10.1 Media use is an important way for older adults to remain engaged and informed
Source: shapechange/iStock

Many other government agencies and nonprofit organizations host sites that provide resources and information on health-related topics as well as topics such as caregiving, housing, and financial management.

Ageism in the Media

One area of research has focused on how media, particularly magazines and popular media, promote the idea of successful aging being associated with sexualized older bodies, particularly heterosexual women. Recall the concept of heterohappiness (Marshall, 2018), discussed in Chapter 4, which refers to the way popular culture cultivates an image of successful aging as a continuation of youthful, attractive, heterosexual, able-bodied, often white couples. Specifically, popular media tends to use these images to not only represent older adults but to communicate the idea that these identities are the only ones that equate to successful, positive, and healthy aging.

Feminist and queer theory lenses have critiqued these rigid conceptualizations of older adults in the media. Further, these critiques point to the dismissal of unrepresented identities in media and structural, systemic inequalities that lead to other circumstances in which people with differing identities are excluded from the successful aging paradigm (Marshall, 2018). Queer gerontology contends that ageist images and representations in the media should be critiqued not just for ageism in and of itself, but also based on the way that normativity affects identity, embodiment, relationships, and how we view aging and our own aging process (Sandberg, 2015).

Social Media

In Chapter 4, we discussed the importance of social engagement and connectedness for well-being in later life. Meeting the human needs for love, belonging, inclusion, and acceptance helps protect older adults from isolation, poor health, and early mortality (Al-Kandari & Crews, 2014; Wakefield et al., 2020). Social media, dating sites, and connection via other online sources can allow older adults to remain engaged with family, friends, and their communities. Social media can play a pivotal role in reducing isolation and stress and increasing connectedness of older adults (Leist, 2013; Zhang, Kim et al., 2020).

The proliferation of social media has provided a way for people of all ages to connect. Research shows that older adults commonly use Facebook, YouTube, Pinterest, Instagram, LinkedIn, and Twitter (Pew Institute, 2018). SeniorPlanet.org from AARP offers opportunities for virtual social engagement via discussion groups, clubs, and other online activities. Like their younger counterparts, many older adults have turned to online dating sites to find partners and companionship. Dating sites targeted to older adults include ourtime.com, seniormatch.com, and silversingles.com.

TECHNOLOGY USE BY OLDER ADULTS

Research suggests that cell phone and smartphone use is ubiquitous among older US adults. Approximately 80 percent of adults aged 65+ own a phone, and 86 percent of adults aged 50+ regularly communicate via text messaging. Among those aged 50+, text messaging has actually surpassed email as a primary way of communicating.

A vast majority (92 percent) of US adults aged 50+ use a laptop or desktop computer, 43 percent use a tablet, 23 percent use e-readers, and 7 percent use an assistive device in the home, such as the Siri personal assistant on Apple devices (AARP, 2018).

CASE 10.1

Emily's Social Media Creativity

Emily is 80 years old and loves to write. When she was younger, she didn't do much with her writing passion except to write in her journal, which she never shared with anyone. In her later years, she decided she wanted to get her writing onto platforms where others could read and comment on it. She started using platforms like Twitter and Facebook to publish her poems and essays. After a few years, she started a blog where she would post longer pieces on her political and other observations. Emily has accumulated thousands of followers over the years who enjoy reading her work.

What benefits do you see for Emily and others in Emily publishing her work on social media sites? What other ways could social media be used in later life to enhance creativity, connection, engagement, and well-being of individuals and their communities?

Internet usage is high among older adults worldwide. Table 10.1 lists internet use by age group in selected countries. These numbers show the wide range of internet access and use among different countries and some of the disparities across age groups and locations.

Access to Technology

Access to technology and online resources can be problematic for many older adults. Research indicates that access barriers fall into one or more of three main areas (Yazdani-Darki et al., 2020):

- Individual barriers such as limitations in education, lack of access to devices or the internet, or unfavorable or fearful attitudes about technology
- Aging-related barriers such as physical or cognitive limitations
- Technology barriers such as devices or resources that are complicated or difficult to use or expensive to obtain or use

Table 10.1 Internet Usage by Adults: Percentage within Each Age Group

Country	Age 50+	Age 30–49	Age 18–29
India	18%	35%	57%
Indonesia	24%	58%	89%
Kenya	25%	43%	64%
Nigeria	31%	51%	65%
Lithuania	47%	97%	100%
Japan	59%	98%	98%
Lebanon	74%	96%	98%
United States	86%	98%	99%
Canada	89%	100%	100%
South Korea	95%	95%	100%

Source: Pew Research Center, 2020.

Particularly problematic is a sense of self-efficacy around technology use. A lack of confidence in using technology can cause stress for older adults, which can be compounded by needing to rely on others to teach them (Yagil, Cohen, & Beer, 2016). For example, although technology can be helpful to people with disabilities or health problems, these challenges can make technology use difficult or cause them to be less likely to use it than people without these challenges (Pew Research Center, 2017).

Research suggests that digital disconnectedness is a serious issue for many older adults, with approximately 22 million older adults in the United States lacking internet access at home. This disconnectedness is exacerbated by inequities associated with race, ability, health, income, education, immigration status, and rural/urban residence. Those without access to the internet or technology face additional challenges. For instance, the 2020 US Census took place online during the COVID-19 pandemic, so those without internet access or digital skills were more likely to not be counted than those with access and skills. Digital disconnection leaves older adults more vulnerable to isolation, which was exacerbated by the pandemic (Older Adults Technology Services, 2020; Stanford Center on Longevity, 2021).

Combating Stereotypes

Older adults, like those in younger generations, use devices to manage health information; track health data; record doctor's visits; conduct telehealth visits; consult with care and other professionals; purchase apps; get information on restaurants, traffic, and directions; and, of course, access news and social media (AARP, 2018). Research suggests that stereotypes of older adults being reluctant or unable to learn to use technology are largely untrue. Many older adults are adopting technologies for a wide range of uses (Hung, Lyons, & Wu, 2020).

Technology Use for Lifelong Learning

Technology offers opportunities for people to learn about numerous topics, such as personal health, genealogy, caregiving, job training, computer skills, financial planning, and home repair. It can make opportunities for lifelong learning accessible for many older adults, including the ability to earn diplomas, degrees, or certificates, and to take courses on subjects of interest.

For example, local libraries, senior centers, and colleges often provide access to computers and online classes for low cost or free of charge. Hundreds of universities offer free massive open online courses (MOOCs). For instance, the New York Public Library offers dozens of free technology courses and operates the Senior Planet Exploration Center, where they provide technology courses, workshops, and talks, along with social and cultural events (New York Public Library, 2021).

Technology Use for Social Connection and Entertainment

Platforms such as FaceTime, Zoom, and Skype have kept people connected, particularly through the COVID-19 pandemic. Older adults were able to use these platforms to stay connected with friends and family, attend remote church services, and even attend funerals when the pandemic made these types of activities all but impossible. Family members who could not visit loved ones who were hospitalized were able to communicate with them via video visits.

Online entertainment and gaming are not just for younger people. Increasingly, older adults are engaging in online gaming and other forms of online entertainment. From 2016 to 2019, the number of gamers aged 50+ increased from 40.2 million to 50.6 million. Much of this gaming activity is focused on puzzles, logic, card, and similar games played on phones and tablets. Almost half (49 percent) of these gamers are women, who report they play regularly. Older adults report gaming for the same reasons as younger adults: for fun, social interaction, and to reduce stress. Older adults also game to keep cognitive skills sharp (Nelson-Kakulla, 2019).

Technology Use to Improve Health
Technology can be used to manage health information and also to support and improve health. It can play a role in allowing people with cognitive or physical disabilities to remain independent to the degree possible. Research indicates that certain technologies used in and for the home can help improve various functions. For example, virtual reality applications can help improve cognitive function after a traumatic brain injury (Alashram et al., 2019). Various types of **electronic assistive technology** (EAT) can help improve cognitive and physical function as well as monitor various functions to alert individuals, caregivers, and health professionals when intervention may be necessary to prevent injury.

Smartphone and tablet apps allow people to control their environment and automate home functions and communication within and outside the home (Jamwal et al., 2018). Homes can also be equipped with devices and communication technology to monitor in-home activities and changes in behavior by producing data analysis algorithms that feed information to older adults and their caregivers. Behaviors that are typically monitored include mobility (walking speed, movement around the home), socialization (emails, phone calls, computer use, driving speed, trips taken out of the home), medication usage and adherence, sleeping habits and patterns, and biological and physiologic functions (BMI, pulse, weight, daily activity) (Oregon Center for Aging and Technology, 2020).

Similarly, web-based services have played an increasingly important role in connecting older adults, people with disabilities or mobility problems, and those who need services such as hospice or palliative care with their caregivers, service providers, and other supports and resources. Web-based resources can also help close equity gaps for people who live in rural areas without many services, people who face transportation barriers, and those who may need access to less costly or in-home services. (Currie, Philip, & Roberts, 2015; Demiris, Parker Oliver, & Wittenberg-Lyles, 2011).

Technology also brings opportunities for older adults to play games and engage in other activities that stimulate cognition. Various companies sell cognitive training programs that promise fun, interactive ways to exercise memory, processing speed, and problem-solving capabilities. Card games, crossword puzzles, and a multitude of other entertaining games can be played digitally as well. Research indicates that playing these games, whether in digital form or not, helps sharpen certain mental skills that tend to decline with age such as planning, reaction time, decision-making, and short-term memory. However, research is unclear on whether they have long-term benefits such as slowing the development or progression of diseases like dementia (Htut et al., 2018).

Figure 10.2 Assistive technology can improve well-being at any stage of life
Source: Diego Cervo/Shutterstock

Many gerontologists criticize the marketing of these "brain training" games as ageist. Similar to the earlier discussion about ageist media images that link heteronormative aging with successful aging, some researchers point out that these games often equate smart, fit, well-functioning brains with successful aging instead of acknowledging the uniquely individual ways our brains age (Katz & Marshall, 2018).

Digital Literacy

The American Library Association defines **digital literacy** as "the ability to use information and communication technologies to find, evaluate, create, and communicate information, requiring both cognitive and technical skills." We learn critical thinking skills when we are young and then build upon those skills as we get older. This includes learning how to think about content we encounter in the media and by using digital technology. For many older adults, digital literacy may not be as straightforward as it is for younger generations who have been exposed to digital content from a very young age. Many organizations serving older adults provide digital literacy education.

Older adults are increasingly engaged in online content. The more time people spend online, regardless of their age, the more they are exposed to scams, hoaxes, conspiracy theories, and false news stories. Thus, it is important for people to be able to identify misinformation (Media Wise, 2021). For example, in the early days of the COVID-19 pandemic, misinformation was widespread. False information about the virus, how it spread, treatment options, and other misleading and nonfactual information was easy to find and difficult to discern from evidence-based facts (Stanford Center on Longevity, 2021). As COVID vaccines were developed and disseminated, the misinformation campaigns continued.

While digital literacy is a concern for people of all ages, it is a particular concern for younger (age 18–34) and older (age 65+) adult cohorts. Indeed, a recent poll indicated that approximately 41 percent of younger and 44 percent of older adults admitted to falling for fake news. This is compared to 37 percent of adults aged 35–49 and 38 percent of adults aged 50–64 (Marzilli, 2018).

Online Safety

Online safety is an issue for people of all ages and particularly for older adults. Recent statistics reveal that cybercrime targeting older adults has increased five times over the past decade, resulting in at least $650 million in losses per year. The actual amount of these losses is probably higher since many cybercrimes are not reported (Fahs et al., 2021). Many older adults do not report cybercrime and other fraud because they do not know the procedures to report it or are too embarrassed about being victims. Further, some older adults may be afraid that family members will think they are incompetent at handling their own financial and other affairs if they fall victim to a crime (Federal Bureau of Investigation, 2021).

Older adults are targets of cybercrime for many reasons. These reasons include:

- Criminals believe that older adults are not savvy enough to spot a scam.
- Older adults often have more financial resources (e.g., homes, savings, and good credit) than younger adults and as such, are more lucrative targets.

Common cybercrimes against older adults include tech support scams (criminals pose as tech support personnel to gain control of devices and sensitive information), romance scams (criminals pose as potential romantic partners), grandparent scams (criminals pose as grandchildren claiming to have a financial emergency), and service scams (criminals post fraudulent online ads to provide services) (Federal Bureau of Investigation, 2021).

Some digital literacy education programs for older adults help them learn how to spot online scams and what to do if they think they have become victims. It is important for all people, including older adults, to know how to protect their security and privacy online. In spite of this, research suggests that many people do not take proactive steps to protect themselves online or the devices they use for health, financial, and other transactions that involve sensitive and personal information (AARP, 2018).

TECHNOLOGY AND END OF LIFE

End-of-life care can be challenging, even when circumstances are ideal, because of our cultural reluctance to talk about death and dying and due to inequities in care and services. Many people wish to die at home, but because of factors such as a lack of communication between patients, caregivers, and providers or a lack of training on end-of-life care, people may end up receiving medical care or interventions they do not want or may die in the hospital or a care facility when they prefer to be at home (Jercich, 2020).

Assistive technology can help to improve communication with and between caregivers, health providers, and those who may be dying at home or in a care facility. Technology can also help people feel more independent and in control of their end-of-life process; shape the narrative and meaning of their end-of-life experience; and ease loneliness that might occur at the end of life. For instance, electronic medical records can alert medical personnel about patients' wishes should they be unable to communicate. Devices such as smart watches and other wearable devices allow remote monitoring for patients and their caregivers and provide data about their health and well-being, including vital signs, physical symptoms, stress levels, and other health indicators (Jones, 2021). Video recordings allow people to record their emergency or end-of-life wishes and instructions (Jercich, 2020).

Technology also is used to train hospice, palliative care, and other healthcare professionals to provide better care to those in pain or who are dying. For example, telemedicine, predictive analytics, artificial intelligence, and virtual reality are assisting professionals to better analyze and monitor patients' symptoms and other health data to improve care, communication, and the dying process to limit pain and suffering and increase comfort (Doolittle et al., 2019; Tashjian et al., 2017).

Technology also has the potential to create problems during illness, injury, or at the end of life. For example, ventilators and other medical devices can substitute for physiological functions such as breathing, pumping the heart, and oxygenating blood to prolong life. In cases where people cannot make their wishes known (e.g., people who are unconscious or in a coma) or who have not made their wishes known through DNR or POLST documents (discussed in Chapter 5), these technologies have the potential to prolong pain and suffering of the patient and their loved ones, particularly if the patient has no chance of recovery (Zitter, 2017). Even if a life-prolonging technology is available, the patient's wishes, as expressed in a living will, advance directive, and other legal documents, should dictate all healthcare choices (Teno et al., 2013).

CHAPTER REVIEW

Media and Older Adults
- Currently, the majority of all adults get their news and other information from modalities other than print.
- Those in younger age groups (18–29) rely more frequently on social media as a news source than people aged 50+; those in older groups rely more heavily on cable, local, and network TV for news.
- Technology offers opportunities older adults to learn about various topics, improve skills, and complete courses and formal educational programs.
- Older adults who want to learn more about health-related topics can find many sites that provide reliable, accurate, and research-based information.
- Social media and dating sites provide ways for older adults to connect with others, find partners and companionship, and reduce isolation.
- Ageism in the media perpetuates the image of successful aging as a continuation of youthful, attractive, heterosexual, able-bodied, often white, sexualized couples.

Technology Use by Older Adults
- Cell phone and smartphone use is ubiquitous among older adults as are computer and internet use.
- Older adults, like younger adults, rely on devices to manage and track health information and manage health issues in the home.
- Digital literacy is important for people of all ages; this involves knowing how to evaluate sources of information and how to discern between fact and misinformation.
- Online safety involves protecting personal and financial information and understanding how to avoid being victimized by online scams.

Technology and End of Life
- Assistive technology is increasingly being used to support people and their care providers in end-of-life processes, including reducing pain and suffering and increasing effective communication.

REVIEW QUESTIONS
1. Discuss various social media and other sites that are marketed to older adults. What advantages and disadvantages do you see with these sites? In what ways might they challenge or perpetuate ageism?
2. Articulate ways that intergenerational teams could assist one another in the use of media and technology.
3. Explore ideas for the use of assistive technology at any stage of life. How can these technologies be used to increase well-being?

KEY TERMS
media
electronic assistive technology (EAT)
digital literacy

CHAPTER 11

Global Trends in Aging

Chapter Outline
Global Aging
    United Nations Initiatives Related to Aging
    Population Aging
    Living Arrangements
    Life Expectancy and Health
    Work and Retirement
    Ageism Worldwide
Culture and Aging
    Cross-National Comparisons
    Cross-Cultural Comparisons
    Cultural Influences on Aging
Aging in the United States in Global Context
    US Life Expectancy
    Foreign-Born Population
Immigration, Migration, and Aging
    Who Migrates and Why?
    Older Adults in Home Countries
    Older Immigrants in Destination Countries
        Early versus Late-Life Immigration
        Older Refugees Fleeing War and Terror
        Legal Status and Threat of Deportation
Aging and Climate Change
    Climate Change and Migration
    Health Impacts of Climate Change
    Climate Change and Natural Disasters

Learning Objectives
After completing this chapter, you will be able to:
- Describe the impact of the aging of the global population with respect to living arrangements, life expectancy, health, work, and retirement.
- Describe the effect of culture on aging and provide examples of insights gained from examining aging from cross-national and cross-cultural perspectives.
- Describe the diversity of the aging population in the United States.
- Explain how global immigration patterns affect older adults.
- Provide examples of how global climate change affects older adults.

In this chapter, we look at aging from a global perspective, examining trends in population aging, including increased life expectancy and the global distribution of the aging population. Aging in the United States is explored in a global and cross-cultural context, along with the interrelated topics of immigration and climate change. All these trends and changes have implications for individual and societal well-being and quality of life as people reach their seventh decades and beyond.

GLOBAL AGING

Globalization refers to the ways in which the world's economies, cultures, and populations influence and depend on one another (Peterson Institute for International Economics, 2021). Populations across the globe are affected by events and phenomena such as economic recession, climate change, population movement, and conflict that cannot be contained within national borders due to the flow of information, ideas, and ideologies via the internet and the ease of international travel (Ritzer, 2019).

United Nations Initiatives Related to Aging
As part of its mission to address international problems and come up with shared solutions, the **United Nations** (UN) collects and disseminates information on population aging and its impact. Differences in life expectancy, demographics, living arrangements, and other indicators of well-being for older adults are connected to the systems and supports provided for them in different countries. Trends in population aging differ by nation and region and are correlated with income levels (Bloom, Canning, & Lubet, 2015).

The UN uses the terms developed economies, economies in transition, and developing economies to classify countries. Developed economies include the United States, Canada, European nations, Australia, New Zealand, and Japan. Economies in transition include countries of south-eastern Europe and the Commonwealth of Independent States and Georgia (i.e., countries the comprised the former Soviet Union). Developing economies include all countries and areas of Africa, Asia (excluding Japan), Latin America and the Caribbean, and Oceania (excluding Australia and New Zealand) (United Nations Department of Economic and Social Affairs Population Division, 2021).

UN efforts draw attention to the pace and impact of global aging and encourage member nations to adopt policies and practices to help people live longer and healthier lives and to recognize their human rights. For example, UN efforts have raised global awareness of the extent and characteristics of elder abuse and neglect.

The Decade of Healthy Ageing is the UN's global collaboration to address rapid population aging by working to improve policies, systems, and services that will help people age in health and dignity (World Health Organization, 2021b). The UN's 17 **Sustainable Development Goals** (SDGs), part of their 2030 Agenda for Sustainable Development, are a call for action to address worldwide problems related to poverty and deprivation, healthcare, education, economic inequality, and to spur economic growth while reducing the impact of climate change. Fifteen SDGs mention the aging population. Three SDGs relate to the impact of living arrangements on the well-being of older adults (United Nations Department of Economic and Social Affairs Population Division, 2020a).

Population Aging

The worldwide population is aging rapidly. The proportion of the world's population aged 60+ will nearly double from 12 percent to 22 percent of the population between 2015 and 2050. Those aged 60+ now outnumber children younger than 5 years (World Health Organization, 2021b). While life expectancy has increased over the twentieth and into the twenty-first centuries, it decreased from 2019 to 2020 in most nations due to the COVID-19 pandemic (Aburto et al., 2021).

Aging populations are concentrated in developed economies such as the United States, Japan, and the nations of Northern Europe. By 2050, 80 percent of the world's older people will live in developing economies. The largest increases in population aging will occur in Eastern and Southeastern Asia, with major increases also expected in Central America, South America, North America, and Europe (United Nations Department of Economic and Social Affairs Population Division, 2020b).

Concepts including **fertility rate** (birth rate within a population), **mortality rate** (deaths within a population), and **migration** (population movement) help us understand how current trends will affect older adults across the world. Developed economies, which have supports in place such as old age pensions, health insurance, and long-term care systems, have a higher proportion of older adults than developing economies. Declining fertility rates and restrictions on immigration have led to increases in the **old age dependency ratio** (OADR) in more developed nations that show that the number of working age people (defined as age 16–64) is shrinking relative to the number of older persons (Vollset et al., 2020).

Declining fertility rates are the predominant contributor to population aging (Bloom et al., 2015). Demographers predict that by 2100 fertility rates in 183 out of 195 countries will be below **replacement level**, the number of births needed to replace the current population (Vollset et al., 2020). Policy interventions to increase fertility rates in developed economies include direct financial support for parents and more availability of childcare. Greater migration into more developed nations could also reduce projected increases in OADR, but many European nations are resistant to immigration as part of a response to population change (McAuliffe & Khadria, 2019).

Interventions such as increased supports for parents may not be feasible or sufficient to ensure that nations can sustain supports and programs for older adults such as Social Security and other social insurance programs, which rely on the contributions of working-age individuals. For example, Japan, where one in three people will be over age 65 in 2030, has a rising OADR. Expenditures on publicly funded pensions will double over the next 40 years. Research suggests that efforts to promote fertility would not significantly lower the predicted OADR, and increased immigration to Japan, which has a very small percentage of foreign-born residents, at a level sufficient to address the problem is unlikely (Parsons & Gilmour, 2018). Countries such as Nigeria and India will see dramatic population growth in addition to greater numbers of older adults, while countries such as Japan will lose population. These changes will affect economic and social conditions and global political situations (Vollset et al., 2020).

Living Arrangements

As discussed in Chapter 8, living arrangements of older adults in the United States have evolved over time due to economic issues, population movement from rural to urban areas, public policies, and smaller family sizes. Global patterns of living arrangements also vary due to prevailing cultural norms and traditions, the need for support, housing costs, and availability of kin. Excluding adults who live in nursing homes and other congregate care facilities, older adults either live independently (alone or with a spouse), with minor and/or adult children, or in extended family households. A higher percentage of older adults live alone or with a spouse in more developed countries such as the United States and Germany, while multigenerational households are more common in developing nations (United Nations Department of Economic and Social Affairs Population Division, 2020b).

The **skip-generation household** is a type of extended family arrangement where children reside with their grandparents without parents present. Reasons for prevalence of skip-generation households vary by nation and region. For example, a high number of grandparents in Malawi and other less developed nations are raising grandchildren due to the parents having died from HIV/AIDS or other illnesses. In contrast, in other nations, skip-generation households result when children are unable to live with their parents due to parental addiction, mental illness, incarceration, military deployment, or the need for working age parents to move to other countries to earn money to send home to their families. While fewer older adults will live in multigenerational households as the twenty-first century progresses, coresidence of older and younger generations will remain an important source of support for older adults in developing countries (United Nations Department of Economic and Social Affairs Population Division, 2020a).

Life Expectancy and Health

Life expectancy has increased dramatically over the past 100 years, though it varies considerably across nations, and it decreased in some nations during the COVID-19 pandemic (Woolf, Masters, & Aron, 2021). In 2021, life expectancy at birth was 77 in the United States, 69 in India, and 55 in Nigeria (Population Reference Bureau, 2021). Since 1995, life expectancy has increased by 7.7 years (12 percent), and it is projected to increase an additional 4.5 years (6 percent) by 2050. The largest increase will occur in sub-Saharan Africa (United Nations Department of Economic and Social Affairs Population Division, 2019).

Increased longevity will be accompanied by either healthier longer lives or longer periods of time when people must deal with chronic disease and require care from family or community supports (Bloom et al., 2015). Additional years of life allow people to continue to fulfill important roles as members of their families and communities. If many of those who are aged 85+ are in poor health and require extensive care, the negative impact on families, communities, and nations will be significant. The growing population of older persons portends a growing disease burden from increases in the incidence of noncommunicable diseases (NCDs), including chronic conditions such as diabetes, cardiovascular disease, and Alzheimer disease that have become the predominant causes of morbidity and mortality worldwide (Bloom et al., 2015). Tobacco use, obesity, unhealthy diets, physical inactivity, and harmful alcohol use contribute to the development of NCDs. While these behaviors and conditions are preventable, they can result from social and economic factors such as lack of access to healthcare and safe options for recreation. Increased chronic disease within a population can slow economic growth due to healthcare costs borne by government, business, individuals, and families.

Work and Retirement

Due to greater longevity and limited economic resources many older adults now have longer working lives. The number of people aged 65+ participating in the labor force in the United States has increased over the past 10 years. The **labor force participation rate** (LFPR) is the proportion of a population that is in the labor force and is helpful in making cross-country and cross-group comparisons (He, Goodkind, & Kowal, 2016). Worldwide, participation in the labor force declines as people age past 50 and accelerates after age 65. Over the life course, the LFPR varies by age, gender, and level of economic development in a country.

As shown in Table 11.1, the LFPR for adults aged 65 and older varies widely between countries. Germany's LFPR of 7.8 percent for adults aged 65 and older reflects its economic resources, policies that encourage early retirement, and generous pension and social insurance benefits. In contrast, the higher LFPR of 20.1 percent for adults aged 65+ in the United States may signal the desire of more Americans than Germans to continue working past 65, or their need to work if they do not have adequate resources to retire. Workers in less developed nations are more likely to be employed past age 65 because formal systems set up to support people in old age are not well developed (He, Goodkind, & Kowal, 2016).

Significant differences in LFPR by gender exist across the life course. For example, in Nigeria, the LFPR of men aged 65+ is 48.1 percent while it is 33.5 percent for women. Reasons for these differences include "traditional norms about the division of labor between males and females" (He, Goodwind, & Kowal, 2016, p. 95); however, the fact that almost half of men aged 65+ and one-third of women aged 65+ are in the labor force suggests that economic necessity keeps people working longer in less developed nations.

Recent trends suggest that LFPR for older adults (both men and women) will increase in more developed countries due to greater longevity, changes in pension

Table 11.1 Comparison of Labor Force Participation Rate in Select Countries, 2019

Country	Total (age 15+)%	Age 55–64%	Age 65+%
More Developed Nations			
Germany	61.2	74.6	7.8
United States	62.6	65.5	20.1
Less Developed Nations			
China	68.2	59.9	21.1
Mexico	61.4	57.4	27.1
Nigeria	55.9	60.3	40.4
Least Developed Nations			
Bangladesh	59.1	57.7	27.6

Source: International Labour Organization, https://ilostat.ilo.org/data/.

systems, and changing social norms about retirement. While there are variations among countries in different regions of the world, LFPR for older adults in less developed nations are predicted to decline (He, Goodwind, & Kowal, 2016).

Ageism Worldwide
Ageism exists across the world. While it manifests differently in different contexts and cultures, ageism is associated with poorer physical and mental health, greater financial insecurity, decreased quality of life, and premature death. Some examples of macro-level ageism are rationing of healthcare according to age, and discriminatory labor and hiring practices. The interaction of ageism with other isms, including racism, sexism, and ableism compounds its impact. The treatment of older persons during the COVID-19 pandemic revealed the impact of ageism worldwide (World Health Organization, 2021). More information on extent of ageism worldwide and better evidence on strategies to reduce its impact on the health, well-being, and human rights of older adults is needed.

CULTURE AND AGING
Globalization has allowed for frequent interaction among people from many nations and cultures. Differing attitudes, practices, and customs shape how older persons are viewed and treated in different contexts. Cross-national and cross-cultural comparisons add to understanding of how people experience the aging process and challenge assumptions based on narrow cultural or national perspectives (Kunkel & Hautz, 2021).

Cross-National Comparisons
Cross-national studies examine differences in social structures and policy. An example of cross-national research is a study that compared goals for retirement among adults ranging in age from their early 20s to their mid-60s in the United States and India (Gupta & Hershey, 2016). The United States has an individualistic cultural orientation, and retirement is a structured state of life for which people actively plan. India has a collectivist orientation with no national system or norms for retirement planning.

Traditionally, older Indians move in with their oldest son or other relatives for care in retirement. Americans view retirement as a reward for hard work but also heed a strong cultural message that retirement is a time to "give back" in terms of volunteerism. In contrast, retirement in India occurs when the self-employed (about 60 percent of workers) or employees (40 percent of workers) can no longer physically work.

The study found that the Indian sample generated fewer goals for retirement and that their goals were less concrete but more self-directed and more focused on financial stability than the goals generated by the American sample. The American sample had a higher percentage of goals that were concrete, particularly goals related to leisure. In both nations, population aging and movement and other social and economic changes present challenges with respect to ensuring "financial, physical, and emotional security, as well as an improved quality of life for older adults" (Gupta & Hershey, 2016, p. 233). These types of studies show that nations and societies draw upon existing cultural traditions and policies to address challenges related to aging.

Cross-Cultural Comparisons
One of the many definitions of **culture** is "the unwritten rules that one must know to function in a given social group" (Whittington et al., 2021, p. 2). These rules influence beliefs, thoughts, feelings, patterns of behavior, customs, values, and social institutions. Cross-cultural comparisons examine different meanings of old age and can highlight what is universal versus what is unique about aging within cultures and countries. As the world has become more interconnected and global changes in the economy and the environment have affected many people, the influence of culture shifts over time.

Cultural influences on aging emerge in different ways including the definition of and what it means to be "old," how older people are treated, beliefs about health and well-being, expectations for how people will be cared for physical, emotionally, and financially in their old age, family obligations related to caregiving, the role of older persons in the community, and ways of coping with grief and loss.

Cultural Influences on Aging
Traditions of **filial piety**, or respect for one's parents, in Asian cultures powerfully influence the sense of duty that adult children feel with respect to caring for parents in their later years. However, filial piety "does not mean that older persons who live in these countries are without challenges or that all children are willing and able to provide care for older parents" (Whittington et al., 2021, p. 5). Cultural beliefs change when worldwide socioeconomic changes require people to alter their behaviors to survive.

The challenges of older adults living in rural areas of China, a world center of manufacturing, illustrate how global economic forces have disrupted cultural traditions of care. Many adult children have left rural villages for work in factories in larger cities, leaving older parents behind to fend for themselves. Researchers who immersed themselves in a remote Chinese village found that the "left behind" older parents had to perform strenuous and risky tasks such as hauling water from a communal well, a task previously performed by their adult children. Contrary to tradition, older men learned to cook and patterns of caring for the very old, traditionally the role of sons, were altered as adult siblings devised new patterns of sharing care (Sun & Dutta, 2016).

Knowledge of cultural context enhances understanding of elder abuse and neglect and of what constitutes humane treatment of older adults in different racial, ethnic, or cultural groups (Jervis, Sconzert-Hall, & The Shielding American Indian Elders Project, 2017; Li, Chen, & Dong, 2020). For example, respect of elder status is a core belief in Native American communities. When questioned about the meaning of elder abuse, Native American respondents included lack of respect, which included relegating older adults to the sidelines and failing to respect the elders' wisdom. This idea broadened more dominant definitions of elder abuse that focus on physical abuse, neglect, and financial exploitation (Jervis et al., 2017).

Cultural beliefs also influence the meaning of successful aging. A comparison of studies on successful aging examined the similarities and differences in definitions of successful aging among diverse groups of older adults in 13 countries. While these studies found that all participants prized social engagement as one important facet of successful aging, the meaning of social engagement varied. While nearly all studies identified the importance of connection to family as one component of social engagement, the importance of other activities such as volunteering, having strong friendship networks, or being a respected elder, differed (Reich et al., 2020).

AGING IN THE UNITED STATES IN GLOBAL CONTEXT

Comparing US aging-related data to data of other nations gives perspective on the challenges of aging and how societies can respond. Compared with developing economies, the United States shares characteristics with other developed economies, including a high proportion of adults aged 65+ and the existence of a social safety net. Older adults comprise a smaller share of the US population (16 percent) than the "oldest" nations of Japan (28.2 percent) or France, Germany, Italy, Portugal, and Greece (over 20 percent) (Population Reference Bureau, 2022). Other nations, such as South Korea, will surpass the United States in their proportions of older adults by 2050 (Federal Interagency Forum on Aging-Related Statistics, 2021). The aging population of the United States is more ethnically and racially diverse than that of other developed nations.

In 2060, a projected 23.4 percent of the US population will be aged 65+. Persons aged 85+ are expected to comprise 4.7 percent of the population in 2060. Older adults in the United States are increasingly diverse in terms of race, ethnicity, and national origin and have a multiplicity of strengths, needs, and concerns. While 77 percent of adults aged 65+ are identified as non-Hispanic white, census projections indicate that by 2060, the older population will be 55 percent non-Hispanic white, 13 percent non-Hispanic Black, 8 percent non-Hispanic Asian, and 21 percent Hispanic, which is the fastest growing group (Federal Interagency Forum on Aging-Related Statistics, 2020).

US Life Expectancy

Life expectancy in the United States, which has been rising steadily over the past 100 years, varies greatly due to gender, race/ethnicity, and socioeconomic status. Income inequality and diverging life-course experiences of older persons mean that some older adults have retired comfortably, while others have had more concerns related to adequacy of income, living arrangements, and availability of long-term care. As the population grows and diversifies, these concerns will increase.

A sobering statistic is the decrease in US life expectancy at birth by 1.8 years between 2018 (78.7) and 2020 (76.9), primarily due to increased numbers of deaths caused by the COVID-19 pandemic. One study estimated that this decrease was 8.5 times the average loss observed in 16 high income democracies. Differences in life expectancy by race and ethnicity in the United States revealed the disproportionate impact of the pandemic on Black and Hispanic populations. Addressing disparities in health and longevity is one challenge for the United States when compared with its peers (Woolf, Masters, & Aron, 2021).

Foreign-Born Population
The United States has the highest foreign-born population in the world. The impact of immigration over time is an increase in the number of older adults who are foreign-born, defined as those who are not citizens at birth and including naturalized citizens, lawful permanent residents, temporary workers, refugees, and undocumented immigrants. The US foreign-born population represented 13.9 percent of the population in 2018 and is expected to increase to almost a quarter (23.3 percent) of the older population by 2060 (Figure 11.1).

Most foreign-born residents live in large metropolitan areas in California, Florida, and New York. By and large, they are not recent immigrants, and three-quarters are US citizens. Four in 10 come from Latin America; 3 in 10 come from Asia, and about one-quarter are from Europe. Less than half of foreign-born older adults speak English at home or "very well," and they also tend to have lower levels of education compared to native-born older adults and foreign-born adults of working age. Foreign-born older adults are more likely to be living in poverty than native-born older adults (Mizoguchi et al., 2019). The diversity of the aging US population poses several challenges for the United States.

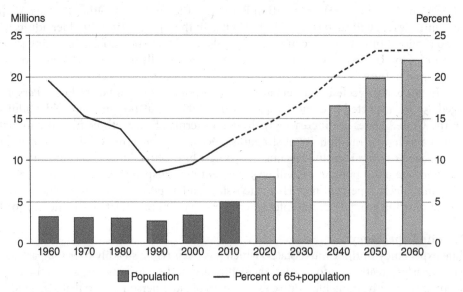

Figure 11.1 Foreign-born population 65 years and older: 1960–2010 and 2020–2060 (projected)
Source: US Census Bureau. Taken from US Census Bureau, American Community Survey Reports, ACS-42, "The Older Foreign-Born Population in the United States: 2012–2016." US Government Printing Office, Washington, DC, 2019.

IMMIGRATION, MIGRATION, AND AGING

Immigration involves many complex political and social issues. Regardless of one's age at immigration, the impact is lifelong. Immigration, also called **international migration**, is the movement of persons away from their place of usual residence and across an international border to a country of which they are not nationals (International Organization for Migration, 2021). In addition to differences in race and ethnicity, older immigrants differ based on their age at arrival in the destination country, the reasons for relocation, legal status, living arrangements, and their economic and social well-being (see, e.g., O'Neil & Tienda, 2015). Immigration also affects the older adults who remain in their home countries after younger family members move.

Who Migrates and Why?

Migration within countries often involves younger people moving to urban areas in search of work and opportunities, leaving older adults with fewer family members to help with caregiving and other types of support (Sun & Dutta, 2016; Willett & Sears, 2020). People who move internationally tend to be younger, wealthier, landowning, and better educated than those who stay behind (Kaczan & Orgill-Meyer, 2020).

There are numerous reasons for why people leave their home countries. **Push factors** are conditions in home countries, such as poverty, environmental degradation, lack of economic opportunity, political instability, and religious or ethnic persecution, which make people want to leave. **Pull factors** are features that attract immigrants to destination countries, such as opportunities for jobs and political freedom and the destination country's need for skills that immigrants possess (Johnson et al., 2020).

Nations accept immigrants for economic reasons (need for labor); social reasons (family reunification); humanitarian reasons (political asylum, settlement of refugees); and for cultural reasons (ethnic or cultural ties between the country of origin and destination country); however, policies vary greatly among nations (Helbling, 2018). The United States, Saudi Arabia, Germany, Russia, and the United Kingdom have the highest numbers of international migrants (Pew Research Center, 2019a). In many developed economies with large populations of older people, immigrants may be economically needed but not culturally welcomed (Faist, 2020). Barriers to immigration result from the desire to preserve jobs for existing residents or anti-immigrant sentiments, including xenophobia (Bloom et al., 2015). As shown in Figure 11.2, the United States historically has alternated between welcoming and excluding immigrants, often based on ethnic or national origin.

An estimated 79.5 million people (1 in 97) are **displaced persons**, people who have been forced from their home by persecution, conflict, or human rights violations. Displaced persons may seek refuge within their home country or outside of it. The number of displaced persons in the world doubled between 2010 and 2019, and the global pandemic added to other complex emergency situations that arise from interactions of climate, conflict, hunger, poverty, and persecution (United Nations High Commissioner for Refugees, 2020).

Refugees, a sub-category of displaced persons, have left their home countries because of persecution due to race, religion, nationality, membership in a particular social or ethnic group, or political opinion (US Department of State, n.d.). Persons outside of the United States can request refugee status, or, if they are in the United States or at the border, they

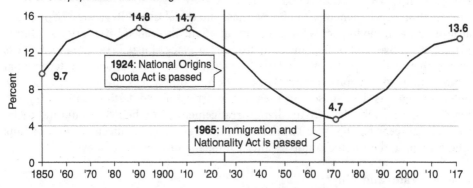

Figure 11.2 Changes in immigrant population in the United States, 1850–2017
Source: US Census Bureau, "Historical Census Statistics on the Foreign-Born Population of the United States, 1850–2000." Pew Research Center, Washington, DC (January 30, 2019) https://www.pewresearch.org/fact-tank/2019/01/30/immigrant-share-in-u-s-nears-record-high-but-remains-below-that-of-many-other-countries/ft_19-01-31_foreignbornshare_immigrantshareofus_2/.

can request political asylum. The number of refugees allowed into the United States was lowered from an average of about 70,000 per year during the Obama administration (2009–2016) to about 30,000 during the Trump administration (2017–2020) and raised again during the Biden administration to 125,000 (Refugee Processing Center, 2021). The number of refugees admitted by other nations has also fluctuated in response to political pressure and capacity to incorporate new populations into existing communities.

Older Adults in Home Countries

International migration presents challenges for older adults left behind when younger family members relocate. **Circular migration**, moving back and forth between home and destination countries for work that supports family members at home, is one

---

CASE 11.1

Chronic Health Conditions Among Older Refugees

The Syrian civil war, the source of most the world's displaced persons in 2019, created a prolonged and difficult refugee and humanitarian situation in that it displaced over 11 million people, including many older adults (United Nations High Commissioner for Refugees, 2020). Many older refugees have unmet needs in addressing chronic conditions such as hypertension and diabetes, which are not prioritized for care in the same way as acute problems and infectious diseases due to numerous challenges in access to care. Health screening data on Syrian refugees and Lebanese citizens aged 40 and over in host communities revealed that nearly two-thirds had hypertension, diabetes, or both. Situations including shortages of medications and supplies such as glucose test strips, insecurity of healthcare facilities due to conflict, and behaviors including smoking and physical inactivity exacerbate chronic illness among older refugees (Sibai et al., 2019).

What are some strategies to address chronic, noncommunicable diseases among older refugees?

reason for a high proportion of skip-generation families in some countries. For example, many adults in the Philippines take jobs in Saudi Arabia and other oil-producing nations of the Middle East or in locales in Asia (Singapore, Malaysia, Hong Kong, and Taiwan) as healthcare workers, domestic servants, and laborers on infrastructure projects (Asis, 2017). Adults from Mexico and Central America cross the US-Mexico border to find work, leaving their parents to care for their children. The financial support sent home is beneficial, but the arrangement can alter family roles, increase caregiver burden, and affect the health and well-being of the older adults left behind (McAuliffe & Khadria, 2019). In the United States, due to increased enforcement, fewer undocumented immigrants travel back and forth across the border, prolonging the separation of families and often leaving grandparents in permanent parental roles (Van Hook & Glick, 2020).

Migration of adult children often leaves older adults without someone to provide care and emotional support. The ability to communicate via the internet and smartphones has helped maintain ties even when family members cannot visit frequently (Bhattacharya & Shibusawa, 2009; Van Hook & Glick, 2020). However, older adults left behind have had to turn to other sources for care to replace support once provided by adult children. More research into the experiences of families trying to maintain intergenerational ties across international borders is needed to increase our understanding of the impact of family disruption due to circular migration (Van Hook & Glick, 2020).

Older Immigrants in Destination Countries
According to the United Nations, in 2019 adults aged 60+ constituted about 12 percent of the world's population, 17 percent of international migrants, 4 percent of internationally displaced persons, 6 percent of internally displaced persons, and 4 percent of refugees (United Nations High Commissioner for Refugees, 2020). Many older adults immigrate to join family members who previously immigrated.

US immigration law prioritizes family members of citizens and legal residents (Johnson et al., 2020). Older immigrants in the United States are diverse in terms of race, ethnicity, socioeconomic status and country of origin, and their experiences vary.

Figure 11.3 Syrian refugee in Zaatari Refugee Camp, Jordan, 2018
Source: Richard Juilliart/Shutterstock

They also differ with respect to when they arrived in the United States and their legal status (e.g., legal resident or undocumented). They often live in immigrant communities in urban areas (Bhattacharya & Shibusawa, 2009; Rodriguez, Paredes, & Hagan, 2017).

The lasting impact of immigration on older adults highlights the diversity of immigration experiences. Cultural expectations of care combined with the stress of caregiving, the need for financial support, and the degree of acculturation may complicate family relationships. **Acculturation** is the process of adaptation to the culture, customs, lifestyle, and expectations of the destination country while keeping or letting go of those of the origin country. Cultural beliefs and expectations may no longer be compatible with the realities and challenges of everyday life, including procuring employment, food, and housing, and addressing health and family caregiving needs. In many cases, older immigrants must deal with anti-immigrant sentiment. **Acculturative stress** is the distress associated with acculturation. External sources include the immigration process, discrimination, and work-related stress; internal sources include issues related to family and marital relationships, language, and health (Cervantes, Gattamorta, & Berger-Cardoso, 2019).

Early versus Late-Life Immigration

Early-life immigrants, many from developing nations, who migrated when younger to take advantage of economic and employment opportunities differ from late-life immigrants from the same countries who moved to join their adult children. For example, immigrants from India who arrived as young adults in the United States after restrictions were lifted in 1965 were well-educated and came to fulfill professional roles such as physicians or engineers. They are now older adults; when compared with their counterparts who arrived later in life, they are more assimilated, have a better ability to navigate health and social service systems, can speak English, are less socially isolated, and less dependent upon their adult children (Bhattacharya & Shibusawa, 2009).

Over half of older foreign-born adults have limited English proficiency (LEP), as defined by US Census data (Mizoguchi et al., 2019). The term **linguistic isolation** is used by the Census Bureau to describe households in which all members have LEP. Linguistic isolation can contribute to difficulties in accessing needed healthcare and social services networks outside of the family Living in a multigenerational household with English-speaking family members reduces isolation because these family members can help with support and service access. One study found that among all groups of US immigrants, those born in India with LEP are the least likely to be linguistically isolated because they live in multigenerational households where younger members speak English; linguistic isolation was high among those born in Ukraine because 33 percent of them lived alone (Gubernskaya & Treas, 2020).

Immigration can affect health status, particularly for older adults with multiple chronic health problems. Ideally, healthcare providers should consider health beliefs and practices and the cultural needs of their patients to ensure optimal care, but this doesn't always happen. Hospitals in Australia attempt to be responsive to the needs of people who represent many nations and cultural traditions by hiring a diverse staff and making interpreters available. Yet a study of 2,180 "acutely unwell" older people admitted to a hospital in Sydney revealed that non-English speakers were more likely to die in the hospital than those able to speak English, suggesting that linguistic isolation may have impeded quality of care and the ability to navigate the hospital system (Basic, Shanley, & Gonzales, 2017).

Older Refugees Fleeing War and Terror
Refugees fleeing war, terror, and threats to their lives often have experiences of trauma that has wide-ranging impact. For example, trauma faced by female refugees from Middle Eastern and African nations who had resettled in Germany included living in a war zone, near-death experiences, witnessing the deaths of family members, domestic violence, and lack of access to healthcare. The refugees differed by age with respect to quality of life, health, and self-perception (e.g., satisfaction with self), with older women reporting poorer health than younger refugees (Jesuthasan et al., 2018). A qualitative study of older refugees from Iraq, Lebanon, Palestine, and Somalia and their adult children living in Denmark revealed tensions arising from differing expectations of the generations. The older adults expected their children to care for them as they aged, while it is typical for older Danish adults needing care to go to nursing homes. The children, while recognizing their duty, were burdened by multiple pressures of providing care and maintaining cultural traditions while trying to integrate into the Danish society (Nielsen et al. 2018).

Legal Status and Threat of Deportation
The population of immigrants who are not legally authorized to live or work in the United States is estimated as 10.5 million, with the majority having lived in the country for more than ten years (Lopez, Passel, & Cohn, 2021). A significant stressor experienced by older immigrants is fear of immigration enforcement actions, including deportation. Due to changes in law, even immigrants with legal residence can be deported for past crimes. They and their family members may be permanently separated because of increased border security that makes travel back and forth risky. This fear may keep them from obtaining needed healthcare and participating in public gatherings (Rodriguez et al., 2017).

AGING AND CLIMATE CHANGE
Climate change refers to changes in average weather conditions that last over multiple decades, including increases and decreases in temperature, changes in patterns of precipitation, and changes in the risk of severe weather events, including heat waves, hurricanes, flooding, and drought (Crimmins et al., 2016). **Anthropogenic** climate change is directly or indirectly caused by the activities of humans, such as the emission of greenhouse gases from motor vehicles or logging in the Amazon rainforest. The results of climate change have both immediate and long-term impacts on the well-being of older adults in terms of migration and immigration, threats to health, destruction of homes and communities, and death.

Climate Change and Migration
Climate change contributes to some within-country and cross-border migration or population movement from rural to urban areas (Faist, 2020). In Kenya, younger adults have left drought-affected rural areas to find work in urban centers, while older adults are more likely stay behind and must adapt to changes (Willett & Sears, 2020). Poverty and lack of resources can prevent people from moving from climate-affected areas. Some countries use planned or forced relocation to address the impact of climate

change, as in areas with increased coastal flooding. In Vietnam, people who were relocated due to coastal flooding caused by climate change lost important social networks and the means for supporting themselves; planners learned "that the proximity of households to livelihoods and maintenance of social networks, as well as people's agency in the decision-making process, are critical in determining the successful restoration of people's lives after resettlement" (Miller & Dun, 2019, p.143). In coming years, more people, many aged 65+, will have to relocate due to environmental impacts such as flooding, drought, and fires caused by climate change.

Health Impacts of Climate Change
While climate change can affect the health of people of every age, many older adults have vulnerabilities related to the normal physiological changes of aging, multiple health conditions, cognitive impairment, or difficulty with mobility. One notable example is increased mortality from extreme heat, especially among socially isolated older adults. Between 1991 and 2018, up to 37 percent of deaths from extreme heat can be attributed to anthropogenic climate change across the globe, though variations by country and region are considerable. Major heat waves occurred in Europe in 2003 (70,000 deaths) and Russia in 2010 (55,000 deaths) and more recently in Britain, Japan, and Sweden (Vicedo-Cabrera et al., 2021). In the summer of 2021, excessive heat in the western United States was responsible for over 200 deaths (Childs, 2021).

Vulnerability to the impact of climate change is a function of exposure, sensitivity, and adaptive capacity. Exposure means contact with the stressor, such as living in an area that disproportionately experiences hurricanes and coastal flooding. Sensitivity is the degree to which one is affected by a stressor, such as having a chronic lung condition that is affected by poor air quality. Adaptive capacity is the ability to deal with a stressor; this includes lack of resources to avoid or mitigate the effects of climate change, such as living in poor-quality housing or lacking air conditioning in housing in areas that experience extreme heat (McDermott-Levy et al., 2019). Table 11.2 provides some examples of the impact of climate change on health.

Climate Change and Natural Disasters
The increase in the number and intensity of natural disasters such as drought, hurricanes, flooding, and extreme heat that are aggravated by rising sea levels and other events associated with climate change do not affect everyone equally (Nicholas & Breakey, 2019). Ageism, often combined with racism and classism, has created conditions that make it more likely that older persons are disproportionately affected by natural disasters (Gullette, 2017). Natural disasters threaten health and safety, property, infrastructure, and national security and lead to insecurity, disruption of life, and economic loss. Some disasters, such as hurricanes, can be predicted; others occur without warning. (US Department of Homeland Security, n.d.).

The effect of Hurricane Katrina on New Orleans in August 2005 revealed that older adults who are poor and/or disabled are very vulnerable when a natural disaster occurs. After Katrina, an AARP survey found that about 13 million people aged 50+ would need help evacuating in the event of a disaster, and about half of those said they would need help from someone outside of their household (Gibson & Hayunga, 2006). Ageism affected who was rescued and the nature of media coverage in the aftermath of

Table 11.2 Climate Change Impact on the Health of Older Adults

Climate change impact	Examples of age-related vulnerabilities	Impact on older adults
More frequent and prolonged heat waves	Body is less able to sense temperature change	Heat-related illness and death
	Living in home without air conditioning	
	Need to take multiple medications to address comorbidities	Medications exposed to heat rendered less effective
Longer pollen season due to higher temperatures	Stronger allergic response	More days with poor air quality
Flooding caused by rising sea levels and more intense precipitation	Mobility impairment	Evacuation more difficult for mobility impaired
	Cognitive impairment	Emergency shelters may not be able to meet needs of older evacuees with no family support
Increased risk of mold in homes and care facilities	Weakened immune response	Increased health risk from exposure to mold spores
Increase in vector-borne diseases (e.g., Lyme disease)	Osteoporosis and osteoarthritis	Increased vulnerability to symptoms of Lyme disease, which include arthritis and pain in tendons, muscles, and bones

Sources: McDermott-Levy & Fick, 2020; McDermott-Levy et al., 2019.

the storm (Gullette, 2017). Some older adults either refused to leave or could not evacuate because of lack of transportation. The 1,833 deaths in New Orleans were mostly due to drowning in flooded areas; 74 percent of the victims were aged 60+, and 50 percent were aged 75+. Some had been through many hurricanes and decided that the risks of evacuating (because of their infirmities) were greater than the risks of staying put. Many deaths occurred because many of the mostly poor and African American older adults were not evacuated early enough. Tragically, 68 deaths also occurred in nursing homes where caretakers abandoned the residents (Gibson & Hayunga, 2006).

Reasons for the high percentage of deaths among older adults included social isolation and lack of social support. Older men were more likely to drown than older women because they were more likely to be socially isolated. In addition, some of those who were evacuated did not survive.

In New Orleans, some people who were evacuated to the Superdome died due to lack of access to treatment and medicine (Gullette, 2017). Staff at other evacuation sites could not always meet the needs of older evacuees with chronic health conditions, physical impairments, limited mobility, or cognitive impairment. After Katrina, health professionals at the Houston Astrodome screened vulnerable elders with pressing needs and found that most needed medical and/or mental health services. They exhibited cognitive impairment, major health problems, or could not perform one or more activities of daily living. Many of these problems existed prior to evacuation. Care systems had been disrupted, and the stress of the disaster likely exacerbated existing disabilities (Dyer et al. 2008). Katrina also had long-term effects on older people who had

CASE 11.2

Aftermath of Superstorm Sandy

Carmen, age 80, lived with her little dog Coco on the 10th floor of a public housing building in a low-lying area of Brooklyn, New York. In 2012, Superstorm Sandy caused widespread power outages in the city and flooding in her neighborhood. Though Carmen had heard the recommendations the evacuate, she chose to stay. She did not believe the storm would be as massive and dangerous as it was, her arthritis made walking difficult, and she did not want to leave Coco. In the aftermath of the storm, she was trapped. She had no family or friends in places with power and lacked the cab fare to get to them. Food that she could not cook rotted in her refrigerator. Her water supply was dwindling, and the nights were terrifying because there was so little light and so much noise and commotion outside. She was frightened to leave and increasingly desperate and disoriented.

What measures are needed to improve the chances that older adults such as Carmen will be willing to evacuate in the event of a disaster such as Superstorm Sandy?

---

deep roots in their community. Whether they returned home or remained elsewhere, Katrina forever altered people's support systems and their way of life.

Since Katrina, many other storms have revealed the vulnerability of older adults. In 2012, Superstorm Sandy caused extensive damage and left many without power for several days. Many were older adults living in high-rise buildings in New York City who were stranded without food and incapable of leaving due to lack of elevator service. Hurricanes Irma and Maria damaged hospitals and limited access to medical care in the Virgin Islands and Puerto Rico in 2017. Health workers in the St. Thomas, US Virgin Islands, reported that older and chronically ill patients were at risk after the hurricane due to disruption in their social support networks and systems. Aging in place is the norm in the Afro-Caribbean culture of St. Thomas, where there are no long-term care or assisted living facilities (Chowdhury et al., 2019).

A spirit of collective responsibility and a commitment to fighting ageism is needed to improve disaster response and addressing the impact of climate change. As the twenty-first century progresses, global climate change will continue to upend lives and harm older persons, particularly those who are vulnerable due to health conditions, socioeconomic status, social identity, or citizenship status. In addition to working to mitigate the worst effects of climate change, social action to achieve change on a global level is necessary to reduce the impact going forward and preserve the world for the older adults of the future, including the readers of this book.

CHAPTER REVIEW

Global Aging

- The United Nations traces trends in global aging and advocates on behalf of older persons worldwide.
- By 2050, people aged 65+ will outnumber children aged five and younger.
- Increases in the old age dependency ratio raise questions about how to support people as they age.

- Global patterns of living arrangements vary, with more adults likely to live alone or with a spouse in developed economies and more older adults living in intergenerational households in developing economies.
- The impact of increased life expectancy will depend on the health and well-being of people living longer lives.
- Labor force participation after age 65 varies by gender, a nation's social safety net for older adults, and level of economic development.
- Eradicating worldwide ageism will allow older adults to live healthier, longer, and more secure lives.

Culture and Aging
- Cross-cultural and cross-national comparisons on aging show what is universal and what is unique about expectations for how people age and how older adults are treated in different contexts.
- Cultural influences on aging, such as the tradition of filial piety in East Asian cultures, change due to global socioeconomic and demographic change.
- Culture influences how people define and view aging-related concepts such as the meaning of elder abuse or successful aging.

Aging in the United States in Global Context
- Like other developed nations, the United States has a high proportion of adults aged 65 and older and a formal social safety net.
- The diversity of the aging population in the United States including the increasing percentage of foreign-born residents is a sign of its global interconnections and distinguishes it from other developed nations.

Immigration, Migration, and Aging
- In 2019, adults aged 60 and over comprised 17 percent of the world's international migrants, including a smaller number of refugees.
- The impact of immigration depends upon the age at immigration, the level of family and social support available, and the degree of acculturation and linguistic isolation.
- Circular migration of working-age adults leaves older adults in less developed nations responsible for their grandchildren.
- Global climate change contributes to within-country and cross-border migration by making living environments dangerous or uninhabitable.

Aging and Climate Change
- Older adults are vulnerable to the effects of climate change because of normal physiological changes of aging, comorbidities, cognitive impairment, and mobility impairments.
- Prolonged heat waves cause excess mortality among older adults. Older adults have been disproportionately affected by hurricanes due to difficulties with evacuation, disruption to social networks, and interrupted access to healthcare and social services.

REVIEW QUESTIONS
1. Describe some of the impacts of the aging of the population worldwide.
2. What are some factors to consider when determining the impact of immigration on older adults?
3. Describe how global climate change can affect health and well-being of older adults. Can you find evidence of the impact of climate change in your community or state?

KEY TERMS

United Nations
Sustainable Development Goals
fertility rate
mortality rate
migration
old age dependency ratio
replacement level
skip-generation household
life expectancy
noncommunicable diseases
labor force participation rate
culture
filial piety
international migration
push factors
pull factors
displaced persons
refugees
circular migration
acculturation
acculturative stress
linguistic isolation
anthropogenic

CHAPTER 12

Legal, Policy, and Economic Issues That Affect Older US Adults

Chapter Outline
Social Policies and Legislation
    Social Policy and Aging Policy
    History of US Aging Policies
    Social Security
        Beneficiaries
        Retirement Age
        Sustainability
    Medicare
    Medicaid
    Affordable Care Act
    Older Americans Act
    Long-Term Care Services and Supports
        Cost of Long-Term Care
        Quality of Long-Term Care
    Elder Justice Act
    Americans with Disabilities Act
    Assistance for Low-Income Older Adults
Poverty, Inequality, and Cumulative Disadvantage
    Poverty Measurement
    Who Is Poor?
        Variance Between Population Groups
        Cumulative Advantage/Disadvantage
Political Participation and Advocacy
    Voting Patterns of Older Adults
    Intersection of Politics and Policy
    Advocacy Organizations
        AARP
        Gray Panthers
        Leadership Council of Aging Organizations
        Other Organizations

Learning Objectives
- Describe landmark US legislation and social policies that address older adults and the aging process, including the Social Security Act, Medicare, Medicaid, and the Older Americans Act.
- Explain how poverty is measured in terms of US government programs and how inequality and cumulative disadvantage affect older adults.
- Describe how political participation and advocacy by and on behalf of older adults can contribute to improved longevity and quality of life in later years.

Previous chapters have included some mention of various laws, policies, and programs that support older adults. In this chapter, we focus on US laws and policies that aim to support older adults, the issues behind those laws and policies, and the outcomes as they have affected the well-being of diverse older adults. We also look at political participation and advocacy by and on behalf of older adults.

SOCIAL POLICIES AND LEGISLATION
In this section, we examine social policy related to aging and provide an overview of the major laws designed to provide vital support to people in their 60s and beyond, including those related to the Social Security, Medicare, and Medicaid programs.

Social Policy and Aging Policy
Social policies are courses of action designed to enhance conditions of social well-being in a society. **Social welfare policies** are laws and regulations that provide protection from certain challenges of modern life when societal institutions such as the family, the economy, and religious organizations are unable to meet people's needs. These policies provide structured ways to address circumstances such as poverty, job or income loss, sickness, disability, and old age. Governments develop and implement social welfare policies to address common human needs (Midgley & Livermore, 2009).

Social welfare policies known as "aging policies" make the services and support we have discussed in earlier chapters possible and have a significant impact on the well-being of older adults. Ideally, they allow people to age with dignity and to maximize self-determination. Social policies also affect decisions people make about employment, marriage, saving for retirement and when to retire, where to live, home ownership, long-term care, and family caregiving. Important policy areas are healthcare, economic security, and meeting the needs of vulnerable older adults.

The services and supports available to older adults are some of the most generous social welfare benefits available in the US social welfare system. However, a sizeable proportion of people are socially isolated as they age and lack sufficient resources for housing, food, and long-term care. Social Security and Medicare, described in later sections, have come under increased fiscal pressure with the number of retiring baby boomers and competition for scarce resources (Reisch, 2019).

History of US Aging Policies
During the colonial period, Poor Laws (based on those in England) specified that families were responsible for the care of children and older family members. When

family members were not available to provide care, the indigent aged were treated as "deserving poor" who received public relief by placement in an almshouse or by being "boarded out" in the households of other community members. By the end of the nineteenth century, almshouses evolved into today's **board and care homes**, which provide personal assistance to older adults and others who cannot live on their own (Haber, 2016).

Despite these supports, older people were largely on their own in ensuring they had enough resources to survive. In a largely rural society, family members cared for older relatives who were no longer able to work. As the population grew and the country became increasingly urbanized and industrialized, people migrated to cities. Men, women, and children worked in factories to provide sufficient resources for their families. By necessity, people continued to work as they aged (Stern & Axinn, 2018). Average life expectancy was shorter; in 1900, average life expectancy at birth in the United States was 46.3 for men and 48.3 for women. At the end of 2021, life expectancy at birth was 77 in the United States (Population Reference Bureau, 2021).

During the Progressive Era (late nineteenth and early twentieth centuries), social reformers sought ways to respond to the hazards and challenges of modern life, including making the workplace safer, providing public education for all children, and making sure that people had support in their old age. The Great Depression sparked the passage of the Social Security Act of 1935, discussed in the following section.

Social Security

In the United States, Social Security is the foundation for economic security for most households of older individuals (Veghte & Schreur, 2019). Nearly every working American participates in this **social insurance** program that requires workers and employers to contribute via a mandatory payroll tax. The funds are used to support workers and their dependents in retirement and in the event of death or disability. The Social Security Act of 1935 has significantly influenced the well-being of older Americans.

During the Great Depression, an estimated 50 percent of the older population lived in poverty. The Social Security Act (SSA) of 1935 established a system that provided retirement income, benefits for survivors, unemployment insurance, and a variety of public assistance programs. The original legislation has been amended many times to expand the categories of beneficiaries and the types of workers covered (Veghte & Schreur, 2019). The original Act provided Old Age Assistance (OAA) so that states could provide cash assistance to older adults meeting a **means test**, which is a determination that income and assets are sufficiently low to qualify for benefits. OAA was converted in 1972 to the Supplemental Security Income (SSI) program, which aids low-income older adults and persons with disabilities who meet eligibility requirements.

The most well-known Social Security program is the Old Age, Survivors, and Disability Insurance (OASDI) program, an **entitlement program** that provides income in retirement for all eligible workers. It also provides benefits for survivors (widows, widowers, and dependents of eligible workers) and for workers who become disabled. Workers who contribute to the Social Security system for at least ten years receive monthly retirement benefits based on their career earnings. Persons with lower lifetime earnings receive more benefits relative to their career average wages. For example, a person who retired in 2020 at age 65 with career average wages of $25,010 would receive yearly benefits that total 51 percent of that amount ($12,825), while a person who earned an average of the maximum taxable amount of $136,710 would receive yearly benefits of 25 percent of that amount ($34,180) (National Academy of Social Insurance, 2021).

The program was originally intended to provide income that would be supplemented by an individual's personal savings and pension(s). In the decades following the original legislation, the US economy and the structure of the labor market went through massive changes; subsequent economic recessions left many retirees and surviving family members with little support in retirement except Social Security income. Family caregiving responsibilities have forced many women to curtail their employment or leave the workforce. This results in lower contributions to Social Security and less-than-adequate retirement income. Divorce, periods of unemployment, and other disruptions have also led to lower income in retirement.

Beneficiaries

One in five individuals and one in four families receive income from Social Security benefits; the majority of these are retired workers. Nine out of ten individuals aged 65+ receive Social Security. Among older beneficiaries, 21 percent of married couples and 45 percent of unmarried individuals receive 90 percent or more of their income from Social Security. Older persons of color are more likely to rely on Social Security for the greater part of their income than white persons (National Academy of Social Insurance, 2021). Figure 12.1 provides a snapshot of those who received benefits in 2020 (Social Security Administration, n.d.a, n.d.b).

Retirement Age

When the Social Security Act was first passed, the full-benefit retirement age was 65. Reforms implemented to control costs raised the retirement age based on an individual's year of birth. The full retirement age is 66 for those born between 1943 and 1954.

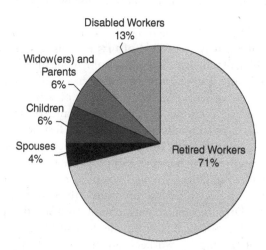

Figure 12.1 Social Security beneficiaries as of November 20, 2020

Source: Data taken from United States Social Security Administration, 2020. Public domain.

It increases in increments (66 years plus a number of months) for those born between 1955 and 1959. Full retirement age is 67 for individuals born in 1960 or later.

People can retire and receive benefits starting at age 62 but they will have a reduced monthly benefit; people who delay retirement receive a credit for their delay up to age 70. People consider many factors in their decision to retire that include their health and family health history, their caregiving responsibilities, and other resources saved for retirement (Veghte & Schreur, 2019).

Sustainability

Future costs for Social Security will increase due to population aging. The contributions to the Social Security trust funds, the Old Age and Survivors Insurance (OASI) trust fund, and the Disability Insurance (DI) trust fund, are separate from the federal budget. The contributions of current workers finance the benefits of current retirees, and the excess is invested in US government securities. While trust fund assets through 2020 exceeded benefits paid, 2021 was the first year when revenue is expected to fall short. This trend will continue because fewer younger people are entering the workforce. The program faces financial pressures to increase reserves due to the large number of retirees eligible for benefits in the coming years. Without actions to improve the long-term financial outlook for Social Security, the trust fund will be exhausted by 2034. Proposed actions include changing the way the cost-of-living adjustments are calculated and raising the maximum taxable income subject to FICA taxes (National Academy of Social Insurance, 2021).

While some policymakers and critics portray Social Security as a budgetary problem, it is also a solution to the problem of poverty. Efforts to maintain the program will ensure that people continue to be protected during the times in their lives when they are not able to be productive (Veghte & Schreur, 2019). In polls, Americans have consistently supported the retention of full benefits offered by Social Security, and the program is politically popular (Newport, 2019).

Medicare

The federal **Medicare** and Medicaid programs were established in 1965 as part of the Great Society legislation of the Lyndon B. Johnson administration (Stern & Axinn, 2018). Both programs provide vital health services to people aged 65 and older. **Medicare** is health insurance for people aged 65+, people under age 65 with certain disabilities, and people with end-stage renal disease. Like Social Security, it is funded through an employer/employee payroll tax, and most recipients are also eligible for Social Security. Over 63 million Americans were enrolled in Medicare in 2021 (Centers for Medicare and Medicaid Services, n.d.a). Although most beneficiaries report good or excellent health, many live with multiple chronic health conditions that limit their activities of daily living. Half of those on Medicare have annual incomes below $26,200 and savings of less than $75,000 (KFF, 2019).

Medicare has four parts:

- Part A is hospital insurance that covers stays in the hospital, skilled nursing facilities (nursing homes and rehabilitation centers), and some home healthcare and hospice care.
- Part B covers doctor visits and outpatient and preventive services.

- Part C refers to optional Medicare Advantage plans. These are managed care health insurance plans offered by private companies approved by Medicare. They cover Part A and Part B services and may include additional benefits such as vision, hearing, and dental care. Most Medicare Advantage plans include Part D coverage.
- Part D, passed in 2003 and also optional, provides prescription drug coverage through a variety of private plans that contract with Medicare (KFF, 2019).

Medicare does not meet all medical needs or pay for some services such as long-term services and supports (LTSS), hearing aids, eyeglasses, and dental care. Figure 12.2 shows the breakout of Medicare benefit payments by type of service. Many beneficiaries pay up to several thousand dollars of their own funds each year to buy supplemental coverage and to cover out-of-pocket expenses such as **deductibles** and **coinsurance**.

Medicare expenditures totaled $799.4 billion in 2019, accounting for 21 percent of national health expenditures. Medicare expenditures will grow over the next several years because more people will reach the age of eligibility, and healthcare costs, including prescription drug costs, will increase (KFF, 2019). Despite rising costs, political support for Medicare is high across political affiliations and generations (Moskowitz, 2018).

Medicaid

Medicaid is a federal-state public assistance program that provides health coverage to eligible low-income adults, children, pregnant women, and people with disabilities. Unlike Medicare, Medicaid is funded from general tax revenues. States administer their own Medicaid programs. They decide which populations and services are covered in accordance with core requirements on eligibility and benefits set by the federal government. Medicaid is the only government-provided funding for long-term care (LTC) services. Originally, Medicaid covered LTC in nursing homes only. Today, due to efforts to reduce the need for institutional care, home- and community-based LTC services are covered via

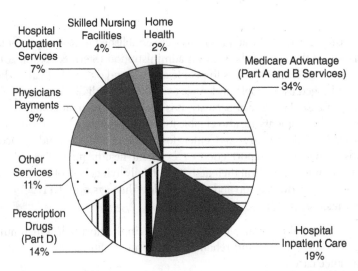

Figure 12.2 Medicare benefit payments by type of service in 2019
Source: Data taken from economic forecast of CBO, January 7, 2020. Public domain.

a process known as community waivers (Rudowitz, Garfield, & Hinton, 2019). People must meet strict income and asset requirements to be eligible for Medicaid.

Medicaid expenditures totaled $671.2 billion in 2020, accounting for 16 percent of national health expenditures (Centers for Medicare & Medicaid Services, n.d.b). Expenditures grew during the pandemic and were expected to fall in 2022 (Williams, 2021). Concern about the impact of the growing population that will be eligible for Medicare and Medicaid coverage has prompted Congress to try to rein in costs, but with limited success. Proposals to cap the cost of Medicaid by turning it into a **block grant** program have not succeeded due to the popularity of the program and the need for coverage of vulnerable populations (Miller, Huberfeld, & Jones, 2021).

Affordable Care Act

The **Patient Protection and Affordable Care Act**, popularly known as Obamacare or the Affordable Care Act (ACA), passed in 2010, altered access to healthcare in the United States and made changes to Medicaid and Medicare. The intent of the ACA was to expand health insurance coverage to more individuals and families and to increase access to care. ACA provisions included requiring employers of businesses with 50 or more full-time employees to provide health insurance, subsidizing privately purchased health insurance, and prohibiting insurance companies from denying coverage to individuals with **pre-existing conditions** such as diabetes, heart disease, and cancer (National Conference of State Legislatures, 2011).

The ACA expanded Medicaid to adults under the age of 65 with incomes of up to 138 percent of the **federal poverty level**, with the federal government paying 90 percent of the cost of the expansion (French et al., 2016). Many people, particularly those in their 50s and 60s, who had avoided seeking care because they could not afford or obtain private health insurance now had access to healthcare services. A 2012 Supreme Court ruling allowed states to opt out of Medicaid expansion. Subsequently, twelve states ended their Medicaid expansion programs, which left those individuals again without health insurance in those states (Flowers & Hado, 2020).

The ACA addressed the rising costs of Medicare through reforms that included reductions in payments to providers. These reforms also made an annual wellness visit and certain preventive services available at no charge to patients. Provisions of the ACA reduced out-of-pocket costs for prescription drugs by fixing a feature of Medicare Part D known as the "donut hole," a gap in coverage for prescription drugs that is activated once a person's total drug costs reach a certain limit ($4,130 in 2021). Strengthened efforts to address racial and ethnic health disparities through the Office for Minority Health also helped older adults (Mauldin, Lee, Tang, Herrera, & Williams, 2020).

Although public support for the ACA has increased over time, its long-term success will depend largely on which political party controls the presidency and Congress. Many in the Democratic party and in the public support ongoing efforts to expand access to care and reduce costs; the Republican party opposes expansion of government-provided benefits and prefers that healthcare remain largely in the private sector.

Older Americans Act

The **Older Americans Act** (OAA) was passed in 1965 to assist individuals aged 65+, was amended in 1973 to include individuals aged 60+, and last reauthorized in 2020.

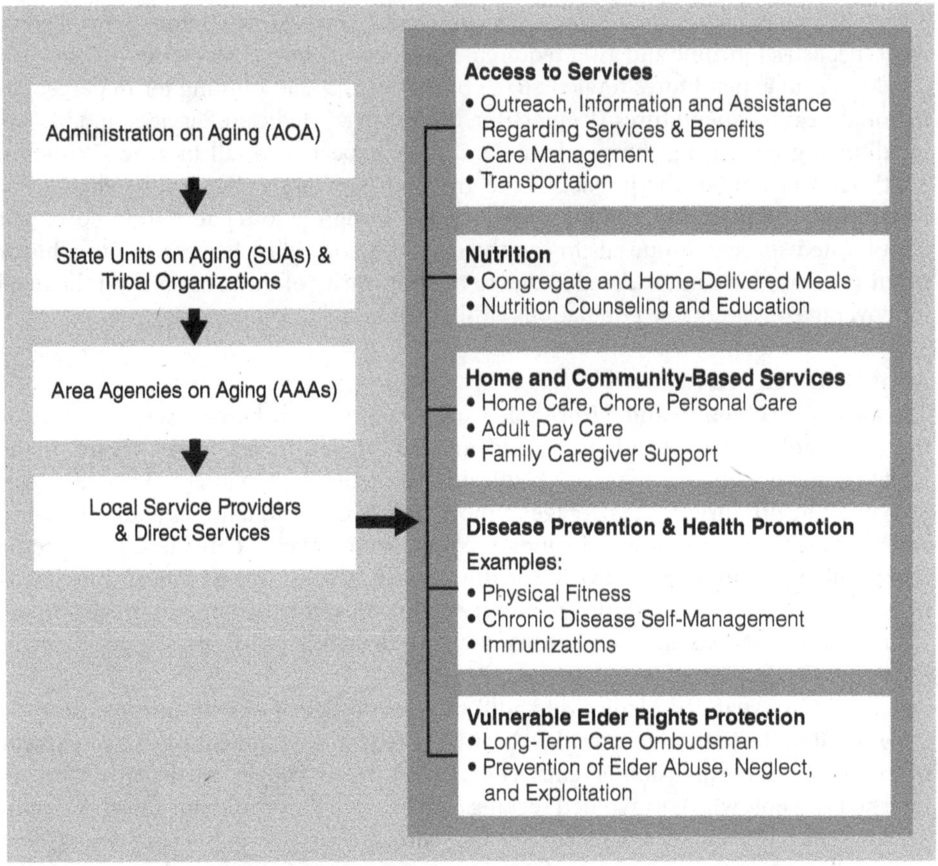

Figure 12.3 Flow of federal, state, tribal, and local funding to local service providers and direct services for older adults
Source: Colello & Napili, 2020. Older Americans Act: Overview and Funding, "Figure 1. The Aging Network." Prepared by the Congressional Research Service. Updated June 23, 2022.

It established the Administration on Aging (AoA) within the Department of Health and Human Services as the chief federal advocate for older Americans. Through the OAA, each state has an Office on Aging and organizes services and programs for those aged 60+ per the terms of this legislation (Colello & Napili, 2020). Services authorized by the OAA include nutrition, personal care, disease prevention and health promotion, legal services, transportation, family caregiver support, and personal care. Figure 12.3 shows the agencies and organizations that comprise the Aging Network.

Total OAA funding in 2020 was $2.1 billion, with the largest portion going to nutrition programs (Colello & Napili, 2020). Formulas established by the legislation determine the amount of funding for each state, which provides a portion of the total funds needed for each type of service. States and localities must provide **matching funds**, and most states provide additional public and private funds to support OAA programs. Federal funding has not kept pace with inflation or the growth of the population of adults aged 60+ and OAA programs do not reach all eligible participants (Ujvari, Fox-Grage, & Houser, 2019). Despite these limitations, OAA-funded programs provide important services that allow people to age in place. Home and community based services (HCBS) include personal care, home-delivered meals, adult day services, and other supports that help people in their own homes as they age.

Long-Term Services and Supports

The United States lacks comprehensive policies and programs to cover pressing long-term care needs. These can include more support for families through paid family leave and flexible workplace policies, programs to pay for long-term care in the home, and programs that support family caregivers when they curtail their work or drop out of the workforce. **Long-term services and supports** (LTSS) comprise "the broad range of paid and unpaid medical and personal care assistance that people may need—for several weeks, months, or years—when they experience difficulty completing self-care tasks as a result of aging, chronic illness, or disability" (Reaves & Musumeci, 2015, para 2).

Cost of Long-Term Care

Policies that help pay for care recognize that the cost of services often exceeds people's resources. Problems in affording care, along with pressures on state budgets for Medicaid and other services, have been growing for decades (Cohen et al., 2020). The ACA attempted to expand long-term care services through the Community Living Assistance Services and Supports (CLASS) Act, a voluntary social insurance program that was repealed in 2012 (Stone, 2019).

LTSS are provided in institutional and home- and community-based settings. Their costs are covered in a variety of ways:

- Out of pocket by the service recipient or a family member
- Private health and long-term care insurance
- Medicaid and other public programs such as those provided under the OAA, including home and community-based services and the Long-Term Care Ombudsman Program

Both Medicare and Medicaid assist with paying for in-home and nursing home care for eligible recipients. Medicaid is the primary payer for LTSS, while coverage provided by Medicare is limited (Reaves & Musumeci, 2015). Medicare covers home healthcare but not personal care services for beneficiaries who are homebound and will pay for up to 100 days in a nursing facility following a hospital stay. Initially, Medicaid covered LTSS in nursing homes only and now pays for the majority of nursing home care in the United States (Rudowitz, Garfield, & Hinton, 2019). The Omnibus Reconciliation Act of 1981 allowed states to pursue Medicaid funding for home- and community-based care through Section 1915(c) waivers, which increased in the 1990s (Miller, Huberfeld, & Jones, 2021). Today, more than half of LTSS provided by Medicaid are for home- and community-based care.

States also provide LTSS to low-income residents through programs that aim to decrease reliance on nursing homes and to avoid or delay involvement in more intensive services funded by Medicaid. State-funded programs often have waiting lists and often compete with other state priorities for funding (O'Brien, Fox-Grage, & Ujvari, 2019).

Some states have developed solutions to finance LTSS for their citizens who cannot afford to pay for long-term care insurance. The state of Washington developed a LTSS social insurance program that is available to all working residents and funded through a mandatory payroll tax. Other states have also explored ways to help pay for long-term care with the goal of reducing the need for resources from Medicaid (Cohen et al., 2020).

Quality of Long-Term Care

The **Nursing Home Reform Act of 1987** addressed poor quality of care in nursing homes through establishing national standards for quality resident care, creating a program to monitor care and ensure that residents' rights were upheld, and establishing certification procedures to ensure that nursing homes meet minimum standards for quality of care. These standards included requirements for staffing, reduction in use of unnecessary drugs or physical restraints, and improvement in physical care with respect to pressure ulcers and incontinence (Sehrawat, 2010).

Gaps exist between the intention of the law and how it has been implemented. For example, the law requires that all nursing homes provide social services to address psychosocial needs of residents and requires that facilities with 120 or more beds have a qualified social worker (with at least a bachelor's degree in social work or a related field) on staff. Most nursing homes have fewer than 120 residents. Given the range of needs of nursing home residents and the fact that the average nursing home has fewer beds, the legislation does not provide enough muscle to ensure that residents will receive high-quality psychosocial services (Sehrawat, 2010).

The certification processes for Medicare and Medicaid also affect the quality of care in nursing homes and assisted-living facilities. These processes examine whether facilities promote residents' rights, including the right to a dignified existence, quality of life, quality of care, and reporting of abuse and neglect. The Long-Term Care Ombudsman Program, established by 1978 amendments to the OAA, provides funding and mandates for the operation of State Ombudsman programs, which in turn designate local agencies to investigate complaints and provide other services to protect residents' well-being and rights (Mauldin et al., 2020).

Elder Justice Act

Efforts to protect and promote the rights of older adults in the community and in institutions have unfolded around elder justice. The Elder Justice Act (EJA), which first passed in 2010 as part of the ACA, focused on establishing a coordinated federal response to elder abuse through health and social service approaches to its prevention, detection, and treatment.

The EJA, which was enacted as part of the Affordable Care Act (ACA) on March 23, 2010, resulted from seven years of efforts by a bipartisan group of lawmakers, lobbyists, practitioners, researchers, and advocates inside and outside the government. It represented Congress's first attempt to pass comprehensive legislation to address abuse, neglect, and exploitation of the elderly at the federal level. Even with bipartisan support, ongoing disputes between Democrats and Republicans over federal spending priorities mean that adequate funding was never obtained to address these goals. In today's Congress, one of the only realistic ways to get legislative proposals related to aging or human services passed is to bundle them with larger bills (Benson, 2018). The ACA passed with Democratic votes only, and most of the authorized expenditures of $777 million dollars were never appropriated (appropriations legislation authorizes federal agencies to spend money previously authorized) (Hubbard, 2020).

The EJA legislated public health and social service approaches to elder abuse under the Department of Health and Human Services in three areas:

- The Elder Justice Coordinating Council includes representatives from 14 federal agencies and offices and meets annually to coordinate activities related to elder abuse at the federal level.
- Programs to Promote Elder Justice involves strengthening existing services, including training of direct care workers, and promoting the use of electronic health records in long-term care, funding for Adult Protective Services, grants to improve and try new approaches to APS programs, and funds to improve the Long-Term Care Ombudsman Program.
- Protection for Residents of Long-Term Care Facilities provides for training government inspectors who investigate complaints of abuse, neglect, and exploitation in LTC facilities that receive Medicare and Medicaid.

The EJA also amended federal law to require federally funded LTC facilities to report crimes against residents or individuals receiving care from those facilities and established a National Nurse Aide Registry, a national database of nursing aides who have completed state-mandated training, and registration requirements that would track those barred from working in LTC facilities due to substantiated findings of abuse, neglect, or exploitation.

Because Congress did not fully fund the EJA, most of its provisions are unfulfilled. As of 2020, about 8 percent of the funds ($66 million) had been appropriated by Congress for elder justice activities. These include Elder Abuse Prevention Intervention Demonstrations, Elder Justice Innovation Grants, the development of the National Adult Maltreatment Reporting System, and other activities related to APS, including demonstration grants and technical assistance.

Elder Justice Reauthorization Acts were introduced in 2020 in the House and the Senate, but no action was taken. However, the momentum to provide more support for elder justice activities has continued. The American Rescue Plan of 2021, one of the most "age-friendly" laws in years, provided $276 million per year in elder justice funding through 2022, allowing APS more resources to prevent and ameliorate elder abuse and to focus on related problems (Blancato & Whitmire, 2021).

Americans with Disabilities Act

Inspired by the Civil Rights movement of the 1960s, the disability rights movement advocated for the **Americans with Disabilities Act** (ADA), passed in 1990. The ADA is designed to protect the civil rights of people with physical and mental disabilities. It focuses on the concepts of disability and accessibility and the philosophy that all people have the right to full participation in society. It mandates the removal of barriers by government and private businesses that deny individuals with disabilities equal opportunity and access to employment, public accommodations, government services, public transportation, and telecommunications (Milne, 2012).

ADA-related policy changes have affected the ways that LTSS are structured, funded, and delivered. The disability rights movement advances a philosophy of **independent living**, based on the premise that services for persons with disabilities should be geared to keeping them in their own homes whenever possible and give them control over how services are provided.

The Supreme Court's Olmstead decision in 1999 ruled that unnecessary institutionalization is discriminatory and in violation of the ADA. Therefore, states must provide services that allow Medicaid recipients to remain in the community. Progress has been uneven due to state budget constraints and the Medicaid program's bias toward institutional care. The Independent Living movement, which has focused on younger adults and children with disabilities, has advocated the expansion of consumer-directed services, affecting services offered by the states (Milne, 2012).

Because long-term care service delivery is largely the same for older adults as it is for younger adults with physical disabilities, many states have refocused LTSS to promote community living in the most integrated setting for adults with disabilities of all ages (Milne, 2012). In April 2012, HHS established the Administration for Community Living (ACL), to better align the federal programs that address community living services and support needs of both the aging and disability populations. The ACL advocates for individuals with disabilities and older adults in its policies, programs, and regulations across the federal government. Formation of the ACL signaled recognition that policy concerns of the aging services network significantly overlap with those of the disabilities service network (Administration for Community Living, 2017).

Assistance for Low-Income Older Adults
Older Americans who meet income guidelines are eligible for other sources of federal assistance. Housing affordability is a concern for older adults who live on fixed incomes (see Chapter 8). The Federal Section 202 Supportive Housing for the Elderly Program, part of the Housing Act of 1959, provides funds to finance construction, acquisition, or renovation of structures for nonprofit organizations that provide supportive housing for persons aged 62+ with very low incomes. It also provides rental subsidies (US Department of Housing and Urban Development, 2021). Many older adults also receive Housing Choice Voucher Assistance known as Section 8, which is open to all ages but unable to assist all eligible persons (Guzman, Sturtevant, & Huaman, 2019).

The Supplemental Security Income (SSI) program, administered through the Social Security Administration, provides income for adults aged 65+ and adults with disabilities who meet eligibility, income, and asset requirements. Unlike Social Security, SSI is funded from general tax revenues. In most states, recipients of SSI also qualify for Medicaid and other benefits such as the Supplemental Nutrition Assistance Program (SNAP), which helps those who meet income guidelines purchase food (Social Security Administration, 2021).

The Low-Income Home Energy Assistance Program (LIHEAP), established in 1981, provides grants to states, tribes, and territories to help with heating and cooling energy costs, bill payment assistance, energy crisis assistance, and weatherization and energy-related home repairs for low-income households. The program prioritizes households with older and disabled adults. Local community-based organizations known as Community Action Agencies often distribute these funds (Perl, 2018).

While 46 percent of the households that receive LIHEAP assistance include at least one member aged 60+, four out of five eligible households do not receive LIHEAP assistance. Annual appropriations for LIHEAP have been curtailed in recent years (Edison Electric Institute, 2021).

Many social services for older adults are funded through Social Services Block Grants (SSBGs), which were established in 1975 with Title XX of the Social Security Act. These grants enable states to fund social services programs. States choose how to allocate their SSBG funds, so programs that serve older adults such as APS must compete with other programs (such as childcare) for funding. In recent years, SSBGs, along with many other programs such as LIHEAP, have been targeted for elimination, making legislative advocacy an important priority (Benson, 2018).

POVERTY, INEQUALITY, AND CUMULATIVE DISADVANTAGE

Social Security and Medicare, combined with pensions and other benefits offered by employers, enabled many adults born between 1920 and 1940 to live comfortably in retirement. The increased number of older adults relative to the rest of the population, fewer employer-funded pensions, changing family structure, greater population mobility, and social isolation have led to greater instability and less financial security for adults aged 65+ now and in the coming decades. This section discusses how poverty is measured, how current policies affect poverty levels, and how inequality and cumulative advantage and disadvantage relate to well-being in later life.

Poverty Measurement

Over the past 50 years, Social Security and SSI have contributed to a nearly 70 percent decline in poverty among Americans aged 65+ (Li & Dalaker, 2019). In 1966, the poverty rate for older adults was 28.6 percent; recent data show that 9.7 percent of adults aged 65+ live in poverty. Without Social Security, an estimated 37.8 percent would live in poverty, meaning that Social Security lifts almost 15 million people above the poverty line (Romig, 2020).

The **federal poverty level** is the official measure that determines the US poverty rate and individuals' eligibility for programs such as Medicaid and SSI. Created in the 1960s, this measure defines poverty based on cash income. The measure is based on the cost of food in 1961 and indexed to inflation. It does not include noncash benefits such as LIHEAP or SNAP or tax credits that are available to low-income adults and families. It also does not consider the higher healthcare costs borne by many older adults. The Supplemental Poverty Measure (SPM) was developed to take these government programs and additional expenses into account. The SPM results in lower poverty rates for children and adults aged 18–64 and a higher poverty rate for adults aged 65+ and older (Li & Dalaker, 2019).

Table 12.1 shows the official poverty guidelines for 2021. They apply to every state except Alaska and Hawaii (which have separate and slightly higher guidelines). The poverty guidelines are well below the actual cost of living in many areas including cities such as New York and San Francisco. People who are "near poor" (i.e., have incomes above the official poverty line) are also challenged by high housing costs, medical expenses, and food insecurity. Research on economic disparities often reports the number of people living at < 200 percent of the federal poverty line, and eligibility for

Table 12.1 2021 Poverty Guidelines

Persons in Family/Household	Poverty Guideline
1	$12,880
2	$17,420
3	$21,960
4	$26,500
5	$31,040
6	$35,580
7	$40,120
8	$44,660

For families/households with more than 8 persons, add $4,540 for each additional person.

Source: Office of the Assistant Secretary for Planning and Evaluation, n.d.

means-tested federal programs is also determined by income levels above the official poverty guidelines.

Who Is Poor?

Because of the increase in the number of older adults, more older adults live in poverty today than 50 years ago. However, the lower poverty rates overall signal greater well-being for a sizeable portion of adults. Examining variations within diverse groups of older adults allows us to consider how poverty can be addressed through policies or other means.

Variance between Population Groups

The poverty rate for individuals aged 65 and older was 8.9 percent in 2019 (Li & Dalaker, 2021). Poverty rates among older adults vary by age, marital status, race, and Hispanic origin, categories identified in the US Census. In 2019 the poverty rate for persons aged 80+ was 11.1 percent; the poverty rate for those aged 75–79 was 9.2 percent, 7.4 percent for those aged 70–74, and 8.4 percent for those aged 65–69. Married adults aged 65+ have lower poverty rates than those who are not married. In 2019, the highest poverty rates occurred among never-married women (17.1 percent) and never-married men (19 percent) without children (Li & Dalaker, 2021).

Between 1975 and 2019, poverty rates decreased for those identifying as non-Hispanic white alone, Black alone, and Hispanic alone (in the Census, questions about Hispanic origin are asked separately from questions on race). For those of Asian origin, poverty rates varied between 7.4 percent and 16.7 percent between 1987 and 2019, with no specific downward or upward trend. In 2019, the non-Hispanic white population had the lowest poverty rate (7.9 percent for women and 5.4 percent for men). The highest poverty rate was among those who identify as Black or African American (20.2 percent for women and 14.9 percent for men) (Li & Dalaker, 2021).

In 2009, researchers conducted the first federally funded study addressing aging among LGBTQ older adults in the United States, working with community-based agencies to recruit a diverse sample. This study, which has continued as a longitudinal study, found that almost 40 percent of the LGBTQ adults aged 80+ in the sample lived at or below 200 percent of the federal poverty line, despite their having higher education levels than the general population (Frederiksen-Goldsen et al., 2019).

The financial well-being of older immigrants depends in part upon when they arrived in the United States. People who are older when they immigrate are likely to have lower incomes and are less likely to work in the United States long enough to access entitlement programs such as Social Security and Medicare. In addition, their access to means-tested programs such as SSI and Medicaid is limited (O'Neil & Tienda, 2015).

Cumulative Advantage/Disadvantage
Financial well-being influences quality of life with respect to health and family stability over the life course. In addition to poverty rates, which count current income, obtaining a full picture of financial well-being requires examination of differences in accumulated wealth over the life span. Income inequality in the United States has risen since the 1980s and widening differences in **cumulative advantage/disadvantage** over the life course mean that the divide between "prosperous elderly and penurious elderly" has intensified over the past 40 years (Crystal, Shea, & Reyes, 2017, p. 915). Over time, the wealthy gain more wealth and the poor become even poorer. These differences result from unequal access to education and opportunity, variation in life-course events such as illness and family formation, and differential impact of world events such as economic recession and war.

POLITICAL PARTICIPATION AND ADVOCACY
The policies and laws described in this chapter came about due to the combined efforts of individuals and groups working to address social problems and voters who elect representatives who create and pass legislation. This section examines older adults' voting behavior and involvement in elections. It also considers grassroots organizations, advocacy coalitions, and organizations that study social problems, propose public policy solutions, and study the impact of existing policies to educate decision-makers and the public.

Voting Patterns of Older Adults
Participation in local, state, and national elections is vital to the functioning of democracy. US citizens exercise one of their most important rights by voting for candidates who will support their priorities. Politicians strive to respond to the needs of older voters with respect to Social Security and Medicare. While people aged 65+ are a politically diverse group, the majority vote for candidates who promise the protect Social Security and strengthen Medicare, support that crosses political lines (Bunis, 2020).

While voter turnout varies with election cycles and tends to be higher during presidential election years, people aged 65+ consistently vote at a higher rate than any other age group. Figure 12.4 shows that about 70 percent of the aged 65+ population voted in the 2016 presidential election, compared to 40 percent of eligible voters aged 18–29 (United States Elections Project, 2020). Voter turnout was even higher in the 2020 presidential election, and younger voters made gains relative to older voters (Pike, 2020).

In 2020, many voters aged 50+ took advantage of early and absentee voting, available in most states, when advocacy groups worked to inform people how they could

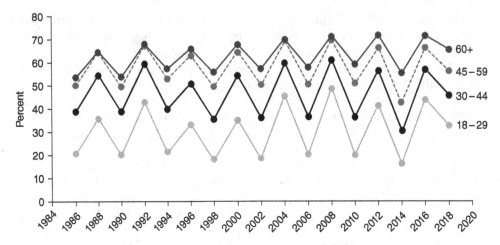

Figure 12.4 Voter turnout by age, US national elections, 1984–2020
Source: Taken from The United States Elections Project. Courtesy of Professor Michael P. McDonald, University of Florida.

cast their ballots before Election Day and avoid polling places where the risk of exposure to COVID-19 would be high. While early and absentee balloting can increase access to voting, and more states have adopted mail-in voting (though some states have since restricted it), many voters aged 65+ may not want to break longstanding voting patterns because of **voter habituation**. The widespread adoption of mail-in voting may also result in fewer neighborhood polling places and eliminate opportunities for people aged 60+ to volunteer as poll workers. Nationally, 58 percent of poll workers are over the age of 60, and 27 percent are over the age of 70 (Gronke et al., 2020). Even though younger poll workers stepped in to work the 2020 election because of the pandemic, many poll workers were in their 70s and 80s.

Intersection of Politics and Policy
People aged 65+ are a diverse group whose concerns arise out of their intersectional social identities. Programs such as Social Security and Medicare that benefit older adults will retain support if most Americans support them. Other programs, such as those funded under the Older Americans Act and programs for low-income Americans of all ages, have less widespread support among the public and among members of Congress. Ageism often determines whether people will actively work to address aging-related needs such as issues related to long-term care and elder abuse. Even though policies benefiting older adults generally have bipartisan support, the number of Congressional staff members with expertise in aging has decreased since the 1990s (Benson, 2018).

Ongoing political advocacy is essential to ensuring that federal aging policies that affect millions of older adults and their families will continue. Advocates and concerned citizens must speak out "loudly and often" (Benson, 2018, p. 73). Voter education on the need to sustain programs that benefit older adults can help. People can also make a difference by pressuring their elected officials through phone calls, emails, letters, and petitions. They can also testify in public hearings and legislative committees. Joining or aligning with advocacy organizations supports these activities and expands the influence of individuals.

Advocacy Organizations

Numerous organizations work to help ensure that laws and policies will best meet the needs of older adults, focusing primarily on those who lack economic and social resources and those who may be harmed by policies and practices that do not prioritize their needs and rights, including the right to autonomy and the right to live free from harm.

Advocacy organizations represent a diversity of interests that converge and intersect. They mobilize political support for policies that address ageism, caregiving, retirement security, healthcare, community support, and the need for meaningful activities in later life. Some organizations focus on ensuring that Social Security, Medicare, and other social policies and programs that address the needs of older adults are maintained and properly implemented. They monitor legislation, conduct research, educate elected officials, the press, and the public about issues, and organize forums and conferences. Their supporters are older adults and those who work on their behalf.

Advocacy organizations use a variety of strategies and tactics, including **lobbying**, **grassroots organizing**, and **coalitions** to mobilize individuals and groups. Many of the organizations described in the following sections employ professional lobbyists to make their case before lawmakers, and they work with **interest groups** to influence policymaking. While some groups are influential and represent a wide range of older Americans, others aim to meet needs that result from the intersection of age and other identities, including gender, race, ethnicity, sexual orientation, socioeconomic class, working status, and immigration status.

AARP

Today, AARP is the largest and most influential membership organization that advocates on behalf of older adults. Formerly known as the American Association of Retired Persons, in 1995, the organization dropped the full wording and became AARP (to broaden membership to all adults aged 50+, regardless of employment status). The membership is politically diverse, with one-third identifying as Democrats, one-third as Republicans, and one-third as independents. In the 1960s, AARP fought against mandatory retirement. The association was instrumental in defeating cuts to Social Security proposed by President Reagan in the 1980s and by President George W. Bush in 2005. AARP supported Medicare Part D and the Affordable Care Act. The organization pushed back against efforts that began in the 1980s to portray older people as "greedy geezers" who claimed an outsize share of federal resources (Day, 2017).

Gray Panthers

Gray Panthers is a grassroots organization with local chapters that is focused on building coalitions to work toward social justice (Day, 2017; Sanjek, 2011). Like AARP, the group originated in the 1960s and opposed mandatory retirement. Founded by activist Maggie Kuhn, the Gray Panthers was a coalition of local organizations concerned about injustice and oppression including the "unjust treatment of citizens because of their age"

(Sanjek, 2011, p. 228). During the 1960s, the Gray Panthers were an intergenerational union of older activists and younger antiwar activists. The Gray Panthers helped end mandatory retirement and helped create the national citizen's coalition that led to nursing home reforms described in this chapter. They also countered ageism by providing a view of old age that differed from the stereotypes of the time. The vision of old age advanced by the Gray Panthers was that older adults were active, connected to others, enjoyed life, and committed to social justice and to being politically engaged (Sanjek, 2011).

Leadership Council of Aging Organizations

AARP founded and today spearheads the Leadership Council of Aging Organizations (LCAO), which consists of 69 organizations committed to representing the interests of older persons in the policymaking arena. The member organizations share information and work together on policymaking on federal, state, and local levels. Members are a diverse array of national organizations including labor unions, identity-based groups, religious and secular social service organizations, groups advocating on behalf of Social Security and Medicare, and groups focused on health and long-term care (Leadership Council of Aging Organizations, 2021).

Other Organizations

Other coalitions and organization focus on specific areas of aging policy. Examples include the Elder Justice Coalition (described in the earlier section on the Elder Justice Act) and Caring Across Generations, which focuses on access to affordable long-term care, support for family caregivers, and improving working conditions for professional caregivers (Caring Across Generations, 2021).

Many organizations advocate on behalf of people for whom the issues of aging intersect with other identities, addressing important needs. Some focus on ensuring that legal rights are upheld with respect to the social policies passed to protect older Americans. Since 1972, Justice in Aging has advocated for the passage of legislation to protect or support low-income older adults. This organization works with state and federal agencies to ensure that governments fairly administer healthcare and economic security programs so that all qualified individuals can access them. It sponsors class-action lawsuits to force changes in program administration when necessary, so that all will have access to services. It also works to advance equity and justice for older adults of color (Justice in Aging, 2021).

SAGE: Advocacy & Services for LGBT Elders is a nationwide policy and advocacy organization that advocates with and on behalf of the LGBT community on the federal, state, and local levels. The group addresses issues such as discrimination, housing, caregiving, healthcare and HIV policy. It aims to educate policymakers and elected officials about the needs of the LGBT aging population and supports laws and policies that affirm their rights (SAGE, 2020).

Generations United focuses on intergenerational collaboration and uses an intergenerational approach to affect policy issues. They recognize the interdependence of the generations and focus on policies that will support grandparents and other relative caregivers, as well as working in partnership with other groups to ensure support of the OAA, healthcare, social services block grants, and other policies (Generations United, 2021).

CASE 12.1

Funding for a Senior Center

In 2021, Antonio, the executive director of a multi-service senior center that provides meal programs, caregiver support, and case management, and recreational and educational services, grew increasingly concerned as the COVID-19 pandemic kept regular participants away from the center, increasing their social isolation. The Elder Justice Reauthorization and Modernization Act of 2021 was introduced to provide funding for programming and activities related to elder justice, including resources for Adult Protective Services and funds to enhance the long-term care workforce. If the law is passed, Antonio's agency would be eligible to apply for funds for programs to reduce social isolation.

Which federal programs are likely sources of funding for the senior center? What can Antonio do to advocate for the passage of this legislation?

CHAPTER REVIEW

Social Policies and Legislation
- Social policies addressing the aging process are structured courses of action enshrined in legislation that are designed to enhance well-being among older adults.
- The landmark Social Security Act of 1935 provided retirement income, benefits for survivors and workers who become disabled, unemployment insurance, and a variety of public assistance programs.
- Social Security has reduced poverty among older adults and has broad support among the American public.
- Medicare is publicly funded health insurance for people aged 65+ that covers services that include hospitalization and doctor visits.
- Medicaid is a government-sponsored health insurance program for low-income people that pays for long-term care in nursing homes and in the community.
- The Affordable Care Act expanded access to health insurance for Americans who cannot obtain health insurance through an employer, such as part-time workers and the self-employed.
- The Older Americans Act supplies structure and federal support for aging services in service access, nutrition, home and community-based services, disease prevention and health promotion, and vulnerable elder rights protection.
- The Americans with Disabilities Act benefited older adults through its emphasis on accessibility and philosophy on independent living.
- The Elder Justice Act established a coordinated federal response to elder abuse through health and social service approaches to its prevention, detection, and treatment.
- Older adults benefit from numerous programs for low-income Americans including assistance with housing, energy, food, and social services.

Poverty, Inequality, and Cumulative Disadvantage
- Social Security and other federal programs have contributed to a 70 percent decline in poverty among older adults since the 1960s.

- Persons at higher risk for poverty in old age include never-married men and women, older women living alone, African Americans, LGBTQ individuals, and immigrants.
- The divide between the poorest and the most prosperous older adults has increased over the past 40 years due to patterns of cumulative advantage and disadvantage.

Political Participation and Advocacy
- Adults aged 65+ participate in the electoral process at higher rates than those who are younger.
- Politicians tend to support policies such as Social Security and Medicare because of their popularity with most voters.
- A variety of advocacy organizations exists to monitor legislation, conduct research, and educate elected officials and the public about issues addressed by aging policy.

REVIEW QUESTIONS
1. Describe how the public programs and resources that people can access as they age are connected to characteristics such as gender, race, sexual orientation, socioeconomic status, and health.
2. What are some factors that make it difficult to establish policies that can provide long-term services and supports for older adults?
3. Which social policies described in this chapter are most likely to have continued bipartisan support? How does voting behavior among older adults affect this support?

KEY TERMS

social welfare policies
board and care homes
social insurance
means test
Social Security
entitlement program
Medicare
deductible
coinsurance
Medicaid
block grant
Patient Protection and Affordable Care Act
pre-existing condition
federal poverty level
Older Americans Act
matching funds
long-term services and supports
Nursing Home Reform Act of 1987
Americans with Disabilities Act
independent living
federal poverty level
cumulative advantage/disadvantage
voter habituation
lobbying
grassroots organizing
coalitions
interest groups

GLOSSARY

acculturation Process of adaptation to the culture, customs, lifestyle, and expectations of the destination country while keeping or letting go of those of the home country

acculturative stress Distress associated with acculturation

active euthanasia Causing death of a terminally ill patient by an act such as administering an overdose of a drug or injection

activities of daily living The tasks of everyday life that include eating, dressing, getting in and out of a bed or chair, bathing, and going to the toilet

activity theory A theory of social development that suggests that rather than "drop out" of life when we grow older, we remain active or engaged in our social lives and roles

adult day care Organized health-supporting care and social engagement and support for people who cannot be left alone during the day

advance directive Legal documents used to communicate a person's wishes about medical treatment when they cannot communicate on their own

age-friendly healthcare A model that advocates for healthcare providers listen and respond to the concerns, goals, wishes, needs, and life experiences of those under their care while also attending to medication, cognitive functioning, and mobility

ageism The prejudice, discrimination, and stereotyping of individuals based on age

agency The proactive and reactive behaviors people use to adjust to their environment

aging in place The ability of people to age in their own home and community safely, independently, and comfortably

aging network The programs and agencies created to help people navigate life as they age, associated with programs established by the Older Americans Act

Americans with Disabilities Act Civil rights law that prohibits discrimination based on disability in all areas of public life including jobs, schools, transportation, and all public and private locations open to the public

andropause A syndrome consisting of decreased sexual satisfaction and general well-being among biological men that can result from decreased testosterone associated with age

anthropogenic Directly or indirectly caused by the activities of humans

assisted living A type of housing that provides personal care and other services designed to assist people with activities of daily living and provide maximum independence

assisted suicide (also called assisted death or assisted dying): a person, usually a physician, takes some type of action (such as providing drugs) to help a patient end their life

autolysis The destruction of cells and tissues by their own enzymes

benevolent ageism Sometimes referred to as positive ageism, it is ageism inherent in positive stereotypes of older adults

bereavement The timeframe in which grief and mourning happen, or the situation of having lost someone or something

blended family A family where one or both parents, who may be in a same sex or heterosexual relationship, have children from a previous relationship and may have children together as well

block grant Federal grant that provides funds to state or local governments to meet broad purposes including social services, law enforcement, or community development

board and care homes Community-based residences that provide personal assistance and meals to residents who were unable to live on their own

bridge job Paid work that spans the time between full-time employment and retirement

caregiver burden The intolerable strain produced by caregiving

caregiver stress The physical, mental, and emotional exhaustion resulting from caregiving

caregiving The act of looking after and attending to the needs of a person who is sick, disabled, or in regular need of care due to age or vulnerability

chronological age Our calendar age, or how many years we have been alive

circular migration Pattern of moving back and forth between one's home country and a foreign country for work opportunities

coalitions Alliances of groups and individuals organized around the achievement of a specific goal, such as supporting passage of legislation or protecting existing programs

cognitive plasticity The brain's ability to change and adapt physically and functionally throughout the life span

coinsurance The amount that an insured person is responsible for paying after health insurance pays its share of eligible expenses

community A group of people with diverse characteristics linked by social ties and who share common perspectives and engage in joint actions, often linked to a geographical setting

community gerontology An area of research, policy, and practice that advances understanding of communities as essential contexts for aging and its diversity

complicated grief Also known as prolonged grief, grief or bereavement that can be problematic for people who may need additional support or intervention

continuing care retirement community A housing option for older adults that offers a range of housing and care options on the same property including independent living, assisted living, and skilled nursing care

continuity theory A theory of social development that posits that personality, relationships, social roles, and patterns of social behavior and engagement established early in life help to predict what our social lives in older age will look like

continuum of care The range of healthcare and living arrangements available as care needs change from being able to care for oneself to needing help with nearly all daily living activities

crossover effect A documented phenomenon whereby throughout the life span, Blacks have higher mortality rates than whites, until about the age of 75–80, when the mortality rates for Blacks become lower than whites

crystallized intelligence Cognitive skills that require manipulation and transformation of information to quickly solve problems

culture Unwritten rules that influence beliefs, thoughts, feelings, patterns of behavior, customs, values, and social institutions and allow one to function in a social group

culture change movement An effort to transform nursing homes from impersonal institutions into person-centered homes that promote autonomy and personal choice in a home-like

cumulative advantage/disadvantage Refers to the accumulation of risks, opportunities, and resources over the life course that are the result of inequality and that affect well-being as people age

deductible The amount an insured person must pay before their insurance company will cover eligible expenses

dementia An umbrella term for a set of diseases or conditions caused by changes in the brain that affect cognitive skills

digital literacy The ability to use information and communication technologies to find, evaluate, create, and communicate information, requiring both cognitive and technical skills

disenfranchised grief Refers to situations when people's reactions to loss are unacknowledged by others around them or by larger society

disengagement theory A theory that posits that we naturally disengage from social roles as we age

displaced persons People who have been forced from their home by persecution, conflict, or human rights violations

distal defense A defense against death anxiety that comes through building a worldview, or system of beliefs and practices, that gives meaning to life and death

do not resuscitate (DNR) form Do not resuscitate orders that direct medical personnel to forgo resuscitative measures in cases of cardiopulmonary arrest

double jeopardy Discrimination based on ageism and one other "ism" like race or gender

durable power of attorney for healthcare A document that appoints a representative who will make healthcare decisions for a person who is unable to communicate or make healthcare decisions

dyads A term used when discussing pairs, such as parent-child, in relation to activities such as caregiving

ecological model A theoretical model that focuses on interacting individual, family, community, and societal factors affecting human behavior

elder abuse A single or repeated act, or lack of appropriate action, occurring within any relationship where there is an expectation of trust, which causes harm or distress to an older person

elder orphans Community-dwelling older adults who are socially and/or physically isolated and who do not have family members or designated caregivers available to assist them

elderspeak Addressing older adults in a high-pitched voice, as if speaking to a child

electronic assistive technology (EAT) Helps to improve cognitive and physical function as well as monitor various functions to alert individuals, caregivers, and health professionals when intervention may be necessary to prevent injury

encore careers Careers that are developed in the pursuit of new, meaningful work in later life

entitlement program Program that requires payments to any person who meets eligibility criteria established by law

environmental gerontology A subdiscipline of gerontology that focuses on how the physical environment influences the aging process and people's sense of belonging to a place and their agency

environmental press How the constraints of the environment influence the ability to adapt as personal competence changes with age

ethnography Qualitative research that relies on extensive observation, in-depth interviews, and the collection of documents and other research evidence to develop a deep understanding of a phenomenon

faith A strong belief in or relationship with God or a higher power, often associated with doctrines, traditions, and values of a specific religion

family A collection of relationships determined by biology, adoption, marriage, and social designation

family development theory A theory that focuses on transitions in and out of family roles over the life cycle

federal poverty level Official measure that determines the US poverty rate and individuals' eligibility for public assistance programs such as Medicaid and SSI; created in the 1960s, this measure defines poverty based on cash income, with the measure based on the cost of food in 1961 and indexed to inflation

feminist gerontology A lens that examines how the intersection of age, gender, and other characteristics affect psychological development over time

feminist theory Explores the experiences of women and other marginalized groups from an intersectional lens

fertility rate Birthrate of a population

fictive kin Consensual family-type relationships, not bases on blood ties or marriage, that are mutually beneficial to family members

filial norms and expectations Expectations that culture and society may place on families in terms of their responsibilities toward family members

filial piety Tradition of respect for parents in Asian cultures that shapes support and care provided by their children in old age

fluid intelligence Cognitive skills that require manipulation and transformation of information to quickly solve problems

formal care Care provided full or part time in the older adult's home by paid care providers such as home health aides, in adult day centers, or in long-term care facilities such as nursing homes

functional age Our age in relation to our overall health status, or how old we seem to be physically

gentrification The process by which the movement of wealthy people into a poor urban area changes its character through improvement in housing and attracting new businesses while displacing current residents

geographical gerontology A subdiscipline of gerontology that focuses on the impact of where people live, patterns of their movement, and how climate change, environmental hazards, and public policy affect the environmental quality and the availability of different housing options

geriatrician A doctor who specializes in the care of older adults and the diseases and conditions that affect them

geriatrics A medical specialty focused on providing care for older adults

gerontologists Those who study or work in the area of gerontology

gerontology The examination of all aspects of later life development including biological, psychological, social, and spiritual facets of growing older

globalization Refers to the ways in which the world's economies, cultures, and populations influence and depend on one another (Peterson Institute for International Economics, 2021).

grassroots organizing Mobilization of individuals and groups at a local level in support of a specific issue or concern

grief A strong, sometimes overwhelming, emotional response to a real or perceived loss

health A state of complete physical, mental, and social well-being and not merely the absence of disease or infirmity

heterohappiness The manner in which popular culture cultivates an image of aging and sexuality in a rigid, heterosexual way, where older adults are able, active, healthy, attractive, and sexually active

heteronormative The worldview that promotes heterosexuality as the normal or preferred sexual identity or orientation

homosociality Social interaction between members of the same sex, typically men

hospice Comfort care that is given to terminally ill people, who, in a doctor's opinion, has fewer than six months to live

hostile ageism Type of ageism that labels all older people as slow, weak, rude, and stubborn

independent living The ability to control and direct one's life and be self-sufficient; in long-term care, an option where people can live autonomously but receive help with housekeeping, transportation, and other amenities when needed

individual ageism Refers to the internalized beliefs and attitudes about age that often lead to discriminatory behaviors between individuals

informal care Care provided to individuals with disabilities, health problems, or functional needs by family members or friends

inpatient Someone who is admitted to and stays in the hospital for medical treatment

institutional ageism Involves ageist beliefs, attitudes, and behaviors that are embedded in our media, organizations, institutions, and larger cultural arenas

instrumental activities of daily living The tasks that are necessary for living independently in the community such as shopping, maintaining the home, managing money, and cooking

interest groups Groups of people that aim to influence public policy based on common interests

intergenerational ambivalence A framework that acknowledges the mixed and contradictory feelings that family members have for each other, particularly as family members age

intergenerational resources exchange How family members exchange resources such as time, money, and emotional support and nurturance among different generations

intergenerational solidarity and conflict A framework that offers insight into positive and negative dimensions of family relationships over the life course

intergenerational stake hypothesis The idea that parents are more devoted to their children and experience better quality parent-child ties than do their children

international migration Movement of persons away from their place of usual residence and across an international border to a country of which they are not nationals

kinship The web of relationships that results from bonds created by biology or marriage

kinship care The raising of children by relatives (often grandparents) or family friends when parents are unavailable or unable to care for them

labor force participation rate Proportion of a population that is in the labor force at a given time

life-course model of social functioning A model of social functionality that acknowledges the importance of prior experiences on shaping our social functioning in later years

life expectancy Estimate of the average number of additional years a person can expect to live at a given age

linguistic isolation A term used to describe households where all members have limited English proficiency

living will A document that states end-of-life wishes for medical care

lobbying Process of educating and persuading lawmakers to develop, support, or rewrite legislation so that the legislation is beneficial to an individual, group, or organization

long-term care The mix of services needed to meet a person's health or personal care needs when they can no longer perform activities of daily living on their own

long-term services and supports Paid and unpaid medical and personal care assistance needed by people who cannot complete self-care tasks because of aging, chronic illness, or disability

macro level Level of interaction in larger systems including government at all levels, regional, national, and global issues, and social forces

matching funds An amount of funding provided by grant recipients that is required to obtain the grant

means test Method to determine eligibility for a government program

media Any means of mass communication, such as radio, television, newspapers, magazines, and online sources such as websites, podcasts, and blogs

Medicaid Joint federal-state health insurance program for low-income people that covers medical costs and long-term care

medical aid in dying (also called physician aid in dying): a physician or other medical professional provides a mentally competent, terminally ill patient (upon the patient's request) a prescription for a lethal dose of medication, which the patient intends to take to end their life

Medicare Health insurance program sponsored by the federal government for adults aged 65+ and adults with disabilities

menopause The cessation of the menstrual cycle, confirmed when 12 consecutive periods are missed, with no other apparent causes

mezzo level Level of interaction that occurs between micro and macro levels, such as the workplace, school settings, or community-based organizations

micro level Level of interaction that occurs among individuals, families, or small groups

microaggressions Subtle, indirect, or unintentional actions or incidents directed toward marginalized people

middle-ageism Ageism targeted toward people in middle age; middle age is often the time many people begin to notice ageism

migration Movement of a population from one country, location, or place to another

model A theoretical model that focuses on interacting individual, family, community, and societal factors affecting human behavior

mortality rate Number of deaths in a population during a given period of time

mourning The way in which grief is expressed

narrative therapy A therapeutic intervention that supports older adults in recounting dominant life stories that are important to their identities and the problems with which they have struggled

naturally occurring retirement communities Places where there is a large concentration of older adults and that often support a mix of services and amenities aimed at older adults

negotiation of boundary ambiguity The way people clarify uncertainties of role expectations, particularly when speaking of family support and obligations for caregiving

neuroageism Ageism associated with neurodegenerative diseases

neurodiversity The range of differences in individual brain function regarded as normal variations within the population

noncommunicable diseases Chronic diseases such as diabetes, cardiovascular disease, and Alzheimer's disease that have become the predominant causes of morbidity and mortality worldwide

norms and expectations Expectations that culture and society may place on families in terms of their responsibilities toward family members

Nursing Home Reform Act of 1987 Passed as part of the Omnibus Reconciliation Act of 1987, established standards and procedures for staffing and oversight of nursing homes

nursing homes A public or private residential facility, also known as a skilled nursing facility, that provides a high level of long-term personal and nursing care for persons (such as the aged or the chronically ill) who are unable to care for themselves

old age dependency ratio The number of persons aged 65 and older relative to the population of working-age adults (age 16–64)

Older Americans Act A law originally passed in 1965 that supports a range of home- and community-based services for adults aged 60+ that focuses on helping people stay as independent as possible

optimal aging the capacity to function across many domains (physical, functional, cognitive, emotional, social, and spiritual) to one's satisfaction and in spite of one's medical conditions

outpatient A patient who visits a hospital or clinic for diagnosis or treatment without being hospitalized overnight

palliative care medical care that aims to provide relief from pain and other symptoms of serious illness

passive euthanasia Withdrawing or withholding life-prolonging medical treatment for terminally ill patients

Patient Protection and Affordable Care Act Federal statute enacted in 2010 that expanded access to health insurance in the United States through individual and employer mandates for insurance coverage, expansion of Medicaid, assistance with paying health insurance premiums, and other efforts to improve access to healthcare and quality of care

patient-centered medical home A model of healthcare coordinated by a primary care doctor that focuses on ensuring that people receive necessary care when and where they need it

peer navigator Trained individuals from the community who assist people in dealing with challenges related to health or caregiving

perimenopause The time frame when the body makes the transition to menopause, with menstruation becoming more irregular

person-and family-centered care An orientation to the delivery of healthcare and supportive services that considers an older adult's needs, goals, preferences, cultural traditions, family situation, and values

physician orders for life-sustaining treatment (POLST) form Physician orders for life-sustaining treatment that can be used to indicate wishes regarding treatments commonly used during medical emergencies

polyvictimization Being a victim or more than one type of abuse or maltreatment

population aging The proportional increase of older adults compared to younger adults and children

positivity effect The tendency to demonstrate a preference toward positive stimuli

pre-existing condition Health condition such as heart disease or cancer that a person has before their health insurance policy coverage begins

primary prevention Intervention to prevent problems or health effects before they occur

proximal defense A mechanism we use to suppress death thoughts and deny personal vulnerability to reduce death anxiety

pull factors Features that attract immigrants to destination countries, such as opportunities for jobs and political freedom and the destination country's need for skills that immigrants possess

push factors Conditions in home countries, such as poverty, environmental degradation, lack of economic opportunity, political instability, and religious or ethnic persecution, which make people want to leave

queer gerontology A specific queer approach to older adulthood that assists in the examination of heterosexist and other dominant norms that define what it means to be older

queer theory A lens through which to examine and critique normalized ways of thinking

refugees People who have left their country of origin because of persecution due to race, religion, nationality, membership in a particular social group, or political opinion

religion An organized and institutionalized tradition of faith and worship.

reminiscence therapy A therapeutic intervention that helps older adults to reflect on and review their lives

replacement level Number of births needed to replace those in the previous generation in a country

respite care Services, such as temporarily institutional care, that provide relief and time off for a person's usual caregiver

secondary prevention Intervention to detect a problem or disease early to prevent it from worsening

self-determination The right of people to make decisions on their own behalf, wherever possible

self-determination theory Addresses simultaneous needs for relatedness, autonomy, and competence

senescence A term that refers to aging or the aging process

senior center Community-based service that provides preventive services including meals, access to social services, exercise and fitness classes, and disease prevention and health promotion activities

skip-generation household Household that consists of grandparents and grandchildren with no one from the intermediate generation (parents of the grandchildren or children of the grandparents)

social convoy model A theory of social aging that posits that we have social networks, or convoys, in which we are embedded throughout our lives and that provide the reciprocity, or give and take, of needed social support

social insurance Public insurance that provides protection against economic risks through mandatory contributions

Social Security US social insurance program that provides retirement, disability, and survivor benefits

social usefulness A term that reflects goal motivations associated with social involvement in activities beneficial to others or society

social welfare policies Laws and regulations that provide protection from poverty and other challenges of modern life

spirituality Related to people's search for what is sacred or what holds meaning, outside of physical concerns

stepfamily A family in which at least one of the parents has a child from a previous relationship

strengths perspective A way of viewing people that focuses on their abilities and potential rather than on their problems or deficits

subjective age How we perceive and experience ourselves as younger or older than our chronological age

subjective age bias The discrepancy between feeling younger than our chronological age

successful aging A way of viewing aging that consists of a low probability of disease and disease-related disability, high cognitive and physical functional capacity, and active engagement with life

support exchanges Emotional support, practical help, and advice traded between parents and their adult children

support groups Formal groups, such as for caregivers, that come together on a regular basis so that members can learn from each other's experiences and benefit from time together

supportive housing Housing that combines affordable housing assistance with supportive services for people with disabilities or those who have experienced homelessness

Sustainable Development Goals A UN blueprint to address worldwide problems including poverty, inequality, lack of access healthcare and education, and the impact of climate change

telemedicine Remote diagnosis or treatment of medical conditions using electronic communication and software

telomeres Nucleotides on the end of chromosomes

tertiary prevention Management of diseases or problems to slow further progression or decline

theory of selective optimization with compensation A theory that posits we can mitigate cognitive functioning difficulties by employing strategies that focus on specific goals using compensatory means to achieve those goals

third places Places where people congregate and socialize in urban and suburban neighborhoods and small towns that create support and connections

triple jeopardy Individuals may face discrimination based on three or more intersecting characteristics

uncomplicated grief A grieving process that usually resolves itself to the point that allows people to carry on their usual relationships and functioning at some point

United Nations International organization consisting of 193 member states, including the United States, that provides a place where nations can gather, address, and discuss common issues such as human rights, disaster relief and humanitarian aid, peacekeeping, climate change, and population aging

voluntary stopping of eating and drinking (VSED) The conscious act of intentionally ceasing eating and drinking, with the goal of ending one's life

voter habituation Habits connected to lifelong voting behavior that determine the manner in which people vote

REFERENCES

AARP. (2018, February 28). *AARP research finds 90 percent of adults 50+ use personal technology to stay connected.* https://press.aarp.org/2018-2-28-AARP-Research-Finds-90-Percent-Adults-50-Use-Personal-Technology-Stay-Connected.

AARP. (2019). *How continuing care retirement communities work.* Retrieved on March 10, 2021, from https://www.aarp.org/caregiving/basics/info-2017/continuing-care-retirement-communities.html.

AARP. (2021). *Top 25 part-time jobs for retirees.* Retrieved on December 23, 2021, from https://www.aarp.org/work/job-search/info-2020/part-time-jobs-for-retirees.html.

AARP Livable Communities. (2020). *AARP network of age-friendly states and communities.* Retrieved on March 1, 2021, from https://www.aarp.org/livable-communities/network-age-friendly-communities/info-2014/member-list.html.

Aburto, J. M., Schöley, J., Kashnitsky, I., Zhang, L., Rahal, C., Missov, T. I., Mills, M. C., Dowd, J. B., & Kashyap, R. (2021). Quantifying impacts of the COVID-19 pandemic through life-expectancy losses: a population-level study of 29 countries. *International Journal of Epidemiology.* https://doi.org/10.1093/ije/dyab207

Academy for Gerontology in Higher Education. (2019). *Gerontology/geriatrics definitions.* Retrieved on March 2, 2019, from https://www.aghe.org/resources/gerontology-geriatrics-descriptions.

Acierno, R., Hernandez, M. A., Amstadter, A. B., Resnick, H. S., Steve, K., Muzzy, W., & Kilpatrick, D. G. (2010). Prevalence and correlates of emotional, physical, sexual, and financial abuse and potential neglect in the United States: The National Elder Mistreatment Study. *American Journal of Public Health, 100*(2), 292–297. doi:10.2105/AJPH.2009.163089

Acierno, R., Hernandez-Tejada, M. A., Anetzberger, G. J., Loew, D., & Muzzy, W. (2017). The National Elder Mistreatment Study: An 8-year longitudinal study of outcomes. *Journal of Elder Abuse & Neglect, 29*(4), 254–269. doi:10.1080/08946566.2017.1365031

Adams, R. G., & Blieszner, R. (1995). Aging well with friends and family. *American Behavioural Scientist, 39,* 209–224.

Addo, F. R., & Lichter, D. T. (2013). Marriage, marital history, and black–white wealth differentials among older women. *Journal of Marriage & Family, 75*(2), 342–362. doi:10.1111/jomf.12007

Adolph, K. E., Karasik, L. B., & Tamis-LeMonda, C. S. (2009). Motor skills. In M. H. Bornsten (Ed.), *Handbook of cultural developmental science* (pp. 61–88). Taylor & Francis.

Administration for Community Living. (2017). *History.* https://acl.gov/about-acl/history.

Administration for Community Living. (2020). *No wrong door: Our story.* Retrieved on March 1, 2021, from https://nwd.acl.gov/our-story.html.

Age Discrimination Info. (2018). *International age discrimination.* Retrieved on February 22, 2021, from http://www.agediscrimination.info/international.

Ajrouch, K. J., Fuller, H. R., Akiyama, H., & Antonucci, T. C. (2017). Convoys of social relations in cross-national context. *The Gerontologist, 58*(3), 488–499. doi.org/10.1093/geront/gnw204

Al-Krenawi, A., & Jackson, S. O. (2014). Arab American marriage: Culture, tradition, religion, and the social worker. *Journal of Human Behavior in the Social Environment, 24*(2), 115–137. https://doi.org/10.1080/10911359.2014.848679

Alashram, A. R., Annino, G., Padua, E., Romagnoli, C., & Mercuri, N. B. (2019). Cognitive rehabilitation post traumatic brain injury: A systematic review for emerging use of virtual reality technology. *Journal of Clinical Neuroscience, 66,* 209–219. doi.org/10.1016/j.jocn.2019.04.026

REFERENCES

Alecxih. L., Shen, S., Chan, I., Taylor, D., & Drabek, J. (2010). *Individuals living in the community with chronic conditions and functional limitations: A closer look*. Office of the Assistant Secretary for Planning and Evaluation, Office of Disability, Aging and Long-Term Care Policy, United States Department of Health and Human Services. Retrieved on July 22, 2019 from http://www.aspe.hhs.gov/daltcp/reports/2010/closerlook.pdf.

Al-Kandari, Y. Y., & Crews, D. E. (2014). Social support and health among elderly Kuwaitis. *Journal of Biosocial Science, 46*(4), S277–285.

Allen, M. S., & Desille, A. E. (2017). Health-related lifestyle factors and sexual functioning and behavior in older adults. *International Journal of Sexual Health, 29*(3), 273–277. https://doi.org/10.1080/19317611.2017.1307301

Alzheimer's Association. (2019). 2019 Alzheimer's disease facts and figures. *Alzheimer's & Dementia: The Journal of the Alzheimer's Association, 15*(3), 321–387. doi:10.1016/j.jalz.2019.01.010

Alzheimer's Association. (2020). Caregiving. Retrieved on March 3, 2021, from https://www.alz.org/help-support/caregiving.

Alzheimer's Association. (2019a). *Types of dementia*. Retrieved on November 17, 2019, from https://www.alz.org/alzheimers-dementia/what-is-dementia/types-of-dementia.

Alzheimer's Association. (2019b). *What is dementia?* Retrieved on November 26, 2019, from https://www.alz.org/alzheimers-dementia/what-is-dementia.

Alzheimer's Society. (2021). *Person centered care*. Retrieved on September 18, 2021, from https://www.alzheimers.org.uk/about-dementia/treatments/person-centred-care.

Ambrey, C. L., Bosman, C., & Ballard, A. (2017). Ontological security, social connectedness and the well-being of Australia's ageing baby boomers. *Housing Studies, 33*(5), 777–812. doi.org/10.1080/02673037.2017.1388912

American Academy of Actuaries. (2021). *Women and Social Security*. Retrieved on March 12, 2021, from https://www.actuary.org/content/women-and-social-security-1.

American College of Physicians. (2020). *Understanding PCMH: What is the patient-centered medical home?* Retrieved on March 3, 2021, from https://www.acponline.org/practice-resources/business-resources/payment/delivery-and-payment-models/patient-centered-medical-home

American Federation for Aging Research. (2019). *Theories of aging*. Retrieved on March 2, 2019, from https://www.afar.org/infoaging/biology-of-aging/theories-of-aging//.

American Heart Association. (2020). *Golfing regularly could be a hole-in-one for older adults' health*. ScienceDaily. https://www.sciencedaily.com/releases/2020/02/200212084405.htm.

American Society for Nutrition. (2019). *Can we prevent muscle loss as we age?* Retrieved on July 28, 2019, from https://nutrition.org/can-we-prevent-muscle-loss-as-we-age/.

American Society of Pension Professionals and Actuaries. (2021). *Retirement: An historical perspective*. Retrieved on January 23, 2021, from https://www.asppa.org/news/browse-topics/retirement-historical-perspective.

American Society on Aging. (2020). *Social and health disparities in America's aging population*. Retrieved on January 2, 2020, from https://www.asaging.org/blog/social-and-health-disparities-americas-aging-population.

American Veterinary Medical Association. (2018). *US pet ownership statistics*. Retrieved on November 17, 2022, from https://www.avma.org/resources-tools/reports-statistics/us-pet-ownership-statistics#companion

Americorps. (2019). *Volunteering helps keep seniors healthy*. Retrieved on March 2, 2021, from https://www.nationalservice.gov/newsroom/press-releases/2019/volunteering-helps-keep-seniors-healthy-new-study-suggests.

Americorps. (2020). *Americorps Seniors Program*. Retrieved on March 3, 2021, from https://www.nationalservice.gov/programs/senior-corps/senior-corps-programs.

Andersen, R. M. (1995). Revisiting the behavioral model and access to medical care: Does it matter? *Journal of Health and Social Behavior, 36*(1), 1–10. doi:10.2307/2137284

Anderson, E., & Fidler, C. O. (2018). Elderly British men: Homohysteria and orthodox masculinities. *Journal of Gender Studies, 27*(3), 248–259.

Annie E. Casey Foundation. (2012). *Stepping up for kids: What government and communities should do to support kinship families*. Retrieved on March 8, 2020, from https://www.aecf.org/resources/stepping-up-for-kids/.

Antonucci, T. C. (2001). Social relations: an examination of social networks, social support, and sense of control. In J. E. Birren & K. W. Schaie (Eds.), *Handbook of the Psychology of Aging*, 5th ed. (pp. 427–453). Academic Press.

Antonucci, T. C., Lansford, J. E., & Akiyama, H. (2001). Impact of positive and negative aspects of marital relationships and friendships on well-being of older adults. *Applied Developmental Science, 5,* 68–75. doi:10.1207/S1532480XADS0502_2

Antonucci, T. C., Lansford, J. E., Schaberg, L., Smith, J., Baltes, M., Akiyama, H., & Dartigues, J.-F. (2001). Widowhood and illness: A comparison of social network characteristics in France, Germany, Japan, and the United States. *Psychology and Aging, 16*(4), 655–665. doi.org/10.1037/0882-7974.16.4.655

Aoyama, M., Sakaguchi, Y., Morita, T., Ogawa, A., Daisuke, F., Kizawa, Y., Tsuneto, S., Shima, Y., & Miyashita, M. (2018). Factors associated with possible complicated grief and major depressive disorders. *Psycho-Oncology, 27,* 915–921.

Arem, H., Moore, S. C., Patel. A., Hartge, P., Berrington de Gonzalez, A., Visvanathan, K. (2015). Leisure time physical activity and mortality: a detailed pooled analysis of the dose-response relationship. *JAMA Internal Medicine, 175*(6), 959–67.

Arensberg M. B. (2018). Population aging: opportunity for business expansion. *Journal of health, population, and nutrition, 37*(1), 7. doi:10.1186/s41043-018-0138-0

Arentshorst, M. E., Kloet, R. R., & Peine, A. (2019). Intergenerational housing: The case of Humanitas Netherlands. *Journal of Housing For the Elderly,33*(3),244–256.doi:10.1080/02763893.2018.1561592

Aries, P. (1981). *The hour of our death*. Vintage Books.

Armstrong, K. (2020). *How age magnifies experience: Deconstructing cross-cultural differences in aging*. Association for Psychological Science. Retrieved on June 15, 2020, from https://www.psychologicalscience.org/observer/how-age-magnifies-experience-deconstructing-cross-cultural-differences-in-aging.

Aronson, L. (2019). *Elderhood*. Bloomsbury.

Asis, M. M. B. (2017). The Philippines: Beyond Labor Migration, Toward Development and (Possibly) Return. *Migration Information Source*. https://www.migrationpolicy.org/article/philippines-beyond-labor-migration-toward-development-and-possibly-return

Aspinall, R., & Lang, P. O. (2018). Interventions to restore appropriate immune function in the elderly. *Immunity & Ageing, 15*(1), 1–8. doi:10.1186/s12979-017-0111-6

Atchley, R. C. (1989). A continuity theory of normal aging. *The Gerontologist, 29,* 183–190.

Atchley, R. C., & Barusch, A. S. (2004). *Social Forces & Aging: Introduction to Social Gerontology* (10th ed.). Thomson/Wadsworth.

Australian Human Rights Commission. (2020). *Age discrimination*. Retrieved on February 22, 2021, https://humanrights.gov.au/our-work/employers/age-discrimination. Ausubel, J. (2020). *Older people are more likely to live alone in the U.S. than elsewhere in the world*. Pew Research Center. Retrieved on July 7, 2021 from https://www.pewresearch.org/fact-tank/2020/03/10/older-people-are-more-likely-to-live-alone-in-the-u-s-than-elsewhere-in-the-world/

Ayalon L (2013) Feelings towards older vs. younger adults: results from the European Social Survey. *Educational Gerontology, 39*(12), 888–901.

Azoulay, P., & Jones, B., Kim, J. D., & Miranda, J. (2018). *Age and high-growth entrepreneurship*. NBER Working Papers 24489, National Bureau of Economic Research.

Balakrishnan, A., & Jordan, N. (2019). The undocumented elderly: Coverage gaps and low health care use. *Journal of Health Care for the Poor and Underserved, 30*(3), 891–898. doi:10.1353/hpu.2019.0062

Balan, E., Decottignies, A., & Deldicque, L. (2018). Physical activity and nutrition: Two promising strategies for telomere maintenance? *Nutrients, 10*(12), 1942. doi:10.3390/nu10121942

Baltes, P. B. (1987). Theoretical propositions of lifespan developmental psychology: On the dynamics between growth and decline. *Developmental Psychology, 23*(5), 611–626.

Baltes, P. B. (1997). On the incomplete architecture of human ontogeny: Selection, optimization, and compensation as foundation of developmental theory. *American Psychologist, 52*, 366–380.

Baltes, P. B., & Baltes, M. M. (1990). Psychological perspectives on successful aging: The model of selective optimization with compensation. In P. B. Baltes & M. M. Baltes (Eds.), *Successful aging: Perspectives from the behavioral sciences* (pp. 1–34). Cambridge University Press.

Band-Winterstein, T. (2015). Whose suffering is this? Narratives of adult children and parents in long-term abusive relationships. *Journal of Family Violence, 30*(2), 123–133. doi:10.1007/s10896-014-9660-z

Banerjee, S., & Ford, C. (2018). *Sensory rooms for patients with dementia in long-term care: Clinical and cost-effectiveness, and guidelines.* Canadian Agency for Drugs and Technologies in Health.

Bansal, A. & Tissenbaum, H. A. (2015). *Quantity or quality: living longer doesn't necessarily mean living healthier.* Retrieved on July 16, 2019, from https://www.the-scientist.com/critic-at-large/quantity-or-quality-35858.

Barak, B. (2009). Age identity: A cross-cultural global approach. *International Journal of Behavioral Development. 29*, 2–11. https://doi.org/10.1177/0165025408099485

Barker, N. N., & Himchak, M. V. (2006). Environmental issues affecting elder abuse victims in their reception of community-based services. *Journal of Gerontological Social Work, 48*(1/2), 233–255.

Basic, D., Shanley, C., & Gonzales, R. (2017). The impact of being a migrant from a non-English-speaking country on healthcare outcomes in frail older inpatients: An Australian study. *Journal of Cross-Cultural Gerontology, 32*(4), 447–460. doi:10.1007/s10823-017-9333-5

Beato, G. (2013). Bridging the generations. *Stanford Social Innovation Review, 11*(4), 61–2.

Beaulaurier, R. L., Seff, L. R., & Newman, F. L. (2008). Barriers to help-seeking for older women who experience intimate partner violence: A descriptive model. *Journal of Women & Aging, 20*(3/4), 231–248. doi:10.1080/08952840801984543

Bengtson, V. L. (2001). Beyond the nuclear family: The increasing importance of multigenerational bonds. *Journal of Marriage & Family, 63*(1), 1–16. doi:10.1111/j.1741-3737.2001.00001.x

Benson, W. (2018). Reflections on aging advocacy— and imperatives for its future. *Generations, 42*(4), 73–78.

Ben-Zvi, A., Miller, E. A., & Morimoto, R. I. (2009). Collapse of proteostasis represents an early molecular event in Caenorhabditis elegans aging. *Proceedings of the National Academy of Sciences, 106*(35), 14914–14919. doi:10.1073/pnas.0902882106

Berk, L. E. (2011). *Exploring lifespan development* (2nd ed.). Pearson.

Bertoni, M., Brunello, G., & Mazzarella, G. (2018). Does postponing minimum retirement age improve health behaviors before retirement? Evidence from middle-age Italian workers. *Journal of Health Economics, 58*, 215–227.

Bhasin, S., Cunningham, G. R., Hayes, F. J., Matsumoto, A. M., Snyder, P.J., Swerdloff, R. S., & Montori, V. M. (2010). Testosterone therapy in men with androgen deficiency syndromes: an Endocrine Society clinical practice guideline. *Journal of Clinical Endocrinology Metabolism, 95*, 2536–2559.

Bhattacharya, G., & Shibusawa, T. (2009). Experiences of aging among immigrants from India to the United States: Social work practice in a global context. *Journal of Gerontological Social Work, 52*(5), 445–462. doi:10.1080/01634370902983112

Bherer, L. (2015). Cognitive plasticity in older adults: effects of cognitive training and physical exercise. *Annals of the New York Academy of Sciences, 1337*(1), 1–6.

Biassoni, F., Cassina, G., & Balzarotti, S. (2019). Autobiographical narration as a tool for the empowerment of older adults' subjective and psychological wellbeing in nursing homes. *Clinical Gerontologist, 42*(3), 334–343. doi:10.1080/07317115.2017.1381867

Bibbo, J. (2019). Caregiving for adult pet owners. In L. Kogan & C. Blazina (Eds.), *Clinician's Guide to Treating Companion Animal Issues* (pp. 143–157). Academic Press. https://doi.org/https://doi.org/10.1016/B978-0-12-812962-3.00009-5

Biography. (2019). *Jack Kevorkian biography*. Retrieved on December 10, 2019, from https://www.biography.com/scientist/jack-kevorkian.

Birditt, K. S., Hartnett, C. S., Fingerman, K. L., Zarit, S. H., & Antonucci, T. C. (2015). Extending the Intergenerational Stake Hypothesis: Evidence of an Intra-individual Stake and Implications for Well-being. *Journal of Marriage and Family*, 77(4), 877–888. doi:10.1111/jomf.12203

Bitterman, A. (2020). Rainbow diaspora: the emerging renaissance of gay neighbourhoods. *The Town Planning Review*, 91(2), 99–107. doi: 10.3828/tpr.2020.6

Blancato, B., & Whitmire, M. P. (2021). *Why the American Rescue Plan is one of the most age-friendly laws in years*. https://www.nextavenue.org/american-rescue-plan-friendly/.

Blieszner, R., Ogletree, A. M., & Adams, R. G. (2019). Friendship in later life: A research agenda. *Innovation in Aging*, 3(1), 1–18.

Blieszner, R., & Voorpostel, M. (2016). Families and aging: Toward an interdisciplinary family-level approach. In V. L. Bengtson & R. A. Settersten (Eds.), *Handbook of Theories of Aging* (pp. 327–348). Springer.

Bloom, D. E., Canning, D., & Lubet, A. (2015). Global population aging: Facts, challenges, solutions, perspectives. *Daedalus*, 144(2), 80–92. https://doi.org/10.1162/DAED_a_00332

Blow, F. C., & Barry, K. L. (2012). Alcohol and substance misuse in older adults. *Current Psychiatry Reports*, 14(4), 310319. doi.org/10.1007/s11920-012-0292-9

Bobitt, J., Kuhne, J., Carter, J., Eliason, S. W., & Twomey, M. S. (2018). Building the adult protective services system of tomorrow: The role of the APS national voluntary consensus guidelines. *Journal of Elder Abuse & Neglect*, 30(1), 93–101. doi:10.1080/08946566.2017.1382414

Boltz, M., Chippendale, T., Resnick, B., & Galvin, J. E. (2015). Testing family-centered, function-focused care in hospitalized persons with dementia. *Neurodegenerative Disease Management*, 5(3), 203–215. https://doi.org/10.2217/nmt.15.10

Bonnie, R. J., & Wallace, R. B. (Eds.). (2003). *Elder mistreatment: Abuse, neglect, and exploitation in an aging America*. National Academies Press.

Boulton-Lewis, G. M. (2010). Education and learning for the elderly: Why, how, what. *Educational Gerontology*, 36, 213–228. doi:10.1080/03601270903182877

Bourassa, K. J. (2015). Women in very low-quality marriages gain life satisfaction following divorce. *Journal of Family Psychology*, 29(3), 490–499.

Bowen, H., Guilan, C., Yanran, D., Siyu, Y., Mingming, Y., Ping, Y., & Hongwei, J. (2019). Gender differences in the association between hearing loss and cognitive function. *American Journal of Alzheimer's Disease and Other Dementias*, 1–8. doi:10.1177/1533317519871167

Brandl, B., & Raymond, J. A. (2012). Policy implications of recognizing that caregiver stress is not the primary cause of elder abuse. *Generations*, 36(3), 32–39.

Bratt, C., Abrams, D., Swift, H. J., Vauclair, C. M., & Marques, S. (2018). Perceived age discrimination across age in Europe: From an ageing society to a society for all ages. *Developmental psychology*, 54(1), 167–80. doi.org/10.1037/dev0000398

Bronson, J., & Carson, E. A. (2019). *Prisoners in 2017*. Retrieved on March 2, 2021, from https://www.bjs.gov/content/pub/pdf/p17.pdf.

Brown, S. L., & Kawamura, S. (2010). Relationship quality among cohabitors and marrieds in older adulthood. *Social Science Research*, 39(5), 777–86. doi:10.1016/j.ssresearch.2010.04.010

Brown, S. L., & Lin, I. (2012). The gray divorce revolution: Rising divorce among middle-aged and older adults, 1990–2010. *Journals of Gerontology: Series B*, 67(6), 731–41. doi:10.1093/geronb/gbs089

Bruder, J. (2017). *Nomadland: Surviving America in the 21st century*. Norton.

Bunis, D. (2019). *Washington State enacts public long-term care insurance*. Retrieved on March 3, 2021, from https://www.aarp.org/politics-society/advocacy/info-2019/washington-long-term-care-law.html.

Bunis, D. (2020). *AARP Polls: Coronavirus, Social Security Cuts top 50+ voter concerns*. Retrieved on March 3, 2021, from https://www.aarp.org/politics-society/government-elections/info-2020/election-poll-issues.html.

Burger, K. (2018). *The new aging family: Older adults and parents*. Retrieved on March 4, 2021, from https://www.nextavenue.org/new-aging-family-older-adults-parents/.

Burnes, D. P., Rizzo, V. M., & Courtney, E. (2014). Elder abuse and neglect risk alleviation in protective services. *Journal of Interpersonal Violence*, 29(11), 2091–113. doi:10.1177/0886260513516387

Burns, V. F., & Sussman, T. (2018). Homeless for the first time in later life: Uncovering more than one pathway. *The Gerontologist*, 59(2), 251–59. doi:10.1093/geront/gnx212

Bussolo, M., Koettl, J., & Sinnott, E. (2015). *Golden aging: Prospects for healthy, active, and prosperous aging in Europe and Central Asia*. World Bank.

Butler, S. M., & Diaz, C. (2016). *"Third places" as community builders*. The Brookings Institution. Retrieved June 4, 2021 from https://www.brookings.edu/blog/up-front/2016/09/14/third-places-as-community-builders/

Calasanti, T. (2005). Ageism, gravity, and gender: Experiences of aging bodies. *Generations*, 29(3), 8–12.

Calasanti, T., & Giles, S. (2020). *The challenge of intersectionality*. American Society on Aging. Retrieved on June 29, 2020, from https://www.asaging.org/blog/challenge-intersectionality.

Calasanti, T. & King, N. (2015). Intersectionality and age. In J. Twigg & W. Martin (eds), *Routledge Handbook of Cultural Gerontology* (pp. 193–200). Routledge.

Canuto, A., Weber, K., Baertschi M, Andreas S, Volkert J, Dehoust MC, Sehner S, Suling A, Wegscheider K, Ausín B, Crawford MJ, Da Ronch C, Grassi L, Hershkovitz Y, Muñoz M, Quirk A, Rotenstein O, Santos-Olmo AB, Shalev A, . . . Härter, M. (2018). Anxiety disorders in old age: Psychiatric comorbidities, quality of life, and prevalence according to age, gender, and country. *American Journal of Geriatric Psychiatry*, 26(2), 174–85.

Cao, Q., Dabelko-Schoeny, H. I., White, K., Maleku, A., & Sheldon, M. (2021). I wanna help, but my hands can be a little tied: The challenges and benefits of formal volunteering among low-income diverse older adults. *Journal of Gerontological Social Work*, 64(3), 388–404. https://doi.org/10.1080/01634372.2021.1897373

Caring Across Generations. (2021). *Policy agenda*. Retrieved on June 6, 2021, from https://caringacross.org/policy-agenda/.

Carney, M. T., Fujiwara, J., Emmert, B. E., Liberman, T., & Paris, B. (2016). Elder orphans hiding in plain sight: A growing vulnerable population. *Current Gerontology and Geriatrics Research*, 2016, 11. doi:10.1155/2016/4723250

Carr, D. C., Fried, L. P., & Rowe, J. W. (2015). Productivity & engagement in an aging America: The role of volunteerism. *Daedalus*, 144(2), 55–67.

Carstensen, L. L. & DeLiema, M. (2018). The positivity effect: A negativity bias in youth fades with age. *Current Opinion in Behavioral Sciences*, 19, 7–12.

Carstensen, L. L., Isaacowitz, D. M., & Charles, S. T. (1999). Taking time seriously: A theory of socioemotional selectivity. *American Psychologist*, 54(3), 165–81.

Carstensen, L. L., & Mikels, J. A. (2005). At the intersection of emotion and cognition: Aging and the positivity effect. *Current Directions in Psychological Science*, 14, 117–21. doi:10.1111/j.0963-7214.2005.00348.x

Cassel, C. (1997). Preface. In *Approaching Death* (pp. v–vii). National Academy Press.

Castelló-Porcar, A. M., & Martínez-Jabaloyas, J. M. (2016). Testosterone/estradiol ratio, is it useful in the diagnosis of erectile dysfunction and low sexual desire? *Aging Male*, 19(4), 254–58. doi-org.libproxy.lib.csusb.edu/10.1080/13685538.2016.1253672

Cattell, R. B. (1967). The theory of fluid and crystallized general intelligence checked at the 5–6 year-old level. *British Journal of Educational Psychology*, 37, 209–24.

Center for Behavioral Health Statistics and Quality. (2017). *2016 National survey on drug use and health: detailed tables*. Substance Abuse and Mental Health Services Administration.

Centers for Disease Control and Prevention. (2018a). *Suicide rising across the US*. Retrieved on October 26, 2020, from, https://www.cdc.gov/vitalsigns/suicide/index.html.

Centers for Disease Control and Prevention. (2018b). *What if I already have hearing loss?* Retrieved on November 27, 2019, from https://www.cdc.gov/nceh/hearing_loss/what_if_i_already_have_hearing_loss.html.

Centers for Disease Control and Prevention. (2020a). *Responding to coronavirus (COVID-19) in nursing homes*. Retrieved on March 3, 2021, from https://

www.cdc.gov/coronavirus/2019-ncov/hcp/nursing-homes-responding.html.

Centers for Disease Control and Prevention. (2020b). *Sexually transmitted disease surveillance 2018*. Retrieved on January 2, 2021, from https://www.cdc.gov/std/stats18/default.htm.

Centers for Medicare and Medicaid Services. (n.d.a). CMS Fast Facts. Retrieved November 22, 2022 from https://data.cms.gov/fact-sheet/cms-fast-facts.

Centers for Medicare & Medicaid Services. (n.d.b). NHE Fact Sheet. Retrieved November 22, 2022 from https://www.cms.gov/Research-Statistics-Data-and-Systems/Statistics-Trends-and-Reports/NationalHealthExpendData/NHE-Fact-Sheet

Cercone, K. (2008). Characteristics of adult learners with implications for online learning design. *AACE Journal*, 16(2), 137–59.

Cervantes, R. C., Gattamorta, K. A., & Berger-Cardoso, J. (2019). Examining difference in immigration stress, acculturation stress and mental health outcomes in six Hispanic/Latino nativity and regional groups. *Journal of Immigrant and Minority Health*, 21, 14–20. doi:10.1007/s10903-018-0714-9

Chen, Y. H., Lin, L. C., Chuang, L. L., & Chen, M. L. (2017). The relationship of physiopsychosocial factors and spiritual well-being in elderly residents: Implications for evidence-based practice. *Worldviews in Evidence-Based Nursing*, 14(6), 484–91.

Cherpak, G. L., & dos Santos, F. C. (2016). Assessment of physicians' addressing sexuality in elderly with chronic pain. *Einstein*, 14(2), 178–84.

Childs, J. W. (2021). *Worst Climate Disasters of 2021 Included Heat, Drought, Flooding – Even a Deep Freeze*. The Weather Channel. Retrieved January 16, 2022 from https://weather.com/news/climate/news/2021-12-17-worst-climate-disasters-2021

Choi, N. G., DiNitto, D. M., Marti, C. N., & Kaplan, M. S. (2017). Older suicide decedents: Intent disclosure, mental and physical health, and suicide means. *American Journal of Preventive Medicine*, 53(6), 772780.

Chonody, J. M. (2016). Positive and negative ageism: The role of benevolent and hostile sexism. *Affilia: Journal of Women & Social Work*, 31(2), 207–18. https://doi.org/10.1177/0886109915595839

Chowdhury, M. A. B., Fiore, A. J., Cohen, S. A., Wheatley, C., Wheatley, B., Balakrishnan, M. P., Chami, M., Scieszka, L., Drabin, M. Roberts, K.A., Toben, A. C., Tyndall, J.A., Grattan, L.M., & Morris, J. G. (2019). Health Impact of Hurricanes Irma and Maria on St Thomas and St John, US Virgin Islands, 2017–2018. *American Journal of Public Health*, 109(12), 1725–32. http://dx.doi.org/10.2105/AJPH.2019.305310

Chrisler, J. C., Barney, A., & Palatino, B. (2016). Ageism can be hazardous to women's health: Ageism, sexism, and stereotypes of older women in the healthcare system. *Social Issues*, 72(1), 86–104.

Ciano, C., King, T. S., Wright, R. R., Perlis, M., & Sawyer, A. M. (2017). Longitudinal study of insomnia symptoms among women during perimenopause. *Journal of Obstetric, Gynecologic, & Neonatal Nursing*, 46(6), 804–13.

Clark, J. L., Phoenix, S., Bilbrey, A. C., McManis, T., Escal, K. A., Arulanantham, R., Sisay, T., & Ghatak, R. (2018). Cultural competency in dementia care: An African American case study. *Clinical Gerontologist*, 41(3), 255–60. https://doi.org/10.1080/07317115.2017.1420725

Cohen, H. L., Thomas, C. L., & Williamson, C. (2018). Religion and spirituality as defined by older adults. *Journal of Gerontological Social Work*, 51(3–4),284–99.

Cohen, M. A., Tell, E. J., Miller, E. A., Hwang, A., & Miller, M. (2020). *Learning from new state initiatives in financing long-term services and supports: Executive summary*. Retrieved on February 3, 2021, from https://www.ltsscenter.org/wp-content/uploads/2020/07/State-LTSS-Financing-Executive-Summary-July-2020.pdf.

Cohn, D. V., & Passel, J. S. (2018). *A record 64 million Americans live in multigenerational households*. Retrieved on July 6, 2019, from https://www.pewresearch.org/fact-tank/2018/04/05/a-record-64-million-americans-live-in-multigenerational-households/.

Colello, K. J. (2020). *The Elder Justice Act: Background and issues for Congress* (R43707). https://crsreports.congress.gov/product/pdf/R/R43707/11.

Colello, K. J., & Napili, A. (2020). *Older Americans Act: Overview and funding*. Retrieved on March 4,

2021, from https://crsreports.congress.gov/product/pdf/R/R43414.

Columbia Public Health. (2021). *The advantages of older workers*. Retrieved on February 17, 2021, from https://www.publichealth.columbia.edu/research/age-smart-employer/advantages-older-workers.

Compassion and Choices. (2019). *Out of hospital DNR and POLST*. Retrieved on December 17, 2019, from https://compassionandchoices.org/end-of-life-planning/plan/dnr/.

Compassion and Choices. (2020). *Voluntarily stopping eating and drinking (VSED)*. Retrieved on June 6, 2020, from https://compassionandchoices.org/end-of-life-planning/learn/vsed/.

Congressional Budget Office. (2020). Medicare—CBO's Baseline as of March 6, 2020. https://www.cbo.gov/system/files/2020-03/51302-2020-03-medicare.pdf.

Conner, K. O., Copeland, V. C., Grote, N. K., Koeske, G., Rosen, D., Reynolds, C. F., & Brown, C. (2010). Mental health treatment seeking among older adults with depression: the impact of stigma and race. *American Journal of Geriatric Psychiatry, 18*(6), 531–43.doi.org/10.1097/JGP.0b013e3181cc0366

Conway, F., Jones, S., & Speakes-Lewis, A. (2011). Emotional strain in caregiving among African American grandmothers raising their grandchildren. *Journal of Women & Aging, 23*(2), 113–28. doi:10.1080/08952841.2011.561142

Coombs, G., and Dollery, B. (2004). The ageing of Australia: Fiscal sustainability, intergenerational equity and inter-temporal fiscal balance. *Australian Journal of Social Issues 39*(4), 459–70.

Correa-de-Araujo, R. (2004). A wake-up call to advance women's health. *Women's Health Issues, 14*, 31–34.

COVID Tracking Project. (2021). *Long-Term-Care COVID Tracker*. The Atlantic Monthly Group. https://covidtracking.com/nursing-homes-long-term-care-facilities

Creighton, A. S., Davison, T. E., & Kissane, D. W. (2016). The prevalence of anxiety among older adults in nursing homes and other residential aged care facilities: A systematic review. *International Journal of Geriatric Psychiatry, 31*(6), 555566.

Cremation Association of North America. (2020). *Cremation rates continue to grow confirming that cremation is the new tradition*. Retrieved on July 19, 2020, from https://www.cremationassociation.org/page/IndustryStatistics.

Cremation Institute. (2020). *Water cremation: Is resomation a green & bio friendly solution?* Retrieved on July 19, 2020, from https://cremationinstitute.com/water-cremation.

Crenshaw, K. (1989). Demarginalizing the intersection of race and sex: A black feminist critique of antidiscrimination doctrine, feminist theory and antiracist politics. *University of Chicago Legal Forum, 1989*(8), 139–67.

Crimmins, A., Balbus, J., Gamble, J. L., Beard, C. B., Bell, J. E., Dodgen, D., Eisen, R.J., Fann, N., Hawkins, M., Herring, S.C., Jantarasami, L. Mills, D.M., Saha, S., Sarofim, M.C., Trtanj, J. & Ziska, L. (2016). *Executive Summary. The Impacts of Climate Change on Human Health in the United States: A Scientific Assessment*. Retrieved from Washington, DC: https://health2016.globalchange.gov/high/ClimateHealth2016_ExecSummary_Standalone.pdf

Crockett, C., Brandl, B., & Dabby, F. C. (2015). Survivors in the margins: The invisibility of violence against older women. *Journal of Elder Abuse & Neglect, 27*(4–5), 291–302. doi:10.1080/08946566.2015.1090361

Cruz-Jentoft, A. J., Baeyens, J. P., Bauer, J. M., Boirie, Y., Cederholm, T., Landi, F., Martin, F. C., Michel, J-P, Rolland, Y, Schneider, S., Topinková, E., Vandewoude, M, Zamboni, M. (2010). European working group on sarcopenia in older people. Sarcopenia: European consensus on definition and diagnosis: Report of the European working group on sarcopenia in older people. *Age and Ageing, 39*(4), 412–23. doi:dx.doi.org/10.1093/ageing/afq034

Crystal, S., Shea, D. G., & Reyes, A. M. (2017). Cumulative advantage, cumulative disadvantage, and evolving patterns of late-life inequality. *Gerontologist, 57*(5), 910–20. doi:10.1093/geront/gnw056

Cumming, E., & Henry, W. (1961). *Growing old: The process of disengagement*. Basic Books.

Currie, M., Philip, L. J., & Roberts, A. (2015). Attitudes towards the use and acceptance of eHealth technologies: A case study of older adults living with chronic pain and implicatitons for rural healthcare. *BMC Health Services Research*, *15*, 162–75.

Cutchin, M. P. (2018). Active relationships of ageing people and places. In M. W. Skinner, G. J. Andrews, & M. P. Cutchin (Eds.), *Geographical Gerontology: Perspectives, Concepts, Approaches* (pp. 216–28). Routledge.

Cutler, David M. (1996). Re-Examining the three-legged stool of retirement income support. In P. A. Diamond, D. C. Lindeman, & H. Young (Eds.), *Social Security: What Role for the Future?* (pp. 125–49). National Academy of Social Insurance.

David, P., & Nelson-Kakulla, B. (2019). *2018 Grandparents Today National Survey: General population report*. Retrieved on June 5, 2019, from https://doi.org/10.26419/res.00289.001.

Day, C. L. (2017). *AARP: America's largest interest group and its impact*. ABC-CLIO.

Dementia Services Information and Development Centre. (2014). *Interventions*. Retrieved on December 2, 2019, from http://dementia.ie/information/interventions.

Dementia Care Central. (2020). *Mini-mental state exam (MMSE) Alzheimer's/dementia test: Administration, accuracy and scoring*. Retrieved on October 3, 2021, from https://www.dementiacarecentral.com/mini-mental-state-exam/.

Demiris, G., Parker Oliver, D., & Wittenberg-Lyles, E. (2011). Technologies to support end-of-life care. *Seminars in Oncology Nursing*, *27*(3), 211–17. doi.org/10.1016/j.soncn.2011.04.006

DePasquale, N., Polenick, C. A., Davis, K. D., Berkman, L. F., & Cabot, T. D. (2018). A bright side to the work–family interface: Husbands' support as a resource in double-and-triple-duty caregiving wives' work lives. *The Gerontologist*, *58*(4), 674–85. doi:10.1093/geront/gnx016

Desmettre, T. J. (2018). Epigenetics in age-related macular degeneration (AMD). *Journal Français d'Ophtalmologie*, *41*(9), e407–e415.

de Vries, B. (2018). The unsung bonds of friendship—and caring—among older adults. *Generations*, *42*, 77–81.

Dewitte, M., & Mayer, A. (2018). Exploring the link between daily relationship quality, sexual desire, and sexual activity in couples. *Archives of Sexual Behavior*, *47*, 1675–86. doi.org/10.1007/s10508-018-1175-x

Diamond, L. M. (2016). Sexual fluidity in males and females. *Current Sexual Health Reports*, *8*, 249–56.

Dignitas. (2019). *End-of-life help and/or regulations*. Retrieved on December 16, 2019, from http://www.dignitas.ch/index.phpoption=com_content&view=article&id=54&lang=en&Itemid=.

DiPrete, T. A., & Eirich, G. M. (2006). Cumulative advantage as a mechanism for inequality. A review of theoretical and empirical developments. *Annual Review of Sociology*, *32*, 271–97.

Doka, K. J. (2002). *Disenfranchised grief: New directions, challenges, and strategies for practice*. Research Press.

Donelan, K., Yuchiao, C., Berrett-Abebe, J., Spetz, J., Auerbach, D. I., Norman, L., & Buerhaus, P. I. (2019). Care management for older adults: The roles Of nurses, social workers, and physicians. *Health Affairs*, *38*(6), 941–49. doi:10.1377/hlthaff.2019.00030

Doolittle, G. C., Nelson, E-L., Spaulding, A. O., Lomenick, A. F., Krebill, H. M., Adams, N. J., Kuhlman, S. J., & Barnes, J. L. (2019). TeleHospice: A community-engaged model for utilizing mobile tablets to enhance rural hospice care. *American Journal of Hospice and Palliative Medicine*, *36*(9), 795–800. doi:10.1177/1049909119829458

Dor, Y., & Cedar, H. (2018). Principles of DNA methylation and their implications for biology and medicine. *The Lancet*, *392*(10149), 777–86. doi:10.1016/S0140-6736(18)31268-6

Dorsey, S., Christopher, C., & Macpherson, D. (1998). *Pensions and Productivity*. W. E. Upjohn Institute for Employment Research.

Drapeau, C. W., & McIntosh, J. L. (2018). *U.S.A. suicide 2018: Official final data*. American Association of Suicidology.

Dunkle, J. S. (2018). Indifference to the difference? Older lesbian and gay men's perceptions of aging services. *Journal of Gerontological Social Work*, *61*(4), 432–59. doi:10.1080/01634372.2018.1451939

Dyer, C. B., Regev, M., Burnett, J., Festa, N., & Cloyd, B. (2008). SWiFT: A rapid triage tool for vulnerable older adults in disaster situations. *Disaster Medicine and Public Health Preparedness*, *2* S45–50. doi:10.1097/DMP.0b013e3181647b81

Edelman, M. & Ficorelli, C. T. (2012). Keeping older adults safe at home. *Nursing*, *42* (1), 65–66. doi:10.1097/01.NURSE.0000408481.20951.e8.

Edemekong, P. F., Bomgaars, D. L., Sukumaran, S., & Schoo, C. (2022). Activities of Daily Living. In *StatPearls*. StatPearls Publishing. Retrieved on November 19, 2022, from https://pubmed.ncbi.nlm.nih.gov/29261878/

Edison Electric Institute. (2021). *Issues & policy: LIHEAP funding*. Retrieved on March 5, 2021, from https://www.eei.org/issuesandpolicy/Pages/liheap.aspx.

Edmonds, G. W., Goldberg, L. R., Hampson, S. E., & Barckley, M. (2013). Personality stability from childhood to midlife: Relating teachers' assessments in elementary school to observer- and self-ratings 40 years later. *Journal of Research in Personality, 47*(5), 505–13.

Eeden-Moorefield, B. V., Martell, C. R., Williams, M., & Preston, M. (2011). Same-sex relationships and dissolution: The connection between heteronormativity and homonormativity. *Family Relations, 60*, 562–71. doi:10.1111/j.1741-3729.2011.00669.x

Ellen, M. E., Demaio, P., Lange, A., & Wilson, M. G. (2017). Adult day center programs and their associated outcomes on clients, caregivers, and the health system: A scoping review. *The Gerontologist, 57*(6), e85–e94. doi:10.1093/geront/gnw165

EngAGE. (2020). *About us*. Retrieved on January 3, 2021, from https://engagedaging.org/about-us.

Erikson, E. (1950). *Childhood and society*. Norton.

Ernst, J. S., & Brownell, P. J. (2013). The United States of America. In A. Phelan (Ed.), *International Perspectives on Elder Abuse* (pp. 206–21). Routledge.

Ernst, J. S., & Smith, C. A. (2015). Departments of public welfare or social services. In B. Berkman & D. Kaplan (Eds.), *The Oxford Handbook of Social Work in Health and Aging* (pp. 131–39). Oxford.

Erosheva, E. A., Kim, H-J., Emlet, C., & Fredriksen-Goldsen, K. I. (2016). Social networks of lesbian, gay, bisexual, and transgender older adults. *Research on Aging, 38*(1), 98–123.

Europa-Kommissionen. (2021). *Age discrimination*. Retrieved on February 22, 2021, from https://ec.europa.eu/info/policies/justice-and-fundamental-rights/combatting-discrimination/age-discrimination_en.

Evans, G. W., Wethington, E., Coleman, M., Worms, M., & Frongillo, E.A. (2008). Income health inequalities among older persons: The mediating role of multiple risk exposures. *Journal of Aging and Health, 20*(1), 107–25. doi:10.1177/0898264307309938

Fagan, R. M. (2013). Pioneer Network: A movement to change the culture of long-term care—Why aren't we there yet? In J. L. Ronch, A. S. Weiner, & K. Greenlee (Eds.), *Culture change in elder care* (pp. 22–49). Health Professions Press.

Fahs, G., Dewan, A., Buccini, S., & Tanner, O. (2021). *Protecting older users online*. Retrieved on May 4, 2021, from https://www.aspentechpolicyhub.org/project/protecting-older-users-online/.

Faigin, C. A., & Pargament, K. I. (2010). Strengthened by the spirit: Religion, spirituality, and resilience through adulthood and aging. In B. Resnick & K. A. Roberto (Eds.), *Resilience in Aging: Concepts, Research, and Outcomes* (pp. 163–80). Springer.

Faist, T. (2020). Commentary: Getting out of the climate migration ghetto: Understanding climate degradation and migration as processes of social inequalities. *International Migration, 58*(6), 247–253. doi:10.1111/imig.12793

Family Caregiver Alliance. (2017). *Caregiving at home: A guide to community resources*. Retrieved on February 3, 2021, from https://www.caregiver.org/caregiving-home-guide-community-resources.

Fang, H., Huang, L., Welch, I., Norley, C., Holdsworth, D. W., Beier, F., & Cai, D. (2018). Early changes of articular cartilage and subchondral bone in the DMM mouse model of osteoarthritis. *Scientific Reports, 8*(2855). doi:10.1038/s41598-018-21184-5

Farage, M. A., Miller, K. W., Berardesca, E., & Maibach, H. I. (2009). Clinical implications of aging skin: cutaneous disorders in the elderly. *American Journal of Clinical Dermatology, 10*(2), 73–86.

Farrell, C. (2016, October 22). Very mobile work force, never far from home. *New York Times*. https://www.nytimes.com/2016/10/22/your-money/retirement-migrant-workers-recreational-vehicles.html

Fassa, P. (2019). *The drugging of American seniors: Big pharma profits depend on sick seniors*. https://healthimpactnews.com/2018/the-drugging-of-american-seniors-big-pharma-profits-depend-on-sick-seniors/.

Feagin, J. R. (1991). The continuing significance of race: Antiblack discrimination in public places. *American Sociological Review, 56*, 101–16.

Federal Bureau of Investigation. (2021). *Scams and safety*. https://www.fbi.gov/scams-and-safety/common-scams-and-crimes/elder-fraud.

Federal Interagency Forum on Aging-Related Statistics. (2020). *Older Americans 2020: Key indicators of well-being*. Washington, DC: U.S. Government Printing Office.

Federal Interagency Forum on Aging-Related Statistics. (2021). Population Aging in the United States: A Global Perspective. https://agingstats.gov/OlderAmericans_AgingPopulation.pdf.

Feinberg, L. F. (2014a). Moving toward person- and family-centered care. *Public Policy & Aging Report, 24*(3), 97–101. doi:10.1093/ppar/pru027

Feinberg, L. F. (2014b). Recognizing and supporting family caregivers: The time has come. *Public Policy & Aging Report, 24*(2), 65–69. doi:10.1093/ppar/pru007

Feinberg, L., Reinhard, S. C., Houser, A., & Choula, R. (2011). *The growing contributions and costs of family caregiving*. Retrieved on February 10, 2021, from assets.aarp.org/rgcenter/ppi/ltc/i51-caregiving.pdf.

Field, A., Robertson, N. A., Wang, T., Havas, A., Ideker, T., & Adams, P. D. (2018). DNA methylation clocks in aging: Categories, causes, and consequences. *Molecular Cell, 71*(6), 882–95. doi:10.1016/j.molcel.2018.08.00

Fileborn, B., Brown, G., Lyons, A., Hinchliff, S., Heywood, W., Minichiello, V., Malta, S., Barrett, C., & Crameri, P. (2017) Safer sex in later life: Qualitative interviews with older Australians on their understandings and practices of safer sex. *Journal of Sex Research, 4499*, 1–14. doi.org/10.1080/00224499.2017.1280121

Fileborn, B., Thorpe, R., Hawkes, G., Minichiello, V., Pitts, M., & Dune, T. (2015). Sex, desire and pleasure: considering the experiences of older Australian women. *Sexual and Relationship Therapy, 30*(1), 117–30.

Fine, A. H. (2019). The human-animal bond over the lifespan: A primer for mental health professionals. In L. Kogan & C. Blazina (Eds.), *Clinician's Guide to Treating Companion Animal Issues* (pp. 1–19). Academic Press. https://doi.org/10.1016/B978-0-12-812962-3.00001-0

Finlay, J. M., Gaugler, J. E., & Kane, R. L. (2020). Ageing in the margins: expectations of and struggles for 'a good place to grow old' among low-income older Minnesotans. *Ageing and Society, 40*(4), 759–83. doi:10.1017/S0144686X1800123X

Fiori, K. L., Antonucci, T. C., & Akiyama, H. (2008). Profiles of social relations among older adults: A cross-cultural approach. *Ageing and Society, 28*(2), 203–31. doi.org/10.1017/s0144686x07006472

Fischer, N., Weber, B., & Riechelmann, H. (2016). Presbycusis—age related hearing loss. *Laryngo-rhinootologie, 95*(7), 497–510.

Flanagan, C., Levine, P., & Settersen, R. (2009). *Civic engagement and the changing transition to adulthood*. Retrieved on March 6, 2021, from http://civicyouth.org/PopUps/ChangingTransition.pdfExternal Web Site Policy.

Flowers, L., & Hado, E. (2020). *Hear their voices: The experiences of midlife adults who gained Medicaid coverage in four expansion states*. Retrieved on February 3, 2021, from https://doi.org/10.26419/ppi.00118.001.

Fredriksen-Goldsen, K. I., Emlet, C. A., Kim, H. J., Muraco, A., Erosheva, E. A., Goldsen, J., & Hoy-Ellis, C. P. (2013). The physical and mental health of lesbian, gay male, and bisexual (LGB) older adults: The role of key health indicators and risk and protective factors. *The Gerontologist, 53*, 664–75. doi:10.1093/geront/gns123

Fredriksen-Goldsen, K. I., Kim, H. J., Barkan, S. E., Muraco, A., & Hoy-Ellis, C. P. (2013). Health disparities among lesbian, gay, and bisexual older adults: Results from a population-based study. *American Journal of Public Health, 103*, 1802–9. doi:10.2105/AJPH.2012.301110

Fredriksen-Goldsen, K. I., Kim, H.-J., Emlet, C. A., Muraco, A., Erosheva, E. A., Hoy-Ellis, C. P., & Petry, H. (2011). *The aging and health report: Disparities and resilience among lesbian, gay, bisexual, and transgender older adults*. Institute for Multigenerational Health.

Frederiksen-Goldsen, K., Kim, H.-J., Jung, H., & Goldsen, J. (2019). The evolution of Aging with Pride—National Health, Aging, and Sexuality/

Gender Study: Illuminating the iridescent life course of LGBTQ adults aged 80 years and older in the United States. *International Journal of Aging & Human Development*, 88(4), 380–404. doi:10.1177/0091415019837591

Freedman, M. (2007). *Finding work that matters in the second half of life*. Public Affairs.

French, M. T., Homer, J., Gumus, G., & Hickling, L. (2016). Key provisions of the Patient Protection and Affordable Care Act (ACA): A systematic review and presentation of early research findings. *Health Services Research*, 51(5), 1735–71. doi:10.1111/1475-6773.12511

Friedman, H. S., Kern, M. L., & Reynolds, C. A. (2010). Personality and health, subjective well-being, and longevity. *Journal of Personality*, 78(1), 179–216.

Friedman, H. S., Tucker, J. S., Schwartz, J. E., Martin, L. R., Tomlinson-Keasey, C., Wingard, D. L., & Criqui, M. H. (1995). Childhood conscientiousness and longevity: Health behaviors and cause of death. *Journal of Personality and Social Psychology*, 68, 696–703. 10.1037/0022-3514.68.4.696.

Fritz, H., Cutchin, M. P., & Cummins, E. R. (2018). Loss of trust in the neighborhood: The experience of older African Americans in Detroit. *Journals of Gerontology: Series B*, 73(7), e108–e119. doi:10.1093/geronb/gby019

Fry, R. (2017). *It's becoming more common for young adults to live at home—and for longer stretches*. Retrieved on March 3, 2021, from https://www.pewresearch.org/fact-tank/2017/05/05/its-becoming-more-common-for-young-adults-to-live-at-home-and-for-longer-stretches/.

Fung, H. H. (2013). Aging in culture. *The Gerontologist*, 53(3), 369–77.

Gallagher, J. (2020). *Here are 7 elder communities that are like living in the gayborhood*. Retrieved July 7 from https://www.lgbtqnation.com/2020/06/7-elder-communities-like-living-gayborhood/.

Gallup. (2021). *Millennials: The job-hopping generation*. Retrieved on December 23, 2021, from https://www.gallup.com/workplace/231587/millennials-job-hopping-generation.aspx.

Ganong, L., & Coleman, M. (2018). Studying stepfamilies: Four eras of family scholarship. *Family Process*, 57(1), 7–24. doi:10.1111/famp.12307

Gass, A. P., Mahan, Z., & Balfour, M. (2018). Definition, background, and case studies of geriatric homeless. In D. Chau & A. P. Gass (Eds.), *Homeless Older Populations: A Practical Guide for Interdisciplinary Care Teams* (pp. 1–22). Springer.

Gawlowska, M., Beldzik, E., Domagalik, A., Gagol, A., Marek, T., & Mojsa-Kaja, J. (2017). I don't want to miss a thing—learning dynamics and effects of feedback type and monetary incentive in a paired associate deterministic learning task. *Frontiers in Psychology*, 8, 935. doi.org/10.3389/fpsyg.2017.00935

Generations United. (2021). *Who we are: Generations United improves the lives of children, youth, and older adults*. Retrieved on November 17, 2022, from https://www.gu.org/who-we-are/.

Generations United and Leading Age. (2017). *Research Snapshot: Intergenerational Programming in Senior Housing*. Retrieved on February 5, 2021, from http://www.ltsscenter.org/resource-library/Research_Snapshot_Intergenerational_Programming_in_Senior_Housing.pdf

Genworth. (2021). Costs of care: Trends & insights. Retrieved on November 17, 2022, from https://www.genworth.com/aging-and-you/finances/cost-of-care/cost-of-care-trends-and-insights.html.

Gerrard, E., & Wilkinson, S. (2005). Passive euthanasia. *Journal of Medical Ethics*, 31, 64–68.

Gheaus, A., & Herzog, L. (2016). The goods of work (other than money!). *Journal of Social Philosophy*. 47(1), 70–89.

Ghisyawan, K. (2016). Social erotics: The fluidity of love, desire and friendship for same-sex loving women in trinidad. *Journal of International Women's Studies*, 17(3), 17–31.

Gibson, M. J., & Hayunga, M. (2006). *We Can Do Better: Lessons Learned for Protecting Older Persons in Disasters*. AARP.

Gironda, M. W., Lefever, K., Delagrammatikas, L., Nerenberg, L., Roth, R., Chen, E. A., & Northington, K. R. (2010). Education and training of mandated reporters: Innovative models, overcoming challenges, and lessons learned. *Journal of Elder Abuse & Neglect*, 22(3/4), 340–64. doi:10.1080/08946566.2010.490188

Gladyshev, V. N. (2014). The free radical theory of aging is dead. Long live the damage theory!

Antioxidants & Redox Signaling, 20(4), 727–31. doi: 10.1089/ars.2013.5228

Gokhale, J. (2004). *Mandatory retirement age rules: Is it time to re-evaluate?* Retrieved on February 28, 2021, from https://www.cato.org/testimony/mandatory-retirement-age-rules-it-time-re-evaluate.

Golant, S. M. (2018). Explaining the realities of aging in place for older adults In M. W. Skinner, G. J. Andrews, & M. P. Cutchin (Eds.), *Geographical Gerontology: Perspectives, Concepts, Approaches* (pp. 189–202). Routledge.

Golden, A. G., Silverman, M. A., & Issenberg, S. B. (2015). Addressing the shortage of geriatricians: What medical educators can learn from the nurse practitioner training model. *Academic Medicine, 90*(9), 1236–40.

Goldsmith, T. C. (2016a). Aging theories: Why modern programmed aging concepts are transforming medical research. *Biochemistry, 81*(12), 1675–84.

Goldsmith, T. C. (2016b). Emerging programmed aging mechanisms and their medical implications. *Medical Hypotheses, 86*(1), 92–96.

Gonzales, E., Matz-Costa, C., & Morrow-Howell, N. (2015). Increasing opportunities for the productive engagement of older adults: A response to population aging. *The Gerontologist, 55*(2), 252–61. doi.org/10.1093/geront/gnu176

Gottlieb, B. H., & Sevigny, A. (2016). Social usefulness: Theory and evidence concerning a late life identity construct. *International Journal of Aging and Human Development, 83*(4), 333–65. doi:10.1177/0091415016655165

Graham, J. (2020, July 24). Technology divide between senior "haves" and "have-nots" roils pandemic response. *Kaiser Health News*. https://khn.org/news/technology-divide-between-senior-haves-and-have-nots-roils-pandemic-response/.

Green Burial Council. (2020). *Green burial defined.* Retrieved on July 20, 2020, from https://www.greenburialcouncil.org/green_burial_defined.html.

Greenberg, J., Solomon, S., & Pyszczynski, T. (1997). Terror management theory of self-esteem and cultural worldviews: Empirical assessments and conceptual refinements. *Advances in Experimental Social Psychology, 29*, 61–139.

Greenfield, E. A., Black, K., Buffel, T., & Yeh, J. (2018). Community gerontology: A framework for research, policy, and practice on communities and aging. *The Gerontologist, 59*(5), 803–10. doi: 10.1093/geront/gny089

Greenfield, E. A., Oberlink, M., Scharlach, A. E., Neal, M. B., & Stafford, P. B. (2015). Age-friendly community initiatives: Conceptual issues and key questions. *The Gerontologist, 55*(2), 191–98. doi: 10.1093/geront/gnv005

Greenlee, K. (2020). Our national shame: Little to no funding for elder abuse prevention and response. *Generations, 44*(1), 117–23.

Greif, G. L., & Woolley, M. E. (2016). *Adult sibling relationships.* Columbia University Press.

Griffin, J. M., Meis, L. A., Greer, N., MacDonald, R., Jensen, A., Rutks, I., Carlyle, M., & Wilt, T. J. (2015). Effectiveness of caregiver interventions on patient outcomes in adults with dementia or Alzheimer's disease: A systematic review. *Gerontology & Geriatric Medicine, 1*, 1–17. https://doi.org/10.1177/2333721415595789

Gronke, P., Manson, P., Lee, J., & Foot, C. (2020). How elections under COVID-19 may change the political engagement of older voters. *Public Policy & Aging Report, 30*(4), 147–53. doi:10.1093/ppar/praa030

Gubernskaya, Z., & Treas, J. (2020). Pathways to linguistic isolation among older US immigrants: Assessing the role of living arrangements and English proficiency. *Journals of Gerontology Series B: Psychological Sciences & Social Sciences, 75*(2), 351–6. doi:10.1093/geronb/gbx178

Guiney, H., Keall, M., & Machado, L. (2021). Volunteering in older adulthood is associated with activity engagement and cognitive functioning. *Aging, Neuropsychology & Cognition, 28*(2), 253–69.

Gullette, M. M. (2004). *Age wise: Fighting the new ageism in America.* University of Chicago Press.

Gullette, M. M. (2017). *Ending ageism, or how not to shoot old people.* Rutgers University Press.

Gullette, M. M. (2018). Against "aging": How to talk about growing older. *Theory, Culture, & Society, 35*(7–8), 251–70.

Gupta, R., & Hershey, D. A. (2016). Cross-National Differences in Goals for Retirement: the Case of India and the United States. *Journal of Cross-*

Cultural Gerontology, 31(3), 221–36. https://doi.org/10.1007/s10823-016-9298-9

Gurchiek, K. (2018). EEOC: *Ageism persists in the workplace.* Retrieved on February 16, 2021, from https://www.proquest.com/tradejournals/eeoc-ageism-persists-workplace/docview/2061840981/se-2?accountid=10359.

Gurera, J. W., & Isaacowitz, D. M. (2019). Emotion regulation and emotion perception in aging: A perspective on age-related differences and similarities. *Progress in Brain Research, 247,* 329–51.

Guzman, S., Sturtevant, L., & Huaman, D. (2019). *Affordable supportive housing fills gap for older adults and people with disabilities.* Retrieved on February 6, 2021, from https://doi.org/10.26419/ppi.00069.001.

Haber, C. (2016). History of long-term care. In G. D. Knowles & P. B. Teaster (Eds.), *Long-Term Care in an Aging Society: Theory and Practice* (pp. 33–60). Springer.

Han, B. H., Moore, A. A., Sherman, S., Keyes, K. M., & Palamar, J. J. (2017). Demographic trends of binge alcohol use and alcohol use disorders among older adults in the United States, 2005–2014. *Drug and Alcohol Dependency, 1,* 170, 198–207. doi:10.1016/j.drugalcdep.2016.11.003

Han, K. T., Kim, D. W., Kim, S. J., & Kim, S. J. (2018). Biological age is associated with the active use of nutrition data. *International journal of environmental research and public health, 15*(11), 2431. doi:10.3390/ijerph15112431

Hannan, M. T., & Kranzberg, M. (2017). *History of the organization of work.* Retrieved on January 31, 2021, from https://www.britannica.com/topic/history-of-work-organization-648000.

Hanson, M. A., Cooper, C., Sayer, A. A., Eendebak, R. J., Clough, G. G., & Beard, J. R. (2016). Developmental aspects of a life course approach to healthy ageing. *Journal of Physiology, 594*(8), 2147–60.

Harding, D. J., & Jencks, C. (2003). Changing attitudes toward premarital sex. *Public Opinion Quarterly, 67*(2), 211–26. https://doi.org/10.1086/374399

Harris, M. A., Brett, C. E., Johnson, W., & Deary, I. J. (2016). Personality stability from age 14 to age 77 years. *Psychology and aging, 31*(8), 862–74. doi.org/10.1037/pag0000133

Harris-Kojetin, L., Sengupta, M., Lendon, J. P., Rome, V., Valverde, R., & Caffrey, C. (2019). *Long-term care providers and service users in the United States, 2015–2016.* National Center for Health Statistics

Harvard Health Publications. (2018). *Aging in place: Special health report.* Harvard Health Publishing.

Harvie, H., & Rumore, R. (2018). Housing and social issues in homeless care. In D. Chau & A. P. Gass (Eds.), *Homeless Older Populations: A Practical Guide for the Interdisciplinary Care Team* (pp. 89–120). Springer.

Hasworth, S. B., & Cannon, M. (2015). Social theories of aging: A review. *Disease-a Month, 61,* 475–79.

Havighurst, R. J., Neugarten, B., & Tobin, S. S (1968). Disengagement and patterns of aging. In B. Neugarten (Ed.), *Middle age and aging: A reader in social psychology* (pp. 161–72). University of Chicago Press.

Hayes, S. M., Alosco, M. L., Hayes, J. P., Cadden, M., Peterson, K. M., Allsup, K., Forman, D. E., Sperling, R. A., Verfaellie, M. (2015). Physical activity is positively associated with episodic memory in aging. *Journal of the International Neuropsychological Society, 21*(10), 780–90.

He, W., Goodkind, D., & Kowal, P. (2016). *International Population Reports, P95/16-1, An Aging World: 2015.* US Government Printing Office. https://www.census.gov/content/dam/Census/library/publications/2016/demo/p95-16-1.pdf

Health Resources and Services Administration. (2021). *Sign up to save lives.* Retrieved on October 10, 2021, from https://www.organdonor.gov/.

Heaphy, B. (2007). Sexualities, gender and ageing: resources and social change. *Current Sociology, 55*(2), 193–210.

Helbling, M. (2018). A Comparison of Immigration Policies 1. *DICE Report, 16*(1), 14–17.

Heller-Sahlgren, G. (2017). Retirement blues. *Journal of Health Economics, 54,* 66–78.

Heo, J., Chun, S., Kim, B., Ryu, J., & Lee, Y. (2017). Leisure activities, optimism, and personal growth among the young-old, old-old, and oldest-old. *Educational Gerontology, 43*(6), 289–99. doi:10.1080/03601277.2017.1289457

Hickenbotham, A., Roorda, A., Steinmaus, C., Glasser, A. (2012). Meta-analysis of sex differences in presbyopia. *Investigative Ophthalmology and Visuals Science*, 53(6), 3215–20.

Hill, P. C., & Pargament, K. I. (2003). Advances in the conceptualization and measurement of religion and spirituality: Implications for physical and mental health research. *American Psychologist*, 58(1), 64–74. doi:10.1037/0003-066X.58.1.64

Hoffmann, R. L., & Mitchell, A. M. (1998). Caregiver burden: Historical development. *Nursing Forum*, 33(4), 5–12. doi:10.1111/j.1744-6198.1998.tb00223.x

Hollis-Sawyer, L., & Cuevas, L. (2013). Mirror, mirror on the wall: Ageist and sexist double jeopardy portrayals in children's picture books. *Educational Gerontology*, 39(12), 902–14. doi:10.1080/03601277.2013.767650

Holt-Lunstad, J. (2017). The potential public health relevance of social isolation and loneliness: Prevalence, epidemiology, and risk factors. *Public Policy & Aging Report*, 27(4), 127–30. doi:10.1093/ppar/prx030

Holt-Lunstad, J. (2018). Why social relationships are important for physical health: A systems approach to understanding and modifying risk and protection. *Annual Review of Psychology*, 69(1), 437–58. doi:10.1146/annurev-psych-122216-011902

Hooyman, N., Browne, C. V., Ray, R., & Richardson, V. (2002). Feminist gerontology and life course. *Gerontology & Geriatrics Education*, 22(4), 3–26.

Hopkins B., & Westra, T. (1988). Maternal handling and motor development: An intracultural study. *Genetic, Social and General Psychology Monographs*, 114, 379–408.

Horngren, B. (2016). Vacationing to make a difference. *Lesbian News*, 42(5), 19–20.

Howarth, R. A. (2011). Concepts and controversies in grief and loss. *Journal of Mental Health Counseling*, 33(1), 4–10.

Htut, T. Z. C., Hiengkaew, V., Jalayondeja, C., & Vongsirinavarat, M. (2018). Effects of physical, virtual reality-based, and brain exercise on physical, cognition, and preference in older persons: a randomized controlled trial. *European Review of Aging and Physical Activity*, 15(1), 10–10. doi.org/10.1186/s11556-018-0199-5

Hubbard, L. A. (2020). *Bob Blancato: Fighting elder abuse through politics.* http://www.silvercentury.org/2020/11/bob-blancato-fighting-elder-abuse-through-politics/.

Hudson, R. B. (1978). The "graying" of the federal budget and its consequences for old-age policy. *The Gerontologist*, 18(5_Part_1), 428–40. doi:10.1093/geront/18.5_Part_1.428

Hughes, M. (2006). Queer aging. *Gay and Lesbian Issues and Psychology Review*, 2(2), 54–59.

Hughes, M. J., Verreynne, M.-L., Harpur, P., & Pachana, N. A. (2020). Companion animals and health in older populations: A systematic review. *Clinical Gerontologist*, 43(4), 365–77. https://doi.org/10.1080/07317115.2019.1650863

Human Rights Watch. (2012). *Old behind bars: The aging prison population in the United States.* Retrieved on March 5, 2021, from https://www.hrw.org/report/2012/01/27/old-behind-bars/aging-prison-population-united-states.

Humphrey, C. (1999). Rituals of death in Mongolia: Their implications for understanding the mutual constitution of persons and objects and certain concepts of property. *Inner Asia*, 1(1), 59–86.

Hung, L-Y., Lyons, J. G., & Wu, C-H. (2020). Health information technology use among older adults in the United States, 2009–2018. *Current Medical Research and Opinion*, 36(5), 789–97.

Huo, M., Graham, J. L., Kim, K., Birditt, K. S., & Fingerman, K. L. (2019). Aging parents' daily support exchanges with adult children suffering problems. *Journals of Gerontology: Series B*, 74(3), 449–59. doi:10.1093/geronb/gbx079

Huo, M., Graham, J. L., Kim, K., Zarit, S. H., & Fingerman, K. L. (2017). Aging parents' disabilities and daily support exchanges with middle-aged children. *The Gerontologist*, 58(5), 872–82. doi:10.1093/geront/gnx144

Ikeuchi, T., Taniguchi, Y., Abe, T., Seino, S., Shimada, C., Kitamura, A., & Shinkai, S. (2021). Association between experience of pet ownership and psychological health among socially isolated and non-isolated older adults. *Animals*, 11(3), 595. https://www.mdpi.com/2076-2615/11/3/595

International Labour Organization. (2016). *Philippines: Equality of opportunity and treatment.*

Retrieved on February 22, 2021, from https://www.ilo.org/dyn/natlex/natlex4.detail?p_lang=en&p_isn=109722&p_count=4&p_classification=05.

International Organization for Migration. (2021). Key migration terms. https://www.iom.int/key-migration-terms#International-migration.

International Osteoporosis Foundation. (2017). *What is osteoporosis?* Retrieved on July 28, 2019, from https://www.iofbonehealth.org/what-is-osteoporosis.

Iversen, T. N., Larsen, L., Solem, P. E. (2009). A conceptual analysis of ageism. *Nordic Psychology*, 61(3), 4.

Jaffe, I. (2017). *Sometimes It Takes A 'Village' To Help Seniors Stay In Their Homes.* National Public Radio. Retrieved on June 21, 2021 from https://www.npr.org/2017/12/15/569529110/sometimes-it-takes-a-village-to-help-seniors-stay-in-their-homes

Jamwal, R., Callaway, L., Winkler, D., Farnworth, L., & Tate, R. (2018). Evaluating the use of smart home technology by people with brain impairment: Protocol for a single-case experimental design. *JMIR Research Protocol, 7*(11), e10451. doi:10.2196/10451

Janhsen, A., Golla, H., Mantell, P. & Woopen, C. (2021). Transforming spirituality through aging: Coping and distress in the search for meaning in very old age. *Journal of Religion, Spirituality & Aging, 33*(1), 38–53. doi:10.1080/15528030.2019.1676362

Jansen, T. (2015). To save on rent, some Dutch college students are living in nursing homes. *The Atlantic.* Retrieved on April 2, 2020 from https://www.theatlantic.com/business/archive/2015/10/dutch-nursing-home-college-students/408976/.

Jercich, K. (2020). *Technology can make end of life care more compassionate.* Retrieved on April 4, 2021, from https://www.healthcareitnews.com/news/technology-can-make-end-life-care-more-compassionate.

Jervis, L. L., Sconzert-Hall, W., & The Shielding American Indian Elders Project, T. (2017). The conceptualization of mistreatment by older American Indians. *Journal of Elder Abuse & Neglect, 29*(1), 43–58. doi:10.1080/08946566.2016.1249816

Jeste, D. V., & Lee, E. E. (2019). The emerging empirical science of wisdom: Definition, measurement, neurobiology, longevity, and interventions. *Harvard Review of Psychiatry, 27*(3), 127–40.

Jesuthasan, J., Sönmez, E., Abels, I., Kurmeyer, C., Gutermann, J., Kimbel, R., Kruger, A., Niklewski, G., Richter, K. Stangier, U., Wollny, A., Zier, U., Oertelt-Prigione, S., & Shouler-Ocak, M. (2018). Near-death experiences, attacks by family members, and absence of health care in their home countries affect the quality of life of refugee women in Germany: a multi-region, cross-sectional, gender-sensitive study. *BMC Medicine, 16*, 15. https://doi.org/10.1186/s12916-017-1003-5

Jiang, D., Hosking, D., Burns, R., & Anstey, K. J. (2019). Volunteering benefits life satisfaction over 4 years: The moderating role of social network size. *Australian Journal of Psychology, 71*, 183–92.

Johannesen, M., & LoGiudice, D. (2013). Elder abuse: A systematic review of risk factors in community-dwelling elders. *Age and Ageing, 42*, 292–98.

John A. Hartford Foundation. (2020). *Age-friendly care: It's about what matters to you.* Retrieved on March 3, 2020, from https://www.johnahartford.org/grants-strategy/current-strategies/age-friendly/age-friendly-care.

Johnson, K. R., Aldana, R., Ong Hing, B., Saucedo, L., & Trucios-Haynes, E. (2020). *Understanding Immigration Law.* Durham, NC: Carolina Academic Press.

Joint Center for Housing Studies. (2019). *Housing America's older adults 2019.* Retrieved on March 3, 2021, from https://www.jchs.harvard.edu/housing-americas-older-adults-2019.

Jones, J. (2021). *How technology is transforming our approach to palliative care.* Retrieved on April 4, 2021, from https://ndocsoftware.com/2019/03/technology-transforming-approach-palliative-care/.

Justice in Aging. (2021). *How we work.* https://justiceinaging.org/how-we-work/.

Kaczan, D. J., & Orgill-Meyer, J. (2020). The impact of climate change on migration: a synthesis of recent empirical insights. *Climatic Change*, 158(3/4), 281–300. doi:10.1007/s10584-019-02560-0

Kahlenberg, R. D. (2019). *How Minneapolis ended single-family zoning*. Retrieved on March 3, 2021, from https://tcf.org/content/report/minneapolis-ended-single-family-zoning/?agreed=1.

Kalfoss, M. H. (2017). Attitudes to ageing among older Norwegian adults living in the community. *British Journal of Community Nursing*, 22(5), 238–45.

Kaslow, F., & Robison, J. A. (1996). Long-term satisfying marriages: Perceptions of contributing factors. *American Journal of Family Therapy*, 24(2), 153–70.

Katz, S., & Marshall, B. L. (2018). Tracked and fit: FitBits, brain games, and the quantified aging body. *Journal of Aging Studies*, 45, 63–68. doi.org/10.1016/j.jaging.2018.01.009

Kaufman, B. G., Thomas, S. R., Randolph, R. K., Perry, J. R., Thompson, K. W., Holmes, G. M., & Pink, G. H. (2016). The rising rate of rural hospital closures. *Journal of Rural Health*, 32(1), 35–43. doi:10.1111/jrh.12128

Kaye, L. W. (2017). Older adults, rural living, and the escalating risk of social isolation. *Public Policy & Aging Report*, 27(4), 139–44. doi:10.1093/ppar/prx029

Kennedy, I. M. (1976). The Karen Quinlan case: Problems and proposals. *Journal of medical ethics*, 2, 3–7.

KFF (Kaiser Family Foundation). (2019). *An overview of Medicare*. Retrieved on March 2, 2020, from https://www.kff.org/medicare/issue-brief/an-overview-of-medicare/.

Kim, K. H. (2011). The creativity crisis: the decrease in creative thinking scores on the torrance tests of creative thinking. *Creative Research Journal*. 23, 285–95. doi:10.1080/10400419.2011.627805

Kirkendall, A. M., Waldrop, D., & Moone, R. P. (2012). Caring for people with intellectual disabilities and life-limiting illness: merging person-centered planning and patient-centered, family-focused care. *Journal of Social Work in End-of-Life & Palliative Care*, 8(2), 135–50. doi:10.1080/15524256.2012.685440

Klass, D., Silverman, P., & Nickman, S. (Eds.). (1996). *Continuing bonds: New understandings of grief*. Taylor & Francis.

Klinenberg, E. (2015). *Heat wave: A social autopsy of disaster in Chicago* (2nd ed.). University of Chicago Press.

Klug, L. A. (2020). *Jewish Funeral customs: Saying goodbye to a loved one*. Retrieved on July 23, 2020, from https://www.jfedgmw.org/jewish-funeral-customs-saying-goodbye-to-a-loved-one.

Kochman, K. (2015). New elements in modern biological theories of aging. Folia Medica Copernicana, 3(3), 89–99.

Koenig, R. (2015). Supportive housing for persons with disabilities: A framework for evaluating alternative models. *Housing Studies*, 30(3), 351–67. doi:10.1080/02673037.2014.953449

Kolodziejczak, K., Rosada, A., Drewelies, J., Duzel, S., Eibich, P., Tegeler, C., Wagner, G. G., Beier, K., Ram. N., Demuth, I., Steinhagen-Thiessen, E., Gerstorf, D. (2019). Sexual activity, sexual thoughts, and intimacy among older adults: Links with physical health and psychosocial resources for successful aging. *Psychology and Aging*, 34(3), 389–404.

Koren, M. J. (2010). Person-centered care for nursing home residents: the culture-change movement. *Health Affairs (Millwood)*, 29(2), 312–17. doi:10.1377/hlthaff.2009.0966

Kotter-Grühn, D., & Hess, T. M. (2012). The impact of age stereotypes on self-perceptions of aging across the adult lifespan. *Journal of Gerontology Psychological Sciences*, 67(5), 563–71. doi:10.1093/geronb/gbr153

Kowald, A., & Kirkwood, T. B. (2016). Can aging be programmed? A critical literature review. *Aging Cell*, 15, 986–98.

Kübler-Ross, E. (1969). *On death and dying*. Macmillan.

Kübler-Ross, E. (1971). *On death and dying*. Macmillan.

Kunkel, S. R., & Hautz, O. (2021). The study of global aging. In F. J. Whittington, S. R. Kunkel, & K. De Medeiros (Eds.), *Global Aging: Comparative Perspectives on Aging and the Life Course* (2nd ed., pp. 27–58). Springer.

Kwak, S., Kim, H., Chey, J., & Youm, Y. (2018). Feeling how old I am: Subjective age is associated with estimated brain age. *Frontiers in Aging Neuroscience*, 10, 168. doi:10.3389/fnagi.2018.00168

Kwong, K., Du, Y., & Xu, Q. (2015). Healthy aging of minority and immigrant populations: Resilience in late life. *Traumatology*, 21(3), 136–44. doi:10.1037/trm0000034

Laal, M. (2011). Barriers to lifelong learning. *Procedia—Social and Behavioral Sciences*, 28, 612–15.

Lachman, M. E., Lipsitz, L., Lubben, J., Castaneda-Sceppa, C., & Jette, A. M. (2018). When adults don't exercise: Behavioral strategies to increase physical activity in sedentary middle-aged and older adults. *Innovation in Aging*, 2(1), 1–12. doi.org/10.1093/geroni/igy007

Lamar, K. L., & Luke, J. J. (2016). Impacts of art museum-based dementia programming on participating care partners. *Journal of Museum Education*, 41(3), 210–19. doi:10.1080/10598650.2016.1193314

Lamers, W. (2017). *Signs of approaching death*. Retrieved on December 4, 2019, from https://hospicefoundation.org/Hospice-Care/Signs-of-Approaching-Death.

Landers, S. & Kapadia, F. (2017). Years of life lost, age discrimination, and the myth of productivity. *American Journal of Public Health*, 107(10), 1535–37.

Lang, P. O., Mendes, A., Socquet, J., Assir, N., Govind, S., & Aspinall, R. (2012). Effectiveness of influenza vaccine in aging and older adults: Comprehensive analysis of the evidence. *Clinical Intervention in Aging*, 7, 55–64.

Langer, N. (2004). Resiliency and spirituality: foundations of strengths perspective counseling with the elderly. *Educational Gerontology*, 30(7), 611–17. doi:10.1080/03601270490467038

Lawrence, R. G. (2012). *Full house: A guide to surviving multigenerational living*. Retrieved on March 3, 2020, from https://www.nextavenue.org/full-house-guide-surviving-multigenerational-living/.

Lawton, M. P., & Nahemov, L. (1973). Ecology and the aging process. In C. Eisdorfer & M. P. Lawton (Eds.), *The psychology of adult development and aging* (pp. 619–74). American Psychological Association.

Lazar, A. (2017). *Feminist gerontology and CSCW*. Retrieved on September 4, 2020, from https://depts.washington.edu/tatlab/intersectionalfutures/wp-content/uploads/2017/02/Lazar_IntersectionalFuturesSubmission.pdf.

Leadership Council of Aging Organizations. (2021). *About LCAO*. https://www.lcao.org/about/.

Le Roux, C., Tang, Y., & Drexler, K. (2016). Alcohol and opioid use disorder in older adults: Neglected and treatable illnesses. *Current Psychiatry Report*, 18, 87. https://doi.org/10.1007/s11920-016-0718-x

Lee, D. M., Nazroo, J., O'Connor, D. B., Blake, M., & Pendleton, N. (2016). Sexual health and well-being among older men and women in England: Findings from the English Longitudinal Study of Ageing. *Archives of Sexual Behavior*, 45, 133–44. doi.org/10.1007/s10508-014-0465-1

Lee, E. S., & Zhang, Y. (2018). Religiosity as a protective factor of psychological well-being among older black, white and Asian Christians in the United States. *Ageing International*, 43(3), 321–335. doi:10.1007/s12126-017-9319-1

Lee, H. J., & Szinovacz, M E. (2016). Positive, negative, and ambivalent interactions with family and friends: Associations with well-being. *Journal of Marriage and Family* 78, 660–679. doi:10.1111/jomf.12302

Lee, Y., & Jean Yeung, W. (2019). Gender matters: Productive social engagement and the subsequent cognitive changes among older adults. *Social science & medicine*, 229, 87–95.

Leedahl, S. N., Brasher, M. S., LoBuono, D., Wood, B. M., & Estus, E. L. (2020). Reducing ageism: Changes in students' attitudes after participation in an intergenerational reverse mentoring program. *Sustainability*, 12, 1–17.

Lehning, A. J., Kim, M. H., & Dunkle, R. E. (2013). Facilitators of home and community-based service use by urban African American elders. *Journal of Aging & Health*, 25(3), 439–458. doi:10.1177/0898264312474038

Leist, A. K. (2013). Social media use of older adults: A mini-review. *Gerontology*, 59, 378–384.

Lester, P. E., Dharmarajan, T. S., & Weinstein, E. (2019). The looming geriatrician shortage: Ramifications and solutions. *Journal of Aging and Health*, 32 (9), 1052–62. https://doi.org/10.1177/0898264319879325

Levin, M. K., Reingold, D., & Solomon, J. (2020). Elder abuse shelter programs: From model to movement. *Generations, 44*(1), 74–80.

Levy, B., Ashman, O., & Dror, I. (2000). To be or not to be: The effects of aging stereotypes on the will to live. *Omega (Westport), 40*(3), 409–20.

Levy, B. R., Slade, M. D., Kunkel, S. R., & Kasl, S. V. (2002). Longevity increased by positive self-perceptions of aging. *Journal of Personality and Social Psychology, 83*(2), 261–270.

Levy, V., & Thayer, C. (2019). *The positive impact of intergenerational friendships.* AARP.

Li, M., Chen, R., & Dong, X. (2020). Elder Mistreatment Across Diverse Cultures. *Generations, 44*(1), 20–25.

Li, Z., & Dalaker, J. (2019). *Poverty among Americans aged 65 and older.* Congressional Research Service.

Li, Z. & Dalaker, J. (2021). *Poverty Among the Population Aged 65 and Older (R45791).* Washington, DC: Congressional Research Service.

Li, Z., & Durgin, F. H. (2017). A large-scale horizontal-vertical illusion produced with small objects separated in depth. *Journal of Experimental Psychology: Human Perception and Performance, 43*(8), 1473–1479.

Li, W., Li, X., Huang, L., Kong, X., Yang, W., Wei, D, Li, J., Cheng, H., Zhang, Q., Liu, Jia. (2015). Brain structure links trait creativity to openness to experience. *Social, Cognitive, and Affective Neuroscience, 10*, 191–198. doi:10.1093/scan/nsu041

Library of Congress. (2017). *Why does hair turn gray?* Retrieved on November 8, 2019, from https://www.loc.gov/everyday-mysteries/biology-and-human-anatomy/item/why-does-hair-turn-gray

Lindenbach, J., Larocque, S., Morgan, D. G., & Jacklin, K. (2019). Mistreated older adults with dementia in the home: Practitioner experience and unattainable professional agency. *Journal of Elder Abuse & Neglect*, 1–29. doi:10.1080/08946566.2019.1657540

Lipnic, V. A. (2018). *The state of age discrimination and older workers in the U.S. 50 years after the Age Discrimination in Employment Act (ADEA).* Retrieved on February 22, 2021, from https://www.eeoc.gov/reports/state-age-discrimination-and-older-workers-us-50-years-after-age-discrimination-employment.

Litwak, E., & Longino, C. F., Jr. (1987). Migration patterns among the elderly: A developmental perspective. *The Gerontologist, 27*(3), 266–72. doi:10.1093/geront/27.3.266

Llanque, S., Savage, L., Rosenburg, N., & Caserta, M. (2016). Concept analysis: Alzheimer's caregiver stress. *Nursing Forum, 51*(1), 21–31. doi:10.1111/nuf.12090

Lloyd-Sherlock, P.G, Ebrahim, S., McKee, M., Prince, M. J. I. (2016). Institutional ageism in global health policy, *BMJ, 354*, 4514.

Lobb, E. A., Kristjanson, L. J. Aoun, S. M., Monterosso, L., Halkett, G. K. B., & Davies, A. (2010). Predictors of complicated grief: A systematic review of empircial studies. *Death Studies, 34*, 673–98.

Löckenhoff, C. E., De Fruyt, F., Terracciano, A., McCrae, R. R., De Bolle, M., Costa, P. T., Aguilar_Vafaie, M.E., Ahn, C., Ahn, H. Alcalay, L., Allik, J., Avdeyeva, T.V., Barbaranelli, C., Benet-Martinez, V., Blatny, M., Bratko, D., Cain, T.R., Crawford, J.T., Lima, M.P., Jr . . . Yik, M. (2009). Perceptions of aging across 26 cultures and their culture-level associates. *Psychology and Aging, 24*(4), 941–54. doi:10.1037/a0016901

Lopez, M. H., Passel, J. S., & Cohn, D. V. (2021). *Key facts about the changing US unauthorized immigrant population.* https://www.pewresearch.org/fact-tank/2021/04/13/key-facts-about-the-changing-u-s-unauthorized-immigrant-population/

Lou, C., Hajkova, P., & Ecker, J. R. (2018). Dynamic DNA methylation: In the right place at the right time. *Science, 28*,1336–40.

Lou, Y., Xu, J., Granberg, E., & Wentworth, W. M. (2012). A longitudinal study of social status, perceived discrimination, and physical and emotional health among older adults. *Research in Aging, 34*, 275–301.

Lowenstein, A. (2010). Caregiving and elder abuse and neglect-developing a new conceptual perspective. *Ageing International, 35*(3), 215–27. doi:10.1007/s12126-010-9068-x

Lu, H., Xu, F., Rodrigue, K. M., Kennedy, K. M., Cheng, Y., Flicker, B., Hebrank, A., Uh, J., Park,

D. C. (2010). Alterations in cerebral metabolic rate and blood supply across the adult lifespan. *Cerebral Cortex 21*, 1426–34. doi:10.1093/cercor/bhq224

Lu, Z., Fischer, T. W., Hasse, S., Sugawara, K., Damenisch, Y., Krengel, S., Funk, W., Berneburg, M., & Paus, R. (2009). Profiling the response of human hair follicles to ultraviolet radation. *Journal of Investigative Dermatology*, 129, 1790–804. doi:10.1038/jid

Lyons, S. T., Schweitzer, L., & Ng, E. S. W. (2015). How have careers changed? An investigation of changing career patterns across four generations. *Journal of Managerial Psychology*, 30(1), 8–21.

MacQueen, K. M., McLellan, E., Metzger, D. S., Kegeles, S., Strauss, R. P., Scotti, R., Blanchard, L., & Trotter, II, R. T., (2001). What is community? An evidence-based definition for participatory public health. *American Journal of Public Health*, 91(12), 1929–38. doi:10.2105/ajph.91.12.1929

Mann, R., Tarrant, A., & Leeson, G. W. (2016). Grandfatherhood: Shifting masculinities in later life. *Sociology*, 50(3), 594–610.

Mansens, D., Deeg, D. J. H., & Comijs, H. C. (2018). The association between singing and/or playing a musical instrument and cognitive functions in older adults. *Aging & Mental Health*, 22(8), 964–71. doi:10.1080/13607863.2017.1328481

Manson, J. E., Chlebowski, R. T., Stefanick, M. L., Aragaki, A. K., Rossouw, J. E., Prentice, R. L. Anderson, G., Howard, B.V., Thomson, C.A., LaCroix, A.Z., Wactawski-Wende, J., Jackson, R.D., Limacher, M., Margolis, K.L., Gass, M., Hsia, J., Johnson, K.C., Kooperberg, C., Kuller, L.H. . . . Wallace, R.B.(2013). Menopausal hormone therapy and health outcomes during the intervention and extended poststopping phase of the Women's Health Initiative. *JAMA*, 310, 1353–68.

Markides, K. S. (1983). Ethnicity, aging and society: Theoretical lessons from the United States experience. *Archives of Gerontology and Geriatrics*, 2(1), 221–28.

Marshall, A. C., Cooper, N. R., Segrave, R., Geeraert, N. (2015). The effects of long-term stress exposure on aging cognition: a behavioral and EEG investigation. *Neurobiology of Aging*, 36(6), 2136–44.

Marshall, B. L. (2018). Happily ever after? "Successful ageing" and the heterosexual inaginary. *European Journal of Cultural Studies*, 21(3), 363–81.

Martin, T. L., & Doka, K. J. (2000). *Men don't cry . . . women do: Transcending gender stereotypes of grief*. Brunner/Mazel.

Martinez, L., Mirza, R. M., Austen, A., Hsieh, J., Klinger, C. A., Kuah, M., Liu, A., McDonald, L., Mohsin, R., Pang, C., Rajewski, J., Salomons, T., Sheikh, I. (2020). More than just a room: A scoping review of the impact of homesharing for older adults. *Innovation in Aging*, 4(2). doi:10.1093/geroni/igaa011

Martinez, P. N., Menendez, S. T., de los Angeles Villaronga, Ubelaker, D. H., Garcia-Pedrero, J. M., & Zapico, S. C. (2019). The big sleep: Elucidating the sequence of events in the first hours of death to determine the postmortem interval. *Science and Justice*, 59(4), 418–24.

Martinson, M., & Berridge, C. (2015). Successful aging and its discontents: A systematic review of social gerontology literature. *The Gerontologist*, 55, 51–57.

Martinson, M., & Minkler, M. (2006). Civic engagement and older adults: A critical perspective. *The Gerontologist*, 46(3), 318–24.

Marzilli, T. (2018). *Old and young US adults most susceptible to fake news*. Retrieved on May 3, 2021, from https://today.yougov.com/topics/media/articles-reports/2018/06/13/old-and-young-us-adults-most-susceptible-fake-news.

Maschi, T., Viola, D., & Sun, F. (2012). The high cost of the international aging prisoner crisis: Well-being as the common denominator for action. *The Gerontologist*, 53(4), 543–54. doi:10.1093/geront/gns125

Maslow, A. H., Frager, R., Fadiman, J., McReynolds, C., & Cox, R. (1970). *Motivation and personality*. New York.

Masotti, P. J., Johnson-Masotti, A., Fick, R., & MacLeod, S. (2006). Healthy Naturally Occurring Retirement Communities: A Low-Cost Approach to Facilitating Healthy Aging [Article]. *American Journal of Public Health*, 96(7), 1164–70. https://doi.org/10.2105/AJPH.2005.068262

Mather, M. (2012). The emotion paradox in the aging brain. *Annals of the New York Academy of Sciences*, 1251(1), 33–49.

Mather, M., & Scommegna, P. (2017). How neighborhoods affect the health and well-being of older Americans. *Today's Research on Aging: Program and Policy Implications, 35*. Retrieved on April 3, 2020, from https://www.prb.org/todays-research-aging-neighborhoods-health/.

Mauldin, R. L., Lee, K., Tang, W., Herrera, S., & Williams, A. (2020). Supports and gaps in federal policy for addressing racial and ethnic disparities among long-term care facility residents. *Journal of Gerontological Social Work, 63*(4), 354–70. doi:10.1080/01634372.2020.1758270

Mayntz, M. (2019). *Definition of a Blended Family: Understanding the Dynamic.* https://family.lovetoknow.com/definition-blended-family

Mayo Clinic. (2020). *What is grief?* Retrieved on June 6, 2020, from https://www.mayoclinic.org/patient-visitor-guide/support-groups/what-is-grief.

Mazzonna, F., & Peracchi, F. (2015). Unhealthy retirement? *Journal of Human Resources, 52*(1), 128–51.

McAuliffe, M., & Khadria, B. (Eds.). (2019). *World Migration Report 2020*. Geneva, Switzerland: International Organization for Migration.

McCarron, H. R., Wright, A., Moone, R. P., Toomey, T., Osypuk, T. L., & Shippee, T. (2020). Assets and unmet needs of diverse older adults: Perspectives of community-based service providers in Minnesota. *Journal of Health Disparities Research & Practice, 13*(1), 106–24.

McDermott-Levy, R., & Fick, D. M. (2020). Advancing gerontological nursing science in climate change. *Research in Gerontological Nursing, 13*(1), 6–12. doi:10.3928/19404921-20191204-02

McDermott-Levy, R., Kolanowski, A. M., Fick, D. M., & Mann, M. E. (2019). Addressing the health risks of climate change in older adults. *Journal of Gerontological Nursing, 45*(11), 21–29. http://dx.doi.org/10.3928/00989134-20191011-04

McHugh M. C., & Interligi, C. (2015). Sexuality and older women: Desirability and desire. In V. Muhlbauer, J. C. Chrisler, & F. L. Denmark (Eds.), *Women and aging: An international, intersectional, power perspective* (pp. 89–116). Springer.

McLaughlin, D., Vagenas, D., Pachana, N. A., Begum, N., & Dobson, A. (2010). Gender differences in social network size and satisfaction in adults in their 70s. *Journal of Health Psychology, 15*, 671–79. doi:10.1177/1359105310368177

Meadows, K. (2020). *Death rituals in Bali*. Retrieved on July 21, 2020, from http://www.mahavidya.ca/2020/05/23/death-rituals-in-bali/.

Media Wise. (2021). *Teaching older Americans how to sort fact from fiction online*. Retrieved on May 2, 2021, from https://www.poynter.org/mediawise-for-seniors/.

Meeks, T. W., & Jeste, D. V. (2009). Neurobiology of wisdom: A literature overview. *Archives of General Psychiatry 66*, 355–65.

Mehrotra, A., Chernew, M., Linetsky, D., Hatch, H., Cutler, D., & Schneider, E. C. (2020). *The impact of the COVID-19 pandemic on outpatient visits: Changing patterns of care in the newest COVID-19 hot spots*. Retrieved on April 1, 2021, from https://www.commonwealthfund.org/publications/2020/aug/impact-covid-19-pandemic-outpatient-visits-changing-patterns-care-newest.

Merghati-Khoei, E., Pirak, A., Yazdkhasti, M., & Rezasoltani, P. (2016). Sexuality and elderly with chronic diseases: A review of the existing literature. *Journal of Research in Medical Sciences, 21*:127–37.

Metaxakis, A., & Partridge, L. (2013). Dietary restriction extends lifespan in wild-derived populations of drosophila melanogaster. PLoS ONE 8(9), e74681. doi:10.1371/journal.pone.0074681

Midgley, J., & Livermore, M. (2009). *The handbook of social policy* (2nd ed.). SAGE.

Milic, J., Muka, T., Ikram, M. A., Franco, O. H., & Tiemeier, H. (2017). Determinants and predictors of grief severity and persistence: The Rotterdam study. *Journal of Aging and Health, 29*(8), 1288–307. doi.org/10.1177/0898264317720715

Miller, E. A., Huberfeld, N., & Jones, D. K. (2021). Pursuing Medicaid block grants with the Healthy Adult Opportunity Initiative: Dressing up old ideas in new clothes. *Journal of Health Politics, Policy and Law, 46*(2), 357–74. doi:10.1215/03616878-8802211

Miller, F., & Dun, O. (2019). Resettlement and the environment in Vietnam: Implications for climate change adaptation planning. *Asia Pacific Viewpoint, 60*(2), 132–47. doi:10.1111/apv.12228

Milne, D. (2012). Olmstead, New Freedom, and Real Choice System Change grants: Bringing the disability movement to older adults. *Generations, 36*(1), 44–51.

Miloyan, B., Byrne, G. J., & Pachana, N. A. (2015). Threshold and subthreshold generalized anxiety disorder in later life. *American Journal of Geriatric Psychiatry, 23*(6), 633641.

Mirmirani, P. (2015). Age-related hair changes in men: Mechanisms and management of alopeica and graying. *Maturitas, 80*(1), 58–62. doi.org/10.1016/j.maturitas.2014.10.008

Mitchell, L. K., & Pachana, N. A., (2020). Psychotherapeutic interventions with older adults: Now and into the future. In A. Etkin, N. Hantke, & R. O'Hara (Eds.), *Handbook of mental health and aging* (pp. 299–314). Elsevier Science & Technology.

Mitteldorf, J. (2016). An epigenetic clock controls aging. *Biogerontology, 17,* 257–65.

Mizoguchi, N., Walker, L., Trevelyn, E., & Ahmed, B. (2019). *U.S. Census Bureau, American Community Survey, ACS-42, The Older Foreign-Born Population in the United States: 2012–16.* U.S. Government Printing Office.

Molony, S. L., Kolanowski, A., Van Haitsma, K., & Rooney, K. E. (2018). Person-centered assessment and care planning. *The Gerontologist, 58*(suppl_1), S32–S47. doi:10.1093/geront/gnx173

Moore, P. H. (2017). A late-night call begins a transformative journey. *Generations, 41*(4), 144–46.

Morrow-Howell, N. (2010). Volunteering in later life: Research frontiers. *Journals of Gerontology Series B: Psychological Sciences and Social Sciences, 65B*(4), 461–69. doi:10.1093/geronb/gbq024

Moses, J. (2018). Road Scholar Caregiver grants: A respite for older adult caregivers. *Generations, 42*(3), 102–3.

Moskowitz, R. L. (2018). Policies for aging Americans: A look at public opinion and the role of government. *Generations, 42*(4), 34–41.

Mueller, S., Wagner, J. & Gerstorf, D. (2017). On the role of personality in late life. In J. Specht (Ed.), *Personality Development Across the Lifespan* (pp. 69–84). Academic Press.

Muller, J. (2004). *How adults learn.* Retrieved on March 7, 2021, from https://cyc-net.org/cyc-online/cycol-0104muller.html#:~:text=Adult%20learning%20is%20life%2Dcentered,be%20by%20trail%20and%20error.&text=Adults%20interpret%20ideas%2C%20skills%20and,the%20purpose%20of%20adult%20education.

Murman, D. L. (2015). The impact of age on cognition. *Seminars in Hearing, 36*(3), 111–21. doi:10.1055/s-0035-1555115

Namazi, M., Sadeghi, R., & Moghadam, Z. B. (2019). Social determinants of health in menopause: An integrative review. *International Journal of Women's Health, 11,* 637–47.

National Academies of Sciences Engineering and Medicine. (2016). *Families Caring for an Aging America.* National Academies Press.

National Academies of Sciences Engineering and Medicine. (2020). *Social isolation and loneliness in older adults: Opportunities for the health care system.* National Academies Press.

National Academy of Social Insurance. (2021). *Social Security benefits, finances, and policy options: A primer.* https://www.nasi.org/research/social-security/social-security-benefits-finances-and-policy-options-a-primer-2021/National Alliance for Caregiving (2020). *Caregiving in the U.S.* Retrieved on February 10, 2010, from https://www.aarp.org/content/dam/aarp/ppi/2020/05/full-report-caregiving-in-the-united-states.

National Center for Health Statistics. (2019). *Health, United States, 2018: Data finder.* Retrieved on March 3, 2020, from https://www.cdc.gov/nchs/hus/contents2018.htm.

National Center on Elder Abuse. (2019). *Prevention strategies.* Retrieved on April 2, 2020, from https://ncea.acl.gov/About-Us/What-We-Do/Practice/Prevention-Strategies.aspx.

National Center on Elder Abuse (n.d.). *Frequently asked questions: What is elder abuse?* Retrieved on November 17, 2022, from https://ncea.acl.gov/FAQ.aspx.

National Conference of State Legislatures. (2011). *The Affordable Care Act: A brief summary.* https://www.ncsl.org/research/health/the-affordable-care-act-brief-summary.aspx.

National Cremation. (2020). *Unique and meaningful ways to scatter ashes*. Retrieved on July 19, 2020, from https://www.nationalcremation.com/cremation-information/unique-and-meaningful-ways-to-scatter-ashes.

National Geographic. (2019). *Neighborhood*. Retrieved on March 3, 2020, from https://www.nationalgeographic.org/encyclopedia/neighborhood/.

National Hospice and Palliative Care Organization. (2019). *History of hospice*. Retrieved on December 16, 2019, from https://www.nhpco.org/hospice-care-overview/history-of-hospice/.

National Institute of Mental Health. (2019). *Mental illness*. Retrieved on October 19, 2020, from https://www.nimh.nih.gov/health/statistics/mental-illness.shtml.

National Institute on Aging (n.d.) *Long distance caregiving*. Retrieved on November 17, 2022, from https://www.nia.nih.gov/health/caregiving/long-distance-caregiving.

National Institute on Aging. (2017). *Long-term care: Residential facilities, assisted living, and nursing homes*. Retrieved on March 3, 2020, from https://www.nia.nih.gov/health/residential-facilities-assisted-living-and-nursing-homes.

National Institute on Aging. (2019). *What are palliative and hospice care?* Retrieved on December 16, 2019, from https://www.nia.nih.gov/health/what-are-palliative-care-and-hospice-care.

National Institute on Aging. (2021). *Sexuality in later life*. Retrieved on January 3, 2021, from https://www.nia.nih.gov/health/sexuality-later-life.

National Institute on Drug Abuse. *Substance use in older adults*. (2020). Retrieved on October 3, 2021, from https://www.drugabuse.gov/publications/substance-use-in-older-adults-drugfacts.

Nelson, T. T. (2005). Ageism: Prejudice against our feared future self. *Journal of Social Issues* 61(2), 207–21.

Nelson, M. K. (2014). Whither Fictive Kin? Or, What's In a Name? *Journal of Family Issues*, 35(2), 201–222. https://doi.org/10.1177/0192513X12470621

Nelson-Kakulla, B. (2019). *Who is the 50+ gamer?* Retrieved on April 19, 2021, from https://www.aarp.org/research/topics/technology/info-2019/2020-gaming-trends-older-americans.html.

New American Economy. (2021). *Undocumented immigrants*. Retrieved on March 12, 2021, from https://www.newamericaneconomy.org/issues/undocumented-immigrants/#economic-contributors,-not-criminals.

New York Public Library. (2021). *NYPL TechConnect classes*. Retrieved on April 16, 2021, from https://www.nypl.org/tech-connect.

Newport, F. (2019). *Polling matters: Social Security and American public opinion*. Retrieved on March 3, 2020, from https://news.gallup.com/opinion/polling-matters/258335/social-security-american-public-opinion.aspx.

Nguyen, A. W., Chatters, L. M., Taylor, R. J., & Mouzon, D. M. (2016). Social support from family and friends and subjective well-being of older African Americans. *Journal of Happiness Studies*, 17, 959–79. doi:10.1007/s10902-015-9626-8

Nicholas, P. K., & Breakey, S. (2019). The Economics of Climate Change and the Intersection with Conflict, Violence, and Migration: Implications for the Nursing Profession. *Nursing Economic$*, 37(1), 23–34.

Nichols, L. O., Chang, C., Lummus, A., Burns, R., Martindale-Adams, J., Graney, M. J., Coon, D. W., Czaja, S. (2008). The cost-effectiveness of a behavior intervention with caregivers of patients with Alzheimer's disease. *Journal of the American Geriatrics Society*, 56(3), 413–20. doi:10.1111/j.1532-5415.2007.01569.x

Nicoll, L. H. (2003). Teaching an old dog new tricks. *Computers, Informatics, Nursing*, 21(2), 59–60. doi:10.1097/00024665-200303000-00001

Nielsen, D. S., Minet, L., Zeraig, L., Rasmussen, D. N., & Sodemann, M. (2018). "Caught in a generation gap": A generation perspective on refugees getting old in Denmark—A qualitative study. *Journal of Transcultural Nursing*, 29(3), 265-273. doi:10.1177/1043659617718064

Nieuwenhuis, A. V., Beach, S. R., & Schulz, R. (2018). Care recipient concerns about being a burden and unmet needs for care. *Innovation in Aging*, 2(3), igy026–igy026. doi:10.1093/geroni/igy026

Nobel, J. (2013). *The spectacular death rituals of the Philippines*. Retrieved on July 21, 2020, from https://www.funeralwise.com/digital-dying/the-spectacular-death-rituals-of-the-philippines/.

Noftle, E. E., & Fleeson, W. (2010). Age differences in big five behavior averages and variabilities across the adult life span: moving beyond retrospective, global summary accounts of personality. *Psychology and aging*, 25(1), 95–107. doi.org/10.1037/a0018199

Noice, T., Noice, H., & Kramer, A. F. (2014). Participatory arts for older adults: A review of benefits and challenges. *The Gerontologist*, 54(5), 741–53. doi:10.1093/geront/gnt138

North, M. S., & Fiske, S. T. (2013). Act your (old) age: prescriptive, ageist biases over succession, consumption, and identity. *Personality & social psychology bulletin*, 39(6), 720–34. doi:10.1177/0146167213480043

North, M. S. & Fiske, S. T. (2015). Modern attitudes toward older adults in the aging world: A cross-cultural meta-analysis. *Psychological Bulletin*. Advance online publication. doi.org/10.1037/a0039469

Northwestern Mutual Life Insurance Company. (2018). *2018 C.A.R.E. Study*. Retrieved on April 4, 2020, from https://news.northwesternmutual.com/2018-care-study.

Novelli C. (2012). Effects of aging and physical activity on articular cartilage: a literature review. *Journal of Morphological Science*, 29(1),1–7.

Nurmi, M. A., Mackenzie, C. S., Roger, K., Reynolds, K., & Urquhart, J. (2018). Older men's perceptions of the need for and access to male-focused community programmes such as Men's Sheds. *Ageing & Society*, 38, 794–816.

O'Brien, E., Fox-Grage, W., & Ujvari, K. (2019). *Home- and community-based services beyond Medicaid: How state-funded programs help low-income adults with care needs live at home*. AARP Public Policy Institute.

O'Donnell, L. (2016). The crisis facing America's working daughters. *The Atlantic*. Retrieved on March 4, 2020, from https://www.theatlantic.com/business/archive/2016/02/working-daughters-eldercare/459249/?utm_source=atlfb.

Office of the Assistant Secretary for Planning and Evaluation. (n.d.) Poverty guidelines. Retrieved May 4, 2021, from https://aspe.hhs.gov/topics/poverty-economic-mobility/poverty-guidelines.

Older Adults Technology Services. (2020). *Aging connected: Exposing the hidden connectivity crisis for older adults*. Retrieved on May 2, 2021, from https://oats.org.

Oliver, A., Tomas, J. M., & Montoro-Rodriguez, J. (2017). Dispositional hope and life satisfaction among older adults attending lifelong learning programs. *Archives of Gerontology and Geriatrics*, 72, 80–85.

O'Neil, K., & Tienda, M. (2015). Age at immigration and the incomes of older immigrants, 1994–2010. *Journals of Gerontology Series B: Psychological Sciences & Social Sciences*, 70(2), 291–302. doi:10.1093/geronb/gbu075

Oregon Center for Aging and Technology. (2019). *About ORCATEC*. Retrieved on November 26, 2019, from https://www.ohsu.edu/oregon-center-for-aging-and-technology/about-orcatech.

Oregon Center for Aging and Technology. (2020). *Our technology*. Retrieved on May 2, 2021, from https://www.ohsu.edu/oregon-center-for-aging-and-technology/our-technology.

Orellano-Colón, E., Mann, W., Rivero, M., Torres, M., Jutai, J., Santiago, A., & Varas, N. (2016). Hispanic older adult's perceptions of personal, contextual and technology-related barriers for using assistive technology devices. *Journal of Racial and Ethnic Health Disparities*, 3(4), 676–86.

Orenstein, G. A., & Lewis, L. (2020). *Erikson's stages of psychosocial development*. Retrieved on August 27, 2020, from https://www.ncbi.nlm.nih.gov/books/NBK556096/.

Orlovic, M., Smith, K., & Mossialos, E. (2019). Racial and ethnic differences in end-of-life care in the United States: Evidence from the Health and Retirement Study (HRS). *SSM-Population Health*, 7, 100331. doi.org/10.1016/j.ssmph.2018.100331

Ortman, J. M., Velkoff, V. A., & Hogan, H. (2014). *An aging nation: The older population in the United States*. US Census Bureau. Retrieved on May 3, 2020, from https://census.gov/content/census/en/library/publications/2014/demo/p25-1140.html.

Ostir, G. V., & Goodwin, J. S. (2006). High anxiety is associated with an increased risk of death in an older tri-ethnic population. *Journal of Clinical Epidemiology*, 59(5), 534540.

Oxman, T. E. (2018). Reflections on aging and wisdom. *American Journal of Geriatric Psychiatry*, 26(11), 1108–18.

Pahl, R. E. (2000). *On Friendship*. Polity.

Palmiero, M. (2015). The effects of age on divergent thinking and creative objects production: A cross-sectional study. *High Ability Studies*, 26, 93–104. doi:10.1080/13598139.2015.1029117

Palmore, E. B. (2013). Typologies. In E. B. Erdman, L. Branch, & D. K. Harris (Eds.), *Encyclopedia of Ageism* (pp. 332–34). Routledge.

Pandey, A., Littlewood, K., Cooper, L., McCrae, J., Rosenthal, M., Day, A., & Hernandez, L. (2019). Connecting older grandmothers raising grandchildren with community resources improves family resiliency, social support, and caregiver self-efficacy. *Journal of Women & Aging*, 31(3), 269–83. doi:10.1080/08952841.2018.1444940

Pardasani, M. (2019). Senior centers: If you build will they come? *Educational Gerontology*, 45(2), 120–33. doi:10.1080/03601277.2019.1583407

Parsons, A. J. Q., & Gilmour, S. (2018). An evaluation of fertility- and migration-based policy responses to Japan's ageing population. *PLOS ONE*, 13(12), 1–14. doi:10.1371/journal.pone.0209285

Partners for Livable Communities. (2020). *Young At Heart Chorus (best practices)*. Retrieved on March 3, 2021, from http://livable.org/livability-resources/591-young-at-heart-chorus.

Pasricha, N. (2016). *Why retirement is a flawed concept*. Harvard Business Review. Retrieved on February 27, 2021, from https://hbr.org/2016/04/why-retirement-is-a-flawed-concept.

Patel, T., & Yosipovitch, G. (2010). The management of chronic pruritus in the elderly. *Skin Therapy Letter*, 15(8), 5–9.

Peck, R. (1955). Psychological developments in the second half of life. In J. E. Anderson (Ed.), *Psychological aspects of aging* (pp. 42–53). American Psychological Association.

Peck, R. (1968). Psychological developments in the second half of life. In B. L. Neugarten (Ed.), *Middle age and aging* (pp. 88–92). University of Chicago Press.

Perl, L. (2018). *LIHEAP: Program and Funding*. Retrieved on April 6, 2020, from https://fas.org/sgp/crs/misc/RL31865.pdf.

Peterson Institute for International Economics. (2021). *What is globalization? And how has the global economy shaped the United States?* https://www.piie.com/microsites/globalization/what-is-globalization

Perone, A. K. (2020). Protecting health care for transgender older adults amidst a backlash of U.S. federal policies. *Journal of Gerontological Social Work*, 1–10. https://doi.org/10.1080/01634372.2020.1808139

Perry, T. E., Andersen, T. C., & Kaplan, D. B. (2014). Relocation remembered: Perspectives on senior transitions in the living environment. *The Gerontologist*, 54(1), 75–81. doi:10.1093/geront/gnt070

Peteet, J. R., Faten, A. Z., & Koenig, H. G. (2019). Integrating spirituality into the care of older adults. *International psychogeriatrics*, 31(1), 31–8. doi:10.1017/S1041610218000716

Petkus, A. J., Reynolds, C. A., Wetherell, J. L., Kremen, W. S., Pedersen, N. L., & Gatz, M. (2016). Anxiety is associated with increased risk of dementia in older Swedish twins. *Alzheimer's & Dementia*, 12(4), 399406. doi.org/10.1016/j.jalz.2015.09.008

Pew Institute. (2018). Social media use in 2018. Retrieved on April 20, 2021, from https://www.pewresearch.org/internet/2018/03/01/social-media-use-in-2018/.

Pew Charitable Trust. (2020). *Americans who get news mainly on social media are less knowledgeable and less engaged*. Retrieved on April 18, 2021, from https://www.pewtrusts.org/en/trust/archive/fall-2020/americans-who-get-news-mainly-on-social-media-are-less-knowledgeable-and-less-engaged.

Pew Research Center. (2015a). *America's changing religious landscape*. Retrieved on April 6, 2020, from https://www.pewforum.org/2015/05/12/americas-changing-religious-landscape/.

Pew Research Center. (2015b). *Parenting in America: 1. The American family today*. Retrieved on October 5, 2019, from https://www.pewsocialtrends.org/2015/12/17/1-the-american-family-today/.

Pew Research Center. (2017). *Tech adoption climbs among older adults*. Retrieved on May 2, 2021, from https://www.pewresearch.org/internet/2017/05/17/barriers-to-adoption-and-attitudes-towards-technology/.

Pew Research Center. (2019a). International migrants by country. Retrieved from https://www.pewresearch.org/global/interactives/international-migrants-by-country/

Pew Research Center. (2019b). *Religion's relationship to happiness, civic engagement and health around the world*. Retrieved on May 8, 2020, from https://www.pewforum.org/2019/01/31/religions-relationship-to-happiness-civic-engagement-and-health-around-the-world/.

Pew Research Center. (2019c). *10 facts about American workers*. Retrieved on January 28, 2021, from https://www.pewresearch.org/fact-tank/2019/08/29/facts-about-american-workers/.

Pew Research Center. (2020). *8 charts on internet use around the world as countries grapple with COVID-19*. Retrieved on April 19, 2021, from https://www.pewresearch.org/fact-tank/2020/04/02/8-charts-on-internet-use-around-the-world-as-countries-grapple-with-covid-19/.

Pew Research Center. (2021). *More than eight-in-ten Americans get news from digital devices*. Retrieved on April 18, 2021, from https://www.pewresearch.org/fact-tank/2021/01/12/more-than-eight-in-ten-americans-get-news-from-digital-devices/.

Phillips, M. L. (2011). *The mind at midlife*. Retrieved on November 6, 2020, from https://www.apa.org/monitor/2011/04/mind-midlife.

Pickering, C., Yefimova, M., & Maxwell, C. (2018). Caregiver stress theory may explain elder abuse but not neglect in dementia family caregiving. *Innovation in Aging*, 2(Suppl_1), 851–51. doi:10.1093/geroni/igy023.3173

Pike, L. (2020, November 7). Why so many young people showed up on Election Day. https://www.vox.com/2020/11/7/21552248/youth-vote-2020-georgia-biden-covid-19-racism-climate-change.

Pillemer, K., Burnes, D., Riffin, C., & Lachs, M. S. (2016). Elder abuse: Global situation, risk factors, and prevention strategies. *The Gerontologist*, 56(Suppl_2), S194–S205. doi:10.1093/geront/gnw004

Poo, A.-j. (2015). *The age of dignity: Preparing for the elder boom in a changing America*. The New Press.

Population Reference Bureau. (2021). International Indicators: Life Expectancy at Birth, Total. Retrieved from https://www.prb.org/international/indicator/life-expectancy-birth-total/snapshot

Population Reference Bureau. (2022). Countries with the Oldest Populations in the World. Retrieved from https://www.prb.org/resources/countries-with-the-oldest-populations-in-the-world/

Portacolone, E. (2017). Structural factors of elders' isolation in a high-crime neighborhood: An in-depth perspective. *Public Policy & Aging Report*, 27(4), 152–55. doi:10.1093/ppar/prx025

Portacolone, E., Perissinotto, C., Yeh, J. C., & Greysen, S. R. (2018). "I feel trapped": The tension between personal and structural factors of social isolation and the desire for social integration among older residents of a high-crime neighborhood. *The Gerontologist*, 58(1), 79–88. doi:10.1093/geront/gnw268

Portacolone, E., Rubinstein, R. L., Covinsky, K. E., Halpern, J., & Johnson, J. K. (2018). The precarity of older adults living alone with cognitive impairment. *The Gerontologist*, 59(2), 271–80. doi:10.1093/geront/gnx193

Prinzinger, R. (2005). Programmed aging: The theory of maximal metabolic scope. *EMBO Reports*, 6(S1), S14–S19.

Proulx, C. M., Curl, A. L., & Ermer, A. E. (2018). Longitudinal associations between formal volunteering and cognitive functioning. *Journal of Gerontology: Psychological Sciences and Social Sciences*, 73, 522–31. doi:10.1093/geronb/gbx110

Putney, J. M., Keary, S., Hebert, N., Krinsky, L., & Halmo, R. (2018). "Fear runs deep:" The anticipated needs of LGBT older adults in long-term care. *Journal of Gerontological Social Work*, 61(8), 887–907. https://doi.org/10.1080/01634372.2018.1508109

Ramsey-Klawsnik, H., & Miller, E. (2017). Polyvictimization in later life: Trauma-informed best practices. *Journal of Elder Abuse & Neglect*, 29(5), 339–50. https://doi.org/10.1080/08946566.2017.1388017

Ranahan, M. E. (2017). Planning for the Residential Needs of Lesbian, Gay, Bisexual, and Transgender Older Adults. *Journal of Community Practice*, 25(2), 159–71. https://doi.org/10.1080/10705422.2017.1307299

Rantanen, T., Volpato, S., Ferrucci, L., Heikkinen, E., Fried. L. P., Guralnik, J. M. (2003). Handgrip strength and cause-specific and total mortality in older disabled women: Exploring the mechanism. *Journal of the American Geriatric Society, 51*(5), 636–41. doi.org/10.1034/j.1600-0579.2003.00207

Ratcliffe, M., Burd, C., Holder, K., & Fields, A. (2016). *Defining rural at the U.S. Census Bureau.* (ACSGEO-1). US Census Bureau

Reaves, E. L., & Musumeci, M. (2015). *Medicaid and long-term services and supports: A primer.* Retrieved on May 4, 2020, from https://www.kff.org/medicaid/report/medicaid-and-long-term-services-and-supports-a-primer/.

Refugee Processing Center. (2021). Admission and Arrivals. https://www.wrapsnet.org/admissions-and-arrivals/

Reich, A. J., Claunch, K. D., Verdeja, M. A., Dungan, M. T., Anderson, S., Clayton, C. K., . . . Thacker, E. L. (2020). What does "successful aging" mean to you? — Systematic review and cross-cultural comparison of lay perspectives of older adults in 13 countries, 2010–2020. *Journal of Cross-Cultural Gerontology, 35*(4), 455–78. doi:10.1007/s10823-020-09416-6

Reinhard, S. C., Feinberg, L. F., Choula, R., & Houser, A. (2015). *Valuing the invaluable 2015 update: Undeniable progress, but big gaps remain.* Retrieved fon May 9, 2020, rom https://www.aarp.org/ppi/info-2015/valuing-the-invaluable-2015-update.html.

Reinhard, S. C., Levine, C., & Samis, S. (2012). *Home alone: Family caregivers providing complex chronic care.* https://uhfnyc.org/publications/publication/home-alone-family-caregivers-providing-complex-chronic-care/.

Reisch, M. (2019). *Social policy and social justice: Meeting the challenges of a diverse society.* Cognella.

Renn, B. N., Arean, P. A., & Unutzer, J. (2020). Epidemiology of selected mental disorders in late life. In A. Etkin, N. Hantke, & R. O'Hara, (Eds.), *Handbook of mental health and aging* (pp. 7–22). Elsevier Science & Technology.

Resnick, B. (2018). Description of the annual wellness visit. *Public Policy & Aging Report, 29*(1), 8–12. doi:10.1093/ppar/pry045

Riddering, A. T. (2008). Keeping older adults with vision loss safe: Chronic conditions and comorbidities that influence functional mobility. *Journal of Visual Impairment and Blindness, 102*(10), 616–20.

Rippon, I., Kneale, D., de Oliveira, C., Demakakos, P., Steptoe, A. (2014). Perceived age discrimination in older adults. *Age and Ageing, 43*(3), 379–86.

Ritzer, G. (2019). Globalization. In M. J. Ryan (Ed.), *Core concepts in sociology* (pp. 123–5). Wiley Blackwell.

Rivera, L. M., & Paredez, S. M. (2014). Stereotypes can "get under the skin": Testing a self- stereotyping and psychological resource model of overweight and obesity. *Journal of Social Issues, 70*, 226–40. doi: 10.1111/josi.12057

Rizzo, V. M., Burnes, D. P., & Chalfy, A. (2015). A systematic evaluation of a multidisciplinary social work–lawyer elder mistreatment intervention model. *Journal of Elder Abuse & Neglect, 27*(1), 1–18. doi:10.1080/08946566.2013.792104

Roberts, A. W., Ogunwole, S. U., Blakeslee, L., & Rabe, M. A. (2018). *The population 65 and older in the United States: 2016.* Retrieved on May 8, 2020, from https://www.census.gov/library/publications/2014/demo/p25-1140.html.

Robinson, D., Valdez, L., Scott, L., & Buchanan, D. (2020). The role of work in gender identity, stress and health in low-income, middle-aged African-American men. *Health Promotion International, 36*(5), 1231–1242. https://doi.org/10.1093/heapro/daaa144

Rodriguez, N., Paredes, C. L., & Hagan, J. (2017). Fear of immigration enforcement among older Latino immigrants in the United States. *Journal of Aging & Health, 29*(6), 986–1014. doi:10.1177/0898264317710839

Romig, K. (2020). *Social Security lifts more Americans above poverty than any other program.* Retrieved on May 9, 2020, from https://www.cbpp.org/research/social-security/social-security-lifts-more-americans-above-poverty-than-any-other-program.

Rosen, T., Lien, C., Stern, M. E., Bloemen, E. M., Mysliwiec, R., McCarthy, T. J., Clark, S., Mulcare, M. R., Ribaudo, D. S., Lachs, M. S., Pilemer, K.,

Flomenbaum, N. E. (2017). Emergency medical services perspectives on identifying and reporting victims of elder abuse, neglect, and self-neglect. *Journal of Emergency Medicine*, 53(4), 573–82. doi.org/10.1016/j.jemermed.2017.04.021

Ross, J. M., Coppotelli, G., Hoffer, B. J., & Olson, L. (2014). Maternally transmitted mitochondrial DNA mutations can reduce lifespan. *Scientific Reports*, 4, 1–3. doi:10.1038/srep06569

Roth, D. L., Skarupski, K. A., Crews, D. C., Howard, V. J., Locher, J. L. (2016). Distinct age and self-rated health crossover mortality effects for African Americans: Evidence from a national cohort study. *Social Science and Medicine*, 156, 12–20. doi:10.1016/j.socscimed.2016.03.019

Rowe, J. W., & Kahn, R. L. (1997). Successful aging. *The Gerontologist*, 37(4), 433–40.

Rowles, G. D. (1983). Place and personal identity in old age: Observations from Appalachia. *Journal of Environmental Psychology*, 3, 299–313.

Rowles, G. D. (1993). Evolving images of place in aging and "aging in place." *Generations*, 17(2), 65–72.

Rowles, G. D., & Teaster, P. B. (2015). The long-term care continuum in an aging society. In G. D. Rowles & P. B. Teaster (Eds.), *Long-Term Care in an Aging Society: Theory and Practice* (pp. 21–37). Springer.

Rubin, A., Parrish, D. E., & Miyawaki, C. E. (2019). Benchmarks for evaluating life review and reminiscence therapy in alleviating depression among older adults. *Social Work*, 64(1), 61–72.

Rubin, D. C., & Bernsten, D. (2006). People over forty feel 20% younger than their age: Subjective age across the lifespan. *Psychonomic Bulletin & Review*, 13(5), 776–80.

Rudowitz, R., Garfield, R. & Hinton, E. (2019). *10 things to know about Medicaid: Setting the facts straight*. https://www.kff.org/medicaid/issue-brief/10-things-to-know-about-medicaid-setting-the-facts-straight/.

Ryu, J., Yang, H., Kim, A. C. H., Kim, K. M., & Heo, J. (2018). Understanding pickleball as a new leisure pursuit among older adults. *Educational Gerontology*, 44(2/3), 128–38. doi:10.1080/03601277.2018.1424507

Sadana, R., Foebel, A. D., Williams, A. N., Beard, J. R. (2013). Population ageing, longevity, and the diverse contexts of the oldest old. *Public Policy Aging Report*, 23(2), 18–25.

SAGE. (2020). *Aging while transgender*. Retrieved on September 24, 2020, from www.sageusa.org/wp-content/uploads/2018/10/.

Sakuraba, R. (2008). *Employment discrimination law in Japan: Human rights or employment policy?* Retrieved on February 22, 2021, from https://www.semanticscholar.org/paper/Employment-Discrimination-Law-in-Japan-%3A-Human-or-Sakuraba/308e2c4ef83a940541640e673ae09ab1e15635c0.

Salthouse T A. (2010). Selective review of cognitive aging. *Journal of the International Neuropsychological Society*, 16(5), 754–60.

Sandberg, L. (2013). Just feeling a naked body close to you: Men, sexuality and intimacy in later life. *Sexualities*, 16, 261–82. doi.org/10.1177/1363460713 48172 6

Sandberg, L. (2015). Towards a happy ending? Positive ageing, heteronormativity and un/happy intimacies. *Lamda Nordica* 4, 19–44.

Sandberg, L. J., & Marshall, B. L. (2017). Queering aging futures. *Societies*, 7(21), doi:10.3390/soc7030021

Sandoval, E., Rashbaum, W. K., Singer, J. E., & Joseph, Y. (2019, October 6). In Chinatown, rampage against sleeping homeless men leaves 4 dead. *New York Times*. Retrieved on March 8, 2020, from https://nyti.ms/2nnK9Bc.

Sanjek, R. (2011). *Gray panthers*. University of Pennsylvania Press.

Sarbey, B. (2016). Definitions of death: brain death and what matters in a person. *Journal of Law and the Biosciences*, 3(3), 743–52.

Schaller, S., Traeen, B., & Kvalem, I. L. (2020). Barriers and facilitating factors in help-seeking: A qualitative study on how older adults experience talking about sexual issues with healthcare personnel. *International Journal of sexual health*, 32(2), 65–80.

Schiamberg, L. B., & Gans, D. (2000). Elder abuse by adult children: An applied ecological framework for understanding contextual risk factors and the intergenerational character of quality of life. *International Journal of Aging & Human Development*, 50(4), 329–59.

Schwenk, T. L. (2016). Substantial decline in tube feeding for U.S. nursing home residents with advanced dementia. *JAMA, 316*, 769–70.

Scullin, M. K., Bliwise, D. L. (2015). Sleep, cognition, and normal aging: Integrating a half century of multidisciplinary research. *Perspectives on Psychological Science, 10*(1), 97–137. doi:10.1177/1745691614556680

Sehrawat, S. (2010). The omission of comprehensive care: An analysis of the Nursing Home Reform Act of 1987. *Journal of Gerontological Social Work, 53*(1), 64–76. doi:10.1080/01634370802609254

Sellon, A. M., Chapin, R. K., & Leedahl, S. N. (2017). Engaging nursing home residents in formal volunteer activities: A focus on strengths. *Ageing International, 42*, 93–114.

Seltzer, J. A. (2019). Family change and changing family demography. *Demography, 56*(2), 405–26. doi:10.1007/s13524-019-00766-6

Serrat, R., Scharf, T., Villar, F., & Gómez, C. (2020). Fifty-Five Years of Research Into Older People's Civic Participation: Recent Trends, Future Directions. *The Gerontologist, 60*(1), e38–e51. https://doi.org/10.1093/geront/gnz021

Settersten, R. A., Jr., & Hagestad, G. O. (2015). Subjective aging and new complexities of the life course. In M. Diehl & H. W., Wahl (Eds.), Subjective aging: New developments and future directions, *Annual Review of Gerontology and Geriatrics, 35* (pp. 29–54). Springer.

Sewdas, R., de Wind, A., van der Zwaan, L. G. L., van der Borg, W., Steenbeek, R., van der Beek, A., & Boot, C. R. L. (2017). Why older workers work beyond the retirement age: A qualitative study. *BMC Public Health, 17*, 672–80.

Shaw, B. H., & Claydon, V, E. (2014). The relationship between orthostatic hypotension and falling in older adults. *Clinical Autonomic Research, 24*(1):3–13.

Shin, H., Ryu, H. H., Yoon, J., Jo, S., Jang, S., Choi, M., Kwon, O., Jo, S. J. (2015). Association of premature hair graying with family history, smoking, and obesity: A cross-sectional study. *Journal of the American Academy of Dermatology, 72*(2), 321–27.

Shinan-Altman, S., & Werner, P. (2019). Subjective age and its correlates among middle-aged and older adults. *International Journal of Aging and Human Development, 88*(1), 3–21.

Sias, P. M., & Bartoo, H. (2007). Friendship, social support, and health. In L. L'Abate (Ed.), *Low-cost approaches to promote physical and mental health* (pp. 455–72). Springer.

Sibai, A. M., Najem Kteily, M., Barazi, R., Chartouni, M., Ghanem, M., & Afifi, R. A. (2019). Lessons learned in the provision NCD primary care to Syrian refugee and host communities in Lebanon: the need to 'act locally and think globally'. *Journal of Public Health, 42*(3), e361–e368. doi:10.1093/pubmed/fdz096

Siegler, E. L., Lama, S. D., Knight, M. G., Laureano, E., & Reid, M. C. (2015). Community-based supports and services for older adults: A primer for clinicians. *Journal of Geriatrics, 2015*. doi:10.1155/2015/678625

Simpson-Kent, I. L., Fuhrmann, D., Bathelt, J., Achterberg, J., Borgeest, G. S., & Kievit, R. A. (2020). Neurocognitive reorganization between crystallized intelligence, fluid intelligence and white matter microstructure in two age-heterogeneous developmental cohorts. *Developmental Cognitive Neuroscience, 41*, 1–15.

Singh P. (2013). Andropause: Current concepts. *Indian journal of endocrinology and metabolism, 17*(Suppl 3), S621–S629. doi:10.4103/2230-8210.123552

Skinner, M. W., Andrews, G. J., & Cutchin, M. P. (2018). Introducing geographical gerontology. In M. W. Skinner, G. J. Andrews, & M. P. Cutchin (Eds.), *Geographical Gerontology: Perspectives, Concepts, Approaches* (pp. 3–10). Routledge.

Smith, A., & Duggan, M. (2013, October 21). *Online dating & relationships*. https://www.pewresearch.org/internet/2013/10/21/online-dating-relationships/.

Smith, J. R. (2015). Expanding constructions of elder abuse and neglect: Older mothers' subjective experiences. *Journal of Elder Abuse & Neglect, 27*(4–5), 328–55. doi:10.1080/08946566.2015.1082527

Smith, M. L., Bergeron, C. D., Goltz, H. H., Coffey, T., & Boolani, A. (2020). Sexually transmitted infection knowledge among older adults: Psychometrics and test-retest reliability. *International Journal of Environmental Research and Public Health, 17*(7), 2462. doi.org/10.3390/ijerph17072462

Smith, R. J., Lehning, A. J., & Kim, K. (2017). Aging in place in gentrifying neighborhoods: Implications for physical and mental health. *The Gerontologist, 58*(1), 26–35. doi:10.1093/geront/gnx105

Smith, S. (2016). *USC Annenberg Film Study: Pop culture stereotypes aging Americans.* Retrieved on May 20, 2019, from https://annenberg.usc.edu/news/faculty-research/usc-annenberg-film-study-pop-culture-stereotypes-aging-americans.

Snelling, S. (2016). *Multigenerational living is back and that's a good thing.* Retrieved on May 6, 2020, from https://www.nextavenue.org/multigenerational-living-is-back-why-thats-a-good-thing/.

Social Security Administration. (n.d.a). *Age 65 retirement.* Retrieved on January 23, 2021, from https://www.ssa.gov/history/age65.html.

Social Security Administration. (n.d.b). Benefits paid by type of beneficiary. Retrieved on May 4, 2021 from https://www.ssa.gov/OACT/ProgData/icp.html

Social Security Administration. (n.d.c). *Understanding Supplemental Security Income (SSI) overview: 2021 edition.* Retrieved on May 4, 2021 from https://www.ssa.gov/ssi/text-over-ussi.htm.

Solomon, D. N., Hansen, L., & Baggs, J. G. (2018). It's all about the relationship: Cognitively intact mother–daughter care dyads in hospice at home. *The Gerontologist, 58*(4), 625–34. doi:10.1093/geront/gnw263

Sone, T., Nakaya, N., Ohmori, K., Shimazu, T., Higashiguchi, M., Kakizaki, M., Kikuchi, N., Kuriyama, S., Tsuji, I. (2008). Sense of life worth living (ikigai) and mortality in Japan: Ohsaki Study. *Psychosomatic Medicine, 70*(6), 709–15. doi:10.1097/PSY.0b013e31817e7e64.

Soriano-Tárraga C., Mola-Caminal M., Giralt-Steinhauer E., Ois A., Rodríguez-Campello A., Cuadrado-Godia E., Gómez-González A., Vivanco-Hidalgo R.M., Fernández-Cadenas I., Cullell N., Roquer, J., Jimenez-Conde, J. (2017). Biological age is better than chronological as predictor of 3-month outcome in ischemic stroke. *Neurology, 89*(8), 830–36. doi:10.1212/WNL.0000000000004261

Spetz, J., Stone, R. I., Chapman, S. A., & Bryant, N. (2019). Home and community-based workforce for patients with serious illness requires support to meet growing needs. *Health Affairs, 38*(6), 902–9. doi:10.1377/hlthaff.2019.00021

Stanford Center on Longevity (2021). *Digital literacy and inclusion for older adults.* Retrieved on May 2, 2021, from https://longevity.stanford.edu/digital-literacy-in-older-adults/.

Starks, H., Dudzinski, D., & White, N. (2013). Physician aid-in-dying. Retrieved on December 11, 2019, from https://depts.washington.edu/bhdept/ethics-medicine/bioethics-topics/detail/73.

Stein, J. (2019, August 14). "This will be catastrophic": Maine families face elder boom, worker shortage in preview of nation's future. *Washington Post.* Retrieved on May 8, 2020, from https://www.washingtonpost.com/business/economy/this-will-be-catastrophic-maine-families-face-elder-boom-worker-shortage-in-preview-of-nations-future/2019/08/14/7cecafc6-bec1-11e9-b873-63ace636af08_story.html.

Stenner, B. J., Mosewich, A. D., & Buckley, J. D. (2020). Why do older adults play golf? An evaluation of factors related to golf participation by older adults. *Journal of Aging & Physical Activity, 28*(3), 399–405. doi:10.1123/japa.2018-0448

Stepler, R. (2015). *5 facts about family caregivers.* Retrieved on March 9, 2020, from https://www.pewresearch.org/fact-tank/2015/11/18/5-facts-about-family-caregivers/.

Stern, M. J., & Axinn, J. (2018). *Social welfare: A history of American response to need.* Pearson.

Stokes, J. E., & Moorman, S. M. (2018). Influence of the social network on married and unmarried older adults' mental health. *The Gerontologist, 58*(6), 1109–13. doi:10.1093/geront/gnx151

Stone, R. I. (2013). What are the realistic options for aging in community? *Generations, 37*(4), 65–71.

Stone, R. I. (2018). The housing challenges of low-income older adults and the role of federal policy. *Journal of Aging & Social Policy, 30*(3/4), 227–43. doi:10.1080/08959420.2018.1462679

Stone, R. I. (2019). Financing long-term services and supports—and the challenge of underlying assumptions. *Generations, 43*(1), 57–59.

Stowe, J. D., & Cooney, T. M. (2014). Examining Rowe and Kahn's concept of successful aging: Importance of taking a life course perspective.

The Gerontologist, 55(1), 43–50. doi:10.1093/geront/gnu055

Stroebe, M., & Schut, H. (2010). The dual process model of coping with bereavement: A decade on. *Omega, 61,* 273–89.

Stroebe, M. S., Hansson, R. O., Schut, H., & Stroebe, W. (Eds.). (2008). *Handbook of bereavement research and practice: Consequences, coping, and care.* American Psychological Association.

Studenski, S., Perera, S., Patel, K., Rosano, C., Faulkner, K., Inzitari, M., Brach, J., Chandler, J., Cawthon, P., Connor, E. B., Nevitt, M., Visser, M., Kritchevsky, S., Badinelli, S., Harris, T., Newman, A., Cauley, J., Ferrucci, L., Guralnick, J. (2011). Gait speed and survival in older adults. *JAMA, 5*(1), 50–58. doi.org/10.1001/jama.2010.1923

Su, L.H., & Chen, T.H. (2007). Association of androgenetic alopecia with smoking and its prevalence among Asian men: a community-based survey. *Archives of Dermatology, 143*(11), 1401–6.

Suanet, B., van der Pas, S., & van Tilburg, T. G. (2013). Who is in the stepfamily? Change in stepparents' family boundaries between 1992 and 2009. *Journal of Marriage & Family, 75*(5), 1070–83. doi: 10.1111/jomf.12053

Sue, D. W. (2010). *Microaggressions in everyday life: Race, gender, and sexual orientation.* John Wiley & Sons.

Sullivan, N. (2003). *A critical introduction to queer theory.* New York University Press.

Sun, K., & Dutta, M. J. (2016). Meanings of care: A culture-centered approach to left-behind family members in the countryside of China. *Journal of Health Communication, 21*(11), 1141–7. doi:10.1080/10810730.2016.1225869

Sun, F., Gao, X., Gao, S., Li, Q., & Hodge, D. R. (2018). Depressive symptoms among older Chinese Americans: Examining the role of acculturation and family dynamics. *Journals of Gerontology: Series B, 73*(5), 870–79. doi:10.1093/geronb/gbw038

Sutherland, A. (2018). "I tried hard to control my temper": Perceptions of older musicians in intergenerational collaboration. *The Qualitative Report, 23*(11), 2670–85.

Symens Smith, A., & Trevelyan, E. (2019). *The older population in rural America: 2012–2016.* Retrieved on March 4, 2020, from https://www.census.gov/library/publications/2019/acs/acs-41.html.

Szanton, S., Roberts, L., Leff, B., Walker, J., Seplaki, C., Soones, T., Thorpe Jr., R. J., Ornstein, K. A. (2016). Home but still engaged: Participation in social activities among the homebound. *Quality of Life Research, 25*(8), 1913–20. doi:10.1007/s11136-016-1245-2

Takahashi, T. A., & Johnson, K. M. (2015). Menopause. *Medical Clinics of North America, 99*(3), 521–53.

Tashjian, V. C., Mosadeghi, S., Howard, A. R., Lopez, M., Dupuy, T., Reid, M., Martinez, B., Ahmed, S., Dailey, F., Robbins, K., Rosen, B., Fuller, G., Danovitch, I., IsHak, W., & Spiegel, B. (2017). Virtual reality for management of pain in hospitalized patients: Results of a controlled trial. *JMIR Mental Health, 4*(1), e9. doi:10.2196/mental.7387

Taylor, S. E. (2012). *Health psychology* (8th ed.). McGraw-Hill.

Taylor, T.N., Munoz-Plaza, C.E., Goparaju, L., Martinez, O., Holman, S., Minkoff, H. L., Karpiak, S. E., Gandhi, M., Cohen, M. H., Golub, E. T., Levine, A. M., Adedimeji, A. A., Gonsalves, R., Bryan, T., Connors, N., Schechter, G., Wilson, T. E. (2016). "The pleasure Is better as I've gotten older": Sexual health, sexuality, and sexual risk behaviors among older women living with HIV. *Archives of Sexual Behavior, 46,* 1137–50. doi-org.libproxy.lib.csusb.edu/10.1007/s10508-016-0751-1

ten Bruggencate, T., Luijkx, K. G., & Sturm, J. (2018). Social needs of older people: A systematic review. *Ageing & Society, 38,* 1745–70. doi:10.1017/S0144686X17000150

Teno, J. M., Gozalo, P. L., Bynum, J. P. W., Leland, N. E., Miller, S. C., Morden, N. E., Scupp, T., Goodman, D. C., & Mor, V. (2013). Change in end-of-life care for medicare beneficiaries site of death, place of care, and health care transitions in 2000, 2005, and 2009. *JAMA, 309*(5), 470–77. doi:10.1001/jama.2012.207624

Terraneo. M. (2015). Inequities in health care utilization by people aged 50+: evidence from 12 European countries. *Social Science Medicine, 126,* 154–63. doi.org/10.1016/j.socscimed.2014.12.028 PMID: 25562311

Thomas, P. A., Liu, H., & Umberson, D. (2017). Family relationships and well-being. *Innovation in Aging*, *1*(3). doi:10.1093/geroni/igx025

Thompson, K. G., Marchitto, M. C., Ly, B. C. K., & Chien, A. L. (2019). Evaluation of physiological, psychological, and lifestyle factors associated with premature graying hair. *International Journal of Trichology*, *11*(4), 153–58.

Tikkanen, R., & Abrams, M. K. (2020). *U.S. health care from a global perspective, 2019: Higher spending, worse outcomes?* Retrieved on March 9, 2019, from https://www.commonwealthfund.org/publications/issue-briefs/2020/jan/us-health-care-global-perspective-2019.

Toossi, M., & Torpey, E. (2017). *Older workers: Labor force trends and career options.* Career Outlook, US Bureau of Labor Statistics. Retrieved on January 28, 2021, from https://www.bls.gov/careeroutlook/2017/article/older-workers.htm.

Topa, G., Depolo, M., & Alcover, C-M. (2018). Early retirement: A meta-analysis of its antecedents and subsequent correlates. *Frontiers in Psychology*, *8*, 1–24.

Topsfield, J., & Rosa, A., (2020). *Life among the dead*. Retrieved on July 21, 2020, from https://www.smh.com.au/interactive/2017/toraja-death-ritual/.

Torres, S., & Cao, X. (2019). Improving care for elders who prefer informal spaces to age-separated institutions and health care settings. *Innovation in Aging*, *3*(3). doi:10.1093/geroni/igz019

Traeen, B., Stulhofer, A., Jurin, T., & Hald, G. M. (2018). Seventy-five years old and still going strong: Stability and change in sexual interest and sexual enjoyment in elderly men and women across Europe. *International Journal of Sexual Health*, *30*(4), 323–36.

Travison, T. G., Araujo, A. B., O'Donnell, A. B., Kupelian, V., & McKinlay, J. B. (2007). A population-level decline in serum testosterone levels in American men. *Journal of Clinical Endocrinological Metabolism*, *92*, 196–202.

Twomey, M. (2018). Breaking the silence on older caregivers and abuse. *Generations*, *42*(3), 71–76.

Tymoszuk, U., Perkins, R., Spiro, N., Williamon, A., & Fancourt, D. (2020). Longitudinal associations between short-term, repeated, and sustained arts engagement and well-being outcomes in older adults. *Journals of Gerontology: Series B*, *75*(7), 1609–19. doi:10.1093/geronb/gbz085

Ujvari, K., Fox-Grage, W., & Houser, A. (2019). *Spotlight: Older Americans Act*. Retrieved on May 9, 2020, from https://www.aarp.org/content/dam/aarp/ppi/2019/02/older-americans-act.pdf.

Ungar, A., Rafanelli, M., Iacomelli, I., Brunetti, M. A., Ceccofiglio, A., Tesi, F., Marchionni, M. (2013). Fall prevention in the elderly. *Clinical Cases in Mineral and Bone Metabolism*, *10*(2), 91–95.

United Health Foundation. (2020). *Volunteerism—ages 65+ in the United States*. Retrieved on March 3, 2021, from https://www.americashealthrankings.org/explore/senior/measure/volunteerism_sr/state/ALL.

United Nations, Department of Economic and Social Affairs, Population Division (2017). *World Population ageing 2017: Highlights* (ST/ESA/SER.A/397). http://www.un.org/en/development/desa/population/publications/pdf/ageing/WPA2017_Highlights.pdf.

United Nations Department of Economic and Social Affairs Population Division. (2019). *World Population Ageing 2019: Highlights*. https://www.un.org/en/development/desa/population/publications/pdf/ageing/WorldPopulationAgeing2019-Highlights.pdf

United Nations Department of Economic and Social Affairs Population Division. (2021). *World Economic Situation and Prospects*. https://www.un.org/development/desa/dpad/wp-content/uploads/sites/45/WESP2021_FullReport.pdf

United Nations Department of Economic and Social Affairs Population Division. (2020a). *World Population Ageing 2020 Highlights: Living arrangements of older persons* (ST/ESA/SER.A/451). https://www.un.org/development/desa/pd/content/publications

United Nations Department of Economic and Social Affairs Population Division. (2020b). *Population Facts, No. 2020/1*. https://www.un.org/development/desa/pd/sites/www.un.org.development.desa.pd/files/files/documents/2020/Oct/undesa_pd_2020_pf_government_policies_population_ageing.pdf

United Nations High Commissioner for Refugees. (2020). *Global Trends: Forced Displacement in 2019*. https://www.unhcr.org/5ee200e37.pdf

United States Census Bureau. (2017). *Profile America facts for features*. Retrieved on March 3, 2019, from https://www.census.gov/content/dam/Census/newsroom/facts-for-features/2017/cb17-ff08.pdf.

United States Elections Project. (2020). *Voter turnout demographics*. Retrieved on May 9, 2019, from https://www.electproject.org/election-data/voter-turnout-demographics.

US Bureau of Labor Statistics. (2016). *Economic news release: Volunteering in the United States—2015*. Retrieved on May 9, 2020, from https://www.bls.gov/news.release/volun.nr0.htm.

U.S. Department of Homeland Security. (n.d.). *Natural disasters*. Retrieved on November 22, 2022 from https://www.dhs.gov/natural-disasters

US Department of Labor. (2021). *Employee Retirement Income Security Act (ERISA)*. Retrieved on January 23, 2021, from https://www.dol.gov/general/topic/retirement/erisa.

US Department of Housing and Urban Development. (2021). *Section 202 Supportive Housing for the Elderly Program*. https://www.hud.gov/program_offices/housing/mfh/progdesc/eld202.

US Department of State. (n.d.). Refugee admissions. https://www.state.gov/refugee-admissions/

USC Center on Elder Mistreatment. (2017). *Supports and tools for elder abuse prevention*. Retrieved on May 9, 2020, from https://eldermistreatment.usc.edu/national-center-on-elder-abuse-ncea-usc/steap/.

van Den Beld, A., Kaufman, J., Zillikens, M., Lamberts, S., Egan, J., & Van Der Lely, A. (2018). The physiology of endocrine systems with ageing. *The Lancet Diabetes & Endocrinology, 6*(8), 647–58.

van der Pas, S., van Tilburg, T. G., & Silverstein, M. (2013). Stepfamilies in later life. *Journal of Marriage and Family, 75*(5), 1065–69. doi:10.1111/jomf.12054

VanderWeele, T. J., McNeely, E., & Koh, H. K. (2019). Reimagining health—flourishing. *JAMA, 321*(17), 1667–68. doi:10.1001/jama.2019.3035

Vandewoude, M., Barberger-Gateau, P., Cederholm, T., Mecocci, P., Salvà, A., Sergi, G., Topinkova, E., Van Asselt, D. (2016). Healthy brain ageing and cognition: Nutritional factors. *European Geriatric Medicine, 7*(1), 77–85.

Van Hook, J., & Glick, J. E. (2020). Spanning borders, cultures, and generations: A decade of research on immigrant families. *Journal of Marriage & Family, 82*(1), 224–43. doi:10.1111/jomf.12621

Varma, V. R., Tan, E. J., Gross, A. L., Harris, G., Romani, W., Fried, L. P., Rebok, G. W., Carlson, M. C. (2016). Effect of community volunteering on physical activity: A randomized controlled trial. *American Journal of Preventive Medicine, 50*, 106–10. doi:10.1016/j.amepre.2015.06.015

Vashi, N. A., de Castro Maymone, M. B., & Kundu, R. V. (2016). Aging differences in ethnic skin. *Journal of Clinical and Aesthetic Dermatology, 9*(1), 31–38.

Veghte, B. W., & Schreur, E. (2019). Social Security: Purpose, evolution, and future prospects. In M. Reisch (Ed.), *Social policy and social justice: Meeting the challenges of a diverse society* (pp. 317–52). Cognella.

Verschuren, J. E., Enzlin, P., Dijkstra, P. U., Geertzen, J. H., Dekker, R. (2010). Chronic disease and sexuality: A generic conceptual framework. *Journal of Sex Research, 47*, 153–170.

Vespa, J., Medina, L., & Armstrong, D. M. (2020). *Demographic Turning Points for the United States: Population Projections for 2020 to 2060*, (P25-1144). https://www.census.gov/content/dam/Census/library/publications/2020/demo/p25-1144.pdf

Vicedo-Cabrera, A. M., Scovronick, N., Sera, F., Royé, D., Schneider, R., Tobias, A., Astrom, C., Guo, Y., Honda, Y., Hondula, D. M., Abrutzky, R., Tong, S., de Sousa Zanotti Stagliorio Coelho, M., Nascimento Saldiva, P. H., Lavigne, Matus Correa, P. Valdes Ortega, N., Kan, H., Osorio, S.... Gasparrini, A. (2021). The burden of heat-related mortality attributable to recent human-induced climate change. *Nature Climate Change, 11*(6), 492–500. doi:10.1038/s41558-021-01058-x

Victor, C. G. P., & Treschuk, J. V. (2020). Critical literature review on the definition clarity of the concept of faith, religion, and spirituality. *Journal of Holistic Nursing, 38*(1), 107–13. doi: 10.1177/0898010119895368

Vollset, S. E., Goren, E., Yuan, C.-W., Cao, J., Smith, A. E., Hsiao, T., ... Murray, C. J. L. (2020). Fertility, mortality, migration, and population scenarios for 195 countries and territories from 2017 to 2100: a forecasting analysis for the Global Burden of Disease Study. *The Lancet, 396*(10258), 1285–1306. doi:10.1016/S0140-6736(20)30677-2

Wahl, H.-W., Iwarsson, S., & Oswald, F. (2012). Aging well and the environment: Toward an integrative model and research agenda for the future. *The Gerontologist, 52*(3), 306–16. doi:10.1093/geront/gnr154

Wahl, H.-W., & Oswald F. (2016). Theories of environmental gerontology: Old and new avenues for ecological views of aging. In V. L. Bengtson & R. Settersten (Eds.), *Handbook of theories of aging* (3rd ed., pp. 621–41). Springer.

Wakefield, J. R. H., Kellezi, B., Stevenson, C., McNamara, N., Bowe, M., Wilson, L., Halder, M. M., & Mair, E. (2020). Social prescribing as "social cure": A longitudinal study of the health benefits of social connectedness within a social prescribing pathway. *Journal of Health Psychology, 27*(20), 1–11.

Walen, H. R., & Lachman, M. E. (2000). Social support and strain from partner, family, and friends: Costs and benefits for men and women in adulthood. *Journal of Social and Personal Relationships, 17*(1), 5–30.

Walter, C. A., & McCoyd, J. L. M. (2015). *Grief and loss across the lifespan, second edition: A Biopsychosocial perspective*. Springer.

Warren, R., & Kerwin, D. (2017). Mass deportations would impoverish us families and create immense social costs. *Journal on Migration and Human Security, 5*(1), 1–8.

Weijer, C. (2005). A death in the family: Reflections on the Terri Schiavo case. *Canadian Medical Association Journal, 172*(9), 1197–98. doi:10.1503/cmaj.050348

Weintraub, D., & Mamikonyan, E. (2019). The neuropsychiatry of Parkinson disease: A perfect storm. *American Journal of Geriatric Psychiatry, 27*(9), 9981018.

West, S., Naar, J. J., Son, J. S., & Liechty, T. (2019). Promoting team sport participation among older women. *Journal of Park & Recreation Administration, 37*(4), 33–50. doi:10.18666/JPRA-2019-9118

Whiteford, H. A., Degenhardt, L., Rehm, J., Baxter, A. J., Ferrari, A. J., Erskine, H. E. (2013). Global burden of disease attributable to mental and substance use disorders: Findings from the Global Burden of Disease Study 2010. *Lancet, 382*(9904), 1575–86.

Whittington, F. J. P., Kunkel, S. R. P., & De Medeiros, K. P. (2021). *Global Aging, Second Edition: Comparative Perspectives on Aging and the Life Course.* Springer.

Wiglesworth, A., Mosqueda, L., Mulnard, R., Liao, S., Gibbs, L. M., & Fitzgerald, W. (2010). Screening for abuse and neglect of people with dementia. *Journal of the American Geriatrics Society, 58*(3), 493–500. doi:10.1111/j.1532-5415.2010.02737.x

Wiles, J. L., Leibing, A., Guberman, N., Reeve, J., & Allen, R. E. S. (2011). The meaning of "aging in place" to older people. *The Gerontologist, 52*(3), 357–66. doi:10.1093/geront/gnr098

Willett, J., & Sears, J. (2020). Complicating our understanding of environmental migration and displacement: The case of drought-related human movement in Kenya. *International Social Work, 63*(3), 364–70. doi:10.1177/0020872818799431

Williams, E. (2021). Medicaid Enrollment & Spending Growth: FY 2021 & 2022 (Issue Brief). https://www.kff.org/report-section/medicaid-enrollment-spending-growth-fy-2021-2022-issue-brief/.

Wion, R. K., & Loeb, S. J. (2015). Older adults engaging in online dating: What gerontological nurses should know. *Journal of Gerontological Nursing, 41*(10), 25–35.

Wise, E. A., Rosenberg, P. B., Lyketsos, C. G., & Leoutsakos, J. M. (2019). Time course of neuropsychiatric symptoms and cognitive diagnosis in National Alzheimer's Coordinating Centers volunteers. *Alzheimer's & dementia (Amsterdam, Netherlands), 11*, 333–9.

Wiseman, R. F. (1980). Why older people move: Theoretical issues. *Research on Aging, 2*(2), 141–54.

Witten, T. M. (2003). Transgender aging: An emerging population and an emerging need. *Review Sexologies, 12*, 15–20.

Women's Budget Group. (2021). *Pushed to more precarity: The uneven impact of lockdowns on mothers and lower income parents*. Retrieved on March 11, 2021, from https://wbg.org.uk/analysis/pushed-to-more-precarity-the-uneven-impact-of-lockdowns-on-mothers-and-lower-income-parents/.

Woody, I. (2016). Mary's House: An LGBTQ/SGL-Friendly, Alternative Environment for Older Adults. *Generations*, *40*(2), 108–9.

Woolf, S. H., Masters, R. K., & Aron, L. Y. (2021). Effect of the covid-19 pandemic in 2020 on life expectancy across populations in the USA and other high income countries: simulations of provisional mortality data. *BMJ*, *373*, n1343. doi:10.1136/bmj.n1343

Worden, J. W. (2009). *Grief counseling and grief therapy* (4th ed.). Springer Publishing Company.

World Health Organization (WHO). (2006). *Defining sexual health: Report of a technical consultation on sexual health, January 28–31, 2002, Geneva.* World Health Organization.

World Health Organization. (2015). *World report on ageing and health.* World Health Organization.

World Health Organization. (2017a). *Elder abuse: What is elder abuse?* Retrieved on March 9, 2020, from http://www.who.int/ageing/projects/elder_abuse/en/.

World Health Organization. (2017b). *Mental health of older adults.* Retrieved on November 5, 2020, from https://www.who.int/news-room/fact-sheets/detail/mental-health-of-older-adults.

World Health Organization. (2018). *World health statistics 2018: Monitoring health for the SDGs, sustainable development goals.* World Health Organization.

World Health Organization. (2019). *Ageism.* Retrieved on March 4, 2019, from https://www.who.int/ageing/ageism/en/.

World Health Organization. (2020). *Constitution.* Retrieved on September 4, 2020, from https://www.who.int/about/who-we-are/constitution.

World Health Organization. (2021a). *Global report on ageism.* https://www.who.int/publications/i/item/9789240016866

World Health Organization. (2021b). UN Decade of Healthy Ageing: 2021-2030. Retrieved from https://www.who.int/initiatives/decade-of-healthy-ageing

World Population Review. (2020). *Average funeral cost by state 2020.* Retrieved on July 19, 2020, from https://worldpopulationreview.com/state-rankings/average-funeral-cost-by-state.

Woźniak, B. (2015). Religiousness, well-being and ageing—selected explanations of positive relationships. *Anthropological Review*, *78*(3), 259–68. doi:10.1515/anre-2015-0021

Yagil, D., Cohen, M., & Beer, J. D. (2016). Older adults' coping with the stress involved in the use of everyday technologies. *Journal of Applied Gerontology*, *35*(2), 131–49.

Yamasoba, T., Lin, F. R., Someya, S., Kashio, A., Sakamoto, T., Kondo, K. (2013). Current concepts in age-related hearing loss: epidemiology and mechanistic pathways. *Hearing Research*, *303*, 30–38.

Yazdani-Darki, M., Rahemi, Z., Adib-Hajbaghery, M., Izadi, F. S. (2020) Older adults' barriers to use technology in daily life: A qualitative study. *Nursing Midwifery Studies*, *3*(9), 229–36.

Yenilmez, I. M. (2015). Economic and social consequences of population aging: The dilemmas and opportunities in the twenty-first century. *Applied Research Quality Life*, *10*(4), 735–52. doi.org/10.1007/s11482-014-9334-2

Yesavage, J.A., Brink, T.L., Rose, T.L., Lum, O., Huang, V., Adey, M.B., & Leirer, V.O. (1983). Development and validation of a geriatric depression screening scale: A preliminary report. *Journal of Psychiatric Research*, *17*, 37–49.

Yonashiro-Cho, J., Meyer, K., & Wilber, K. H. (2017). The aging network. In X. Dong (Ed.), *Elder Abuse: Research, Practice, and Policy* (pp. 297–315). Springer.

Zayed, A. A., Shahait, A. D., Ayoub, M. N., & Yousef, A. M. (2013). Smokers' hair: Does smoking cause premature hair graying? *Indian Dermatology Online Journal*, *4*(2), 90–92. doi:10.4103/2229-5178.110586

Zhang, K., Kim, K., Silverstein, N. M., Song, Q., Burr, J. A., (2020). Social media communication and loneliness among older adults: The mediating roles of social support and social contact. *The Gerontologist*, *gnaa197*. doi.org/10.1093/geront/gnaa197

Zhang, X., Yin, C., Tian, W., Lu, D., Yang, X. (2020). Effects of cognitive behavioral therapy on anxiety and depression in patients with chronic obstructive pulmonary disease: A meta-analysis and systematic review. *Clinical Respiratory Journal, 14,* 891–900. doi.org/10.1111/crj.13226

Zitter, J. N. (2017). *How the rise of medical technology is worsening death.* Retrieved on April 6, 2021, from https://www.healthaffairs.org/do/10.1377/hblog20171101.612681/full/.

Zizza, C. A., Ellison, K. J., & Wernette, C. M. (2009). Total water intakes of community-living middle-old and oldest-old adults. *Journals of Gerontology. Series A, Biological Sciences and Medical Sciences, 64*(4), 481–86. doi:10.1093/gerona/gln045

INDEX

Note: Tables, figures or photographs, and boxes are indicated by *t*, *f*, and *b* following the page number.

AARP, 102, 116, 144, 174, 176, 179, 217
    described, 217
    Leadership Council of Aging Organizations (LCAO), 218
AARP Livable Communities, 142
ableism, 10
Aburto, J. M. et al., 184
Academy for Gerontology in Higher Education, 2
"accelerated aging," 147
acculturation, 194
acculturative stress, 194
Acierno, R. et al., 108, 109
active adult communities, 131
active euthanasia, 75
activities, for preserving healthy brain function, 46, 47*f*
activities of daily living (ADL), 104
    residential facilities and, 131
activity theory, 60–61, 60*f*
Adams, R. G., & Blieszner, R., 64
adaptability and resiliency, 52
adaptive grief patterns, 82
Addo, F. R., & Lichter, D. T., 94
Administration for Community Living (ACL), 158, 212
Administration on Aging (AoA), 208–9, 208*f*
Adolph, K. E., Karasik, L. B., & Tamis-LeMonda, C. S., 22
adult children
    death of, 98
    "difficult", and elder abuse, 110
    with mental health challenges, 97
    parents and, 96–97, 97*f*
    with special needs, 97
    with substance use disorders, 97
adult day care, 167
Adult Protective Services (APS), 111–12
    abuse allegations, 167
    EMS referrals, 162
    long-term care workforce, 219
adults living alone, 130, 130*f*, 133, 142
advance directives, types of, 78
advertising, ageism in, 10–11, 11*f*
advocacy organizations, 217–18

Affordable Care Act, 207
    Community Living Assistance Services and Supports (CLASS) Act, 209
    Elder Justice Act (EJA), 210–11
    Medicare coverage and, 163
affordable housing, 130, 143, 144, 148
African American populations
    end-of-life disparities, 78
    entrepreneurship, 158
    memory support program, 107
    mortality and crossover effect, 53
    older versus younger grandparents, 103
    postponing retirement, 121
    resilience in high-crime neighborhood, 140
    women and marriage, 94
    work experiences, 117
age
    chronological, 20
    defining, 20–22
    functional, 20
    human development and, 22
    intersectional factors affecting, 21
    "old old" and "young old," 132
    self-perceptions and, 20
    significance of, 20
    subjective, 21
age discrimination, 118
Age Discrimination Info, 119*t*
Age-Friendly Community Initiative, 142
age-friendly healthcare, 165, 165*t*
age-friendly policies, 136
ageism, 7–8
    activity theory and, 60–61
    "brain training" games as, 178
    case study, 10
    consequences of, 12–14
    costs of, 118, 187
    diversity of needs, 153
    global trends, 187
    in the medical profession, 164
    natural disaster rescues and media coverage, 196–97
    older versus younger grandparents, 103
    politics and policy, 216

INDEX

ageism (*Cont.*)
    sexual activity and, 67–68, 69
    types of, 8–9, 10b
    use of term, 7
ageist language, avoiding, 16
agency, 134
aging. *See also* population aging
    "accelerated aging," 147
    additional perspectives, 5–7
    cultural influences, 188–89
    more positive view of, 15–16
    role of place in, 133
    unique issues, 4
aging genes, 25
aging in place, 130, 132–34
    choices analyzed, 132
    importance of place, 132–33
    research on, 133
    theories and approaches, 134–36
    village model, 142
aging network, 165
aging policies, 202
Ajrouch, K. J. et al., 63
Alashram, A. R., 177
alcohol use
    misuse and abuse, 59
    treatment programs, 165
Alecxih. L., 33
Al-Kandari, Y. Y., & Crews, D. E., 63, 174
Al-Krenawi, A., & Jackson, S. O., 94
Allen, M. S., & Desille, A. E., 68
allow natural death (AND) forms, 78
Alzheimer's Association, 30, 31t, 104, 105t, 167–68
Alzheimer's disease, 31t. *See also* dementia
    caregiver stress, 108
    caregiving for, 104, 105t, 167–68
    information about community resources, 168
    prison populations, 147
    scans of brains, 32f
Alzheimer's Society, 32
Ambrey, C. L., Bosman, C., & Ballard, A., 63
American Academy of Actuaries, 123
American College of Physicians, 163
American Federation for Aging Research, 23
American Heart Association, 158
American Rescue Plan of 2021, 211
American Society for Nutrition, 27, 28
American Society of Pension Professionals and Actuaries, 122t
American Society on Aging, 34
Americans with Disabilities Act (ADA), 211–12
American Veterinary Medical Association, 103

Americorps, 123, 161
AmeriCorps Senior, 161
Andersen model of healthcare utilization, 163
    access to services, 166
Andersen, R. M., 163
Anderson, E., & Fidler, C. O., 65
androgenetic alopecia, 25
andropause, 30
animal companionship, 103–4
Annie E. Casey Foundation, 102, 103
anthropogenic climate change, 195
antidiscrimination laws for workplace, 119t
Antonucci, T. C., 61
Antonucci, T. C., Lansford, J. E., & Akiyama, H., 63, 65
Antonucci, T. C., Lansford, J. E., Schaberg, L. et al., 63
anxiety, 49
Aoyama, M. et al., 80
Appalachia, 132
Area Agencies on Aging (AAAs), 165, 168, 208f
Arem, H. et al., 36
Arensberg M. B., 4
Arentshorst, M. E., Kloet, R. R., & Peine, A., 144b
Aries, P., 75
Armstrong, K., 22
Aronson, L., 163, 164
the arts, 159–60, 160f
Asian people, premature gray hair, 26
Asis, M. M. B., 193
Aspinall, R., & Lang, P. O., 28
assisted living facilities
    formal care in, 106
    intergenerational living, 144
    overview of, 145
assisted suicide, 75
assistive devices
    access to, 35
    selective optimization with compensation, 47
assistive technology, 174, 177, 178f, 179
Atchley, R. C., & Barusch, A. S., 121
Atchley, R. C., 61
Australia
    antidiscrimination laws for workplace, 119t
    immigrant healthcare, 194–95
Australian Human Rights Commission, 119t
Ausubel, J., 133
autobiographical insideness, 132
autolysis, 74–75
Ayalon L., 7
Azoulay, P. et al., 8

baby boom generation, substance use among, 49
Balakrishnan, A., & Jordan, N., 163
Balan, E., Decottignies, A., & Deldicque, L., 24

Balinese funeral practices, 87b
Baltes, P. B., & Baltes, M. M., 47
Baltes, P. B., 15, 16, 40
Band-Winterstein, T., 110, 111
Banerjee, S., & Ford, C., 32
Bansal, A. & Tissenbaum, H. A., 23, 33
Barak, B., 21
Barker, N. N., & Himchak, M. V., 166
Basic, D., Shanley, C., & Gonzales, R., 195
Beato, 143
Beaulaurier, R. L., Seff, L. R., & Newman, F. L., 147
behavioral accommodations, 36
beliefs and perceptions of age and aging
    cross-cultural commonalities, 11–12, 12b
    in other cultures, 11
    physical health and, 22
beneficiaries, 204f
benevolent ageism, 8
Bengtson, V. L., 91, 93, 94
Benson, W., 211, 213, 216
Ben-Zvi, A., Miller, E. A., & Morimoto, R. I., 24
bereavement, 78
    uncomplicated, 80
Berk, L. E., 42
Bertoni, M., Brunello, G., & Mazzarella, G., 121
Bhasin, S. et al., 30
Bhattacharya, G., & Shibusawa, T., 193, 194
Bherer, L., 46
Biassoni, F., Cassina, G., & Balzarotti, S., 52
Bibbo, J., 104
Biography, 76
biological aging
    cross-cultural perspectives, 22–23
    theories, 23–25
biological theories, 5, 6t
biopsychosocial theories, 5
Birditt, K. S. et al., 97
Bitterman, A., 132, 138
Blancato, B., & Whitmire, M. P., 211
Blieszner, R., & Voorpostel, M., 91, 93, 94
Blieszner, R., Ogletree, A. M., & Adams, R. G., 64
block grants, 207
    Social Services Block Grants (SSBGs), 213
blogs, 173
Bloom, D. E., Canning, D., & Lubet, A., 183, 184, 186, 191
Blow, F. C., & Barry, K. L., 49
board and care homes, 203
Bobitt, J. et al., 111
body appearance, age and gender, 43
body donation, 85
body transcendence, 42
Boltz, M. et al., 107
bone mass, 28
Bonnie, R. J., & Wallace, R. B., 109

Boulton-Lewis, G. M., 124
boundary ambiguity
    negotiation of, 99
    role expectations, 99
    stepfamilies, 99
Bourassa, K. J., 96
Bowen, H. et al., 27
brain, 30–32
    total brain death, 74
Brandl, B., & Raymond, J. A., 110
Bratt, C. et al., 12b
bridge job, 117, 117f
bridge jobs, 116–17, 117f
Bridge Meadows, 143
Bronson, J., & Carson, E. A., 131
Brown, S. L., & Kawamura, S., 95
Brown, S. L., & Lin, I., 96
Bruder, J., 148, 159
Bunis, D., 106, 215
Burger, K., 98
burial, 83
    green burials, 84–85
Burnes, D. P., Rizzo, V. M., & Courtney, E., 167
Burns, V. F., & Sussman, T., 148
business opportunities, population aging and, 3–4
Bussolo, M., Koettl, J., & Sinnott, E., 7, 14, 15
Butler, Robert, 7
Butler, S. M., & Diaz, C., 161

Calasanti, T., & Giles, S., 34
Calasanti, T. & King, N., 6, 9, 21
Calasanti, T., 8, 10
cannabis use, 50
Canuto, A. et al., 49
Cao, Q. et al., 161
careers in gerontology, 4
    examples of, 5t
caregiver burden, 107, 108
caregiver stress, 107
caregiving, 104–8. See also elder abuse
    adult children with special needs, 131
    care recipient fears, 108
    family relationships and, 92
    formal care, 104, 105–7, 107t
    impact on caregivers, 107–8
    informal care, 104–5
    long-distance, 105
    older adults in home countries, 193
    older pet owners, 104
    people with Alzheimer's disease, 104
    person and family-centered care (PFCC), 108
    quality of care, 108
    reasons for, 105
    respite care, 167
    rewards and challenges, 105

caregiving (Cont.)
    risk for abuse, 109–10, 110t
    sibling relationships, 98
    support for caregivers, 106
    support groups, 167
    support services, 167–68
    travel as respite for, 159
    work and, 119–20
Caring Across Generations, 105t, 218
    as advocacy group, 218
Carney, M. T. et al., 133
Carr, D. C., Fried, L. P., & Rowe, J. W., 54
Carstensen, L. L. & DeLiema, M., 45
Carstensen, L. L., & Mikels, J. A., 9, 23
Carstensen, L. L., Isaacowitz, D. M., & Charles, S. T., 45, 61
cartilage changes, 28
case studies
    ageism on campus, 10
    assisted living, 135
    chronic health conditions among refugees, 192
    Daniel's care plan, 34
    heat wave in Chicago, 139
    high-crime neighborhoods, 140
    involuntary movers, 135
    long-distance relationships, 92
    multigenerational living, 101
    overcoming limited mobility issues, 47
    post-retirement careers, 117
    post-retirement socializing, 66
    senior centers, 219
    social engagement benefits, 168–69
    social media, 175
    Superstorm Sandy, 198
    terminal illness, 79
Cassel, C., 75
Castelló-Porcar, A. M., & Martínez-Jabaloyas, J. M., 30
cataracts, 27, 27f
Cattell, R. B., 30
cellphone and smartphone use, 174
    apps for home use, 177
cemeteries, 85
Center for Behavioral Health Statistics and Quality, 48
Centers for Disease Control and Prevention, 36, 50, 69, 147
Centers for Medicare and Medicaid Services, 205, 207
central nervous system, brain, 30–32
Cercone, K., 125
Cervantes, R. C., Gattamorta, K. A., & Berger-Cardoso, J., 194
Chen, Y. H. et al., 54
Cherpak, G. L., & dos Santos, F. C., 68
Cheyne-Stokes breathing, 74
children
    caregiving grandparents, 103
    exposure to attitudes, 11
    motor skills, 22, 22f
Childs, J. W., 196
China, 188
Chinese immigrants, 101
Choi, N. G. et al., 9, 50
Chonody, J. M., 8
Chowdhury, M. A. B. et al., 198
Chrisler, J. C., Barney, A., & Palatino, B., 13
chronic illness or disability
    active social aging and, 61
    Americans with Disabilities Act (ADA), 211–12
    among refugees, 192
    continuum of care for, 131
    end-of-life decisions, 78
    healthcare services and, 161–62
    impact of increased, 186
    increased longevity and, 186
    Katrina evacuees, 197–98
    noncommunicable diseases (NCDs), 186
    sexual activity and, 68
    social development and, 61
    social networks and, 64
chronological age, 20
Ciano, C. et al., 29
circular migration, 192–93
civic engagement and participation, 123–24, 124f
Clark, J. L. et al., 107
climate change, 195–98
    anthropogenic, 195
    health impacts, 196, 197t
    health vulnerabilities, 196
    migration and, 195–96
    Superstorm Sandy, 198
coalitions, 217
cognitive behavioral therapy (CBT), 51
cognitive functioning
    factors affecting, 46
    overcoming barriers to learning, 46–47
    preserving healthy brain function, 46, 47f
cognitive plasticity, 46
Cohen, H. L., Thomas, C. L., & Williamson, C., 54
Cohen, M. A. et al., 209, 210
Cohn, D. V., & Passel, J. S., 100, 101, 130
coinsurance, 206
Colello, K. J., & Napili, A., 165, 208, 208f
Columbia Public Health, 118
communities, definition of, 152–53
Community Action Agencies, 212
community gerontology, 153
community involvement, recreation and, 157–61
community or civic engagement, 123–24
community resources, 153

INDEX 269

access to information about, 168
access to services, 166
adult day care, 167
for healthcare, 162
in-home personal services, 167
overview of, 152
prevention services, 166–67
religious involvement as, 157
resource brokerage and linkage, 168
social isolation and, 154
socializing in third places, 161
support services, 167–68
types of services (overview), 166
volunteering and, 161
community waivers, 207
companion animals, 103–4
Compassion and Choices, 76, 78
compensatory means to overcome barriers, 47, 48f
case study, 47
complicated grief, 80
computers, 174–75
Congressional Budget Office, 206f
connectedness
cultural beliefs and, 189
importance of, 152
spiritual, 157
Conner, K. O. et al., 51
conservation cemeteries, 85
continuing bonds model of grief, 82
continuing care retirement communities (CCRCs), 141, 142, 144
dementia care, 144
continuity theory, 61
social connectedness and, 62
continuum of care, housing and care options, 131
Conway, F., Jones, S., & Speakes-Lewis, A., 103
Coombs, G., and Dollery, B., 14
COPD (chronic obstructive pulmonary disease), anxiety and depression related, 51
coping skills, 53
core social networks, 64
Correa-de-Araujo, R., 13
COVID-19 pandemic
complicated grief and, 80
connectedness online, 176
depression and, 48
differences between population groups, 190
impact on funerals, 86
informal resources and networks, 154
life expectancy and, 185, 190
misinformation online, 178
online connections and, 70, 176
senior centers and social isolation, 219
social engagement during, 159

social isolation during, 154, 154f
technology access, 155b
telemedicine, 162
term care facilities and, 146–47
treatment of older persons, 187
US Census, 176
COVID Tracking Project, 146
creativity, 53
and productivity, 52–53
Creighton, A. S., Davison, T. E., & Kissane, D. W., 49
cremation, 83–84
options for ashes, 84, 84f
rates, 83
Cremation Association of North America, 83
Cremation Institute, 84
Crenshaw, K., 6
CreUnited Statesfeldt-Jakob disease, 31t
Crimmins, A. et al., 195
critical thinking skills, 178
Crockett, C., Brandl, B., & Dabby, F. C., 111, 147
cross-cultural perspectives
on aging, 22–23
antidiscrimination laws for workplace, 119t
cultural and religious traditions at death, 87b
culture and aging, 187–89
marriage, 94
personality traits and, 45
crossover effect, 53
Cruz-Jentoft, A. J. et al., 27
cryonics, 85
crystallized intelligence, 30
Crystal, S., Shea, D. G., & Reyes, A. M., 215
cultural ageism, 12
culture
acculturation, 194
definition of, 188
mental health stigmas, 51, 52b
perceptions of aging, 10–12, 12b
culture change movement, 146
Cumming, E., & Henry, W., 59
cumulative advantage/disadvantage, 215
Currie, M., Philip, L. J., & Roberts, A., 177
Cutchin, M. P., 132, 134
Cutler, David M., 122
cybercrime, 178–79

Dali, Salvador, 53
dark spots, 25
David, P., & Nelson-Kakulla, B., 102
Day, C. L., 217
death
of adult children, 98
awareness of death, 83
defining physical death, 73–74

death (*Cont.*)
    grief and loss, 78–83
    memorializing people after, 83, 85–86, 87*b*
    as natural part of living, 75
    perceptions of, 75
    physical process of dying, 74–75
    taking care of the dead, 83–86
    total brain death, 74
death with dignity legislation, 76–77
Decade of Healthy Ageing, 184
deductibles, 206
dementia, 30–31. *See also* Alzheimer's disease
    adult day care, 167
    arts programs, 160
    caregiver abuse and, 110
    caregiving for, 104
    continuing care retirement communities (CCRCs), 144
    geriatricians and, 164
    impact on caregivers, 107–8
    online cognitive programs, 177
    PFCC principles and, 108
    reminiscence therapy for, 52
    rural services and, 137
    screening and diagnosis, 50
    therapies, 32, 52
    treatment, 31–32
    types of, 31*t*
Dementia Care Central, 50
Dementia Services Information and Development Centre, 32
Demiris, G., Parker Oliver, D., & Wittenberg-Lyles, E., 177
DePasquale, N. et al., 106
deportation and senior care, 195
depression, 48–49
    COVID-19 pandemic and, 48
    geriatric depression scale (GDS), 50
    outcomes of volunteering and, 161
    rates of, 48–49
    spiritual connectedness and, 157
    women's friendship networks, 65
Desmettre, T. J., 27
Detroit, neighborhoods in, 140
de Vries, B., 64
Dewitte, M., & Mayer, A., 67
Diamond, L. M., 68
digital disconnectedness, 176
digital literacy, 178
    online scams and, 179
Dignitas, 77
DiPrete, T. A., & Eirich, G. M., 44
Disability Insurance (DI) trust fund, 205
disability rights movement, 212

discrimination
    ageism in the workplace, 118
    antidiscrimination laws for workplace, 119*t*
    double discrimination, 118
    housing options, 143
disenfranchised grief, 81
disengagement theory, 59–60
displaced persons, 191
distal defense, 82
divorce, 96
    blended families, 98–99
DNA, genetic (programmed) theory, 23–25, 24*f*
DNA methylation, 24
Doka, K. J., 81
domestic abuse, 110–11
    Adult Protective Services (APS), 167
    older victims of, 147
    shelter programs, 147
Donelan, K. et al., 163
do not resuscitate (DNR) forms, 78
Doolittle, G. C. et al., 180
Dorsey, S., Christopher, C., & Macpherson, D., 121
Dor, Y., & Cedar, H., 24
double discrimination, 118
double jeopardy, 8
Drapeau, C. W., & McIntosh, J. L., 50
drug insurance coverage (Part D), 205–6, 206*f*, 207, 217
dual-process of coping model of grief, 82
Dunkle, J. S., 161
durable power of attorney for healthcare, 78
dyads, 108
Dyer, C. B. et al., 197

early retirement, 120
ecological model of elder abuse, 109, 110*t*
economies, 183
Edelman, M. & Ficorelli, C. T., 134
Edemekong, P. F. et al., 131
Edison Electric Institute, 213
Edmonds, G. W. et al., 45
educational and entertainment media, 173–74
Eeden-Moorefield, B. V., et al., 65
ego integrity, theory of, 42
ego transcendence, 42
elder abuse, 108–12
    defined, 109, 109*t*
    ecological model, 109
    long-term family patterns and, 110–11
    multidisciplinary teams, 112
    Native American view of, 189
    prevention and intervention strategies, 111–12
    trends, 108
Elder Justice Act (EJA), 210–11

Elder Justice Reauthorization and Modernization Act of 2021, 219
elder orphans, 133
elderspeak, 14
electronic assistive technology (EAT), 177
Ellen, M. E., et al., 167
emergency medical services (EMS), 162
emotional development, 45–46
emotion and aging, 45–46
employment
    disengagement theory, 59, 60
    divorce and, 96
encore careers, 116
    case study, 117
endocrine system, 28–30, 29f
    genetic theory and, 24–25
end-of-life decisions, preparing for, 78
end-of-life options, 75–76
    disparities, 78
    hospice care, 77, 77f
    technology and, 179
end-of-life wishes, 13
EngAGE, 159
entitlement programs, 203
environment
    cremation considered, 84
    green burials, 84–85
environmental accommodations, 36
environmental gerontology, 134–35
environmental press, 134
Erikson, E., 40–42, 41t
Erikson, Joan, 41
Ernst, J. S., & Brownell, P. J., 111
Ernst, J. S., & Smith, C. A., 165, 167, 168
Erosheva, E. A., et al., 65
ethnography, 132
Europa-Kommissionen, 119t
European Union, antidiscrimination laws for workplace, 119t
euthanasia, 75–77
exercise, 158. *See also* physical activity
extroversion, 45

Fagan, R. M., 145, 146
Fahs, G., et al., 179
Faigin, C. A., & Pargament, K. I., 159
Faist, T., 191, 195
faith, use of term, 155
falls
    preventive measures, 36
    risks of, 28
family
    blended families, 98–99
    caregiving role reversal, 105
    caring for older adults, 104–8
    defining, 91–93
    dependence on adult children, 97
    divorce impact, 96, 98–99
    elder abuse dynamics and, 108–12
    filial norms and expectations, 100
    intergenerational resource exchange, 99
    intergenerational solidarity and conflict, theory of, 93
    LGBT older adults and, 65
    multigenerational, 100–101, 110
    negotiation of boundary ambiguity, 99
    nontraditional, 98–99
    nuclear, 91
    parents and adult children, 96–97, 97f
    rights to grieve, 81
    roles and relationships, 91, 94–104
    sibling relationships, 98
    theories of family and aging, 93–94
    theory of intergenerational ambivalence, 93–94, 110
Family and Medical Leave Act (FMLA), 106
Family Caregiver Alliance, 167
family development theory, 93
family networks/systems, overview of, 94
Fang, H., et al., 28
Farage, M. A., et al., 25
Farrell, C., 159
Fassa, P., 13
Feagin, J. R., 53
Federal Bureau of Investigation, 179
Federal Interagency Forum on Aging-Related Statistics, 189
Federal Nursing Home Reform Act of 1987, 145
federal poverty level, 207. *See also* poverty
    as official measure, 213
    Supplemental Poverty Measure (SPM), 213
Federal Section 202 Supportive Housing for the Elderly Program, 212
Feinberg, L., et al., 116, 119
Feinberg, L. F., 106, 108
feminist gerontology, 42
feminist theories, 6, 6t
    ageism in the media, 174
    intersection of age and gender, 43
fertility rates, 184
    replacement level, 184
fictive kin, 92
Field, A., et al., 23, 24
Fileborn, B., et al., 67, 69, 70
filial norms and expectations, 100
filial piety, 188
Final Exit Network, 76
financial support, in retirement, 121–23, 122t
Fine, A. H., 104

Finlay, J. M., Gaugler, J. E., & Kane, R. L., 137, 139, 140, 148, 161
Fiori, K. L., Antonucci, T. C., & Akiyama, H., 63
Fischer, N., Weber, B., & Riechelmann, H., 27
fitness and sports, 158
Flourishing Measure, 161, 162*t*
Flowers, L., & Hado, E., 207
fluid intelligence, 30
foreign-born population, 190, 190*f*
forgiveness, 157
formal care, 104, 105–7, 107*t*
    background checks, 111
France, social networks in, 64
Fredriksen-Goldsen, K. I., et al., 65, 215
Fredriksen-Goldsen, K. I., Kim, H. J., et al., 65
Freedman, M., 116
French, M. T., et al., 207
Freud, Sigmund, 40
Friedman, H. S., Kern, M. L., & Reynolds, C. A., 45
friend groups, 64, 66*f*
    female versus male, 65–66
friendships
    among LGBT older adults, 65
    cross-cultural perspectives, 63–64
    female versus male friend groups, 65–66
    intergenerational, 66–67, 67*f*
    as one form of social network, 64
    online social groups, 70
    social connectedness and, 64–67, 67*f*
    three circles of, 62
Fritz, H., Cutchin, M. P., & Cummins, E. R., 139, 140
Fry, R., 97
functional age, 20
funeral homes, 86
funerals
    alternatives to traditional services, 86
    cost of, 83–84
    cross-cultural perspectives, 87*b*
    impact of COVID-19 pandemic, 86
    as memorializing tradition, 85
    perceptions of death, 75
Fung, H. H., 23

Gallagher, 144
Gallup, 115
gaming, online, 177–78
Ganong, L., & Coleman, M., 91, 96, 99
Gass, A. P., Mahan, Z., & Balfour, M., 131, 148
Gates, Bill, 8
Gawlowska, M., 47
gayborhoods, 138
gender. *See also* women
    caregiver stress, 108
    friend groups and, 65–66

    grip strength, 28
    labor force participation, 116, 186
    sexual activity and, 68
    signs of aging, 8
    suicide attempts and, 50
    work experiences, 117
gender discrimination, 53
generational perspective, labor force participation, 115, 117
Generations United, 218
Generations United and Leading Age, 143
genetic (programmed) theory, 23–25, 24*f*
gentrification, 138–39
Genworth, 107*t*
geographical gerontology, 135–36
geriatric depression scale (GDS), 50
geriatric homeless population, 148
geriatricians
    health care and, 164, 164*f*
    shortage, 12
geriatrics, definition of, 2
Germany, 186
    immigrant trauma, 195
    social networks in, 64
gerontology
    as career field, 2, 4, 5*b*
    community, 153
    definition of, 2
    environmental gerontology, 134–35
    geographical gerontology, 135–36
    gerontologist roles, 4
    population aging, 2–3
    research design overview, 2
Gheaus, A., & Herzog, L., 115
Ghisyawan, K., 68
Gibson, M. J., & Hayunga, M., 196, 197
Gironda, M. W. et al., 111
Gladyshev, V. N., 23
glaucoma, 27
globalization
    culture and aging, 187
    use of term, 183
global population aging, 3, 4*f*, 184–85
    living arrangements, 185
Gokhale, J., 120
Golant, S. M., 9, 132, 133
Golden, A. G., Silverman, M. A., & Issenberg, S. B., 12
Goldsmith, T. C., 24
golf, 158
Gonzales, E., Matz-Costa, C., & Morrow-Howell, N., 3
Gottlieb, B. H., & Sevigny, A., 153
Graham, J., 155*b*

grandfathers, 66
grandparents
    caregiving grandchildren, 103
    divorce impact, 96
    grandchildren and, 93, 101–3
    roles, 92–93
    Temporary Assistance for Needy Families (TANF)
        program, 144
grassroots organizing, 217
gray hair
    age-related changes, 25, 26
    physical factors, 22
    timing of, 26
Gray Panthers, 217–18
Greenberg, J., Solomon, S., & Pyszczynski, T., 83
Green Burial Council, 85
green burials, 84–85
Greenfield, E. A., et al., 142, 152, 153
Green House Model, 146
Greif, G. L., & Woolley, M. E., 98
grief, 78–83, 79f
    adaptive grieving model, 82
    awareness of death, 83
    complicated, 80
    continuing bonds model, 82
    disenfranchised, 81
    dual-process of coping model, 82
    five stages of, 81–82
    prolonged, 80
    tasks of mourning model, 82
    theories and models, 81–82
    types of, 80–81
    uncomplicated, 80
Griffin, J. M., et al., 107
Gronke, P., Manson, P., Lee, J., & Foot, C., 216
Gubernskaya, Z., & Treas, J., 194
Guiney, H., Keall, M., & Machado, L., 123
Gullette, M. M., 7, 8, 13, 14, 15, 16, 93, 109, 196, 197
Gupta, R., & Hershey, D. A., 187, 188
Gurchiek, K., 118
Gurera, J. W., & Isaacowitz, D. M., 45
Guzman, S., Sturtevant, L., & Huaman, D., 212

Haber, C., 141, 203
hair
    age-related changes, 25–26, 26f
    early graying, 22
    hair loss, 25–26, 26f
half-siblings, 98
Han, B. H., et al., 50
hand grip as indicator, 27, 28
Han, K. T., et al., 20
Hannan, M. T., & Kranzberg, M., 116
Hanson, M. A. et al., 7

Harding, D. J., & Jencks, C., 94
Harris-Kojetin, L., et al., 131
Harris, M. A., et al., 45
Harvard Health Publications, 132
Harvie, H., & Rumore, R., 148
Hasworth, S. B., & Cannon, M., 60, 61
Havighurst, R. J., Neugarten, B., & Tobin, S. S., 60
Hayes, S. M., et al., 46
health
    climate change and, 196, 197t
    definition of, 161
    increased longevity and, 186
healthcare
    advance directives, 78
    age-friendly, 165, 165t
    effect of ageism, 12–13
    end-of-life decisions and, 179
    Flourishing Measure, 161, 162t
    geriatricians and, 164, 164f
    intersectional factors and, 34
    "normal" processes of aging, 13
    potential problems with technology, 180
    in rural areas, 137
healthcare insurance, 207. See also Affordable Care
    Act; Medicaid; Medicare
healthcare professionals
    age-friendly healthcare, 165, 165t
    beliefs of, 12–13
    formal caregiving, 106–7, 107t
    immigrant patients, 194
    training technology, 179–80
healthcare services, 161–69
    access to, 162–63
    Andersen model of healthcare utilization, 163
    community-based, 162
    factors promoting access, 163
    locations for, 162
health disparities, 33–35, 190
health promotion, concept of, 35
health, promotion of, 33–36
    recommendations, 35
health-related topics online, 173
Health Resources and Services Administration, 85
Heaphy, B., 44
hearing and vision, access to preventive care, 35
hearing loss, 26–27
    accommodations, 36
heart disease, premature gray hair, 26
heat waves
    Chicago, 139
    climate change and, 196, 197t
Helbling, M., 191
Heller-Sahlgren, G., 121
Hemlock Society, 76

Heo, J., et al., 157, 158
heterohappiness, 68
    in the media, 174
heteronormative sexuality, 68
heterosexist norms, 44
He, W., Goodkind, D., & Kowal, P., 186, 187
Hickenbotham, A., et al., 27
Hispanic older adults, assistive device access, 35
HIV infection, 69
Hoffmann, R. L., & Mitchell, A. M., 107, 108
Hollis-Sawyer, L., & Cuevas, L., 11
Holt-Lunstad, J., 154
home assessments, for safety and mobility, 36
home care workers, 107, 107t
homelessness
    geriatric homeless population, 148
    living arrangements and, 148, 148f
    special needs adults, 131
home sharing, as housing options, 143
homosociality, 65
Hooyman, N., et al., 43
Hopkins B., & Westra, T., 22
hormone replacement therapy (HRT), 30
hormones. See endocrine system
Horngren, B., 159
hospice care, 77, 77f, 108
hostile ageism, 8
housing and care options, 129–31, 141–47
    adults living alone, 130, 130f, 133, 142
    Age-Friendly Community Initiative, 142
    aging in place, 130, 132–34
    assisted living facilities, 131, 145
    communal living, 143
    continuing care retirement communities (CCRCs), 141, 144
    continuum, 141–42
    continuum of care, 131
    costs associated, 141–42
    decisions to move considered, 134
    environmental press and, 134
    historical background, 141
    home safety and accessibility, 134
    home sharing, 143
    housing affordability, 212–13
    innovative solutions, 142–43, 144b
    intergenerational communities, 143–44
    intergenerational programming, 143
    involuntary movers/stayers, 135
    LGBT 65+ housing initiatives, 142–43
    for low-income older adults, 144
    needs changing over time, 133–34
    neighborhoods, importance of, 137–41
    nursing homes, 145–46
    residential facilities and communities, 131
    supportive housing, 145, 145t
    theories and approaches, 134–36
    types of relocations, 135
    urban and rural, 136–37, 136f
    villages, 142
    for vulnerable populations, 147–48
Housing Choice Voucher Assistance, 212
housing models, 3
Howarth, R. A., 80
Htut, T. Z. C., et al., 177
Hubbard, L. A., 211
Hughes, M., 44
Hughes, M. J., et al., 103
human development lenses, 6t 7
    physical age and, 22
Humanitas, 144b
Human Rights Watch, 147
Humphrey, C., 87b
Humphry, Derek, 76, 76f
Hung, L-Y., Lyons, J. G., & Wu, C-H., 176
Huntington's disease dementia, 31t
Huo, M., et al., 97
Hurricane Katrina, 196–98
hybrid cemeteries, 85

Ikeuchi, T., et al., 104
immigrants. See also migration
    acculturation and acculturative stress, 194
    changes over time, 191, 192f
    climate change and, 195–96
    deportation and senior care, 142
    displaced persons, 191
    early-life versus late-life immigration, 194–95
    healthcare, 194–95
    legal status and threat of deportation, 195
    limited English proficiency (LEP), 194
    linguistic isolation, 194
    migration, 184
    older, in destination countries, 193–94
    political asylum, 192
    poverty rates, 215
    priorities of US law, 193
    refugees, 191–92, 193f
    religious involvement and, 157
    Social Security benefits and, 122, 123
    undocumented, 193, 195
    urban neighborhoods, 137, 138, 139
    who migrates and why, 191–92
immune system, 28
immunosenescence, 28
independent living, 212
independent living communities, 131
Independent Living movement, 212
India, 187–88, 194
individual ageism, 9
Indonesian funeral practices, 87b

inequality, discrimination and, 43–44
inflammation, immune system and, 28
informal care, 104–5
in-home health care, Medicare and Medicaid, 209
in-home personal services, 167
inner circle of friendship, 62
    cross-cultural perspectives, 63
inpatient settings, 162
institutional ageism, 9
institutions, ageist attitudes, 12
instrumental activities of daily living (IADLs), 104
    residential facilities and, 131
integrity vs. despair, 41, 41t
interest groups, 217
intergenerational ambivalence, theory of, 93–94
intergenerational communities, 143, 143–44
intergenerational community orchestras and choruses, 160
intergenerational families, violence and elder abuse, 110–11
intergenerational friendships, 66–67, 67f
intergenerational programming, 143
intergenerational resource exchange, 99
intergenerational solidarity and conflict, theory of, 93
intergenerational stake hypothesis, 97
intergenerational work teams, 118
internalized ageism, 11
    consequences of, 12
internalized attitudes, 9
internalized cultural values, 22–23
International Labour Organization, 187t
international migration, 191. *See also* immigrants; migration
International Organization for Migration, 191
International Osteoporosis Foundation, 28
Internet use, 175, 175t
intersectional factors
    activity expectations, 60–61
    age and gender, 43, 44f
    age-friendly healthcare, 165
    age-related psychological changes, 42–43
    anxiety disorders and, 49
    dementia, 30–31
    Erikson's theory and, 42
    healthcare access and, 163
    healthcare and, 34
    health disparities, 33–35
    hearing and vision, 27
    neighborhoods, importance of, 138
    other characteristics, 43–44
    Peck's theory and, 42
    political advocacy, 216–17
    reactions to loss, 80
    relocation or aging in place, 132
    resiliency and, 53
    rights to grieve, 81
    volunteering and, 161
    work while caregiving, 119
intersectional identities, life-course model of social functioning and, 61
intersectional lenses, 6, 6t
    factors that affect aging, 21–22
    resiliency, 53
intimacy and sexuality, 67–70
    beliefs about sexuality, 67–68
    types of intimacy, 67
involuntary movers/stayers, 135
    case study, 135
Irish wake and funeral customs, 87b
irritable bowel syndrome, premature gray hair, 27
"isms," 7, 44
isolation and loneliness. *See also* social isolation
    adults living alone, 133
    contributing factors, 63
    impact during heat waves, 139
    natural disasters and, 197
    online connections, 70
    social connectedness and, 63
    theory of Intergenerational Solidarity and Conflict, 93
    transgender older adults, 65
    trends, 63
Iversen, T. N., Larsen, L., Solem, P. E., 7

Jaffe, I., 142
Jamwal, R., et al., 177
Janhsen, A., et al., 54
Jansen, T., 144b
Japan
    antidiscrimination laws for workplace, 119t
    family-focused networks, 63
    OADR in, 185
    retirement and, 120
Jercich, K., 179
Jervis, L. L., Sconzert-Hall, W., & The Shielding American Indian Elders Project, 189
Jeste, D. V., & Lee, E. E., 54
Jesuthasan, J., et al., 195
Jewish funeral practices, 87b
Jiang, D., et al., 123
Johannesen, M., & LoGiudice, D., 109
John A. Hartford Foundation, 165, 165t
Johnson, K. R., et al., 191, 193
Joint Center for Housing Studies, 130, 136, 141
Jones, J., 179
Judson Manor, 144b
Justice in Aging, 218

Kaczan, D. J., & Orgill-Meyer, J., 191
Kahlenberg, R. D., 136
Kalfoss, M. H., 23
Kaslow, F., & Robison, J. A., 94
Katz, S., & Marshall, B. L., 177
Kaufman, B. G., et al., 137
Kaye, L. W., 137
Kennedy, I. M., 74
Kevorkian, Jack, 76, 76f
KFF (Kaiser Family Foundation), 205, 206
Kim, K. H., 53
kinship, 92
kinship navigator programs, 103
Kirkendall, A. M., Waldrop, D., & Moone, R. P., 104
Klass, D., Silverman, P., & Nickman, S., 82
Klinenberg, E., 139
Klug, L. A., 87b
Kochman, K., 25
Koenig, R., 131, 145, 145f
Kolodziejczak, K., et al., 67, 68, 69
Koren, M. J., 146
Kotter-Grühn, D., & Hess, T. M., 9, 11
Kowald, A., & Kirkwood, T. B., 25
Kübler-Ross, E., 81–82
Kuhn, Maggie, 217
Kunkel, S. R., & Hautz, O., 187
Kwak, S., et al., 21
Kwong, K., Du, Y., & Xu, Q., 154

Laal, M., 125
labor force participation, 115
labor force participation rate (LFPR), 186–87, 187t
Lachman, M. E., et al., 36
Lamar, K. L., & Luke, J. J., 160
Lamers, W., 74
Landers, S. & Kapadia, F., 9, 53
Langer, N., 96
Lang, P. O., et al., 28
language use
  avoiding ageist language, 16
  discomfort with death, 75
  foreign-born population, 190
  limited English proficiency (LEP), 194
  linguistic isolation, 194
  microaggressions, 13–14
  normalizing terms for aging, 16
  rhetoric and policy changes, 14
Lawrence, R. G., 101
Lawton, M. P., & Nahemov, L., 134
Lazar, A., 43
Leadership Council of Aging Organizations (LCAO), 218
learning, 46–47
  barriers to continued, 125
  cognitive plasticity, 46

creativity and, 53
  lifelong learning, 124–25, 125f
  neurodiversity, 46
  overcoming barriers to, 46–47
  preserving healthy brain function, 46, 47f
Lebanon, social networks in, 64
Leedahl, S. N., et al., 67
Lee, D. M., et al., 68
Lee, E. S., & Zhang, Y., 157
Lee, H. J., & Szinovacz, M E., 64, 65
Lee, Y., & Jean Yeung, W., 54
Lehning, A. J., Kim, M. H., & Dunkle, R. E., 163
Leist, A. K., 174
Le Roux, C., Tang, Y., & Drexler, K., 49
Lester, P. E., Dharmarajan, T. S., & Weinstein, E., 164
Levin, M. K., Reingold, D., & Solomon, J., 147
Levy, B., Ashman, O., & Dror, I., 12
Levy, B. R., et al., 22
Levy, V., & Thayer, C., 67
Lewy body dementia, 31t
LGBT older adults
  arts programs, 160
  care in later years, 94
  communal living, 143
  continuing care retirement communities (CCRCs), 144
  discrimination in caregiving, 107
  friendships among, 65
  LGBT 65+ housing initiatives, 142–43
  poverty rates, 214–15
  relocation at retirement, 132
  resiliency, 53
  SAGE: Advocacy & Services for LGBT Elders, 43, 218
  urban neighborhoods and, 138, 139
Library of Congress, 26
life-course model of social functioning, 61, 62
life expectancy
  earlier trends, 203
  global trends, 185–86
  impact of COVID-19 pandemic, 185, 190
  rates, 164
  US trends, 189–90, 203
lifelong learning, 124–25, 125f, 176
life review therapy, 52
life-span development, 7
  individual differences, 15
  personality traits, 45
life-span theorists, 40
Li, M., Chen, R., & Dong, X., 53, 189
limited English proficiency (LEP), 194
Lindenbach, J., et al., 137
linguistic isolation, 194
Lipnic, V. A., 118, 119t
literature, 11

Litwak, E., & Longino, C. F., Jr., 135
living arrangements
    changes in, 129
    global patterns, 185
    overview of, 129
    place, importance of, 129
    skip-generation household, 185
    of vulnerable populations, 147
living wills, 78
Li, Z., & Dalaker, J., 213, 214
Li, Z., & Durgin, F. H., 54
Llanque, S. et al., 107
Lloyd-Sherlock, P. G., et al., 9
Lobb, E. A., et al., 80
lobbying, 217
Löckenhoff, C. E. et al., 12
longevity
    divorce and, 96
    effects of increased, 98
    extended life and health outcomes, 33
    family structure and, 91
    global trends, 185–86
    "oldest old" caregiving, 104
    physical activity and, 36
    promotion of, 33–36
    sense of purpose in retirement, 120
    Social Security benefits and, 123
    trends, 164
long-term care
    cost of, 209–10
    long-term services and supports (LTSS), 209–10
    Medicare and, 206–7
    "No Wrong Door" initiative, 168
    Protection for Residents of Long-Term Care Facilities, 211
    quality of, 210
    workforce, 219
Long-Term Care Ombudsman Program, 210
long-term partnerships, 94
long-term services and supports (LTSS), adults with disabilities, 212
Lopez, M. H., Passel, J. S., & Cohn, D. V., 195
loss and grief, 78–79
    disenfranchised grief, 81
    variation in reactions, 82
Lou, C., Hajkova, P., & Ecker, J. R., 12, 24
Lowenstein, A., 6
Low Income Home Energy Assistance Program (LIHEAP), 168, 212–13
low-income older adults
    housing options, 144
    other assistance for, 212–13
    social services for, 168
    state-funded LTSS, 209–10

Lu, H., et al., 53
Lu, Z., et al., 26
Lyons, S. T., Schweitzer, L., & Ng, E. S. W., 116

McAuliffe, M., & Khadria, B., 184, 193
McCarron, H. R., et al., 161, 163
McDermott-Levy, R., & Fick, D. M., 197t
McDermott-Levy, R., et al., 196, 197t
McHugh M. C., & Interligi, C., 13
McLaughlin, D., et al., 65
MacQueen, K. M., et al., 152
macro settings
    ageism, 187
    community gerontology, 153
    effects of ageism, 12
    examples of careers, 5b
macular degeneration, 27
    training, 36
male pattern baldness, 25–26
mandatory retirement, 118–19, 120
    opposition to, 217
Mann, R., Tarrant, A., & Leeson, G. W., 66
Mansens, D., Deeg, D. J. H., & Comijs, H. C., 159
Manson, J. E., et al., 30
marriage
    arranged, 94
    cross-cultural perspectives, 94
    defining a good marriage, 94–95
    divorce and, 96, 98–99
    familial roles and relationships, 94
    reasons for, 94
marriage history of older adults, 95f
Marshall, A. C., et al., 46
Marshall, B. L., 67, 174
Martinez, L., et al., 143
Martinez, P. N., et al., 75
Martinson, M., & Berridge, C., 15
Martinson, M., & Minkler, M., 124
Martin, T. L., & Doka, K. J., 82
Mary's House, 143
Marzilli, T., 178
Maschi, T., Viola, D., & Sun, F., 147
Maslow, A. H., et al., 63
Masotti, P. J., et al., 137
massive open online courses (MOOCs), 176
matching funds, 208
Mather, M., & Scommegna, P., 138, 152
Mather, M., 46
Mauldin, R. L., et al., 207, 210
Mayntz, M., 99
Mayo Clinic, 79
Mazzonna, F., & Peracchi, F., 121
Meadows, K., 87b
meal programs, 166–67
Meals on Wheels, 167

means test, 203
media
    ageism in, 9, 9f, 174
    educational and entertainment, 173-74
    natural disaster coverage, 196-97
    news media, 172-73
    overview of, 172
    social media, 172-73
    successful aging in, 174
    use of term, 172
    views of older adults, 10-11
Media Wise, 178
Medicaid, 206-7
    expansion, 207
    home healthcare, 167, 209
    housing options, 141
medical aid in dying, 75, 76
medical orders for lifesustaining treatment (MOLST), 78
Medicare
    ACA and rising costs, 207
    benefit payments by type of service, 206f
    coinsurance, 206
    deductibles, 206
    healthcare availability, 162
    long-term care, 141
    overview of, 205-6
    primary care and, 163
    voting patterns and, 215
medications
    caregiving and, 106
    for decreased sexual desire, 68
    for mental illness, 52
Meeks, T. W., & Jeste, D. V., 54
Mehrotra, A., et al., 162
memory
    other cognitive functions and, 30
    support program, 107
men
    married, and friendship ties, 65-66
    sexual activity and, 68
menopause
    cultural attitudes compared, 22-23
    endocrine system and, 29
mental health, 48-52
    adult children with special needs, 97
    ageism consequences, 12
    anxiety, 49
    benefits of social connectedness, 63
    civic engagement and participation, 123-24, 124f
    cognitive behavioral therapy (CBT), 51
    cultural stigmas and, 51, 52b
    depression, 48-49
    elder abuse and, 110
    familial social networks and, 64

narrative therapy, 52
psychotherapeutic approaches, 51-52, 51f
reminiscence therapy, 52
screening and diagnosis, 50
substance use disorders, 49-50
suicide, 50
treatment, 50-51, 165
trends, 48
volunteering and, 123
Merghati-Khoei, E., et al., 68
Metaxakis, A., & Partridge, L., 33
Mexico, social networks in, 63-64
mezzo settings
    community gerontology, 153
    examples of careers, 5b
microaggressions, 13-14, 14f
micro settings
    community gerontology, 153
    examples of careers, 5b
middle-ageism, 8
middle circle of friendship, 62
    cross-cultural perspectives, 63
Midgley, J., & Livermore, M., 202
migration. See also immigrants
    circular, 192-93
    climate change and, 195-96
    older adults in destination countries, 193-94
    older adults in home countries, 192-93
    push/pull factors, 191
    use of term, 184
    who migrates and why, 191-92
Milic, J., et al., 80
Miller, E. A., Huberfeld, N. & Jones, D. K., 207, 209
Miller, F., & Dun, O., 196
Milne, D., 211, 212
Miloyan, B., Byrne, G. J., & Pachana, N. A., 49
Mini-Mental State Exam (MMSE), 50
Minneapolis, 136, 140-41
minoritized groups
    age discrimination among, 118
    effect of ageism on healthcare, 13
    end-of-life disparities, 78
    health disparities, 33-35
    poverty rates, 214
    projected trends, 189
    successful aging and, 15
    urban neighborhoods and, 139
Mirmirani, P., 25
Mitchell, L. K., & Pachana, N. A., 51
mitochondria, 25
Mitteldorf, J., 24, 25
mixed dementia, 31t
Mizoguchi, N., et al., 190, 194
Molony, S. L., et al., 108

Mongolian funeral practices, 87b
Moore, P. H., 158
Morrow-Howell, N., 161
mortality rates
    compared, 53
    extreme heat and, 139, 196
    global, 184
Moses, J., 159
Moskowitz, R. L., 206
mourning, 79
    tasks of mourning model, 82
Mueller, S., Wagner, J. & Gerstorf, D., 45
multigenerational families and households, 100, 100f
    benefits and drawbacks, 100–101
    case study, 101
    demographics, 100
    global trends, 185
    housing and, 130, 142
    immigrants in, 194
Murman, D. L., 30
muscle mass, 27, 28
musculoskeletal system, 27–28
music, importance of, 159–60

Namazi, M., Sadeghi, R., & Moghadam, Z. B., 23
narrative therapy, 52
National Academies of Sciences Engineering and Medicine, 63, 93, 105, 106, 133, 154
National Academy of Social Insurance, 204, 205
National Alliance for Caregiving, 119
National Center on Elder Abuse, 105t, 109t, 111
National Conference of State Legislatures, 207
National Cremation, 84
National Geographic, 137
National Hospice and Palliative Care Organization, 77
National Institute of Mental Health, 48
National Institute on Aging, 68, 105, 105t, 145
National Institute on Drug Abuse, 49–50, 51
National Social Life Health and Aging Project, 95
Native American communities, 189
natural disasters, 196–97
naturally occurring retirement communities (NORCs), 137
negative ageism, 8
negativity bias, 45
neglect, elder abuse and, 109t, 110
negotiation of boundary ambiguity, 99
neighborhoods, importance of, 137–41
    in aging in place, 134
    in Detroit, 140
    different neighborhoods compared, 140–41
    features associated with healthy aging, 138, 138f
    gentrification impact, 138–39
    geographical gerontology lens, 135
    high-crime, 139, 140
    losing trust in neighborhood, 140
    in Minneapolis, 140–41
    naturally occurring retirement communities (NORCs), 137
    sense of community and, 152–53
    urban neighborhoods analyzed, 139
    zoning laws and, 135–36
Nelson-Kakulla, B., 177
Nelson, M. K., 92
Nelson, T. T., 12
Netherlands, 144b
neuroageism, 8
neurodegenerative diseases, 8
neurodiversity, 46
New American Economy, 123
Newport, F., 205
news media, 172–73, 178
New York Public Library, 176
New Zealand neighborhoods, 137–38
Next Avenue, 105t
Nguyen, A. W., et al., 65
Nicholas, P. K., & Breakey, S., 196
Nicoll, L. H., 124
Nielsen, D. S., et al., 195
Nieuwenhuis, A. V., Beach, S. R., & Schulz, R., 108
Nobel, J., 87b
Noftle, E. E., & Fleeson, W., 45
Noice, T., Noice, H., & Kramer, A. F., 159
noncommunicable diseases (NCDs), 186
North American culture, positivity effect, 23
North, M. S., & Fiske, S. T., 8, 12
Northwestern Mutual Life Insurance Company, 106
Novelli C., 28
"No Wrong Door" initiative, 168
nuclear family, 91, 92f, 98–99
Nurmi, M. A., et al., 65
Nursing Home Reform Act of 1987, 210
nursing homes
    culture change movement, 146
    formal care in, 106
    as housing option, 145–46
    intergenerational living, 144b
    Medicare and Medicaid for, 209
    psychosocial services in, 210
    quality of care, 145–46, 210
nutrition
    common issues, 35
    programs, 208, 208f

Obamacare, 207
O'Brien, E., Fox-Grage, W., & Ujvari, K., 209
O'Donnell, L., 105, 106
Office of the Assistant Secretary for Planning and Evaluation, 214t
old age dependency ratio (OADR), 184–85

280 INDEX

Old Age, Survivors, and Disability Insurance (OASDI) program, 203, 205
Oldenburg, Ray, 161
Older Adults Technology Services, 176
Older Americans Act, 165
   amendments to, 210
   caregiver support programs, 167
   delivery of services, 166
   elder abuse programs, 111
   funding flows, 208, 208f
   home and community based services (HCBS), 209
   overview of, 207–9
Oliver, A., Tomas, J. M., & Montoro-Rodriguez, J., 124
Olmstead decision, Supreme Court, 212
O'Neil, K., & Tienda, M., 191, 215
online dating, 70, 174
online entertainment and gaming, 177–78
online safety, 178–79
online social groups, 70
optimal aging, 15–16, 16f
   adaptation and, 16
Oregon Center for Aging and Technology, 36, 177
Orellano-Colón, E., et al., 35
Orenstein, G. A., & Lewis, L., 41, 42
organ, tissue, and whole-body donation, 85
Orlovic, M., Smith, K., & Mossialos, E., 78
Osher Lifelong Learning Institute (OLLI), 125
osteoporosis, 28
Ostir, G. V., & Goodwin, J. S., 49
othering
   defined, 13
   stereotypes and, 13
outer circle of friendship, 62
   cross-cultural perspectives, 63
outpatient basis, 162
Oxman, T. E., 54

Pahl, R. E., 64
palliative care, 77
Palmiero, M., 53
Pandey, A., et al., 103
Pardasani, M., 166
parents and adult children, 96–97, 97f
   children at least 65 years old, 98
Parkinson disease dementia, 31t
Parsons, A. J. Q., & Gilmour, S., 185
Partners for Livable Communities, 160
part time employment
   prdouctivity and, 54
   trends, 116–17
Pasricha, N., 120
passive euthanasia, 75
Patel, T., & Yosipovitch, G., 25
patient-centered medical home, 163
Patient Protection and Affordable Care Act, 207

Peck, R., 42
peer navigators, 103
pensions, 121–23, 122t
   overview of, 213
   publicly funded, 185
perimenopause, 29
Perl, L., 212
Perone, A. K., 165
Perry, T. E., Andersen, T. C., & Kaplan, D. B., 134, 135
personality and emotion, 44–46
   aging, 44–45
   emotion, 45–46
person and family-centered care (PFCC), 108
person-centered care, 32
Peru, antidiscrimination laws for workplace, 119t
Peteet, J. R., Faten, A. Z., & Koenig, H. G., 155
Peterson Institute for International Economics, 183
Petkus, A. J., et al., 49
pets, 103–4
Pew Charitable Trust, 173
Pew Institute, 174
Pew Research Center, 92f, 115, 155, 156, 156t, 172, 175t, 176, 191
Philippine funeral practices, 87b
Philippines, antidiscrimination laws for workplace, 119t
Phillips, M. L., 46
physical activity, 36
physical changes of aging, cultural attitudes compared, 23
physical death, 73–74
physical health
   consequences of ageism, 12
   internalized attitudes and, 22
   intersectional characteristics, 15
   subjective age and, 21
physician aid in dying, 75, 77
physician orders for life-sustaining treatment (POLST) forms, 78
Piaget, Jean, 40
Picasso, Pablo, 53
Pickering, C., Yefimova, M., & Maxwell, C., 110
pickleball, 158
Pike, L., 215
Pillemer, K., et al., 108, 109, 112
Pioneer Network, 146
place, importance of, 129, 132–33
   as symbols of identity, 133
plastination, 85, 86f
podcasts, 173
political asylum, 192
political participation and advocacy, 215–18
poll workers, 216
polyvictimization, 109
Poo, A.-j., 107
poorer countries, health challenges, 34

Poor Laws, 202-3
population aging, 2-3. *See also* aging
    consequences of, 3-4
    costs for Social Security, 205
    global, by age group, 3, 4f, 184
    increases, 3, 3f
    negative views of, 14
    trends overview, 183
Population Reference Bureau, 138f, 185, 189, 203
Portacolone, E., 140, 143
Portacolone, E., Perissinotto, C. et al., 139, 154
Portacolone, E., Rubinstein, R. L. et al., 168
positive ageism, 8
positive health outcomes, productivity and, 54
positivity effect, 23
    emotions and, 45-46
pottery, 160f
poverty. *See also* federal poverty level
    anxiety and, 49
    cumulative advantage/disadvantage, 215
    federal poverty level, 207, 213
    foreign-born population, 190
    housing and, 142
    measuring, 213-15, 214t
    migration and, 191, 195
    "near poor," 213-14
    official guidelines, 213, 214t
    overview of, 213
    retirement and, 123
    social isolation and, 63
    Social Security, 14, 203, 205
    trends, 213, 214
    UN policies, 184
    variance between population groups, 214-15
pre-existing conditions, 207
presbycusis, 26-27
prescription and nonprescription medications, misuse and abuse, 49-50
prespbyopia, 27
prevention services, 166-67
preventive measures, 36
primary care, 163
primary care physicians, access to, 163
primary prevention services, 166
print media, 172
Prinzinger, R., 25
prison, older adults in
    compassionate release, 147
    living arrangements of, 147
    rates of incarceration, 147
    sentencing policies and, 131
    special needs and, 131
problem solving, 46
productivity, 52, 53-54
    work related to, 115

Programmed aging theory, 23-25, 24f
prolonged grief (disorder), 80
Protection for Residents of Long-Term Care Facilities, 211
protective services, 167. *See also* Adult Protective Services
Proulx, C. M., Curl, A. L., & Ermer, A. E., 124
proximal defense, 83
psychological age, theories of, 40-44
    global perspectives, 52b
psychological theories, 5, 6t
psychosocial stages of development, 40-42, 41t
psychotropic medications, 52
pull and push factors, 191
purpose in life, 120
Putney, J. M., et al., 107

quality of life, longevity and, 33
queer gerontology, 44
    ageism in the media, 174
queermisia, 7
queer theory, 6, 6t
    ageism in the media, 174
    on heterohappiness, 68
    psychological aspects of aging, 44

race and ethnicity
    religious participation, 156t
    spiritual connectedness and, 157
    suicide attempts and, 50
radio and TV, 172
Ramsey-Klawsnik, H., & Miller, E., 109
Ranahan, M. E., 143
Rantanen, T., et al., 27
Ratcliffe, M., et al., 136
Reaves, E. L., & Musumeci, M., 209
recreation
    the arts, 159-60, 160f
    community involvement and, 157-61
    sports and fitness, 158
    travel, 159
recreational vehicles (RVs), 148, 159
Refugee Processing Center, 192
refugees, 191-92, 193f
    fleeing war, terror, and threats to their lives, 195
Reich, A. J., et al., 189
Reinhard, S. C., Levine, C., & Samis, S., 106
Reisch, M., 202
relationships, 59. *See also* family; friendships; social networks
    continuity theory and, 51
    long-distance, 92
    parents and adult children, 96-97, 97f
    siblings, 98
    social convoy model, 61-62, 62f
    "trust," 109

religion
  involvement and health, 157
  use of term, 155
religious communities, 155–56, 156t
  benefits of religious involvement, 157
reminiscence therapy, 52
Renn, B. N., Arean, P. A., & Unutzer, J., 48
replacement level, 184
residential facilities and communities, 131
  anxiety issues and, 49
  assisted living facilities, 131
  long-term care, 131
  nursing homes, 131
resiliency, 52, 53
  community identity and resources, 154
  crossover effect, 53
  in distressed neighborhoods, 139, 140
Resnick, B., 163
resources. See also community resources
  availability of, 21, 21f
respite care, 167
retirement
  early, reasons for, 120
  effects of, 120–21
  financial support in, 121–23, 122t
  global trends, 186
  goals compared, 188
  lifelong learning, 124–25, 125f
  longevity and health, 120
  mandatory, 118–19, 120
  phases or transitions, 121
  postponing, 121
  poverty and, 123
  purpose in life, 120
  regular happy hours, 66
  relationship changes, 62
  relocation or aging in place, 132
  social network changes, 64
  urban neighborhoods during, 137
  volunteerism and civic engagement, 123–24, 124f
retirement age for Social Security, 204–5
Riddering, A. T., 36
"right to die" movement
  famous cases, 74
  Hemlock Society, 76
  proponents of, 76, 76f
rigor mortis, 75
Rippon, I. et al., 7
Ritzer, G., 183
Rivera, L. M., & Paredez, S. M., 12, 13
Rizzo, V. M., Burnes, D. P., & Chalfy, A., 112
Road Scholar, 159
Roberts, A. W., et al., 131
Robinson, D. et al., 121

Rodriguez, N., Paredes, C. L., & Hagan, J., 194, 195
roles for older adults
  disengagement theory, 59
  reimagined, 3–4
Romig, K., 213
Rosen, T., et al., 162
Ross, J. M., et al., 24
Roth, D. L., et al., 53
Rowe, J. W., & Kahn, R. L., 15
Rowles, G. D., & Teaster, P. B., 131
Rowles, G. D., 132, 133
Rubin, A., Parrish, D. E., & Miyawaki, C. E., 52
Rubin, D. C., & Bernsten, D., 21
Rudowitz, R., Garfield, R. & Hinton, E., 207, 209
rural and urban environments, 136–37, 136f
rural services, for healthcare, 163
Russia, antidiscrimination laws for workplace, 119t
Ryu, J., et al., 158

Sadana, R. et al, 7, 14, 15
SAGE: Advocacy & Services for LGBT Elders, 43, 218
St. Thomas, US Virgin Islands, 198
Sakuraba, R., 119t
Salthouse T. A., 30
Sandberg, L., 68, 69, 174
Sandberg, L. J., & Marshall, B. L., 6, 61
Sandoval, E. et al., 148
Sanjek, R., 217, 218
Sarbey, B., 73, 74
sarcopenia, 27
Saunders, Cicely, 77
Schaller, S., Traeen, B., & Kvalem, I. L., 69
Schiamberg, L. B., & Gans, D., 109
Schwenk, T. L., 13
screening and diagnosis, physical and mental health problems, 50
Scullin, M. K., Bliwise, D. L., 46
secondary prevention services, 166
Sehrawat, S., 210
selective optimization with compensation, theory of, 47, 48f
self-determination, client, 111–12
self-determination theory, 153
self-directed learning, 124–25
self-neglect, 109, 109t
self-worth, measuring, 42
Sellon, A. M., Chapin, R. K., & Leedahl, S. N., 123
Seltzer, J. A., 100, 101
senescence, defined, 23
senescent alopecia, 26
senior centers, 161
  case study, 219
  delivery of services, 166

senior communities, 131
SeniorPlanet.org, 174
sense of purpose, 120
Serrat, R., et al., 161
Settersten, R. A., Jr., & Hagestad, G. O., 43
sexuality and intimacy, 67–70, 69f
    beliefs examined, 67–68
    decreased activity, 68
    differences between population groups, 68–69
    influence of technology, 69–70
    nonintercourse activities, 69
    sexually transmitted disease and, 69
sexually transmitted infections (STIs), 69
Shaw, B. H., & Claydon, V, E., 28
shelter programs, 148
Shinan-Altman, S., & Werner, P., 21
Shin, H., et al., 26
Sias, P. M., & Bartoo, H., 64
Sibai, A. M., et al., 192
siblings
    half-siblings, 98
    relationships, 98
    sibling rivalry, 98
    stepsiblings, 98
Siegler, E. L., et al., 167
Simpson-Kent, I. L., et al., 30
Singh P., 30
skilled nursing facilities, 131
skin, age-related changes, 25
Skinner, M. W., Andrews, G. J., & Cutchin, M. P., 135
skip-generation household, 185
Smith, A., & Duggan, M., 70
Smith, J. R., 110
Smith, M. L., et al., 69
Smith, R. J., Lehning, A. J., & Kim, K., 139
Smith, S., 11
Snelling, S., 101
Snoezelen room, 32, 33f
snowbirds, 134
social connectedness, 59, 62–64
    across cultures, 63–64
    benefits of social engagement, 168–69
    friendships and, 64–67, 67f
    mental health benefits, 63
    physical well-being and, 63
    sexuality and intimacy, 67–70
social convoy model, 61–62, 62f
    circles of reciprocity, 61–62
    cross-cultural perspectives, 63–64
social distancing, 154, 154f
social engagement, meanings across cultures, 189
social insurance, 203
social isolation. *See also* isolation and loneliness

    access to services, 166
    poverty and, 63
    social connection and, 154
socially constructed concepts about aging, 22
social media, 70, 172–73
    case study, 175
    connectedness and, 174
social networks, 61–62
    cross-cultural perspectives, 63–64
social policy
    aging policy, 202
    effect of ageism, 14
    history of aging policies, 202–3
    overview of, 202
    Social Security, 203–4
Social Security, 122–23, 122t, 203–4
    beneficiaries, 204
    benefits, 203–4
    debates over, 14
    means tests, 203
    poverty levels and, 213
    retirement age, 204–5
    sustainability, 205
    voting patterns and, 215
Social Security Act (SSA) of 1935, 203
    social services programs, 213
Social Security Administration, 122t, 123, 204, 204f, 212
social services, 165–68
Social Services Block Grants (SSBGs), 213
social usefulness, 153
social welfare policies, 202
socioemotional selectivity theory, 45
    social network changes, 52
sociological theories, 5, 6t
    activity theory, 60–61
    continuity theory, 61
    disengagement theory, 59–60
    life-course model of social functioning, 61
    social convoy model, 61–62, 62f
sociology of aging, overview of, 59
Solomon, D. N., Hansen, L., & Baggs, J. G., 108
Sone, T., et al., 120
Soriano-Tárraga C., et al., 20
special needs, adults with, overview of, 131
Spetz, J., et al., 107
spiritual connectedness, 157
spirituality
    benefits of involvement, 157
    described, 54
    as evolving process, 54
    role of, 54, 55f
    spiritual practices, 156, 156f
    use of term, 155
sports and fitness, 158

stage theories, 40–42, 41t
Stanford Center on Longevity, 176, 178
Starks, H., Dudzinski, D., & White, N., 75
State Units on Aging (SUAs), 208, 208f
Stein, J., 107
Stenner, B. J., Mosewich, A. D., & Buckley, J. D., 158
stepfamily, 99
Stepler, R., 96
stepparent responsibilities, 99
stepsiblings, 98
stereotypes
    aging process and decline, 8
    in benevolent ageism, 8, 10b
    disengagement theory and, 59–60
    intergenerational friendships and, 67
    language use and, 10
    negative, in media, 11
    personality and emotion, 44–45
    as self-fulfilling prophesies, 13
    sports and fitness, 158
    traditional senior centers, 166
    use of technology, 176
    in Western culture, 44
Stern, M. J., & Axinn, J., 203, 205
Stokes, J. E., & Moorman, S. M., 95
Stone, R. I., 130, 136, 141, 142, 144, 209
Stonewall Gardens, 144
Stowe, J. D., & Cooney, T. M., 91
strengths-based lenses, 6t, 7
strengths perspective, 96
stress
    effects on cognition, 46
    family members and, 93
    friendships and, 64
Stroebe, M., & Schut, H., 82
Studenski, S., et al., 28
Suanet, B., van der Pas, S., & van Tilburg, T. G., 100
subjective age, 21
subjective age bias, 21
subsidized meal programs, 166–67
substance use disorders, 49–50
    adult children with special needs, 97
    physical symptoms and, 51
    treatment programs, 165
successful aging, 15
    activity theory and, 60–61
    "brain training" games as ageist, 178
    critiques of, 15
    cultural beliefs and, 189
    exclusions from paradigm, 174
    in the media, 174
    representations of sexuality, 67–68
Sue, D. W., 13
suicide, 50
Su, L. H., & Chen, T. H., 26

Sullivan, N., 6
Sun, F., et al., 101
Sun, K., & Dutta, M. J., 188, 191
Supplemental Nutrition Assistance Program (SNAP), 168, 212
Supplemental Poverty Measure (SPM), 213
Supplemental Security Income (SSI) program, 212
support exchanges, 97
supportive housing, 145, 145t
support networks
    multigenerational families and households, 101
    stepfamilies, 99
Supports and Tools for Elder Abuse Prevention (STEAP) Initiative, 111
support services, 167–68
    respite care, 167
Sustainable Development Goals (SDGs), 144
Sutherland, A., 160
Symens Smith, A., & Trevelyan, E., 136, 136f
Syrian civil war, 192, 193f
Szanton, S., et al., 152

Takahashi, T. A., & Johnson, K. M., 29
Tanzania, antidiscrimination laws for workplace, 119t
Tashjian, V. C., et al., 180
tasks of mourning model of grief, 82
Taylor, S. E., 13
Taylor, T. N., et al., 69
technology
    access during pandemic, 155b
    access to, 175–76
    assistive, 174, 177, 178f179
    cybercrime, 178–79
    digital literacy, 178
    end of life and, 179–80
    in the home, 36
    to improve health, 177–78
    for lifelong learning, 176
    misinformation online, 178
    monitoring health functions, 177
    online safety, 178–79
    overview of, 172
    scams, 179
    for social connection and entertainment, 176
    use by older adults, 174–79
    web-based resources, 177
technology industry, middle-ageism, 8
telemedicine, 162
telomeres, 24, 24f
Temporary Assistance for Needy Families (TANF) program, 144
ten Bruggencate, T., Luijkx, K. G., & Sturm, J., 64
Teno, J. M., 180
terminal illness, case studies, 79
Terraneo. M., 33

terror management theory, 83
tertiary prevention services, 166
testosterone levels, 29, 30
The Conversation Project, 105t
theories of aging, 5–7, 6t
    deficit-based, 6
theory of intergenerational ambivalence, 93–94
    elder abuse and, 110
theory of selective optimization with compensation, 47, 48f
third places, 161
Thomas, P. A., Liu, H., & Umberson, D., 92, 94, 95
Thompson, K. G., et al., 26
Tibetan funeral practices, 87b
Tikkanen, R., & Abrams, M. K., 163
Toossi, M., & Torpey, E., 115
Topa, G., Depolo, M., & Alcover, C-M., 120
Topsfield, J., & Rosa, A., 87b
Torres, S., & Cao, X., 161
Traeen, B., et al., 68
transgender older adults
    age-friendly healthcare, 165
    discrimination impact, 43
    friendship networks among, 65
transmisia, 7
travel, 159
Travison, T. G., et al., 30
treatment
    mental health disorders, 50–52
    reminiscence therapy, 52
triple jeopardy, 8
trust relationship, 109
TV and radio, 172
Twomey, M., 109
Tymoszuk, U., et al., 159

Ujvari, K., Fox-Grage, W., & Houser, A., 209
uncomplicated grief, 80
Ungar, A., et al., 28
United Health Foundation, 123
United Nations
    classifications of nations, 183
    initiatives related to aging, 183–84
    Sustainable Development Goals (SDGs), 144
United Nations, Department of Economic and Social Affairs Population Division, 3, 3f, 4f, 183, 184, 185, 186
United Nations High Commissioner for Refugees, 191, 192, 193
United States
    aging-related data compared, 189
    antidiscrimination laws for workplace, 119t
    Chinese immigrants, 101
    cultural orientation compared, 187–88
    diversity trends, 189
    foreign-born population, 190, 190f
    indigenous and immigrant populations, 34
    labor force participation, 186
    long-term services and supports (LTSS), 209
    pervasive ageism in, 7
    projected trends, 189
    skip-generation households, 185
    social network patterns, 63
United States Census Bureau, 3, 95f, 190f, 192f
United States Elections Project, 215, 216f
urban and rural environments, 136–37, 136f
US Bureau of Labor Statistics, 161
USC Center on Elder Mistreatment, 111
US Department of Homeland Security, 196
US Department of Housing and Urban Development, 144, 212
US Department of Labor, 122t
US Department of State, 191

van Den Beld, A., et al., 29
van der Pas, S., van Tilburg, T. G., & Silverstein, M., 96, 99, 100
VanderWeele, T. J., McNeely, E., & Koh, H. K., 161, 162t
Vandewoude, M. et al., 46
Van Hook, J., & Glick, J. E., 193
Varma, V. R., et al., 124
vascular atrophy, effects of, 25
vascular dementia, 31t
Veghte, B. W., & Schreur, E., 203, 205
Verschuren, J. E., et al., 67
Vespa, Medina, & Armstrong, 164
Vicedo-Cabrera, A. M., et al., 196
victimhood, 111
Victor, C. G. P., & Treschuk, J. V., 155
Vietnam, 196
villages, as housing options, 142
virtual communities, 153
vision changes, 27
    access to preventive care, 35
Vollset, S. E., et al., 184, 185
voluntary stopping of eating and drinking (VSED), 75
volunteerism, 123
    community resources and, 161
    retirement and giving back, 188
    trends, 161
"volunturists," 159
voter education, 216–17
voter habituation, 216
voting behavior, 215–16, 216f
vulnerable populations
    living arrangements of, 147
    older adults in prison, 147

Wahl, H.-W., & Oswald F., 16
Wahl, H.-W., Iwarson, S., & Oswald, F., 130, 132, 133

Wakefield, J. R. H., et al., 63, 174
Walen, H. R., & Lachman, M. E., 64
Walter, C. A., & McCoyd, J. L. M., 98
Wang, Vera, 53
Warren, R., & Kerwin, D., 142
wear-and-tear mitochondrial theories, 25
web-based resources, 177
Weijer, C., 74
Weintraub, D., & Mamikonyan, E., 50
welfare. *See* social welfare policies
West, S., et al., 158
Whiteford, H. A., et al., 49
Whittington, F. J. P., Kunkel, S. R. P., & De Medeiros, K. P., 188
Wiglesworth, A., et al., 110
Wiles, J. L., et al., 134, 138
Willett, J., & Sears, J., 191, 195
Williams, E., 207
Wion, R. K., & Loeb, S. J., 70
wisdom, 11
  expressions of, 54
Wise, E. A., et al., 50
Wiseman, R. F., 134, 135
Witten, T. M., 65
women
  ageism and, 7
  as caregivers, 106
  caregiver stress, 108
  COVID-19 pandemic and, 119–20
  domestic abuse and, 147
  effects of ageism, 13
  friendship networks among, 65
  healthcare access, 13
  impact of caregiving, 119
  menopause, 22–23, 29
  retirement income, 123
  sexual activity and, 68
  sexualized older bodies, 174
  team sports, 158
Woody, I., 143
Woolf, S. H., Masters, R. K., & Aron, L. Y., 185, 190
Worden, J. W., 82
work
  abilities and skill sets, 118
  bridge jobs, 116–17, 117*f*
  caregiving and, 119–20
  encore careers, 116
  generational perspective, 115, 117
  global trends, 186–87
  labor force participation rate (LFPR), 186–87, 187*t*
  nature of, 116
  perceptions of, 115
workforce
  ageism in, 118
  discrimination in, 14
  global trends, 115
  population aging and, 3
  retirement benefits, 121–23, 122*t*
  US trends, 116–17
World Elder Abuse Awareness Day, 111
World Health Organization (WHO), 7, 12, 14, 15, 28, 34, 35, 50, 52*b*, 67, 109, 118, 119, 161, 184, 187
World Population Review, 84
worldview, 83
Woźniak, B., 157

Yagil, D., Cohen, M., & Beer, J. D., 176
Yamasoba, T., et al., 27
Yazdani-Darki, M., et al., 175
years and physical age, 20
Yenilmez, I. M., 3
Yesavage, J. A., et al., 50
yoga, 156, 156*f*, 158
Yonashiro-Cho, J., Meyer, K., & Wilber, K. H., 165, 166
Young@Heart Chorus, 160
younger individuals, depression compared, 48–49
youthful appearance, among men, 21

Zayed, A. A., et al., 22
Zhang, K., Kim, K. et al., 174
Zhang, X., Yin, C. et al., 51
Zitter, J. N., 180
Zizza, C. A., Ellison, K. J., & Wernette, C. M., 20
zoning laws, 135–36
Zuckerberg, Mark, 8